KNOWLEDGE DISCOVERY FROM LEGAL DATABASES

T0180545

Law and Philosophy Library

VOLUME 69

KNOWLEDGE DISCOVERY FROM LEGAL DATABASES

by

ANDREW STRANIERI

University of Ballarat, Ballarat, Victoria, Australia.

and

JOHN ZELEZNIKOW

Victoria University, Melbourne, Victoria, Australia.

 Springer

A C.I.P. Catalogue record for this book is available from the Library of Congress.

ISBN-13 978-90-481-6771-5 (PB)
ISBN-13 978-1-4020-3037-6 (e-book)

Published by Springer,
P.O. Box 17, 3300 AA Dordrecht, The Netherlands.

Printed on acid-free paper

springeronline.com

Printed in the Netherlands.

CONTENTS

ACKNOWLEDGEMENTS

There are many people who have helped contribute towards this book. When he came to La Trobe University in July 1991, Don Berman managed to excite the authors of this text about the possibilities of using Artificial Intelligence and Legal Reasoning. His advice, drive and mentoring helped sustain us in this project even though his unfortunate demise came before we started writing this book.

We need to thank four PHD students from the Donald Berman Laboratory for Information Technology and Law at La Trobe University. Mark Gawler and Bryn Lewis helped program the Split Up system, whilst Emilia Bellucci provided advice with regards to negotiation support systems and Jean Hall supported us in evaluating many of the systems we developed. Sasha Ivkovic, a PHD student at the University of Ballarat provided valuable insights into the use of association rules in law.

Kevin Ashley of the University of Pittsburgh Law School provided many useful comments that helped us structure the proposal that ultimately led to the writing of this book. An Australian Research Council grant helped sustain Andrew Stranieri during his writing of the book. La Trobe University, the University of Edinburgh Law School and Victoria University supported John Zeleznikow. We also acknowledge the assistance of Domenico Calabro from Victoria Legal Aid, John Yearwood and Rosemary Hay from the University of Ballarat and Hilary Luxford from Victoria University.

But most of all we must thank our families for their unswerving devotion during our authorship of this book.

For Andrew, this book owes its existence to the love and patience of his wife Giselle and our children Elan and Eleanor. Without their enduring support this text would not have seen the light of day. I cherish every day together and find that, as time goes on, I am appreciating our common journey much more than the milestones.

For John's part, this book is dedicated to his wife Lisa and children Ashley, Sarah, Annie, Eva and Joseph. Despite three-year-old Joseph regularly stating "I no like Daddy working on his computer", somehow I managed to complete the viii

manuscript. Without the warmth, generosity, love and numerous cups of tea from my darling wife Lisa, I would not have envisaged starting this process, let alone completing it.

PREFACE

1. THE IMPORTANCE OF INVESTIGATING DATA MINING IN LAW

Over the past two decades, there has been considerable research in the cross-disciplinary domain loosely defined as Information Technology and Law. Much of this work has focussed upon the Law of Information Technology, and can be generally classified as belonging to the domain of Intellectual Property.

In this book, we will focus upon how information technology can help improve legal practice. [Susskind 2000] outlines the past use of Information Technology (IT), and indicates probable future uses of IT by the legal profession. He indicates that until recently, there was only limited use of IT by legal professionals. Whilst the use of word processing, office, automation, case management tools, client and case databases, electronic data/document interchange tools and fax machines is now standard, only recently have legal firms commenced using knowledge management techniques. The use of applied legal decision support systems is in its infancy.

[Zeleznikow and Hunter 1994] investigated the development of intelligent systems in legal practice. They noted that most commercially successful systems have employed rules. The major reasons for this occurrence include that it is easy to model rules and there are many tools for building rule-based systems.

Although many commentators including [Moles and Dayal 1992] clearly express reservations about this approach for the majority of fields of law, rule-based reasoning is still the predominant basis for constructing legal decision support systems. The fundamental limitation not addressed by this view of law can be reduced to two significant omissions: (a) the failure to model open texture, and (b) the failure to provide an analysis of how justification differs from the process used to arrive at decisions.

A decade later, in his description of commercial legal decision support systems build at the Donald Berman Laboratory for Information Technology and Law at La Trobe University, [Zeleznikow 2003] noted that the majority of commercially available legal decision support systems model fields of law that are complex but not discretionary. There seems little doubt that the trend toward rule based systems to encode large and complex legislation will continue to a substantial extent. This is assured by the increasing public demand for more transparency and consistency in government decision-making alongside with the continuing enactment of increasingly complex legislation.

Given that rule-based systems are inadequate for modelling legal reasoning, [Zeleznikow and Hunter 1994] considered how case-based reasoning and hybrid reasoning have been used to develop legal knowledge-based systems.

In this text we wish to go one step further and illustrate how the newly emerged field of Knowledge Discovery from Databases (KDD), sometimes called data mining can be used to model reasoning in discretionary legal domains. Then, by applying KDD to build legal knowledge-based systems on the World Wide Web, we can help improve access to justice and provide support for alternative dispute resolution.

2. THE STRUCTURE OF THIS BOOK

To discuss whether Knowledge Discovery from Databases is feasible in the legal domain, we first need to examine basic concepts of KDD. We note that KDD can be categorised into four categories:
   a) classification,
   b) clustering,
   c) series analysis and
   d) association.

The process has five phases:
   a) data selection,
   b) data pre-processing,
   c) data transformation,
   d) data mining, and
   e) evaluation.

Although KDD with data from law is not prevalent, important examples of classification, clustering, series analysis and association have been performed. Throughout the book, we claim that KDD can be gainfully used in discretionary legal domains. To demonstrate this, we commence with an examination of the concepts of open-texture and discretion. We discuss the concept of stare decisis, and the notion that even in legal domains in Common law countries, in which stare decisis is not strictly followed, many judges still adhere to the notions of personal stare decisis and local stare decisis.

KDD involves the mining of legal cases. We hence next ask, is it feasible to mine cases in Civil Law domains, since Civil Law does not apply precedent, to the same extent as Common Law. [Ashley 2003] argues that judges in civil law jurisdictions do reason with legal cases, but in a very different way from their common law counterparts.

In Chapter two we discuss legal issues relating to the data selection phase. These include the importance of open-texture in choosing tasks suitable for the use of Knowledge Discovery from Database techniques and assessing the degree of open texture of a problem. This will lead us to investigate which cases are suitable for use in the KDD process and the distinction between commonplace and landmark cases.

Once we have chosen the appropriate cases and variables for our KDD task, we need to pre-process our data to ensure it is ready for further phases of the KDD process. This task requires attention to two main factors; missing values and erroneous data and is discussed in Chapter three. Issues addressed will include: a) missing data, b) inconsistent data, c) noise, d) judicial error, e) coping with contradictory data and f) inconsistencies due to new legislation or precedents.

Data that has been selected and pre-processed may not necessarily be ready for exposure to a data-mining algorithm. Some transformation of the data may dramatically enhance the benefit of the subsequent data-mining phase. Transformation can be performed in five ways: a) Aggregation of data values, b) Normalisation of data values, c) Feature reduction. d) Example reduction and e) Restructuring. In chapter four we examine the notion of data transformation and suggest that Argumentation can be gainfully used to restructure data. The benefits of using argumentation to support legal KDD will be a recurring theme in this book.

Having performed data cleaning, data pre-processing and data transformation we are now ready to mine our legal data sets. In Chapters five to eight, we will investigate appropriate data-mining algorithms.

The first data-mining algorithm we will discuss is rule induction. Inductive reasoning is the process of moving from specific cases to general rules. A rule induction system is given examples of a problem where the outcome is known. When it has been given several examples, the rule induction system can create rules that are true from the example cases. The rules can then be used to assess other cases where the outcome is not known.

New knowledge can be inferred with rule induction. Once rules have been generated they can be reviewed and modified by the domain expert, providing for more useful, comprehensive and accurate rules for the domain. ID3 and C4.5 use information theory to learn decision trees from data sets. These decision trees can then be turned into rules of the form IF <condition(s)> THEN <consequent>.

We will discuss how rule induction has been used in legal domains to: a) generate indices into cases, b) analyse a domain in order to detect a change in the way a legal concept is used by courts, c) estimate the number of days that are likely to elapse between the arrest of an offender and the final disposition of the case.

In Chapter six we will investigate data-mining with uncertainty. This involves the use of many statistical techniques. Association rules are not intended to be viewed as generalisations from data, but indicate that an association between the condition(s) and the consequent exists. Associated with each rule, is a confidence factor, that is how likely is the rule to be true and the support of the rule which states how many of the items in the data set are affected by this rule. We will consider examples of association rules that a) advise upon the distribution of marital property following divorce in Australia, b) the distribution of legal aid grants in Victoria, Australia.

Fuzzy rules are based on fuzzy set theory and attempt to capture the degree of uncertainty inherent in a rule. Fuzzy logic is a many-valued propositional logic where each proposition P rather than taking the value T or F has a probability attached (thus between 0 and 1) of being true. It would take the value 0 if it were false and 1 if it were true. Logical operators and probability theory are then combined to model reasoning with uncertainty. Fuzzy rules capture something of the uncertainty inherent in the way in which language is used to construct rules. We will see that fuzzy logic has been used in modelling traffic accident law and to construct a case-based reasoner to provide advice about contracts under the United Nations Convention on Contracts for the International Sale of Goods.

Other statistical techniques we will consider include genetic algorithms, Bayesian classification and Dempster-Shafer Theory. Our final data-mining technique to be investigated is neural networks. A neural network consists of many self-adjusting processing elements cooperating in a densely interconnected network. Each processing element generates a single output signal that is transmitted to the other processing elements. The output signal of a processing element depends on the inputs to the processing element: each input is gated by a weighting factor that determines the influence that the input will have on the output. The strength of the weighting factors is adjusted autonomously by the processing element as data is processed. Neural networks are particularly useful in law because they can deal with a) classification difficulties, b) vague terms, c) defeasible rules and d) discretionary domains.

Although the focus of this book is on data mining from structured databases, we provide an overview of text mining approaches in Chapter 8. Substantial applications of information retrieval and neural network algorithms toward text clustering, summarisation and categorisation in law are surveyed.

Throughout this book we will provide a detailed examination of one particular legal domain – the distribution of marital property following divorce in Australia. Split-Up is a hybrid rule-based/neural network that offers decision support in this domain. Many of the legal principles discussed in this book have been used in the Split-Up project.

One of the major concerns in using Knowledge Discovery from Databases is that the process of determining whether a pattern is interesting. A pattern is interesting if it is a) easily understood by humans, b) valid (with some degree of certainty) on new or test data, c) potentially useful and d) novel. A pattern is also interesting if it validates a hypothesis that the user sought to confirm. In Chapter nine we look at issues of the evaluation of systems that must be considered to justify the use of results and systems developed from the process of Knowledge Discovery from Legal Databases.

CHAPTER 1

INTRODUCTION

Data is now collected in a variety of commercial and scientific fields in such quantities that the problem of automating the elicitation of meaningful knowledge from data has become pressing. For example, data sets from astronomical observations were once manually scanned by experts searching for anomalies or interesting patterns. However, as [Fayyad *et al* 1996] note, the manual analysis of data in astronomy is no longer feasible since data sets in this field often exceed many thousands of millions of records.

In the legal domain information is often stored as text in relatively unstructured forms. Primary statutes, judgments in past cases and commentaries are typically stored as text based documents. In contrast, scientific and commercial information is collected in a more structured manner. Grocery items at most supermarkets are bar-coded and scanned at purchase. Computer systems link retailers with suppliers and suppliers with distribution centres in order to streamline the provision of goods. The data collected about each item is used to closely monitor sales and the performance of processes within those organisations.

In contrast, many applications for Court hearings are paper based, though the use of case management systems is becoming increasingly common. Judgments record relevant findings of fact and rulings in the form of a narrative but fact values are rarely stored in a structured format such as a database. This has consequences for the future retrieval of similar cases, for the management of Courts, and for the analysis and prediction of legal decisions using knowledge discovery from database techniques.

If judgments are stored as a narrative, the retrieval of a past case involves scanning the text of past cases. Commercial search engines such as Lexis and Westlaw search for multiple keywords using Boolean AND, OR and NOT operators. Nevertheless, retrieving all the cases that are relevant to a query and none that are irrelevant is very difficult. [Rose 1993] identifies the limitations of keyword search and describes a technique for converting the narrative judgment into a semi-structured representation which has been derived from artificial intelligence. Retrieval performance is significantly enhanced by this approach.

The focus of this text is in on the potential that knowledge discovery from database techniques have to improve the prediction and analysis of case outcomes. According to [Frawley *et al* 1991] knowledge discovery from databases (KDD) is the 'non trivial extraction of implicit, previously unknown and potentially useful information from data'. Data mining is a problem-solving methodology that finds a logical or mathematical description, eventually of a complex nature, of patterns and regularities in a set of data [Fayyad *et al* 1996].

The Victorian (Australia) Parliamentary Committee on Law Reform [Parliament of Victoria 1999] identified many ways in which technology can improve the efficiency and effectiveness of the legal profession and judiciary. Many of their recommendations involve the storage of data in a more structured form.

Law has not yet been characterised with data collected in structured formats in the quantities apparent in other fields. However, knowledge discovery techniques have begun to be applied to legal domains in useful ways. Existing attempts in this direction provide important insights into the benefits for the practice of law in the future and also illustrate problems for KDD unique to the legal domain.

According to [Fayyad *et al* 1996] KDD techniques, in general can be grouped into four categories:

a) Classification. The aim of classification techniques is to group data into predefined categories. For example, data representing important case facts from many cases may be used to classify a new case into one of the pre-defined categories, 'pro-plaintiff' or 'pro-defendant'.

b) Clustering. The aim of clustering techniques is to analyse the data in order to group the data into groups of similar data. For example, a clustering technique may group cases into six main clusters that an analyst would interpret in order to learn something about the cases.

c) Series Analysis. The aim of series analysis is to discover sequences within the data. Sequences typically sought are time series. For example, past cases over a time period may be analysed in order to discover important changes in the way a core concept is interpreted by Courts.

d) Association. The objective of association techniques is to discover ways in which data elements are associated with other data elements. For example, an association between the gender of litigants and the outcome of their cases may surprise analysts and stimulate hypotheses to explain the phenomena.

e) Text mining. This refers to information retrieval methods, the automated generation of a document summary, the extraction of concepts such as case factors from judgements, the assignment of a document to a category and other approaches that deal with large repositories of textual documents.

Although KDD with data from legal databases is not prevalent, important examples of classification, clustering, series analysis, association and time series have been performed. These examples are presented in the next section.

1. KNOWLEDGE DISCOVERY FROM DATABASES IN LAW

The application of knowledge discovery techniques to law has been limited to a handful of applications and a relatively small range of data mining techniques. In this section we provide a brief summary of notable efforts in this field in order to provide a flavour for KDD approaches in law and to illustrate the differences between classification, clustering, series analysis and associational KDD.

1.1   Classification

As we shall demonstrate in chapter 5, techniques exist for the automatic discovery of knowledge in the form of rules that take the general form IF A and B and C. THEN D. A number of researchers have applied KDD techniques to automatically extract IF-THEN rules from data in order to make a prediction.

[Wilkins and Pillaipakkamnatt 1997] examined large numbers of cases in order to estimate the number of days that are likely to elapse between the arrest of an offender and the final disposition of the case. The time to disposition depends on variables such as the charge, offender's age, and the county where the arrest was made. Values on more than 30 variables from over 700,000 records from 12 U.S states were used. Rules were automatically extracted using the rule induction algorithm ID3. Although [Wilkins and Pillaipakkamnatt 1997] themselves had hoped for rule sets that predicted the time to disposition more accurately than their results indicate, this study remains an impressive demonstration of the potential for KDD techniques to contribute to the delivery of legal services.

[Vossos *et al* 1993] and [Zeleznikow *et al* 1994], in conjunction with a legal firm, developed the Credit Act Advisory System, CAAS. This is a rule based legal expert system that provides advice regarding the extent to which a credit transaction complies with the Credit Act 1984 (Vic). Although the majority of rules derive directly from the statute, some factors remain vaguely defined in the Act. For example, the factor 'credit was for a business purpose' is not defined by the statute. In this instance, a rule induction algorithm was invoked to discover new rules from a database of facts from past cases that involved credit for a business purpose. A rule induction technique discovers rules from past cases where a judge had decided whether credit was extended for a business purpose. These rules help a user determine whether a new, current situation involves credit for a business purpose or not.

In another innovative application of knowledge discovery to law, [FeuRosa 2000], a Supreme Court Judge in Brazil has initiated a program for the resolution of traffic accident disputes. His 'Judges on Wheels' program involves the transportation of a judge, police officer, insurance assessor, mechanical and support staff to the scene of minor motor vehicle accidents. The team collects evidence, the mechanic assess the damage, and the judge makes a decision and drafts a judgement with the help of a program called the 'Electronic Judge' before leaving the scene of the accident. The 'Electronic Judge' software uses a KDD approach that involves data mining tools called neural networks. Neural networks are discussed at length in chapter 7. These tools learn patterns of decision making from judges in previous traffic accidents and suggest an outcome for the current accident that is consistent with previous ones. No rules are induced. Although, the judge is not obliged to follow the suggestion offered by the 'Electronic Judge', the software is used by judges in 68% of traffic accidents in the state of Espirito Santo. The system plays an important role in enhancing the consistency of judicial decision-making.

[Hobson and Slee 1994] study a handful of cases from the UK Theft Act and use neural networks to predict the outcome of theft cases. They used a series of leading cases in British theft law to train a network to predict a courtroom outcome. The results they obtained were less than impressive, which they attributed to flaws in the use of neural networks in legal reasoning. As we shall argue throughout this text, this criticism was unduly harsh. Neural networks have much to offer KDD. However, any application of KDD to data drawn from the legal domain must be carefully performed. Due attention is required, so that key assumptions made at each phase of the KDD process are clearly articulated and have some basis in jurisprudence. For example, the cases used in the Hobson and Slee study involved leading cases. In the next chapter, we argue that leading cases are not well suited to a KDD exercise.

[Bench-Capon 1993], drawing on hypothetical data from a social security domain, was guarded in his appraisal of the benefits of using neural networks to model reasoning in legal domains. Similar concerns regarding the use of neural networks in law have been advanced by [Hunter 1994]. However, as we shall demonstrate in subsequent chapters, the appropriate application of KDD involves steps that include data selection, data pre-processing, data transformation, data mining and evaluation. At each phase, assumptions that are consistent with jurisprudential theories must be made. If assumptions are clearly articulated and carefully drawn, neural networks, in addition to other KDD techniques can be adapted to provide accurate predictions.

[Chen 2000] describes an automated detective that scans web pages for criminal activity. In that study, the data is text on a web page. Processes they have developed seek to classify the page into one of two pre-defined categories, illegal or not illegal.

In the Split Up project, [Stranieri et al 1999] collected data from cases heard in the Family Court of Australia dealing with property distribution following divorce. The objective was to predict the percentage split of assets that a judge in the Family Court of Australia would be likely to award both parties of a failed marriage. Australian Family Law is generally regarded as highly discretionary. The statute presents a 'shopping list' of factors to be taken into account in arriving at a property order. The relative importance of each factor remains unspecified and many crucial terms are not defined. The age, state of health and financial resources of the litigants are explicitly mentioned in the statute as relevant factors yet their relative weightings are unspecified. The Act clearly allows the decision-maker a great deal of discretion in interpreting and weighing factors.

The relative importance judges have placed on relevant factors in past cases can, to some extent be learnt with the use of KDD. This knowledge enables the user of Split Up to predict the outcomes of future cases. As we shall discuss throughout this work, important issues to be taken into account include which cases should be included in a KDD sample, how do we deal with cases in which a judge has perhaps erred, how do we evaluate the results of our systems, and how do we know which factors are important.

[Oatley and Ewart 2003] describe the OVER Project as a collaboration between West Midlands Police, UK and the University of Sunderland that aimed to assist police with the high volume crime, burglary from dwelling houses. A software system they developed enables the trending of historical data, the testing of 'short term' hunches, and the development of 'medium' and long term' strategies to burglary and crime reduction, based upon victim, offender, location and details of victimisations. The software utilises mapping and visualisation tools and is capable of a range of sophisticated predictions, tying together statistical techniques with theories from forensic psychology and criminology. The statistical methods employed (including multi-dimensional scaling, binary logistic regression) and data-mining technologies (including neural networks) are used to investigate the impact of the types of evidence available and to determine the causality in this domain. The final predictions on the likelihood of burglary are calculated by combining all of the varying sources of evidence into a Bayesian belief network. This network is embedded in the developed software system, which also performs data cleansing and data transformation for presentation to the developed algorithms.

[Oatley *et al* 2004a] note that computer science technology that can support police activities is wide ranging, from the well known geographical information systems display ('pins in maps'), clustering and link analysis algorithms, to the more complex use of data mining technology for profiling single and series of crimes or offenders, and matching and predicting crimes. They present a discussion of data mining and decision support technologies for police, considering the range of computer science technologies that are available to assist police activities.

1.2   Clustering

The aim of clustering techniques is to group data into clusters of similar items. In practice, legal data about persons, cases or situations is typically stored as text based documents rather than structured databases. Discovering knowledge by the automatic analysis of free text is a field of research that is evolving from information retrieval research and is often called text mining. [Hearst 1999] proposes that text-mining involves discovering relationships between the contexts of multiple texts and linking this information together to create new information.

Many text-mining applications involve clustering. The application of a type of neural network known as Self Organising Maps (SOM) to group European Parliament cases into clusters has been described by [Merkl and Schweighofer 1997], [Schweighofer and Merkl 1999] and [Merkl *et al* 1999]. Each cluster contains only cases that are similar according to the SOM. The SOM, used in this way have proven to accurately discover groupings for many thousands of cases.

In the SOM application [Merkl *et al* 1999] were interested in identifying clusters and the issue of selecting a cluster centre was not important. [Pannu 1995] engaged in knowledge discovery by identifying the centre point in a cluster. This took the form of identifying a prototypical exemplar of pro-defendant and pro-plaintiff cases within a domain. An exemplar pro-defendant case has features that are most like those cases in which the defendant won and most unlike the cases the defendant lost. This technique can be applied to assist a lawyer to structure an argument in a current case.

1.3   Series analysis

Very few studies have been performed that analyse sequences of data in law. However, the study by [Rissland and Friedman 1995] provides a good indication of the potential utility in doing so. They collected data from US Bankruptcy cases over a ten-year period and asked whether knowledge discovery techniques could be applied to automatically discover significant shifts in judicial decision-making. Data represented variables known to be relevant for the concept of 'good faith' in bankruptcy proceedings. Their aim was to discover a method for detecting a change in the way the concept of 'good faith' was used by Courts. The onset of a leading decision was automatically detected from case data using a metric they devised.

1.4   Association

Association rules depict an association between specific variable values. For example, an association rule that claims that if gender is female, then case is won on 10% of cases highlights a link between two variables, gender and outcome. The link is not necessarily causal and may not even be interesting. Typically, the discovery of all possible association rules from data from many cases is computationally infeasible. However, an algorithm discussed in Chapter 6, called *Apriori* advanced by [Agrawal *et al* 1993] makes the automatic generation of rules tractable. [Stranieri *et al* 2000] have illustrated that association rule generators can highlight interesting associations in a small dataset. In an example of KDD in law that aims to analyse a legal domain rather than making specific predictions regarding judicial outcomes, [Ivkovic *et al* 2003] has generated association rules from over 300,000 records drawn from database of applicants for government funded legal aid in Australia. In that country, applicants for legal aid must not only pass an income and assets test but must also demonstrate that their case has some merit for success. Consequently considerable data is recorded about the applicant and the case. The purpose of the association rules study performed by [Ivkovic *et al* 2003] was to determine whether this data mining technique could automatically analyse the data in order to identify hypotheses that would not otherwise have been considered. For example, as a result of this study, an association between the applicant's age and categories of legal aid applied requested was discovered. It can be summarised as follows: 89% of applicants between 18 and 21 applied for legal aid for criminal offences whereas 57% of applicants between 40 and 50 applied for aid for criminal offences. This result surprised experts in the field who did not expect young applicants to be so highly represented in criminal law matters. This result is not, of itself used to explain much, but is advanced to assist in the formulation of hypotheses to explain the associations observed.

The four categories of KDD techniques, classification, clustering series analysis and association detection are useful categories in the practical process of applying KDD to data, because they help an analyst determine the desired outcome of a KDD exercise. The next section discusses the nature and types of data, before exploring the KDD phases in depth

1.5   Text mining

Text mining includes techniques for clustering documents discussed above, summarising and categorising documents and extracting information from text. A common application of text categorisation is the assignment of keyword lists to categorise cases.   Typically legal publishers expend considerable resources to manually determine the most appropriate list of keywords for each published case. For example, judgments available on-line from WESTLAW [Westlaw 2004], the American legal publisher, are categorised manually into 40 high level categories such as bankruptcy.   [Thompson 2001] describe comparative trials with three different data mining techniques, one that applies clustering and two that involve classification by rule induction.

Other approaches that involve text mining involve sophisticated case matching techniques that are not simple examples of clustering or classification approaches because other processes are also involved.   For example, [Bruninghaus and Ashley 2001] sought to elicit case factors automatically from a summary of a case.   The motivation for doing so was to enable the most time consuming phase of case based reasoning methods [Ashley 1991], the elicitation of factors to be performed automatically.   This involved sophisticated natural language parsing of sentences.

[Yearwood 1997] reports a technique for the retrieval of similar cases. His work involves the automatic identification of which sections of refugee law judgments feature most prominently in the retrieval of cases that match a current one.   This work was also successfully applied to more structured documents taken from hospital records [Yearwood and Wilkinson 1997].

In the SALOMAN project, [Moens et al 1997] and [Moens 2000] generated a summary of a judgments.   This was done by combining text matching using information retrieval algorithms with expert knowledge about the structure of judgments.   SPIRE, developed by Daniels and Rissland [Daniels and Rissland 1997] integrates a case based reasoner with information retrieval techniques to locate the passage within a document where a query concept is likely to be found.

[Dozier et al 2003] used text-mining techniques to create an on-line directory of expert witnesses from jury verdict and settlement documents.   The supporting technologies that made the application possible included information extraction from text via regular expression parsing, record linkage through Bayesian based matching and automatic rule-based classification.   Their research shows that text-mining techniques can be used to create useful special-purpose directories for individuals involved in legal proceedings.

Common application areas of text mining include:
a)   Homeland Security and Intelligence – I) Analysis of terrorist networks. i) Rapid identification of critical information about such topics as weapons of mass destruction from very large collections of text documents and iii) Surveillance of the Web, e-mails, or chat rooms.
b)   Law Enforcement such as the structuring of narrative reports written by federal, state, and local law enforcement agents to aid the analytical process by identifying previously unnoticed trends, links, and patterns.

The Coplink project [Hauck et al 2002] does not use entity extraction techniques because they drew the data from a structured database system. Yet many police records systems contain large collections of unstructured text and structured case reports. These textual sources often contain volumes of information that are not captured in the structured fields. A future research direction in the project is to develop textual mining approaches that support knowledge retrieval from such sources. The development of linguistic-analysis and textual-mining techniques for performing fine-grained content analysis could help to make intelligent use of large textual collections in police databases.

Although text-mining approaches are discussed in Chapter 8, the focus of this work is on the description of the process of discovery of knowledge from structured databases and not from free text.

2. CONCEPTUALALISING DATA

The conceptual view of data that we will take can be described as a spreadsheet model. Table 1 illustrates a spreadsheet model of data where each row is a record. A record can be regarded as a snapshot of the world and is also called a case, an example, or, in database terminology, a tuple. The columns represent variables. A variable defines a feature that is expected to be relevant for a data set. Table 2 illustrates names that are often used interchangeably for data elements.

Table 1. Spreadsheet view of data

		Wife's age	Wife's Health	Age of eldest child	Percentage of Assets awarded to the wife
1	Marriage	35	Good	4	65
2	Marriage	24	Excellent	?	50
3	Marriage	82	?	0	40
4	Marriage	82	Good	0	40

Table 2. Terminology for data

Equivalent terms	Description	Example
Row, record, tuple, example, value, itemset	Data values	35, Good, 4, 65
Column, variable, feature, attribute	Data variables	Wife's age, Age of eldest child

A variable's type describes the kind of values that records can take. For example, the variable Wife's age in Table 1 is an integer. Figure 1 presents a hierarchy of data types.

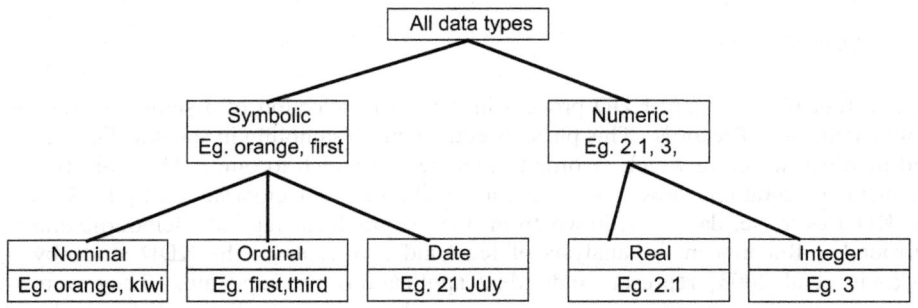

Figure 1. Types of data values

Raw data often contains data that has been recorded in inconsistent ways. For example, date fields are stored in 01/01/2001 formats in some records and in Jan 1, 2001 formats in other records.

Data within a field may be stored consistently, but is recorded in a way that is likely to be too fine grained. For example, variable age, recorded as an integer, is likely to be too fine grained for most applications. A rule discovered by a data mining algorithm from that data may read as:

If 'age = 25' then 'Favourite movie' is 'Sound of Music'
If 'age = 26' then 'Favourite movie' is 'Sound of Music'
If 'age = 27' then 'Favourite movie' is 'Sound of Music'

Binning, or collapsing the age values into distinct categories such as child, teenager, young adult, middle aged and elderly may be more appropriate for the task at hand. Furthermore, important patterns or rules may not be discovered for specific age groups because sufficient records do not exist for each year.

In the next section, phases of any KDD exercise are described. Each chapter in this text expands on phases in the KDD process by articulating jurisprudential and other assumptions that are required for the application of KDD to law.

3. PHASES IN THE KNOWLEDGE DISCOVERY FROM DATABASE PROCESS

The KDD process begins with the analysis of data stored in a database or data warehouse and ends with the production of new knowledge. [Fayyad et al 1996] describe knowledge discovery as a process with five distinct stages:

3.1 Data selection.

The first phase of any KDD process involves the selection of a sample of data from a database of records. This phase is equivalent to sampling in statistical circles and involves selecting which records to include and which to omit. There are two distinct considerations; how to select records and how to select variables. In the Split Up KDD exercise, data was drawn from one geographical region; Melbourne and surrounds. Records in the analysis of legal aid applicants in the KDD study by [Ivkovic et al 2003] represent individual applications for legal aid. They were selected on a temporal rather than geographical or jurisdictional basis, by considering all Victorian applications for legal aid within a three year period. The selection of relevant variables is an important aspect of the data selection phase. The age of the husband and wife in a family law dispute are relevant by virtue of the principle statute and because experts in the field clearly indicate that age impacts on property allocation decisions.

3.2 Data pre-processing.

Sample data from any real world data set can be expected to contain records that are erroneous and may, if used, distort the knowledge discovered. Errors may derive from the incorrect transcribing of case facts from a judgement to a structured database. However, other errors may reflect mistakes that judges have made. The assumptions made concerning the nature of judicial error are important in determining how best to deal with judgements that are apparently mistaken.

3.3 Data transformation.

Data may need to be transformed in order to discover useful knowledge. Transformation can involve changing the categories of values a variable may have. Age may be collected in years, but transformed into three values; young, middle aged and elderly. Another way that data may be transformed is to decompose the problem. In Split Up, the task of predicting the percentage split of assets awarded to the parties was decomposed into smaller tasks. KDD was applied to each smaller problem to discover knowledge that could not have been obtained had the problem not been decomposed.

3.4   Data mining.

According to [Fayyad et al 1996] data mining is a problem-solving methodology that finds a logical or mathematical description, eventually of a complex nature, of patterns and regularities in a set of data. Data mining techniques derive from four different sources;
a) artificial intelligence
b) database theory
c) inferential statistics, and
d) mathematical programming.
Artificial intelligence research has contributed techniques such as neural networks, rule induction and association rules. Linear logistic and multiple regression in addition to algorithms such as K-means and K-medians have been developed by statisticians. Mathematical programming has contributed techniques such as the min-max method from optimisation theory.

3.5   Evaluation/Deployment

This phase involves the evaluation and interpretation of knowledge discovered as a result of the data-mining phase. The evaluation of any legal system is fraught with theoretical and pragmatic obstacles. Assumptions regarding the nature of knowledge impact on how knowledge discovered using the process is evaluated.
Each chapter in this text focuses on an aspect of the KDD process. Examples will be drawn from KDD projects in a variety of legal domains with a special emphasis on experiences learned from the Split Up project. Our main aim is to illustrate that the KDD process can be successfully applied to predict and analyse legal decisions. This is more easily apparent in fields of law broadly regarded as discretionary. The way in which we view discretion is critical in framing assumptions we need to make in each phase of the KDD process. In light of this, we discuss the nature of discretion before commencing a detailed view of each KDD phase.
A central theme of this text is that the application of KDD to data from the legal domain involves considerations that are specific to law. In this sense, legal databases are different from other datasets. Law is characteristically open textured and for many centuries, significant thinkers have advanced concepts of jurisprudence that can guide the data miner.

4. DIFFERENCES BETWEEN LEGAL AND OTHER DATA

The KDD process is particularly well suited to the discovery of decision making patterns in fields of law that involve some discretion. In the next chapter, the concepts of open texture, discretion and the related concept of stare decisis are discussed in relation to KDD.

From a theoretical perspective, [Tata 1998] argues that legal reasoning cannot be decomposed or deconstructed to a set of variables inter-linked together in a similar way from one case to another. Rather, legal reasoning is a holistic process where a decision-maker selects and processes facts of interest in a way that cannot be pre-specified before a case is encountered. As a holistic process, any attempt to systematically encode a judgment as a chain of reasoning steps that link facts to conclusions is, at best, superficial. Any KDD attempt to glean some unknown knowledge from data from many superficially encoded judgments can lead to the discovery of so-called knowledge that is quite misleading.

Although there is a risk that misleading conclusions can be drawn as a result of a KDD exercise, these risks are offset against potential gains. Currently, the analysis of judicial decisions occurs in a non-transparent manner. Practitioners develop experience in understanding judicial decision-making processes in specific jurisdictions. This experience is transferred informally to colleagues and is rarely subjected to rigorous analysis. Further, even the busiest practitioner can know of only a small number of cases. Legal scholars analyse major decisions and trends in greater detail. However, rarely do they regularly explore thousands of cases. Judges cannot easily allay public concerns that decisions are inconsistent. Furthermore, their decisions are not always readily predictable. KDD can promise to make law more transparent, and predictable.

Perhaps the greatest obstacle to the widespread use of KDD techniques is the absence of large structured datasets. As society becomes more information-based data will inevitably be collected in a structured fashion. Currently, legal firms, Courts and related professionals, are rapidly utilising case management systems. Non—profit organisations such as LegalXML ([LegalXML 2001] and [Leff 2001]) are developing standards for legal documents. Such standards, which use the extensible mark-up language (XML), vastly facilitate the storage of data in structured ways.

5. CHAPTER SUMMARY

Techniques for the discovery of knowledge from databases are becoming increasingly important, since data continues to be collected in vast quantities. In this chapter, we have described how the collection of data in the legal domain lags behind other fields of human endeavour. However, the trend toward increased collection of legal data is nevertheless apparent. The need to organise and analyse large data sets for interesting patterns or knowledge becomes pressing as data is collected in abundance. In this chapter, we have provided an overview of the steps involved in the discovery of knowledge from legal data. In each step, data selection, data pre-processing, data transformation, data mining and evaluation, the characteristics of the domain of law must be taken into account in order to avoid mis-interpretation of data. The over-arching claim we make is that KDD techniques are particularly adept at discovering patterns of judicial reasoning in discretionary fields of law, provided the data that reflects the reasoning processes is collected. In the next chapter, we explore the first phase of the KDD exercise; the selection of data.

CHAPTER 2

LEGAL ISSUES IN THE DATA SELECTION PHASE

The first phase of the KDD process involves collecting sample data. Decisions must first be made regarding the nature of the problem of interest in order to assess its suitability for the KDD process. Some problems are more suited to the use of KDD than others, whilst some are not suitable at all. Broadly speaking, fields of law that involve considerable judicial discretion at the level of a first instance decision-maker are more suited to a KDD exercise than ones where discretion is limited. However, the assessment of the extent to which a field of law is suitable for a KDD exercise involves a number of considerations that are outlined in this chapter.

Once the problem area is defined, decisions must be made regarding the source of data for the KDD exercise. In practice, this may be an academic exercise because broadly speaking; in the legal domain, data that reflects reasoning processes is not regularly collected in a structured way.

Nevertheless, where data is available, decisions regarding what data is appropriately collected must be made. For example, if the KDD exercise involves predicting judicial outcomes, then the past cases must be sought and variable/value pairs or factors must be extracted from the cases. Decisions regarding the number and types of cases, the identification of relevant variables and the extraction of values for relevant variables from case text must be made.

It is our contention that KDD process are particularly well suited to the discovery of decision making patterns in fields of law that involve some discretion. A discussion of discretion and the related concept of open texture is an important preamble to the identification of appropriate fields of law, and the prudent selection of data once a field has been identified.

1. OPEN TEXTURE, DISCRETION AND KDD

Legal reasoning is characteristically indeterminate. [Bench-Capon and Sergot 1988] view the indeterminacy in law as a specific consequence of the prevalence of open textured terms. Open texture was a concept first introduced by [Waismann 1951] to assert that empirical concepts are necessarily indeterminate. To use his example, we may define gold as that substance which has spectral emission lines X, and is coloured deep yellow. However, because we cannot rule out the possibility that a substance with the same spectral emission as gold, but without the colour of gold, will confront us in the future, we are compelled to admit that the concept we have for gold is open textured.

We view judicial reasoning that involves a degree of discretion, as a manifestation of open texture. Furthermore, a recurring theme throughout this text is that the concept of open texture is apt in the legal domain, because new uses for terms, and new situations constantly arise in legal cases. Thus, as [Berman and Hafner 1988] indicate, legal reasoning is essentially indeterminate because it is open textured. [Bench-Capon and Sergot 1988] view the indeterminacy in law as a specific consequence of the prevalence of open textured terms. They define an open textured term as one whose extension or use cannot be determined in advance of its application. The term 'vehicle' in an ordinance discussed by [Hart 1958] in his seminal work on legal positivism, can be seen to be an open textured term because its use in any particular case cannot be determined prior to that case. ([Prakken 1993] and [Prakken 1997]) collates and analyses the substantial artificial intelligence literature on open texture to point out that situations that characterise law as open textured include reasoning which involves defeasible rules, vague terms or classification ambiguities. This analysis of open texture is central to our discussion because we argue that the existence of judicial discretion is a form of open texture that is distinct from the situations considered by ([Prakken 1993] and [Prakken 1997]). This is important for us, because other models of legal reasoning can perhaps best be applied to deal with the forms of open texture considered by Prakken. However, KDD is particularly suitable for discretion.

The distinct types of situations that [Prakken 1993] notes are difficult to resolve because of the open textured nature of law are:

a) **Classification difficulties**. [Hart 1958] presents a local government ordinance that prohibits vehicles from entering a municipal park. He argues that there can be expected to be little disagreement that the statute applies to automobiles. However, there are a number of situations for which the application of the statute is debatable. What of roller blades, for instance? [Fuller 1958], in a response to Hart posed the situation of a military truck mounted in the park as a statute. Considerable open texture surrounds the use of the term 'vehicle' in this case even though there is no doubt that the truck is a vehicle.

b) **Defensible rules**. Another type of open texture arises from the defeasibility of legal concepts and rules. Any concept or rule, no matter how well defined, is always open to rebuke. Rarely do premises or consequents exist in law that are universally accepted. Driving whilst drunk is definitively prohibited by a Victorian statute, though few courts would convict a drunk forced to drive at gunpoint.

c) **Vague terms.** Legal tasks are often open textured because some terms or the connection between terms are vague. A judge finds the various interpretations of terms such as reasonable or sufficient stems from the vagueness of these terms and not from classification dilemmas or defeasibility requirements. [Brkic1985] labels this a gradation of totality of terms which he claims is one reason that deduction is an inappropriate inference procedure for many problems in law.

The existence of judicial discretion contributes to the open textured nature of law. Yet situations that involve discretion cannot always be described as instances of classification difficulties, defeasible rules or the presence of vague terms. We thus argue that the existence of discretion is a distinct form of open texture.

Consider a hypothetical panel of Family Court judges who agree on all the facts of a family law property dispute. Members of the panel can conceivably arrive at different percentages of the assets that ought to be awarded to the wife. The different outcomes may partly be due to the presence of vague terms that are interpreted differently by various judges. In part, the different outcomes may be due to classification type anomalies. One judge classifies a lottery win as a contribution to the marriage whereas another disagrees with this decision. Different outcomes may even be the result of defeasible rules. One judge applies the principle of an asset-by-asset approach, whereas another considers that principle irrelevant and adopts the global approach.

While these scenarios describe situations that are open textured, there are situations, common in family law cases, that are not captured by these instances of open texture. We can imagine a panel of judges, where vague terms are interpreted in much the same way by all judges. There are no classification anomalies and all judges have used the same principles. In this scenario the outcomes may still be different because judges apply different weights to each relevant factor. No judge is wrong at law, because the statute clearly affords the decision-maker precisely this sort of discretion. Thus, an additional situation is apparent; one where the decision-maker is free to assign weights to relevant factors, or combine relevant factors in a manner of her own choosing. This discretion will certainly contribute to the open textured nature of law and to indeterminacy.

[Dworkin 1977] presents a systematic account of discretion by proposing two basic types of discretion, that he called strong discretion and weak discretion. Weak discretion describes situations where a decision-maker must interpret standards in her own way, whereas strong discretion characterises those decisions where the decision-maker is not bound by any standards and is required to create his or her own standards. [MacCormick 1981] does not dispute this conceptualisation but contends that Dworkin's distinction between typologies is one of degree and not of type.

The discretion apparent in Australian family law exemplifies the weak discretion of Dworkin. The vast majority of decisions in the Family Court of Australia do not introduce new standards, set new precedents nor invoke new factors that have not previously been considered. Consequently, the majority of such decisions cannot be seen to involve strong discretion. Most cases are those that [Zeleznikow *et al* 1997] call commonplace cases. The distinction between commonplace and landmark cases is important in the data selection phase of the KDD process.

We claim that there are degrees of discretion depending on the domain. We hold this view because there exist domains such as property division in Australian Family Law, in which two decision makers may be applying identical rules and principles to facts interpreted in the same way yet both arrive at different, yet legally valid outcomes. Typically, the statute that underlies these domains presents a list of factors to be considered by the decision maker but does not indicate the relative weighting of each factor. [Christie 1986] calls these types of statutes shopping list Acts. Judges, in such domains exercise discretion by assigning a importance to each factor. The principle statute governing Australian family law, The Family Law Act (1975) is an example of a shopping list Act.

The statute presents a 'shopping list' of factors to be taken into account in arriving at a property order. The relative importance of each factor remains unspecified and many crucial terms are not defined. For example, the nature of a contribution is left unspecified. Similarly, what weight the retrospective element assumes relative to the prospective element, is left unspecified. The age, state of health and financial resources of the litigants are explicitly mentioned in the statute as relevant factors, yet their relative weightings are also unspecified. The Act clearly allows the decision maker a great deal of discretion in interpreting and weighing factors.

[Christie 1986] describes different situations that involve discretion in order to claim that its exercise inevitably involves power relationships within a political system. His approach is particularly useful for us, not because of the socio-political conclusions he draws, but because he specifically identifies statutes that provide a decision-maker with a shopping list of factors, as fields of law that necessitate a kind of Dworkian weak discretion. His main example is reproduced here to draw a parallel between the discretion that Australian family law mandates and the discretion given to decision-makers regarding US hazardous wastes. The relevant legislation is Section 520 of Second Restatement of Torts [1977].

In determining whether an activity is abnormally dangerous, the following factors are to be considered:
a) The existence of a high degree of risk of some harm to the person land or chattels;
b) The likelihood that the harm that results from it will be great;
c) The inability to eliminate the risk by the exercise of reasonable care;
d) The extent to which the activity is not a matter of common usage;
e) The inappropriateness of the activity to the place where it is carried on; and
f) The extent to which its value to the community is outweighed by its dangerous attributes.

As [Christie 1986] notes, an enormous range of legal decisions could be plausibly justified under Section 520. Some decisions that are no doubt plausible to the decision-maker may be appealed to higher Courts. They may conceivably choose to fetter the discretion at the lower level by imposing standards to guide the way the relevant factors are to be weighted and, by so doing, enforce a rigid stare decisis.

Ultimately, the concept of stare decisis underpins the use of KDD in law and warrants special discussion. Before discussing stare decisis, we give a brief introduction to Australian Family Law and the Family Court of Australia. This will help us understand the nature of property distribution in Australian Family Law.

Australia has a federal system of government. The Australian Constitution divides authority between the States and the Commonwealth and gives the Federal Parliament the power to make laws about marriage and divorce. The principal aim of the Family Law Act (1975) was to reform the law governing the dissolution of marriage. The new Act superseded State and Territory laws about 'guardianship, custody, access and maintenance' of children of a marriage. The Family Law Act (1975) as well as making significant changes to the law relating to divorce in Australia, created the Family Court of Australia to interpret and apply that law to individual cases.

According to [Kovacs 1992] family law in Australia differs from other legal domains in that the principle of stare decisis, that like cases should be treated alike, is only superficially applied in family law. For example, the Full bench of the High Court of Australia determined in Mallet vs. Mallet[1], that trial judges cannot base their assessment of property matters by assuming a 50/50 split between husband and wife and deviating from this starting point on the basis of contribution and needs. Trial judges are encouraged by the High Court to take all factors indicated in the statute into account.

[Kovacs 1992] contends that the High Court in Mallet vs. Mallet failed to take the opportunity to place specific constraints on the way in which trial judges determine property matters.   High Court justice Gibbs, C. J. made this point succinctly in Mallet. He said, *"It is proper, and indeed often necessary for the Family Court, in dealing with the circumstances of a particular case, to discuss the weight which it considers should be given, in that case, to one factor rather than another. It is understandable that practitioners, desirous of finding rules or even formulae, which may assist them in advising their clients as to the possible outcomes of litigation, should treat the remarks of the court in such cases as expressing binding principles, and that judges, seeking certainty or consistency, should sometimes do so. Decisions in particular cases of that kind can, however, do no more than provide a guide; they cannot put fetters on the discretionary power which the Parliament has left largely unfettered"*

In Norbis vs. Norbis[2], another opportunity arose for the High Court to lay down specific guidelines. According to [Kovacs 1992], the High Court went some way towards establishing some specific constraints. [Ingleby 1993] largely concurs with the views of [Kovacs 1992] and notes an appeal to the first appellate Court, the Full Bench of the Family Court of Australian is not permitted if the only ground for appeal is that the appeal court would have arrived at a different result had it heard the case. Permissible grounds for appeal include:

    a) the first instance judge did not include reasons for a discretionary decision

    b) the trial judge acted on a wrong principle

    c) the trial judge allowed irrelevant matters to guide him or her

    d) the trial judge did not take relevant matters into account or did not afforded them appropriate weight.

    e) the trial judge mistook the facts.

2. STARE DECISIS

Stare decisis is a fundamental principle in common law legal systems. The principle dictates that the reasoning, loosely, ratio decidendi used in new cases must follow the reasoning used by decision-makers in courts at the same or higher level in the hierarchy. Both [Kovacs 1992] and [Ingleby 1993] observe that stare decisis is

---

[1] [1984] 156 CLR 185

[2] [1986] 161 CLR 513

not as rigorously applied in family law as it is in other domains. However, the concept of stare decisis is a difficult one and warrants further focus in order to identify the ramifications that a departure from stare decisis has for KDD.

If, for instance, fields of law such as property division in Australian family law are so discretionary that leading commentators convincingly argue that stare decisis does not apply, then can case outcomes be predicted? If outcomes cannot be accurately predicted, then any attempt at doing so using KDD techniques is futile.

Perhaps outcomes in discretionary fields cannot be predicted because the discretion that is inherently placed in the hands of the judge encourages so much uncertainty that predictions can only ever be educated guesses. However, if this were the case, we would expect practitioners in Australian family law to be consistently inaccurate with their own predictions. On the contrary, we find that practitioners are very accurate in predicting outcomes, despite the discretion available to judges. This apparent paradox is resolved by looking more closely at the concept of stare decisis.

[Wassestrom 1961] identifies three types of stare decisis which [Lawler 1964] illustrates. Lawler's diagrams are reproduced below as Figure 1, Figure 2 and Figure 3. Figure 1 represents traditional stare decisis. Under this type of stare decisis, a court is bound by prior decisions of courts of equal or higher level. It is this kind of stare decisis that [Kovacs 1992] and [Ingleby 1993] claim has not occurred fully in family law, because the High Court has failed to lay down specific constraints for trial judges to follow.

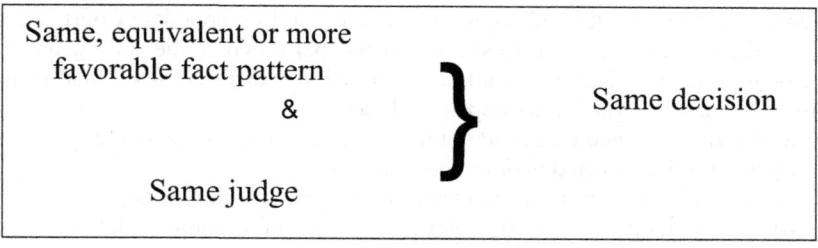

Figure 1. Traditional Stare Decisis

Another type of stare decisis, called personal stare decisis, is used to describe the observation that most judges attempt to be consistent with their previous decisions. This manifests itself in the Family Court, as the tendency an individual judge has to be consistent with the way he or she exercised discretion in past, similar cases. Figure 2 depicts personal stare decisis.

The third type of stare decisis represents the tendency of a group of judges that make up a current court to follow its own decisions. This type of stare decisis is represented in Figure 3 and manifests itself in property division in Australian family law, as a desire for Family Court judges to exercise discretion in a manner that is consistent with other judges of the same registry of the Court, at the same time.

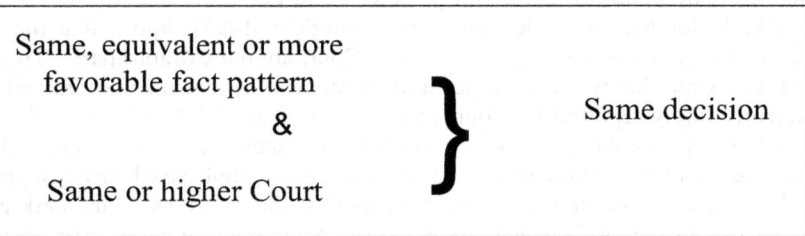

Figure 2. Personal Stare Decisis

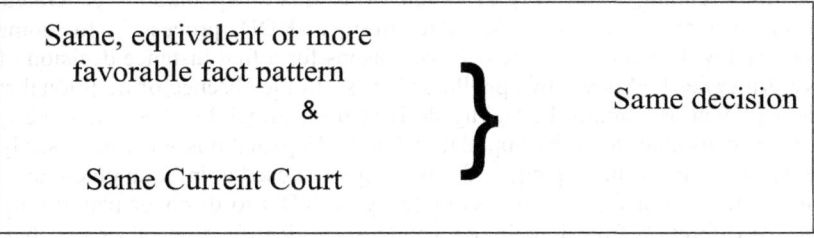

Figure 3. Local stare decisis

[Lawler 1964] reminds us that predicting the outcome of a case cannot be possible without the concept of stare decisis. Furthermore, the ability to predict an outcome with some accuracy is important if the law is to be respected within the community.

Although family law in Australia has been controversial, by and large, practitioners experienced with the way in which the Court and individual judges exercise discretion can predict outcomes in property proceedings with some degree of accuracy. As [Kovacs 1992] and [Ingleby 1993] point out, this level of predictability is not due to traditional stare decisis. We take the view that the predictability must be the result of the remaining two forms of stare decisis, local and personal stare decisis.

This has ramifications for the data selection, data pre-processing and evaluation phases of KDD. Some case outcomes in discretionary domains are so far removed from other similar cases that it is reasonable to assume the judge has erred. In domains characterised by traditional stare decisis, a judge can err by failing to follow the constraints laid down by equal or superior Courts. In personal and local stare decisis, judges err by failing to be consistent with other judges currently in the same Court or with themselves in earlier like decisions.

Another ramification of local and personal stare decisis relates to the types of cases suitable for the data selection phase. [Ingleby 1993] argues that the vast majority of cases that come before the Family Court are not extraordinary. They do not involve extraordinary facts, do not have outcomes that are unexpected and are, consequently rarely reported by Court reporting services. [Zeleznikow *et al* 1997] calls such cases commonplace cases and distinguishes them from landmark or leading cases. In fields where traditional stare decisis is emphasised, any case that is currently viewed as commonplace could be used in the future as a landmark case. This blurs the distinction between landmark and commonplace cases. However, in domains where traditional stare decisis is not strongly followed, if a case is regarded as commonplace at the time of decision, it is extremely unlikely to be invoked in the future as a landmark case. An ordinary case impacts by adding to the body of cases for personal and local stare decisis.

Our traditional, local and personal stare decisis conceptualisation also has ramifications relating to the way in which we evaluate explanations generated by computer systems that use knowledge from a KDD process. In domains characterised with traditional stare decisis, reasons for a first instance decision often involve principles laid down by appellate Courts. In the absence of traditional stare decisis, explanations cannot be rigidly derived from principles, because none have been specifically laid down by appellate Courts. Explanations must necessarily be further removed from the sequence of reasoning steps used to infer an outcome.

Our starting point for the process of applying KDD to discover patterns in the exercise of discretion from judicial decisions is an identification of factors that are currently, or have, in the past been relevant in the determination of judicial outcomes. Once relevant factors have been identified and a structure of the reasoning within the field of law ascertained, data mining algorithms can learn to weight factors in a similar manner to the way in which judges undertake this task. This applies equally to common law and civil law jurisdictions though differences between the two types of jurisdictions impact on the identification of a suitable field of law and the selection of data for a KDD exercise. This is discussed in the next section.

3. CIVIL AND COMMON LAW

Since we hope that the use of KDD in law has applications beyond the common law domains in which the authors of this text are familiar, we need to investigate decision-making in a variety of legal systems. Because KDD involves learning from cases, we focus upon the significance of cases in common law, civil law and hybrid legal systems.

Common law is the legal tradition that evolved in England from the 11th century onwards. Its principles appear for the most part in reported judgments, usually of the higher courts, in relation to specific fact situations arising in disputes that courts have adjudicated. The common law is usually much more detailed in its prescriptions than the civil law. Common law is the foundation of private law, not only for England, Wales and Ireland, but also in forty-nine U.S. states, nine Canadian provinces and in most countries that first received that law as colonies of the British Empire and which, in many cases, have preserved it as independent States of the British Commonwealth.

Civil law may be defined as that legal tradition which has its origin in Roman law, as codified in the Corpus Juris Civilis of Justinian[3] and as subsequently developed in Continental Europe and around the world [Tetley 1999]. Civil law eventually divided into two streams: the codified Roman law (as seen in the French Civil Code of 1804 and its progeny and imitators - Continental Europe, Québec and Louisiana being examples); and uncodified Roman law (as seen in Scotland and South Africa). Civil law is highly systematised and structured and relies on declarations of broad, general principles, often ignoring the details.

Statutory law, or law found in legislation other than civil codes, is basic to both the civil and common law. In common law jurisdictions, most rules are found in the jurisprudence and statutes complete them. In civil law jurisdictions, the important principles are stated in the code, while the statutes complete them.

[David and Brierly 1985] note that common law and civil law legal traditions share similar social objectives (individualism, liberalism and personal rights) and they have in fact been joined in one single family, the *Western law* family, because of this functional similarity. [Tetley 1999] explores the sources, concepts and style of the two Western sources of law. He classifies differences with regards to:

1. *Order of priority: jurisprudence and doctrine* – A major difference between the civil law and common law is that priority in civil law is given to doctrine (including the codifiers' reports) over jurisprudence, while the opposite is true in the common law.

2. *Doctrine* - The civil law doctrine's function is to draw from the cases, books and legal dictionaries, the rules and the principles which will provide both the practice and the courts with a guide for the solution of particular cases in the future. The civil code focuses on legal principles. It identifies their function, determines their domain of application, and explains their effects in terms of rights and obligations. The common law doctrine's function is more modest: authors are encouraged to distinguish cases that would appear incompatible in civil law, and to extract specific rules from these cases. The common law author focuses on fact patterns. He or she analyses cases presenting similar but not identical facts, extracting from the specific rules, and then, through deduction, determines the often very narrow scope of each rule, and sometimes proposes new rules to cover facts that have not yet presented themselves.

3. *Jurisprudence* - Common law jurisprudence sets out a new specific rule to a new specific set of facts and provides the principal source of law, while civil law jurisprudence applies general principles, and is only a secondary source of law and explanation

---

[3] The *Corpus Juris Civilis* is the name given to a four-part compilation of Roman law prepared between 528 and 534 AD by a commission appointed by Emperor Justinian and headed by the jurist Tribonian.

4. *Statutes* - Although statutes have the same primacy in both legal traditions, they differ in their functions. Civil law codes provide the core of the law - general principles are systematically and exhaustively exposed in codes and particular statutes complete them. Common law statutes, on the other hand, complete the case law, which contains the core of the law expressed through specific rules applying to specific facts.

5. *Style of drafting of laws* - Civil law codes and statutes are concise, while common law statutes are precise. Indeed, civil law statutes provide definitions, and state principles in broad, general phrases. Common law statutes, on the other hand, provide detailed definitions, and each specific rule sets out lengthy enumerations of specific applications or exceptions, preceded by a catch-all phrase and followed by a demurrer such as *notwithstanding the generality of the foregoing*. This difference in style is linked to the function of statutes. Civilian statutory general principles need not be explained, precisely, because they are not read restrictively (not being exceptions), but need to be stated concisely if the code is to be exhaustive. Common law statutory provisions need not be concise, because they cover only the specific part of the law to be reformed, but must be precise, because the common law courts restrict rules to the specific facts they are intended to cover.

6. *Interpretation of laws* - In civil law jurisdictions, the first step in interpreting an ambiguous law is to discover the intention of the legislator by examining the legislation as a whole, as well as the provisions more immediately surrounding the obscure text. In common law jurisdictions, by comparison, statutes are to be objectively constructed according to certain rules standing by themselves, such as that an enactment must be read as a whole, and that special provisions will control general provisions, so as to meet the subjects' reasonable understandings and expectations.

7. *The appointment of judges* - Common law judges, who are called to play an important role in deciding what the law is, are appointed from among experienced practising lawyers. Civil law judges, whose main function is adjudicating, are appointed fresh from specialised schools.

8. *The role of legal rules* - Civil law categories are based on the rules themselves[4], while common law categories were founded on the law that was administered by different courts[5]. Civil law systems are **closed**, in the sense that every possible situation is governed by a limited number of general principles, while common law systems are **open**, in the sense that new rules may be created or imported for new facts.

9. *Rights versus remedies* - Civil law focuses on rights and obligations, while common law is oriented toward the jurisdiction of particular courts to grant the sought-after remedy (*remedies precede rights*).

---

[4] Such as private law and public law
[5] Such as common law courts and the court of Equity

10. *Stare decisis* - Stare decisis is a fundamental principle in common law legal systems. The principle dictates that the reasoning, loosely, *ratio decidendi[6]*, used in new cases must follow the reasoning used by decision-makers in courts at the same or higher level in the hierarchy. Stare decisis is unknown to civil law, where judgments rendered by judges only enjoy the *authority of reason*;

Because of the essential role of stare decisis in common law countries, analogical reasoning and reasoning with cases is commonly performed by legal professionals operating in such countries. Hence, legal decision support systems have often used case-based reasoning[7].

Given these differences, is there any value to be gained from using case-based models of legal reasoning in a civil law context? [Ashley 2003] claims that judges in civil law jurisdictions do reason with legal cases, but in a very different way from their common law counterparts.

We claim, that whilst case-based reasoning is particularly suited for modelling reasoning in common law, Knowledge Discovery from Databases is equally suited for use in civil law domains. The reason for our claim is that KDD is primarily used to understand how judges exercise discretion. Even in civil law countries, with their emphasis on codifying the law, there exist what [Black 1990] defines as discretionary acts. In such Acts, judges must exercise their discretion. The use of KDD in civil law countries can help support transparency and consistency in such countries.

4. SELECTING A TASK SUITABLE FOR KDD: THE IMPORTANCE OF OPEN TEXTURE

Essentially, tasks suited to a KDD exercise are those that involve:
a) many ambiguous or vaguely defined concepts
b) many coarse grained rather than fine grained concepts
c) tasks underpinned by statutes that embed a *shopping list* of factors
d) an analyst who adheres to jurisprudential perspectives that are more consistent with critical legal studies, legal realism, post modern, or to somewhat of a lesser degree positivist schools of thought, and certainly to a lesser degree German conceptualist schools.
e) a socio-political environment that encourages ambiguity or discretion
f) a complete list of relevant concepts for the task.

An assessment of the extent to which a KDD exercise is suitable in a given field of law requires a clear articulation of the objective of the KDD exercise. The specification of an objective in a form that is clearly operationalised is a key element for a successful KDD exercise. For example, an objective within the field of

---

[6]   The ground or reason for the decision. The point in a case that determines the judgement.

[7]   Case based reasoning is the process of using previous experience to analyse or solve a new problem, explain why previous experiences are or are not similar to the present problem and adapting past solutions to meet the requirements of the present problem.

Australian family law could be the prediction of the percentage split of marital assets a judge is likely to determine. For reasons to be discussed below, a task within the same field of law that is less suitable for KDD involves the prediction of the actual property order a judge is likely to construct to realise a particular percentage split.

An assessment of the extent to which KDD is suitable for a task involves identifying the extent to which a task involves open texture. In the discusson of Hart's article on legal positivism [Hart 1958] above, the argument was advanced that predicting whether a judge will or will not allow roller blades in the park, involves the open textured concept *vehicle*.

Although every possible extension for an open textured concept cannot be completely known in advance, it is plausible to estimate the extent to which the extensions known represent all possible uses. Practitioners seem to estimate the degree to which a field of law is open textured, in order to offer a prediction. Few practitioners would argue that the concept of *vehicle* that arises in Hart's scenario seems less subject to new uses than the concept of *a social group* that arises in the determination of refugee status according to the United Nations Convention Relating to the Granting of Refugee Status (1958).

A gradation of open texture may seem at first sight, to defy the notion of open texture. However is pragmatically appealing particularly for identifying suitable applications of KDD. As [Waismann 1951] claims, most empirical concepts are, and will remain open textured. However, a family law expert, aware that a judge may interpret concepts such as a) marriage length, b) financial contributions, c) health needs and other factors in many possible ways; or will exercise discretion in weighting the factors; will suggest a likely outcome with some caution.

An expert on road traffic law will suggest that a judge will interpret the terms driver, blood alcohol test and legal limit in only one way. Because it is less open textured than family law, the law relating to drink driving appears to be more predictable than family law. Open texture may be an all or nothing affair for theoreticians but, for practitioners, there are degrees of open texture.

The open textured continuum cannot have definite end-points. No task is completely open textured and no task in law is totally well defined. To say that a task is totally well defined is to say that only one interpretation alone can ever be found. This may occur in systems such as mathematics, where one can prove theorems from axioms by the use of inference rules. But, this is not the case in law, at least according to most jurisprudence theorists. To propose that a legal concept can be tightly defined presumes a preposterous knowledge of future events. At the other extreme, no task is totally open textured. To be so would be to interpret the task and terms in any way whatsoever.

A determination of the degree of open texture inherent in a task involves the following considerations:

  a) Ambiguity: the extent to which statutes, cases and concepts used in the field contain ambiguous or vague definitions;
  b) Granularity: the extent to which terms in the domain are coarse grained;
  c) Discretionary statutes: the extent to which a field of law is underpinned by shopping list type of statutes;

d) Jurisprudence: the jurisprudential perspective presumed. Some perspectives presume virtually no open texture whereas others presume it is prevalent;
e) Socio-political environment: the social and political context of the reasoning;
f) Completeness of knowledge: the extent to which key elements in a reasoning process within a field of law are known.

An assessment of the degree to which a field of law is open textured is necessarily subjective. Different KDD analysts may classify the same task in different ways. A determination is not made on the basis of clear metrics that measure criteria derivable in an objective fashion from theory. Rather, the determination of the degree of open texture involves some subjective judgment and thus leads to the conclusion that the KDD exercise is as much an art as it is a science. We will now briefly discuss each consideration in the assessment of the degree of open texture of a legal task.

4.1   Ambiguity

A field of law may be regarded as well defined if definitions for most terms within the environment are provided in the statute or in past cases. For example, Section 5(1) of the Victorian Credit Act (1984) contains seventy-four definitions for terms that appear within the act. Furthermore, a number of schedules included with the act serve to refine terms within the definitions. In addition to this, there have been a small number of decisions that have served to further clarify remaining ambiguities.

In contrast, the United Nations Convention for the Determination of Refugee Status (1955) contains almost no definitions for terms such as well-founded fear, persecution and religion. Most practitioners perceive this Convention as quite open textured, yet few perceive the Victorian Credit Act to be open textured to the same extent.

[Kovacs 1992] notes that fundamental terms in the principle statute governing family law in Australia, the Family Law Act (1975) are left open ended and subject to various interpretations. According to her, principles have been written into the Act to guide a judicial decision maker in the alteration of custody or property rights, but these only act as broad guidelines and not as specific constraints on decisions.

4.2   Granularity

A task is likely to be perceived as quite open textured if it contains a number of terms that are course grained or broad in scope. The terms, financial resources, past contributions and health are included in the Family Law Act (1975). Most experts regard these as open textured terms because they are very abstract and can be instantiated to refer to a great many scenarios. In contrast, the term blood alcohol level in a road traffic statute is more specific in scope and cannot be made to apply to many other terms.

4.3   Jurisprudence

An assessment of the degree of open texture within a field of law depends heavily on the jurisprudential perspective adopted. For example, the movement prevalent over one hundred years ago, sometimes called German conceptualism, assumes that judges are almost totally constrained by rules. Every attempt is made by adherents to that view to determine one single correct meaning for every term in any rule in a legal system. Most terms can be expected to be perceived as considerably better defined by German conceptualists than would be the case for adherents to other theories.

For example, the critical legal studies movement exemplified by [Kennedy 1986], is in stark contrast to the German conceptualists. Kennedy asserts that the interpretation of terms within statutes is very much dependent on the case outcome a judge desires. For an adherent to critical legal studies, far more terms will be subject to more extensions in any legal field than is the case for German conceptualists.

4.4   Socio-political environment

The extent to which a real world task is open textured is dependent on the social and political context of the reasoning. In the past, the term, *sexual harassment* was extended to cover only grave violations of human rights. The same term is far more open textured in the current socio-political climate than was previously the case.

A field of law that regulates vehicular access to a municipal park may not be considered appreciably open textured under normal circumstances. However, in a scenario where racial unrest leading to riots is commonplace, terms such as the race of the driver, the race of park frequenters or the insignia displayed on the driver's jacket may be far more relevant for determining whether the vehicle is prohibited from the park than whether the vehicle is a tank.

4.5   Discretionary environment

Whilst investigating the discretionary environment, we need to identify the relevant factors. Section 79(4) and Section 75(2) of the Family Law Act (1975) list a number of factors that must be considered when devising a property order. Section 79(4) refers to the prospective element included in Section 75(2). These sections are summarised here in order to illustrate that this statute presents a list of factors to be taken into account. In considering what order (if any) should be made under this section, following proceedings with respect to any property of the parties to a marriage, the court shall take into account:

a)   the financial contribution made directly or indirectly by a party to the marriage to the acquisition, conservation or improvement of any of the property of the parties;

b)   the contribution (other than a financial contribution) made by a party to the marriage to the acquisition, conservation or improvement of any of the property of the parties;

c) the contribution made by a party to the marriage to the welfare of the family including any contribution made in the capacity of homemaker or parent;

d) the effect of any proposed order upon the earning capacity of either party to the marriage;

e) the matters referred to in sub-section75(2) so far as they are relevant (eg age and state of health of parties);

f) any other order made under this Act affecting a party to the marriage or a child of the marriage.

The statute presents a 'shopping list' of factors to be taken into account in arriving at a property order. The relative importance of each factor remains unspecified and many crucial terms are not defined. For example, the nature of a contribution is left unspecified. What weight the contributions assume relative to future needs is similarly left unspecified. The age, state of health and financial resources of the litigants are explicitly mentioned as relevant factors in the statute, yet their relative weightings are not specified.

The Act clearly allows the decision maker a great deal of discretion in interpreting and weighing factors. The Family Court of Australia has argued that discretion in family law is appropriate because appellate Court decisions provide a constant source of guidelines for first instance decision makers. However, [Kovacs 1992] argues that the discretion of trial judges is so unfettered that stare decisis cannot be said to apply to Australian family law in the same way it applies in other domains of law. The concept of stare decisis is central to any attempt at predicting case outcomes. In Chapter 3, we discuss, at length, how this concept relates to data mining.

One of the Section 75(2) paragraphs, subsection 75(2)o allows a judge, in the interests of justice, to consider any factor not mentioned elsewhere in the Act. The presence of discretionary provisions such as 75(2)o tends to sway an expert toward viewing a task which references those sections as one that is more discretionary than would otherwise be the case.

4.6   Completeness

At any given time, a reasoner can assign a belief in the completeness of its knowledge of the environment. A student introduced to an environment correctly perceives her knowledge to be limited. On receiving a task, it is reasonable to expect the student to believe the solution may require concepts which are, at that time, not known to be relevant. As experience in solving problems within that environment increases, the confidence in the completeness of knowledge of the domain also increases.

In any field of law, the extent to which concepts are relevant for reaching a conclusion, can conceivably, be estimated. For example, in practice, judges of the Family Court of Australia follow a five-step process in order to arrive at a property order. (see [Dickey 1990] and [Ingleby 1993]):

a) Ascertain the property of the parties.

b) Value all property of both parties.
c) Discern those properties that will not be subject to a Court order altering interests from those that may be the subject of a Court order.
d) Property that may be subject to a Court order is referred to as common pool property. This task is known as the common pool determination task. Determine a percentage of the common pool property to be awarded to each party.
e) Create an order altering property interests to realise the determined percentage split of the common pool property.

Relevant features for the common pool determination task include the type of asset, which party acquired the asset, when it was acquired, from whom, and whether funds were used to maintain or improve the asset. The colour and cost of the asset may be integral features of an asset, yet are not relevant for the common pool determination exercise.

Completeness reflects the extent to which concepts relevant for a problem solution are explicit. For example, key terms for the percentage split determination task in Australian family law are specified clearly in the principal statute, though many of the terms are ambiguous.

Once a percentage split has been decided, a judge attempts to realise that percentage by creating a property order that distributes the actual property. Judges in general avoid forcing a sale of any asset and attempt to minimise the disruption to the everyday life of children. However the statute provides no guidance to do with the construction of a property order. Furthermore, there have been few, if any contested cases that specifically relate to the court order created. Therefore, knowledge regarding the creation of a property order is not considered as complete as that regarding, for example, the assessment of a percentage split of assets.

5. SAMPLE ASSESSMENT OF THE DEGREE OF OPEN TEXTURE

A task that is not appreciably open textured has terms that are fine grained and unambiguous; is underpinned by statutes that do not include lists of factors to be taken into account without providing guidance as to how factors are to be combined and; clearly articulates all relevant considerations.

Tasks that are not appreciably open textured are typically not good candidates for a KDD exercise because heuristics that reflect reasoning inherent in the task are likely to be more readily available manually through structured interviews with experts or other knowledge acquisition devices. To use KDD in these tasks is to attempt to do automatically what can be easily and accurately performed manually.

The common pool task in property proceedings is not appreciable open textured. Factors that have been elicited from domain experts as relevant for a determination of common pool inclusion include a) acquisition date of a property, b) the registered proprietor, c) the source of the property, d) the outlay of funds on the property, and e) the duration of the marriage. None of the relevant terms are totally well defined. For example, the acquisition date of a business may be the date the business was first registered with authorities, the date attempts were made to initiate the business or the date the business began operating. However, experts agree that, by and large, most terms in the task, are reasonably well defined. Furthermore, experts expect that these factors are quite complete in that they do not expect a judicial decision maker to take new factors not previously encountered into account in a determination of common pool assets.

This assessment depends to some extent on our jurisprudential theory. An adherent to critical legal studies or post-modern jurisprudence may be inclined to deny the importance of any expert's opinion in this regard and to regard the common pool task as extremely open textured. However, from our non-post-modern point of view, the task is quite well defined.

Tasks underpinned by discretionary statutes, that adopt ambiguous terms, but are essentially complete, are well suited to a KDD exercise. The task of determining a percentage split of marital assets to be awarded to each party of a failed marriage is not so well defined. There are three factors identified as relevant for the determination of a final percentage: i) the relative contributions by the parties, ii) the relative future needs and iii) the level of wealth of the marriage. Experts do not consider other factors to be relevant at this level, so we consider this task to be relatively complete. However, we are obliged to regard the task as quite open textured in that the way the factors combine is subject to judicial discretion.

Tasks that are not complete or involve concepts that are not clearly known, are not suited to a KDD exercise, because of the suspicion that relevant variables for the task are not known. The task of predicting the Family Court property order a judge will arrive at, in order to distribute assets of a marriage to realise a desired percentage split, is an example of a task that is considerably open textured, because it is not complete. Judges in general avoid forcing a sale of any asset and attempt to minimise the disruption to the everyday life of children. However, there is little indication about the reasoning steps used by judges beyond these basic heuristics. The statute provides no guidance and there have been very few contested cases that specifically relate to the court order created.

The first step in the application of KDD to a legal domain involves the articulation of a specific task that is a required objective of the KDD. The actual task can then be investigated to determine the extent to which reasoning within the task is open textured. The key criteria are the extent to which ambiguous terms and concepts are prevalent, the extent to which the underlying statutes are discretionary, the granularity of terms, the completeness of knowledge, the socio-political environment and the jurisprudence perspective. The task can be assessed according to these criteria and can help to determine whether the task is suited to KDD.

Once the task is regarded to be suitable for KDD, a sample data set must be selected. This involves two distinct steps, the selection of relevant variables and the selection of a sufficient number of prior records or cases. These steps are discussed in the next section.

6. SELECTING DATASET RECORDS

Data in the legal domain can represent attributes of persons, processes or legal cases. For example, Victoria Legal Aid[8], a government funded legal aid organisation stores values for up to 800 variables relating to an application for legal aid. Attributes such as the name of an applicant, the type of charge, the date of birth and the nationality can be seen to be features of the application. These features are useful in a data mining exercise such as that performed by [Wilkins and Pillaipakkamnutt 1997] for estimating time to disposition of a case.

In contrast to attributes of persons or processes, data can be stored that is useful in supporting the reasoning processes of a legal decision maker. For example, the data collected from over one hundred family law cases by [Stranieri et al 1999] represents facts, conclusions and decisions made by a Family Court judge in the process of reaching a decision. The data derives directly from case judgements as delivered by judges.

The considerations involved in the selection of records from a domain depend to a large extent on whether the data derives from, and represents reasoning processes used by decision makers or whether the data represents descriptive features of a domain.

The key distinction to be made if data represents the reasoning process used in cases is that between commonplace cases and landmark cases. Commonplace cases are far more suitable for a KDD exercise than landmark cases. The distinction between these two types of cases as far as KDD, is concerned is made in the next section.

6.1   Commonplace cases vs Landmark cases

[Kolodner 1993] incorporates context in her definition of a case for case-based reasoning systems. She states that 'a case is a contextualised piece of knowledge representing an experience that teaches a lesson fundamental to achieving the goals of the reasoner'. [Zeleznikow et al 1997] notes that even in non-contentious areas, Kolodner's definition provides scope for considerable problems. They disagree with Kolodner that a case necessarily '...teaches a lesson fundamental to...the reasoner'. Certainly some cases do fit this description. Most notably within law, those decisions from appellate courts which form the basis of later decision and provide guidance to lower courts do provide a fundamental lesson, or normative structure for subsequent reasoning. [Pound 1908] considers such cases to be formal, binding and inviolate prescriptions for future decision-making, whilst [MacCormick 1978] sees them as beacons from which inferior or merely subsequent courts navigate their way through new fact situations. The common name for such cases is landmark cases.

---

[8]   VLA based in Victoria, Australia is a government-funded provider of legal services for disadvantaged clients (_www.legalaid.vic.gov.au_).   Its goals include providing legal aid in the most effective, economic and efficient manner and pursuing innovative means of providing legal services in the community

However, most decisions in any jurisdiction are not landmark cases. Most decisions are commonplace, and deal with relatively minor matters such as vehicle accidents, small civil actions, petty crime, divorce and the like. These cases are rarely, if ever, reported upon by court reporting services, nor are they often made the subject of learned comment or analysis. More importantly, each case does not have the same consequences as the landmark cases.

Landmark cases are therefore of a fundamentally different character from commonplace cases. Landmark cases will individually have a profound effect on the subsequent disposition of all cases in that domain, whereas commonplace cases will only have a cumulative effect, and that effect will only be apparent over time.

Take, for example, the case of *Mabo v Queensland (No.2)*[9]. Prior to *Mabo*, the indigenous people of Australia, the Aborigines, had few, if any, proprietary rights to Australian land. Under British colonial rule, their laws were held to be inchoate and Australia itself was held to be *terra nullius*, 'empty land' at the time of white settlement. Hence, the only property laws applicable were those stemming from the introduction of white rule, laws which were less than generous in their grant of land to Aborigines. In *Mabo*, the High Court held that previous decisions holding that Australia was *terra nullius* at settlement, and decisions holding that Aborigines had no property laws affecting land, were simply wrong at law. Hence, the High Court said, Aborigines had sovereignty over parts of Australia under certain conditions. Whether one agrees with the High Court's interpretive technique, it is indisputable that this is the landmark case in the area, and has formed the basis of future decisions in the area. Indeed, *Mabo*, like many other leading cases, was the spur for political action and ultimately led to the introduction of the Federal *Native Title Act*[10]. Thus, landmark cases have the dual effect of determining (to some degree) the interpretation of subsequent fact situations as well as influencing the invocation of normative legislative processes.

Two leading United States landmark cases *Plessy v. Ferguson*[11] and *Brown v. Board of Education. of Topeka*[12], deal with the issue of segregated schools. Following the defeat in battle in 1865 of the Confederate States, whose decision in 1861 to leave the Union, prompted the US Civil War, the thirteenth and fourteenth amendments to the US constitution were passed.

Section 1 of the Thirteenth Amendment to the US constitution states,

Neither slavery nor involuntary servitude, except as a punishment for crime whereof the party shall have been duly convicted, shall exist within the United States, or any place subject to their jurisdiction.

Section 2 of the Thirteenth Amendment to the US constitution states,

Congress shall have power to enforce this article by appropriate legislation.

Section 1 of the Fourteenth Amendment to the US constitution states,

---

[9] (1992) 175 CLR 1
[10] Commonwealth Consolidated Acts - An Act about native title in relation to <u>land</u> or <u>waters</u>, and for related purposes 1993
[11] 163 US 537 (1896)
[12] 347 U.S. (1954)

All persons born or naturalized in the United States, and subject to the jurisdiction thereof, are citizens of the United States and of the state wherein they reside. No state shall make or enforce any law which shall abridge the privileges or immunities of citizens of the United States; nor shall any state deprive any person of life, liberty, or property, without due process of law; nor deny to any person within its jurisdiction the equal protection of the laws.

In 1896, in the case of *Plessy v. Ferguson* the United States Supreme Court ruled that the demands of the Fourteenth Amendment were satisfied if the states provided separate but equal facilities and the fact of segregation alone did not make facilities automatically unequal. In 1954, in *Brown v. Board of Education of Topeka* the Supreme Court seemingly overturned the decision made in *Plessy v. Ferguson.* In *Brown v. Board of Education of Topeka*, in the opinion of [Black 1990], the Supreme Court declared racial segregation in public schools to be in violation of the equal protection clause of the Fourteenth Amendment. They did so, not by overturning *Plesy v. Ferguson* but by using sociological evidence to show that racially segregated schools could not be equal [Dworkin 1986].

To further indicate the similarity between landmark cases and rules we note that in *Miranda v Arizona*[13] the United States Supreme Court ruled that prior to any custodial interrogation the accused must be warned:

1. That he has a right to remain silent;
2. That any statement he does make may be used in evidence against him;
3. That he has the right to the presence of an attorney;
4. That if he cannot afford an attorney, one will be appointed for him prior to any questioning if he so desires.

Unless and until these warnings or a waiver of these rights are demonstrated at the trial, no evidence obtained in the interrogation may be used against the accused. Miranda v Arizona is a landmark case with regards to the rights of the accused in a United States criminal trial. This case has assumed such significance that its findings are known as the Miranda rule.

Landmark cases rarely occur in common practice and are reported and discussed widely. These cases set a precedent that alters the way in which subsequent cases are decided. In the last two decades, the number of landmark cases in the Family Court of Australia is in the order of hundreds while the number of commonplace cases is in the order of multiple tens of thousands.

It should be noted that or notion of a landmark or commonplace case, is relevant to the system in which it is used. Hypo [Ashley 1991] has a case knowledge base consisting of thirty legal cases in the domain of trade secrets. None of these cases has a particular legal significance, and thus legal scholars may consider these cases as commonplace cases. However, because HYPO reasons from these cases, for the purpose of the HYPO system, these cases can be considered as landmark cases.

Some critics believe the use of legal case-based reasoners is limited. [Berman 1991] believed legal case-based systems must by necessity simulate rule-based systems and that factors emulate rules. He stated: *'For developers, as contrasted to researchers, the issue is not whether the resulting rule base is complete or even*

[13] 384 U.S. 436 (1966)

accurate or self-modifying — but whether the rule base is sufficiently accurate to be useful'. We believe that jurisprudes and developers of legal decision support systems use landmark cases as norms or rules. Commonplace cases can be used to learn how judges exercise discretion.

6.1.1   Commonplace Cases in Civil Law and Mixed Legal Systems

In section 3 we discussed the differences between common law and civil law codes, and indeed noted that there are indeed many hybrid legal systems. We also posed the question: is there any value to be gained from using Knowledge Discovery from Databases in a Civil Law Context?

Mixed jurisdictions and mixed legal systems, their characteristics and definition, have become a subject of very considerable interest and debate in Europe, no doubt because of the European Union, which has brought together many legal systems under a single legislature, which in turn has adopted laws and directives taking precedence over national laws. In effect, the European Union is a mixed jurisdiction or is becoming a mixed jurisdiction, there being a growing convergence within the Union between Europe's two major legal traditions, the civil law of the continental countries and the common law of England, Wales and Ireland [Markesinis 1993].

[Lundmark 1998] claims that there are reasons to believe that at least some European legal systems are converging in their use of precedents. Given the *Europeanisation of Europe*, courts are beginning *to rely upon decisions not only of the European Court of Justice but also of other Member State courts*. As judges in one European State confront *foreign values* from the others, *they need to question and then to articulate underlying assumptions*. As a result, the style of opinion writing is becoming less ministerial, bold, and declaratory and more discursive, cautious and fact-oriented. In short, judicial reasons are becoming more amenable to distinguishing and to ... use of the fact-based result of the decision in addition to the announced rationale and the discernable principles.

[Ashley 2003] also believes that the proliferation of computers and density of legal regulation will lead to a greater use of case reports in civil law domains. [MacCormick and Summers 1997] conducted a five-year study of nine civil law and two common law domains. They concluded that all these systems accommodate justified legal change through judicial as well as legislative action that is through precedent. [Lundmark 1998] concluded that a self-imposed adherence to precedent will help judges to reduce political disapproval, and to forestall legislative measures to restrict their ability to stray from precedent.

Thus with the development of a European Legal System, and UN conventions and courts (such as the UN Convention on the International Sale of Goods, the International Court of Justice, the International Criminal Court and International Criminal Tribunals for the former Yugoslavia and Rwanda) there is a need for a uniform application of the same law. As long as sufficiently many and sufficiently detailed case descriptions exist, we argue that it feasible to use KDD to model the manner in which civil law judges exercise discretion.

6.2   Using Commonplace cases in training sets for KDD Algorithms

The vast majority of cases that come before a first instance decision maker in family law are never published, are never appealed, and establish no new principle or rule. They do not revolve around a new legal interpretation, nor do they involve circumstances that are legally interesting to experienced practitioners. They are commonplace cases.

Commonplace cases are suitable for the discovery of knowledge about how judges exercise discretion in family law, whereas landmark cases are not suitable. The distinction between commonplace and landmark cases is not one based on clear definitional categories since any case that is currently viewed as commonplace could conceivably be used in the future as a landmark case. For example, perhaps the most significant leading case in family law, Mallet vs Mallet[14] was not particularly extraordinary at the first instance court.

The trial judge in Mallet vs Mallet awarded 20% of the business assets from a long marriage to the wife after taking the contributions and needs of both parties into account. The Full Bench of the Family Court increased the wife's percentage split to 50% by making explicit the principle that equality should be the starting point. That Court commenced with 50% and deviated according to contributions and needs. Following this decision, the husband appealed to the High Court. The High Court overruled the Full Bench of the Family Court and reinstated the trial judge's decision. As indicated previously, this case became a landmark case in that it firmly endorsed unfettered trial Court discretion.

Although a case cannot be definitely categorised as either commonplace or landmark, the distinction between them is a useful one when applying selecting cases for inclusion in a KDD exercise. Most landmark cases are not suitable for the assembly of training sets for data mining, because these cases typically revolve around a definitional issue or they attempt to resolve a classification ambiguity so that a precedent for subsequent cases may be set.

Landmark cases heard by appeal courts typically establish a new rule or principle. In a domain where traditional stare decisis is less influential than in standard Common law domains, Appeal Courts can more readily be seen to establish broad principles or resolve classification ambiguities. For example, in the Full Court decision in the Marriage of Elias[15] a precedent was established that deemed entrepreneurial prowess as a form of contribution to a marriage. Debts have been admitted as negative contributions in The Marriage of Anttman[16]. Both these leading cases can be seen to refine the open textured concept of a contribution to a marriage.

The objective in applying machine learning in the discretionary domain of family law is to model the way, in which judges weight factors which are known to be relevant. A leading case may introduce a new factor that subsequent trial decisions must accommodate. Data about the factor could not have been recorded in cases

[14] (1984) 156 CLR 185
[15] (1977) Fam LR, cited in [Ingleby 1993]
[16] (1980) 6 Fam LR

prior to the landmark case. For example, prior to Elias, no trial judge would have mentioned a contribution in the form of entrepreneurial prowess, because that issue was not known to be relevant.

[Hunter 1994] illustrated that most applications of the data mining technique neural networks, to law, use landmark cases. For example, [Hobson and Slee 1994] used a series of leading cases in British theft law to train a network to predict a courtroom outcome. Results they obtained highlighted flaws in the use of neural networks in legal reasoning. However, we agree with Hunter in noting that their results are partly due to the use of landmark cases rather than commonplace cases.

A distinction between commonplace and landmark decisions can also be seen in the ratio decidendi or rationale of a decision. The ratio decidendi in reported and appellate Court decisions can be seen to have a different purpose from the ratio in commonplace cases. The purpose of the ratio of an appellate court judge is to convince subsequent trial judges to accept a change in the interpretation of legal principles or rules. This is so even if a case sets no dramatic precedent but reinforces existing, and commonly held principles. The purpose of the ratio in unreported cases is slightly different.

First instance decision makers aim to explain to litigants (and others) that the reasoning used was in accordance with the appropriate statutes and principles and that an appeal is not warranted. The ratio in unreported cases is thus more likely to reflect the reasoning actually used in assimilating all facts to determine a conclusion. The ratio in a reported case is more likely to revolve only around those facts that are contentious. The discussion centres on which of a number of possible interpretations of principles is most appropriate as a precedent for making future decisions.

Commonplace cases are more appropriate than landmark cases, for inclusion in the training set of a data mining algorithm[17]. However, discerning a commonplace case from a landmark case is problematical given that a past commonplace case may become a future landmark case if it happens to be appealed or, perhaps even refered to, in an appealed decision. A concept of 'interesting' is advanced in order to guide the discernment of a commonplace case from a landmark case. If a case is not interesting, it is a commonplace case. For a first instance decision to be interesting it must:

a) be appealed, or
b) includes a new principle, rule or factor in its ratio decidendi, or
c) exhibits an outcome vastly at odds with other similar cases

It is not sufficient to admit only appealed cases to the category of interesting cases, because a litigant may choose to avoid an appeal for a variety of reasons. Thus, not all interesting cases are appealed.

The concept of 'interestingness' of a case can be operationalised relatively easily by noting that senior judges of the Family Court make precisely this sort of judgement in deciding which cases are to be published by Court reporting services. These services do not publish the judgements of all cases, because the majority of

---

[17] Such as neural networks or rule induction algorithms.

cases are of little interest to readers. Thus, the more appropriate cases from which to extract data for inclusion in a training set are unreported cases. These cases are those in which a senior judge of the Family Court has ruled as uninteresting. These cases are not published, so it is difficult for a future practitioner to invoke one of these cases as backing for an argument.

Reported cases are of great importance for identifying relevant factors (described above) in the Split Up system. A reported case may set a precedent; invalidating a factor that had previously been considered relevant, or alternatively, it may introduce a new factor.

Accessing a random sample of cases is not straightforward and requires some assumptions. For example, the Family Court operates throughout Australia, yet it seems unreasonable to assume that decisions have no regional differences. A classifier trained with data from one region may perform poorly when predicting a case from another region. Another assumption we make is that decisions made by appeal Courts are not necessarily representative of decisions made by first instance judges. We also make the assumption that decisions made more than four years ago are not necessarily representative of decisions made recently, or that are likely to be made in the near future. Data for the original Split Up project was gathered from unreported Family Court cases decided between 1992 and 1994 in the Melbourne region of Australia. Each of the cases examined was decided by one of eight different judges. Judgments from these eight judges were examined in preference to limiting ourselves to those from only one judge in order to encourage the network to mimic a composite of all judges and also because no one judge had decided a sufficient number of cases[18] during that period.

The identification of an appropriate field of law and set of cases is a key first step in a KDD exercise. Another early step involves the identification of relevant variables or factors.

6.3   Identifying relevant variables

The identification of relevant variables for performing inferences is an important early step in the process for discovering knowledge in law. [Tata 1998] discusses attempts at providing computer-based support for judges engaged in sentencing. He claims that reasoning in that domain involves far more than merely listing relevant variables. For instance, both [Lovegrove 1999] and [Schild 1998], in identifying the relevant variables judges use when making sentencing decisions, work from an assumption that there is a straightforward relationship between case facts and the sentence due. While neither may advocate rigid sentencing guidelines or a mandatory sentencing process, their analyses and criticisms still reflect a belief in what [Hart 1964] calls *treating like cases alike and different cases differently*, the principle of stare decisis.

In contrast, [Tata 1998] has clearly articulated the absence of a simple relationship between case facts and the sentence. This is particularly apparent in

---

[18]   For both completeness and to train the neural network.

sentences concerning multiple offences. For Tata, a narrative process that is iterative, in that an initial story is first constructed, more aptly represents reasoning by sentencing experts. Facts are then sought that are consistent with the story. He characterises legal decision-making in sentencing as a holistic process that involves more than collecting a list of relevant variables.

The exercise of discretion in this model suggests that the phenomena and strategies incorporated into a story is broader than a pre-specified list of case features and will include any number of real life phenomena. A corollary of this is that discretionary decision-making in law is qualitatively the same as many forms of discretionary decision-making outside legal domains. Although it is difficult to imagine a computationally feasible model that is based on this perspective of discretionary decision-making, it is reasonable to assume that a computer based system that supports decision-making is plausible. If such a system were to be developed, the way in which discretion and consistency is actually operationalised in the system will depend very heavily on the structures used to represent a narrative. This leads us to surmise that, at some level in the computer program, a list of variables will need to be identified.

[Quinlan 1997] claims that the mere identification of relevant variables is not, by itself sufficient to warrant the use of data mining techniques that aim to induce general rules from data. For this to occur meaningfully, a number of other conditions must be met. Values must be able to be associated with variables. For example, the variable age, when representing a litigant's age may take on any numeric value from 0 to a predefined maximum. Note, that a variable-value analysis is not the only way reasoning in law can be modelled. The case based reasoning approach developed by [Ashley 1991] in his HYPO system uses factors rather than variable-value pairs. For example, the *{Bought-Tools}* factor represents the fact situation where the plaintiff's former employer brought the plaintiff's notes and tools to the defendant. [Bruninghaus and Ashley 2001] reports methods for the automatic extraction of HYPO style factors directly from the text of judgements. As such, their work represents an instance of knowledge discovery from databases called text mining. Text mining adopts methods from information retrieval and linguistics and is discussed in detail in chapter eight

[Quinlan 1997] claims that the induction of rules also requires sufficient data, predefined classes and discrete classes. The requirement of sufficient data is obvious, however identifying how many records are sufficient for the task, is far from clear. This task inevitably depends on the number of variables present and on how simply they are combined. Typically, datasets in the hundreds and thousands are considered minimal in most domains. However, it is quite difficult to capture data from thousands of cases in most fields of law. In chapter four we discuss a way to model the reasoning used in law in a way that transforms the knowledge discovery problem into one that requires a fairly small number of cases.

Statutes and cases are typical sources for extracting relevant factors in a legal domain. When we examine Australian family law, we find that the age of both parties to a family law dispute is considered to be a relevant factor because the Family Law Act, section 75(2) explicitly identifies age as a relevant consideration. The wealth of the marriage is not mentioned as a factor in the statute, but a series of leading cases identify this as a factor that impacts on how contributions to the marriage are assessed. The hair colour of the judge or the month of the year the trial takes place is not mentioned in any statute or leading case and practitioners do not consider that these factors are taken into account by judges in inferring an outcome.

Identifying relevant factors involves the parallel use of statutes, judgments made in past cases, textbooks in the specialised area and interviews with experts. Written judgments of commonplace cases are very useful source materials, because the explanations for decisions detail factors that the judge has used, even if the way the factors have been combined or weighted is often left unspecified. However, a written judgment will not necessarily make explicit every factor a judge uses in order to reach a decision. For example, commonly assumed knowledge is necessarily used by judges in reaching a property decision, but is unlikely to be made explicit in a written judgment. A judge may argue that the wife, at seventy years of age, is elderly. The judge will rarely elaborate on this argument, because it is commonly believed that people of age seventy or more should classified as elderly.

The statute underpinning a discretionary domain is often a primary source of relevant factors. Statutes such as the Family Law Act (1975) present a list of factors that are to be considered. For example, the Act clearly indicates that the contributions and future resources are relevant factors. However, as described in the previous chapter, most statutes of this type also include a section that enables the decision maker to take into account other relevant consideration. Thus, the statute alone is not a sufficient source for relevant factors.

Written judgements augment the search for relevant factors. For example, Mullane J in the Marriage of Coulter[19] writes: *"Her lack of employment experience in that area, and her other skills provide only a very limited future earning capacity relative to that of the husband. "*

It is clear from this judgement that employment experience and future earning capacity are relevant factors. Yet, how these factors inter-relate with others, if they do so at all, is unclear from the judgements. Furthermore, it may be the case that factors are mentioned in a judgment in a way that places undue emphasis on their role. This is less often the case with judges whose writing style is particularly terse.

The way in which factors inter-relate can be ascertained in consultation with domain experts and specialised texts. In the Split Up project, relevant factors are inserted into a hierarchy of factors in a tree like diagram. Figure 4 below illustrates an initial tree of relevant factors that are apparent from a preliminary analysis of statutes and excerpts of the judgments above.

Figure 4 illustrates that future needs, past contributions and the wealth of the marriage are the most important factors for a percentage split inference. The health and financial resources of each party are considerations for a future needs inference.

[19] (1989) 13 Fam LR 421

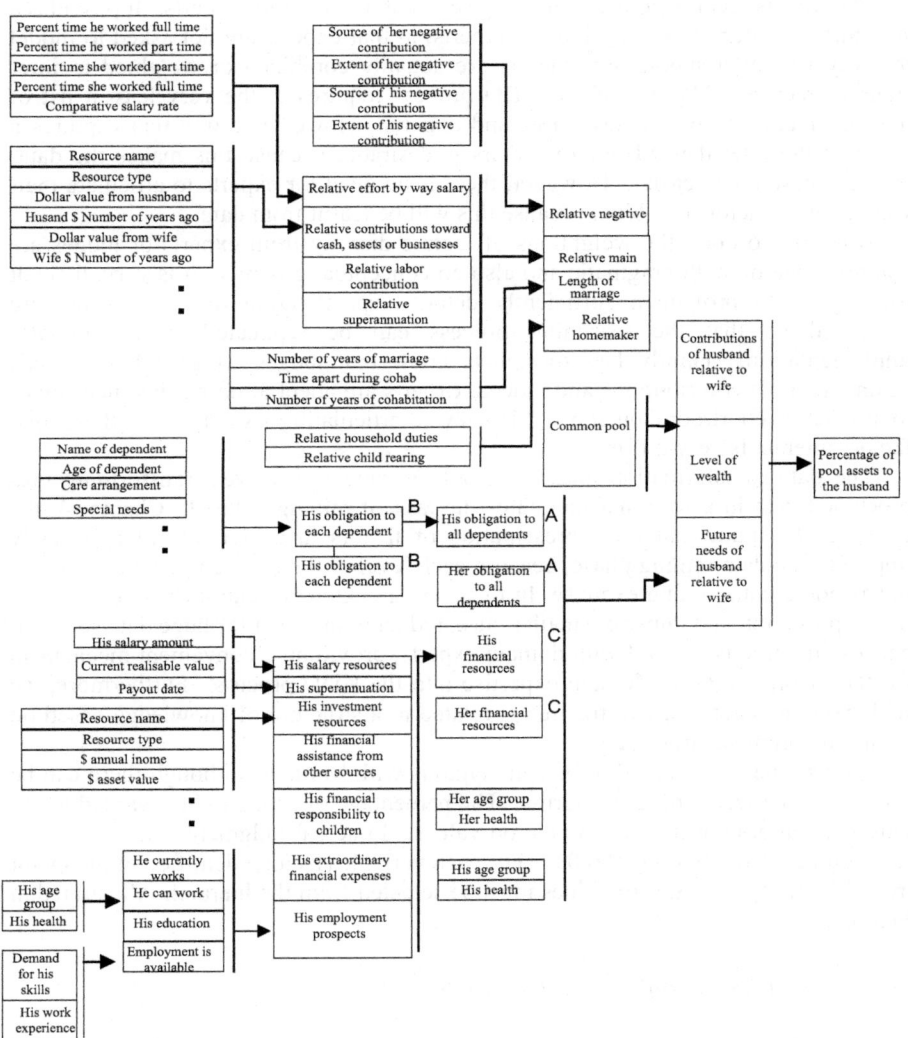

Figure 4. Tree of factors in Split Up

The tree, is ideally, constructed in close collaboration with experts. It provides a structure for interviews with domain experts, in that experts are not asked to model the way in which subordinate factors are actually combined or weighted to infer superior factors. The use of the KDD process requires at the very least a list of relevant factors from statutes, cases and experts. However, a tree that captures a sense of the inter-dependence of factors is desirable because this makes the data-mining phase much easier. However, there is no need for experts to articulate their view on how factors combine, because this will be learnt from data.

Attempts to elicit the weightings of factors directly from experts or judges are inappropriate on both pragmatic and also on conceptual grounds. It is very difficult for experts to provide a sufficiently detailed specification of how factors are combined so that the reasoning process can be replicated in a computer implementation. Family law specialists know that judges weigh relative needs against relative contributions and indeed, experts are adept at doing this themselves to predict a courtroom outcome. However, articulating exactly how these two factors interact is very difficult.

The data transformation phase of a KDD exercise involves transforming pre-processed data in a way that facilitates the task of mining data. In Chapter 4, the case will be made that the representation of factors in a hierarchical tree vastly improves the data-mining phase, because each level of the tree can be taken to be an independent data-mining exercise. In this way, an extensive data-mining exercise is decomposed into a number of smaller ones, reducing the need for huge data sets and, because the tree is derived with domain experts, providing a convenient mechanism for the incorporation of domain expertise into the KDD process. Furthermore, we will show in chapter 4, that the tree is related to a structure of knowledge based on Toulmin argument structures.

We use the term 'factor' to be synonymous with 'variable' although there can be differences between these two terms. The percentage of assets to be awarded to the wife is a variable in that it can take on values. In actual judgments, the values are real numbers from 0.0% to100.0%. For each variable (factor) identified in the factor tree, the appropriate type of values must be selected from the hierarchy illustrated in Figure 4.

6.4   Identifying possible values for variables

Once variables relevant for the KDD process have been identified it is necessary to discern possible values for each variable. Values can be categorised in the following way:
a) Nominal. Nominal values represent unordered categories. Values for an offence variable maybe 'theft', 'robbery', 'drink-driving'. These values are not ordered in any way.
b) Ordinal. Ordinal values represent order categories. Order may be represented using qualitative categories such as 'much more', 'more', 'about the same', 'less' and 'much less'. Alternatively, order may be represented using a number scale.

This may be a real, integer or interval scale. An interval scale need not be based on equal intervals. For example, the percentage split variable in the Split Up KDD exercise has assigned values, '0-9, 10-19, 20-29, 30-34, 35-39, 40-44, 45-49, 50-54, 55-59, 60-64,65-69, 70-79, 80-89, 90-100'.

c) Fuzzy. Fuzzy variables derive from fuzzy set theory developed by [Zadeh 1965]. In classical set theory an item is either a member of a set or it is not. In fuzzy set theory an item belongs to a set with a degree of membership that varies from 0 for not in the set, to 1 in the set. Zadeh notes that variables we use in language are often fuzzy. The person who is 85 maybe said to belong to the set of elderly people with a degree of membership equal to 1, and to the set of young people with a degree of membership equal to 0. A person who is 40 years of age may belong to young set with a degree of membership equal to 0.5 and to the set of elderly people with a degree 0.4. Later in Chapter 6, we discuss data mining techniques with fuzzy sets.

In many data mining exercises, there is little choice of variable type because data is sourced from databases where types and possible values have already been defined. These can, to some extent, be transformed during the transformation phase discussed in Chapter 4. However, if data is to be collected for the first time, deciding what values to assign to variables is difficult. For example, common sense tells us that recording the age of parties in months is unnecessary for divorce proceedings; years will suffice. However, what if a data-mining algorithm automatically detects that, in the vast majority of cases, where the husband is older than the wife the contributions favour the husband. This association is not noticed when the husband is the same age as the wife. A more fine-grained analysis may prove interesting but is not possible if age has only been recorded in years[20].

Discerning appropriate values for ordinal variables often requires some attention. First of all, if new data is to be collected, then should a variable such as age be an integer or an ordinal value? In Split Up, we recorded the husband and wife's age as an integer in years and also recorded the judges assessment of their age, whenever one was made, as an ordinal variable with "elderly", "quite elderly", "middle aged", "quite young" and "young" as values. How did we arrive at these values and not others in the Split Up project?

As indicated previously, data for the Split Up project came from written judgements of unreported family law cases. We selected an ad-hoc sample of these cases and noted what adjectives judges to used to describe the values for each variable. For example, judges almost always used one of the following words with regard to age: "elderly", "quite elderly", "middle aged", "quite young" and "young". When describing the extent to which one party of a marriage contributed relative to the other party, terms such as "much more", "more", "on an equal basis", "less" and "much less" were discerned. Though actual adjectival phrases varied, a five member ordered list of possible values was most appropriate. Furthermore, a three point scale for contributions seemed intuitively insufficient to capture the intended meaning underpinning judges' statements. A seven point scale for contributions seemed too fine-grained.

---

[20] Of course on may argue that an age difference of months is negligible.

The identification of relevant variables and their types represents the first part of the data selection phase. The next part is more commonly associated with sampling. The central objective is to select a data sample that will enable knowledge about the whole population of interest to be gleaned from the sample. In a KDD process in law, this amounts to selecting cases from a bank of earlier cases.

In the next chapter, we further elaborate on our theme that the KDD process is particularly suited to capturing the way in which judges weigh relevant factors in discretionary legal domains. However, to apply the process appropriately, we need to draw a distinction between commonplace cases and landmark cases and claim that the KDD process is far more appropriately applied to a sample of commonplace cases than it is to landmark cases.

In the Split Up project, three raters manually extracted data from one hundred and three cases. The template for data extraction derived from the hierarchy of arguments presented in Figure 4. The three raters extracted data from these cases by reading the text of the judgment and recording values for ninety-four variables.

Inter-rater agreement tests were performed informally. Any variable that seemed ambiguous or unclear was highlighted, so that a consensus among the raters could be reached. Most variables were not obviously subject to inter-rater disagreement. For example variables that represent each applicant's age, number and age of children, dollar value of the common pool determined by the judge, the length of the marriage and the percentage of assets awarded to each party were unambiguously indicated in each judgement.

Some rater interpretation was required for a number of variables. For example, our template represents five possible values to capture the contributions of the husband relative to those of the wife; Husband contributed much more, more, about the same, less, much less than the wife. Different judges, writing in natural language express the relative contribution assessment in different ways. For example, Hannon J. in The Marriage of B [21]states: *"I assess their respective contributions as to 60 per cent to the husband and 40 per cent to the wife"*

Another judge may phrase a similar sentiment as: *"I assess the contributions to favour the husband to some extent"*. The raters reached a consensus and coded the two assessments as *"Husband contributed more than Wife"*. Few disagreements between raters arose after discussions surrounding the first few cases.

7. CHAPTER SUMMARY

The first phase of a KDD exercise involves the collection of data. In law, this involves the selection of a task suitable for the exercise. We claim that KDD is particularly well suited to model discretionary fields of law. A classification scheme is presented that indicates what tasks are suited to KDD. Key dimensions of the scheme relate to the concept of open texture.

Once a task is regarded suitable for KDD, appropriate cases must be sought. In this chapter, we claim that a distinction between commonplace and landmark cases

---

[21] (1995) ML4336

is usefully drawn and that cases to be used in the KDD process are most appropriately selected from commonplace cases. The identification of relevant variables and possible values for each variable is particularly important in the legal domain, since so many information sources are text based. In this chapter, we discussed approaches for the identification of variables from judgements.

Issues that impact on the data selection phase of KDD were also discussed in this chapter. However, data collected from cases cannot be directly used in a data-mining endeavour. Such data must be pre-processed. In the next chapter we describe the method we use to pre-process data.

CHAPTER 3

LEGAL ISSUES IN THE DATA PRE-PROCESSING PHASE

Data pre-processing involves preparing the sample data for further phases of the knowledge discovery from database process. This requires attention to two main factors;
   a) missing values and,
   b) inconsistent data.

If many records have missing values for key features then any data-mining method will not accurately discover patterns from those records. If the sample includes cases where a decision maker has erred, then the data-mining technique that aims to predict the outcome of new cases will be compromised by past decisions that are, in fact, erroneous. In this chapter we examine strategies for identifying and dealing with errors. Assumptions about legal reasoning that must be made with each strategy are articulated.

In practice, data about persons, cases or situations is typically stored as text based documents rather than structured databases. Data stored in most text databases is neither completely structured (as in databases) nor completely unstructured. Indeed, it is semi-structured. Text-mining is a field of research that involves discovering knowledge by the automatic analysis of free text and that is evolving from information retrieval research. We discuss this important topic in detail in chapter eight.

1. MISSING DATA

An item may be missing for a variety of reasons. It may never have been collected, or if it was collected, may not have been collected in all cases. The item may not be relevant for all cases. For example, Table 1 has missing data in two records, 'Wife's health' in Marriage no. 3 and 'Age of eldest child' in Marriage No. 2. However, the value in Marriage No.2 is missing because there were no children in that marriage. The value in Marriage No.3 is missing because it was never collected. The source of missing values can be summarised as follows:

a) **Appropriately missing.** A missing value represents the true state of the world. For example, a missing value on an address field is appropriately missing for homeless persons.
b) **Erroneously Missing.** A value exists but has not been collected. This can occur in two ways.
   - **Instrument error.** The instrument collecting the value is at fault. Examples include an automatic scanner that occasionally malfunctions or a poorly constructed survey in which some respondents miss questions.
   - **Intentionally omitted.** The value is intentionally omitted. For example, survey respondents who wish to keep their income private may omit an income field. Intentionally omitted values may be associated with values maintained on other variables. If men are more sensitive than women, about the privacy of their income, then a missing value on income will tend to co-occur with a value 'Male' on gender.

The factor tree described in chapter two eliminates missing values that arise because a value is not appropriate. For example, domain experts are certain that an estimate of the contributions to the marriage, the future needs of both parties and the wealth level of the marriage are needed in order to determine a percentage split outcome. All of the unreported cases used for Split Up included a percentage split outcome and values for contributions, needs and wealth. However, not all cases involved a business. The dataset for the Individual business resources network comprised all cases that did involve a business, so there was no missing data.

The two cases may vary on a factor that has not been identified as relevant. For example, the two cases in Table 1 may be distinguished by a fourth factor that is unknown or unspecified.

Table 1 Table with missing data

	Wife's age	Wife's Health	Age of eldest child	Percentage of Assets awarded to the wife
Marriage 1	35	Good	4	65
Marriage 2	24	Excellent	?	50
Marriage 3	82	?	0	40
Marriage 4	82	Good	0	40

Missing values that are due to collection deficiencies can, in general, be dealt with in the following ways:

a) ignoring the missing data;
b) removing the entire record;
c) estimating an appropriate value by:
   - inserting a variable mean,

− finding a record most similar[22] on all the other variables and using the data value of the retrieved record[23] for the missing value.

Each of these methods has shortcomings. [Quinlan 1989] compared numerous approaches for dealing with missing values and concluded that taken over all datasets, no approach is uniformly better than others. Ignoring the missing data is feasible for some data-mining methods but not for others. For example, mining with feed forward neural networks requires values for all variables, whereas mining with the C4.5 algorithm has no such requirement. Removing the entire record is a strategy that cannot be readily considered unless there are a substantial number of cases. Even so, the elimination of those records that contain missing data may easily also remove a class of cases that contain an important pattern.

A more effective strategy than removing the entire record, involves estimating an appropriate value for the missing attribute. The simplest way to achieve this goal is to insert the mean value of the variable. Doing this minimises the gap between the true value and the value used, assuming the values are distributed equally around the mean. However, this is not often the case. A variant on this strategy includes using the mode, rather than the average, as an appropriate value for the missing attribute. The mode is the value that is present in more records than any other value.

A value for missing data may be estimated by searching for a similar record that does not have missing values. For example, record 4 has identical values for all variables in record 3, except for the missing value in record 3. Therefore, the value for the 'Wife's health' variable in record 4 in Table 1 can be assigned to the missing value in record 3. This is, of course only a pragmatic measure and cannot be taken as foolproof. If a record with identical values on all other variables cannot be found then value of the relevant attribute with the record with the closest match, is taken as the missing value.

2. INCONSISTENT DATA

Legal databases are likely to contain records that reflect inconsistencies. A simple and hypothetical example illustrates this. Consider a task where the decision maker concludes outcome X whenever facts A, B and C are present. This may have occurred in many cases, so be captured many times in a legal database. However, if a new case decides Y from facts A, B and C, then this is at odds with the first pattern. The reasons for this can include:

a) Noise. The data collection procedure was inaccurate.
b) Judicial error. The decision maker may have erred.
c) Change. Legislation, precedent cases (in common law countries) or judicial behaviour may have changed.

A concern with inconsistent data is important for the KDD process within law, because data-mining techniques might tend to learn incorrect or inappropriate

---

[22] To the record with the missing value
[23] On that variable

patterns. For example, a data-mining technique will learn incorrect patterns if exposed to sufficiently many cases in which a judge had not followed personal or local stare decisis. Similarly if elements of a case such as the length of the marriage are wrongly recorded in a database, the dataset is considered noisy. Furthermore, law is always in flux, so changes in legislation, precedents, judicial or community values will similarly impact on patterns learnt. In this chapter, noise, error and change are discussed.

2.1   Noise

Noise is typically assumed to consist of random discrepancies in data that are due to measurement anomalies and are not a feature of the distribution of data. For example, a faulty scanner may introduce noise into industrial data. Noise may explain outliers. Inconsistencies between the categorisation of values for the Split Up template, by the three raters in the Split Up project, introduce noise into the training sets. [Eliot 1993] surveys neural network research to point out that generalisation performance and training time degrade if the dataset contains noisy data. [Liang and Moskowitz 1992] have quantified the effect of noise on neural network performance and have introduced a method based on semi-markov models to detect noisy examples.

Data objects that are grossly different from or inconsistent with the remaining set of data are called **outliers**. [Han and Kamber 2001] note that many data-mining algorithms attempt to minimise the influence of outliers or totally eliminate them. However, such action can lead to the loss of important hidden information – such as in the case of fraud detection, where outliers may indicate fraudulent activity.

The outlier mining problem can be viewed as two subproblems: a) define what data can be considered as inconsistent in a given data set; and b) find an efficient method to mine the outliers so defined. The problem of defining outliers is nontrivial. If a regression model[24] is used for data modelling, than an analysis of the residuals can provide a good estimate for 'extremeness'. The task is more difficult when finding outliers in time-series data, as they may be hidden in trend, seasonal or other cyclic changes. Data visualisation methods are weak in detecting outliers in data with many categorical attributes or in data of high dimensionality, since human eyes are good at visualising numeric data of only two to three dimensions.

Computer-based methods for outlier detection can be categorised into three approaches:
a) **Statistical-Based Outlier Detection** – this approach assumes a distribution or probability model for the given data set (normal distribution) and then identifies outliers with respect to the model using a discordancy test. Application of the test requires knowledge of the data set parameters (such as the assumed data distribution), knowledge of distribution parameters (such as the mean and

---

[24]   In linear regression, data is modelled using a straight line of the form $y = \alpha x + \beta$. α and β are determined using the method of least squares. Polynomial regression models can be transformed to a linear regression model.

variance) and the expected number of outliers. A statistical discordancy test examines two hypotheses: a working hypothesis and an alternative hypothesis. The hypothesis is retained if there is no statistically significant test supporting its rejection. A major drawback of the statistical approach is that most tests are for single attributes, yet many data mining problems require finding outliers in multidimensional space. Moreover, the statistical approach requires knowledge about parameters of the data set, such as the data distribution. However, in many cases, the data distribution may not be known. Statistical methods do not guarantee that all outliers will be found for the cases where no specific test was developed, or the observed distribution cannot be adequately modelled with any standard distribution. [Wang and Gedeon 1995] describe a statistical detection method and report improvements over other methods to detect and remove outliers. However, these methods are not trivial to implement and can be costly in terms of computer resources.

b) **Distance-Based Outlier Detection** – the notion of distance-based outliers was introduced to counter the main limitations imposed by statistical methods. Rather than relying on statistical tests, we can think of distance-based outliers as those objects who do not have 'enough' neighbours, where neighbours are defined based on their distance from the given object. In comparison with statistical-based methods, distance-based outlier detection generalises the ideas behind discordancy testing for various standard distributions. Distance-based outlier detection avoids the excessive computation that can be associated with fitting the observed distribution into some standard distribution and in selecting discordancy tests. Several efficient algorithms for mining distance-based outliers have been developed: i) index-based algorithm; ii) nested-loop algorithm; and iii) cell-based algorithm.

c) **Deviation-Based Outlier Detection** – deviation-based outlier detection does not use statistical tests or distance-based measures to identify exceptional objects. Instead, it identifies outliers by examining the main characteristics of objects in a group. Objects that deviate from this description are considered outliers.

In the next section we discuss judicial error as a source of contradictory data, particularly within a domain that affords a decision maker much discretion.

2.2   *Judicial error*

Judicial error is conceptualised differently by prevailing jurisprudential theories. Utilitarianism was first advanced by Jeremy Bentham[25]. Bentham argued that the purpose of a legal system is to advance the greatest degree of happiness to the greatest number of people. There is little place for natural law or natural rights in his legal philosophy. For utilitarians, an error in legal reasoning occurs if a judge

---

[25] Bentham (1748-1832) was a leading theorist in Anglo-American philosophy of law and one of the 'founders' of utilitarianism. His most important theoretical work is the *Introduction to the Principles of Morals and Legislation* (1789), in which much of his moral theory--which he said reflected 'the greatest happiness principle'--is described and developed.

determines an outcome which cannot, ultimately, contribute to the well being of the largest number of people.

According to perspectives advanced by ([Dworkin 1977] and [Dworkin 1986]), a judge errs, albeit in a minor way, by failing to discover the ideal way in which to apply precedents to a current fact situation. This view led to the concept of an ideal judge; a concept that was perhaps attacked most strongly by adherents to the critical legal studies movement.

For legal positivists such as [Hart 1994], a judge may err by failing to discern a core from a penumbra case or by failing to apply appropriate rules to resolve a current penumbra case. For German conceptualists, a judge errs by failing to reason deductively from facts to a conclusion.

The concept of judicial error that can be drawn from major theories of jurisprudence, pre-supposes a failure in adherence to the doctrine of stare decisis. However, the type of stare decisis that most neatly fits into these theoretical perspectives advanced is what we define as traditional stare decisis.

The right of appeal in common law jurisdictions provides a safeguard against judicial error. However, the grounds for appeal against a first instance decision vary so markedly across jurisdictions that a general specification of erroneous decisions is very difficult. For instance, according to [Dickey 1990], the acceptable grounds for appeal a first instance decision-maker in the Family Court of Australia include:

a) a failure on the part of the trial judge to provide reasons for a judgement, or
b) the use of an inappropriate principle in reaching a decision, or
c) incorrect findings of fact or,
d) the inappropriate weighting of factors.

The requirement to give reasons has been imposed on first instance judges by a number of High Court decisions. In these cases, traditional stare decisis was operative, in that the High Court was firm in laying down constraints to ensure trial judges included reasons for their decisions. Traditional stare decisis is also clear in the *Marriage of Gronow*[26] in establishing a right to appeal if the trial judge acted on a wrong principle or allowed irrelevant factors to influence her.

Another ground for appeal involves the inappropriate weighting of a relevant factor. We indicated above[27], that the High Court has been reluctant to fetter the discretion of trial judges by laying down guidelines to control the way in which factors are weighted. The fact that experienced practitioners can predict Family Court outcomes, demonstrates that personal stare decisis and local stare decisis apply in the Family Court of Australia.

This arises because of a desire on the part of first instance decision-makers to weight relevant factors in a manner that is consistent with the decisions of other judges. A hypothetical Family Court judge can be imagined as one who whenever she is presented with cases with identical facts, the judge would determine precisely the same percentage split of assets to both parties. That is, the exercise of discretion

---

[26] (1979) 5 Fam LR 719
[27] In the case Mallet vs Mallet (1984) 156 CLR 185.

is perfectly consistent with other judges and, perfectly consistent with the same judge over time.

However, the ideal judge does not exist in the real world. Individual judges are not perfectly consistent with other judges, even on the same set of facts. An informal study with Family Court judges exposed to the same case facts, revealed substantial variance in percentage split outcomes. This concurs with experiences reported by family law practitioners. If it were possible to expose a large number of judges to the same set of facts, then we can imagine that a mean outcome would emerge and individual judgments would fall on both sides of the mean.

A conceptualisation of judicial error is important for the application of the knowledge discovery process to legal reasoning, because the goal of a machine learning system is to predict outcomes that judges will consider acceptable. The performance of such algorithms can be expected to degrade if exposed to large numbers of decisions in which a judge has actually erred.

If the entire set of cases used in a KDD exercise, contains a significant amount of errors, then data mining algorithms cannot be expected to accurately predict outcomes. But, how are we to determine whether an actual judicial outcome is an unacceptable exercise of discretion for the purposes of KDD? To what extent can two judges offer divergent decisions on cases with very similar findings of fact before one (or both) is considered to have erred? Furthermore, to which authority should we turn, to make this determination? We shall first discuss the issue of which authority is best placed to make a determination on acceptable bounds of discretion.

The most obvious authorities for the discernment of acceptable exercises of discretion from unacceptable exercises of discretion are appellate Courts. However, this authority is not totally suitable because decisions that fail local stare decisis may never be appealed for a variety of reasons including:

a) An appeal to a higher court is expensive and the possible gain may not warrant the additional expense.

b) Gender or other cultural factors may impact on the decision to appeal. For example, [Alexander 1992] has illustrated that women tend to be more reluctant than men to continue conflict and are therefore more reluctant to pursue an appeal.

Furthermore, according to [Kovacs 1992], a demonstration that a relevant factor was not given appropriate weight by a trial judge is extremely difficult to prove, because standards for the exercise of discretion in family law have not been laid down by the High Court. Experienced practitioners typically advise against an appeal unless a decision was patently unjust.

An appeal Court is not ideally situated to determine issues of local stare decisis, because the main function of an appeal Court is to determine whether a lower Court has appropriately applied legal rules and principles. The issue of determining local, or personal stare decisis is only indirectly addressed.

[Schild 1998] explores these issues in depth when considering the field of the sentencing of Israeli criminals. To ensure more consistent sentencing decisions, he recommended the establishment of panels of experts specifically formed to provide feedback. This approach raises many issues that warrant discussion. However, this discussion is beyond the scope of this text.

The task at hand is pragmatic, in that we are concerned with the impact judicial error has on the knowledge discovery from database process. If some cases from which we collect data, fail to adhere to local (or personal) stare decisis, then data-mining techniques cannot be expected to learn useful patterns.

Cases in the dataset that are inconsistent with other cases need to be identified and dealt with in the pre-processing phase. If the inconsistency is due to judicial error, then we are compelled to attempt to identify them and adopt a strategy such as modifying offending records, or removing or ignoring such records. If the inconsistency is due to a change in legislation or the emergence of a precedent case, then other mechanisms may need to be invoked.

Contradictory examples are, in general, examples that have different outcomes despite identical inputs. Contradictory cases are necessarily present in discretionary domains, because judges cannot be expected to weight factors in the same way on every case throughout their career. Nor can they be expected to be perfectly consistent with the weightings used by other judges.

2.3   Dealing with contradictory data

There are a number of ways to deal with extreme contradictions. Most simply, the contradictions can be ignored. [Wang and Gedeon 1995] note that a small proportion of contradictory examples will not dramatically effect the performance of a neural network. However, the performance of other data-mining techniques depends more heavily on the proportion of contradictory examples. The first step in dealing with contradictions, if they are not to be ignored, involves their detection. This is not trivial in a KDD exercise in law. The data in Table 2 illustrates a sample contradictory data.

Table 2 Sample contradictory data

Marriage Number	Wife's age (yrs, mths)	Wife's Health	Age of eldest child	Suburb	Percentage of Assets awarded to the wife
1	35,1	Good	4,1	Delacombe	65
2	35,1	Good	4,1	Delacombe	30
3	35,1	Good	4,1	Delacombe	64
4	35,5	Good	?	Delacombe	50
5	34,9	Good	4,2	Gold Point	40
6	34,9	Good	4,2	Sebas	40

Marriage 1 and Marriage 2 in Table 2 have identical values on input attributes but differ dramatically on the value on the output attribute (percentage of assets awarded to the wife). A casual observer might conclude that these two records clearly contradict each other. However, Marriage 3 does not contradict Marriage 1 despite identical input values because the output percentage is 64 and not 65.

In the next chapter we discuss the data transformation methods used in the Split Up project. In this chapter, we will see, that a fundamental transformation performed on the values of variables is to map an ordinal value onto a binary string. We shall see how that transformation assisted us in the deployment of neural networks for making predictions. Another benefit of the transformation adopted was that we could more easily develop a metric for determining the extent to which two examples are contradictory. We briefly describe the nature of variables and the transformation we performed in order to illustrate the metric.

An ordinal variable such as the contributions of the husband relative to the wife has five possible values, ["much more", "more", "same as", "less", "much less"]. This was mapped to a binary string 5 places long, where each character is either 1 or 0. The string [1,0,0,0,0] represents the value "much more" whereas the string, [0,0,1,0,0] represents between "the same as".

Two binary outcomes can be compared by noting the position of the set bit in each outcome. Thus, a binary outcome, [1 0 0 0 0], differs from [0 0 0 0 1] by four place units. The set bit in the second number is four places away from the set bit in the former outcome. We call this a four-place contradiction. The average number of examples across all twenty datasets in the Split Up study that had identical inputs and outputs that differed by three or more bit positions totalled 9.37% of the population. However, this ranged from 0% for one dataset to 29.4% for another.

Plausible explanations for the high proportions of contradictions in the financial resources dataset are illustrative of the kinds of issues that emerge when dealing with contradictory data:

a) **Sampling error**. The sample drawn was not representative of the population of cases with respect to financial resources determination.

b) **Local stare decisis.** Local stare decisis with respect to financial resources in the Melbourne registry is quite poor.

c) **Incomplete knowledge.** Relevant factors that predict financial resources are missing. Salary, superannuation, business and resources from family or new partners may not be the only relevant items. Data collection occurred at the wrong level of granularity.

The most likely explanation for the quality of the datasets in the Split Up study is that of sampling error, because the sample size is so small it does not allow us to learn patterns. However, it is interesting to note that the factors considered relevant for determining financial resources are a matter of on-going controversy. One Family Court judge clearly indicated that resources a party receives from his or her family or new partners are irrelevant. However, domain experts are quite adamant that judges do indeed take this factor into account. One practitioner extols female clients to dress modestly for Court appearances in case judges take the view that the prospects for remarriage of a well-dressed divorcee are high and consequently the wife will have inflated financial resources prospects. This might lead to the judge concluding that a well groomed wife requires a lesser split of the common pool than a woman who is more modestly attired, because the judge believes the latter woman has greater future needs.

It is unwise to conclude that local stare decisis has failed merely because of the existence of contradictions. The number of contradictions reflects those examples with identical inputs and outputs that differed by more than 3 bit places. This is a rather crude measure of the level of contradictions. It may suffice for the data-mining purposes of identifying interesting patterns in datasets, but is not sufficient as the basis of sociological inferences.

A more sophisticated measure of contradictions would be to introduce a metric of input similarity. The criteria of 3 [or more bit] places may be too severe for some training sets and too relaxed for others. However, despite these considerations, it seems most plausible to assume that the anomaly noted in the financial resources network is due to sampling error.

2.4 Inconsistencies due to new legislation or precedents

Broadly speaking, new legislation and new precedent cases impact on the way in which judges make decisions in the following ways:
a) Making a factor relevant that was previously not mentioned in the decision-making context, or was previously considered irrelevant. So, for example, domestic violence in family law property proceedings was not a relevant consideration prior to Kennon v Kennon[28].
b) Making a factor that was once relevant, irrelevant. For example, the ethnic background of a child was once a factor in determining child welfare issues in Australia[29]. It often led to the forcible removal of many aboriginal children from their families. Ethnic background is now no longer considered relevant
c) Changing the way an outcome is inferred without changing relevant factors. If a new factor is introduced as a relevant consideration by a statue or precedent, then cases prior to the precedent have no data collected about that factor and the way in which the factor impacts on the other factors may be so severe that it invalidates any previous knowledge gleaned from a KDD exercise. In this case, there is little alternative but to re-expose the data to the data-mining exercise. However, this course of action is problematic, because soon after the introduction of the new factor, there are very few cases decided where the factor plays a prominent role. For example, even though domestic violence is clearly an issue in property proceedings since the case Kennon v Kennon, there have been such a small number of cases since that precedent that involve domestic violence, that the very little data exists[30].

The constantly changing nature of law would seem, at first sight, to make KDD in law a fruitless process. However, this is not the case. The data transformation act, based on argumentation theories, and described in the next chapter, has the effect of decomposing a major problem into small units. Any change caused by the

---

[28] Kennon V. Kennon FLC 92-757 (1997)

[29] See for example, **Royal Commission into Aboriginal Deaths in Custody**, *National Report*, vol. 1, p. 6 Accessible on the internet world wide web site http://www.austlii.edu.au/cgi-bin/disp.pl/au/journals/AILR/1997/disp269

[30] See for example Farmer and Bramley [2000] FamCA 1615 (13 December 2000).

introduction of a relevant new factor, can be localised to one argument, without impacting on other arguments. It is however, the case that knowledge within the effected argument cannot be relied upon once a change occurs. However, we demonstrate in the next chapter that the impact of this change is not significant as long as argumentation is used to decompose the task into smaller units.

2.5   Dealing with inconsistent data

Once detected, inconsistent data may be dealt with in one of three ways:
a)   All contradictory cases are removed from the dataset.
b)   No contradictory cases are removed from the dataset.
c)   Some contradictory cases are removed from the dataset, through the use of predefined criteria.

The strategy adopted in the Split Up project was to remove all contradictory cases from the dataset. Although this strategy is less than ideal, it avoids some of the drawbacks of other approaches.

Leaving contradictory examples in the dataset is not appropriate if the sample size is small. If sufficient data is collected, then we could have a greater confidence that the contradictions noted reflect the exercise of discretion in the population and are not anomalies due to the sample selected. For example, if the sample size is increased tenfold, then we would have considerably more confidence that the proportion of contradictions noted in the sample was the proportion that existed in the true population. This would mitigate toward leaving the contradictory cases in the dataset.

When presented with identical inputs, a neural network learns to produce an outcome that is between the contradictory outputs. Whilst this strategy is acceptable, it relies on the existence of substantially large datasets, which is often not feasible in law. The examples used in the Split Up system are by no means plentiful and sampling error cannot be ruled out. A concrete example may clarify this assertion.

The strategy of removing all contradictory examples is preferred to one in which we attempt to determine which of the contradictory cases are unacceptable exercises of discretion. As discussed above, [Schild 1995] highlights the need for panels of experts and judges to regularly determine boundaries for acceptable exercises of discretion. Such a panel would have the authority to rule that one or more of the contradictory cases was unacceptable and thus mandate the removal of only those cases.

However, such panels do not exist in most fields of law,. The authority to determine which of the contradictory outcomes are acceptable and which are unacceptable, does not reside with any one person or group. It should not be taken by data analysts engaged in the knowledge discovery process. If contradictory cases cannot remain in the dataset and unacceptable examples cannot be discerned from acceptable ones, then the relatively conservative strategy of removing all contradictory cases is the most appropriate one.

In domains that are not appreciably less discretionary than Australian family law, it could be said that if two judges arrive at different conclusions after a finding of identical facts, then the judges are using different legal principles or standards. Simply removing contradictory cases from consideration when modelling a domain, runs the very serious risk that important rules, or principles that discern one case from another, are overlooked. However, as illustrated above, two judges in family law could conceivably agree on the facts of a case and also on the appropriate legal principles, yet still reach different conclusions. This is because the principal statute affords the first instance decision maker flexibility in the weighting and combining of factors.

Family law disputes are unusual in that any extreme exercise of discretion is equally undesirable if it favours the husband or the wife[31]. However, in other matters, an extreme exercise of discretion in favour of the plaintiff may be worse (or better) than one in favour of the defendant.

3. CHAPTER SUMMARY

In this chapter issues that arise in the data pre-pre-processing phase of a knowledge discovery from databases exercise have been discussed. Missing values can be dealt with by ignoring all missing values, removing all records that contain missing values or by invoking techniques for estimating the required values. Each approach has its limitations and strengths. Many records will be inconsistent with other records. This could be due to data collection anomalies, inconsistent decision making practices or changes in legislation or precedents. Decision-making practices are particularly likely to be inconsistent in discretionary domains of law, because the decision maker has the freedom to weigh factors in his or her own way. However, extreme outcomes can occur and are appropriately labelled errors. Although judicial error has not been the focus of much attention in jurisprudence, a conceptualisation of this problem is important for the application of KDD to legal databases. A conceptualisation of judicial error enables us to articulate bounds of acceptable discretion in sophisticated ways, so that decisions outside those bounds do not unduly influence the data-mining phase. In the next chapter, we discuss issues associated with transforming the data so that it is ready for the data-mining phase.

---

[31] In many legal domains, there is an onus on a specific party to prove its claims. For example, in criminal law, the prosecution must prove the defendant is guilty beyond reasonable doubt. In taxation law, the taxpayer must prove he met all the guidelines.

CHAPTER 4

LEGAL ISSUES IN THE DATA TRANSFORMATION PHASE

Data that has been selected and pre-processed may not necessarily be ready for exposure to a data-mining algorithm. Some transformation of the data may dramatically enhance the benefit of the subsequent data mining phase. Transformation can be performed in five ways:

a) **Aggregation of data values**. This involves transforming values into categories or groups. Values on an age variable captured in years and months, for example, may be transformed into five pre-defined age groups.

b) **Normalisation of data values**. A variable with large values measured, for instance in the thousands could dominate a variable with very small values measured in the thousandths in the data mining phase. Normalising involves transforming both sets of values so that they fall within the same range.

c) **Feature reduction.** This involves the removal of features that are not relevant or make no sizeable contribution to the data mining exercise.

d) **Example reduction.** Example reduction involves eliminating records from the data set. Data-sets in law are typically too small to contemplate example reduction.

e) **Restructuring.** Restructuring involves decomposing the data-set into smaller parts for independent data mining exercises.

Restructuring a data set into smaller parts for independent mining exercises is particularly important for mining from data sets in law. This is due to the lack of availability of large data sets that reflect judicial reasoning. For example, 94 variables were identified by specialist family lawyers as relevant for determining property outcomes in Australian family law. A data mining exercise with so many variables requires data from many thousands of cases for meaningful results. However the mining exercise was decomposed into 35 independent, small and manageable data mining exercises. Most of these smaller exercises involved less than five variables, so that mining was possible, though not ideal, with data from around one hundred cases.

1. AGGREGATING VALUES

Aggregating values is also known as binning because it involves transforming values of a feature into a small number of categories. A date of birth feature, represented in the dataset in a dd/mm/yyyy format may be more usefully aggregated into a year value. Daily sales may be binned into 12 categories, representing sales in each month of the year.

Aggregating values is performed so that more meaningful patterns emerge from the data-mining phase. A specific date of birth is unlikely to be directly associated with or predict other values. However, the transformation of a date of birth value into an age in years, or an age in qualitative categories such as elderly, middle aged or young is far more likely to yield interesting patterns.

Specific expertise in the field of law at hand is required for effective aggregation. The actual percentage of assets a Family Court of Australia judge awarded the husband is represented in the original Split Up data set as a number between 0 and 100 with one decimal point. Table 1 illustrates that aggregation of values need not be equal across all bins.

Table 1. Aggregation of values for percentage split

1	0-10%
2	11-20%
3	21-30%
4	31-35%
5	36-40%
6	41-45%
7	46-50%
8	51-55%
9	56-60%
10	61-65%
11	66-70%
12	71-80%
13	81-90%
14	91-100%

The Table 1 bins are not of equal size. The first and last three bins range over ten percentage points, whereas the values in between range over five points. This was done because specialists in the field advised that predictions within an accuracy of 10% at the extremes were acceptable, given the relative infrequency of these cases.

Decisions regarding binning are invariably subjective. Often, the data-set contains data in categories, that according to field specialists, need not be binned further. However, there is no simple way to determine if the existing bins will yield meaningful results in the mining phase. Typically, values are binned according to advice and then re-binned if results from the mining phase prove un-interesting. Normalising, discussed in the next section involves more objectivity.

2. NORMALISING

Normalisation involves scaling values so that they fall within a specified range. This is particularly important if two or more features have vastly different ranges. For example, the dollar value of assets may range from $0 to $20,000,000 whereas the marriage length may range from 1 to 40 years. If both sets of values were exposed to a data mining method such as a neural network (discussed in Chapter 7), even small differences in the asset value would overwhelm differences in the length feature. [Han and Kamber 2001] provide a formula for normalising values presented here as Equation 4.1

Equation 4.1

*New = ((Old– Min)/(Max - Min) * (New_max – New_min)) + New_min*

Where:

New is the new, normalised value for an example
Old is the dataset value for an example
Min is the smallest value for the feature in the data-set
Max is the largest value for the feature in the data-set
New_Min is the smallest value for the normalised range
New_Max is the largest value for the normalised range

The normalisation that is performed with the use of Equation 4.1 is linear in that the values on one range are scaled down or up to values on another scale. No notice is taken of the average or the variance of the values. In Z-score normalisation, values for a feature are normalised based on the mean and standard deviation of the values. This is depicted in Equation 4.2.

Equation 4.2

New = (Old – Mean) / Standard_deviation

Where:
New is the new, normalised value for an example
Old is the dataset value for an example
Mean is the average value for the feature
Standard_deviation is the standard deviation for the values of the feature

3. FEATURE OR EXAMPLE REDUCTION

Feature reduction involves the removal of features that are irrelevant or will not contribute to the data mining exercise. Irrelevant features may clutter the data mining phase making the discovery of meaningful patterns difficult or at worst, impossible. There are three main ways that feature reduction is performed:

a) **Expert heuristics.** Legal specialists well acquainted with the jurisdiction the data-set derives from often have a clear view of the extent to which a feature may be irrelevant and warrant removal. The articulation of a reason for each feature's relevance presents as a simple and effective, yet not foolproof mechanism for the identification of irrelevant features. In law, the relevance of a feature typically derives directly from a statute, precedent case, regulation or commonly accepted practice. However, this is not always the case. Most family law specialists claim the wife's hair color is irrelevant and should not play a role in mining aimed at predictive property split orders. In contrast, some specialists claim hair color is entirely relevant in property proceedings as judges may, correctly or not, regard that blond women have better prospects for re-marriage and therefore ought to be awarded fewer marital assets.

b) **Statistical techniques.** Statistical techniques can be applied to the data-set to identify features that do not contribute to the prediction. Principal components analysis (PCA) is the technique most often used to determine such features. PCA involves the analysis of variance between features and the class variable in a prediction exercise. PCA requires specialist statistical software, since the calculations are cumbersome. PCA is applicable only to features that are numeric[32].

c) **Data mining.** The third approach used in feature reduction involves the application of a data mining technique in order to discover features that do not contribute to the mining. The rule induction algorithm is often applied in this way because features that are irrelevant do not appear in rules derived with this algorithm. [Skabar *et al* 1997] applied a different method with excellent results. He used a search method called genetic algorithms to look for the best subset of features of the Split Up data-set for neural network training. He found a subset of 17 features predicted percentage split in property proceedings as well as the original 94 featured data-set.

The use of expert heuristics is the best of the three approaches when using a data-set that derives from legal databases. The statistical and data-mining approach may yield counter-intuitive results that while correct, are not readily explained or accepted. For example, many of the features found to be unnecessary by [Skabar

---

[32] Suppose that we have N tuples from k-dimensional space to compress. [Han and Kamber 2001] say PCA searches for c k-dimensional orthogonal vectors that can be best used to represent the data, where c <= k. The original data is projected onto a much smaller space, resulting in data compression. PCA can be used as a form of dimensionality reduction. Unlike attribute subset selection, which reduces the attribute set size by retaining a subset of the initial set of attributes, PCA 'combines' the essence of attributes by creating an alternative smaller set of variables. The initial data can then be projected onto this smaller set.

1997] in predicting percentage split outcomes such as the contributions made by the husband are central in statutes and common-sense reasoning in family law. Specialist lawyers, judges and other commentators explain virtually every judgement with reference to this feature. The fact that a data-mining method does not need this feature in order to make good predictions cannot be taken to mean that the feature is not taken seriously by judges in reaching decisions. It is more likely that this is an artefact that arises because the inter-dependence between this feature and other features results in accurate predictions when using a combination of other features.

3.1   Example reduction

Example reduction involves the removal of cases from the data-set. This is less likely to occur in knowledge discovery from legal databases than in other databases, because legal data-sets are typically small. However, the removal of examples may have occurred during the data-processing phase, as a result of missing values or inconsistent values. Example reduction in the data transformation phase may occur in order to eliminate examples prior to a key event such as a new statute or landmark case. As in all phases of the knowledge discovery process, the participation of legal specialists is critical.

The remaining method in the transformation phase involves restructuring the problem so that separate and independent data mining exercises can be performed. Restructuring is particularly important for KDD from legal databases because data-sets are relatively small. The remaining sections of this chapter discuss an approach to restructuring that involves concepts drawn from argumentation theories.

4. THE USE OF ARGUMENTATION FOR RESTRUCTURING

Figure 1 illustrates a partial tree that illustrates 6 of the 94 features used to model how judges of the Family Court of Australia distribute marital property. The top-level feature in the tree is the percentage split of assets a judge awards the husband and the wife. Specialist lawyers indicate that three variables substantially determine the asset split: future needs, past contributions and the level of marital wealth of the marriage. Leading cases and sections from relevant statutes are cited to support the relevance of these factors. Figure 1 also illustrates that past contributions are inferred by considering direct contributions, negative contributions and homemaker contributions.

A data mining exercise that aims to discover the way in which the percentage split is inferred from future needs, past contributions and wealth is relatively small. Indeed, there are only $5 * 6 * 5 = 150$ possible different combinations of values in the three variables that determine the percentage split. A judge's finding on contribution, wealth and needs can be used as input into a neural network in the data-mining phase. A sample of cases that number in the hundreds rather than tens of thousands provides an adequate sample for good predictions.

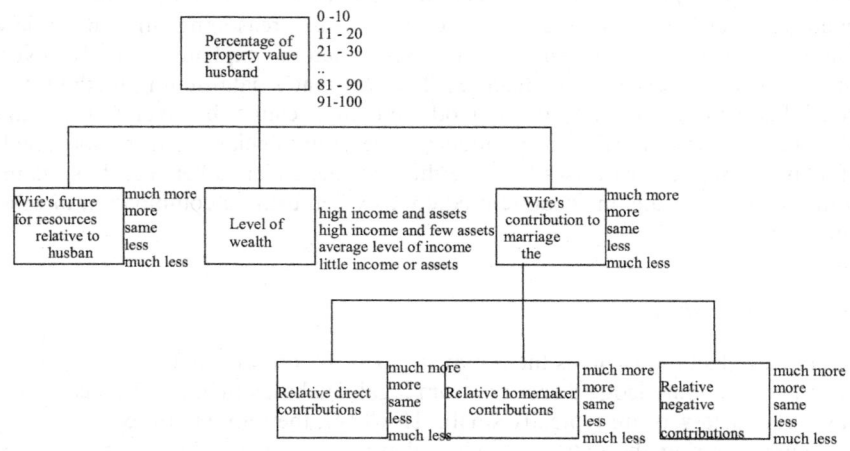

Figure 1. Partial tree for Split Up

Trees that represent a hierarchy of factors in a legal case have been used in law in numerous ways. [Wigmore 1937] advanced a representation that included a hierarchy of factors in a schema now called a Wigmore diagram. [Aleven and Ashley 1995] extended the Hypo case based reasoning system by drawing on a hierarchy of factors called a factor tree. A factor in Cato is not a variable but is equivalent to a variable-value pair in the scheme advanced here. [Bench-Capon 1999] illustrated the use of partial order in combining trees of factors that represented arguments opponents make.

As described above, in the Split Up project, the trees were derived in consultation with specialist lawyers. The consultation proceeded in the following way:

a) Commencing at the top most variable, specialists were asked to identify possible values for the variable. A 100 point scale was considered too fine-grained whereas a scale with 5% intervals was considered appropriate.

b) Specialists were asked to draw on precedents, statutes and their own experience in the field to identify those factors that would be sufficient for an inference of the top most variable. The three factors identified as most directly relevant for a percentage split determination related to contribution, needs and wealth. These are known as children of the top most node.

c) Appropriate values for each child variable were identified. For instance, contribution values were "much more", "more", "about the same", "less", "much less".

d) The fourth step involved ascertaining a reason for the relevance of the variable. Doing so provided the knowledge engineer with a degree of confidence that the factors identified were indeed relevant factors. Typically, a reason for relevance in law, relates the variable to a statute, a precedent or common practice in the field. The reason for relevance concept derives from an argumentation model described by [Yearwood and Stranieri 2004] and is summarised in the next section. We shall see that this model is useful for data mining exercises in law, because it provides a mechanism for integrating domain knowledge supplied by specialists with automated data mining algorithms.

e) Each child variable was visited and specialists were asked to identify factors for it. Relevant factors for determining the husband's contribution relative to that of the wife were; *the direct contributions, the homemaker contributions* and *negative contributions*. The *negative contributions* variable is a recent addition following a series of precedent cases involving gambling debts and domestic violence. Steps 4 and 5 are repeated until the specialist indicates that the variable can no longer be reduced. For instance, all specialists agreed that the variable age, measured in whole years could not be decomposed.

The hierarchy of relevant factors derives from the Generic Actual Argument model described in [Yearwood and Stranieri 2004]. This model provides a natural framework for decomposing a task during the data transformation phase. It provides a mechanism for integrating domain knowledge to constrain and enhance the data mining phase. The model is introduced in the next section.

[Stranieri *et al* 2001] note that argumentation, in general involves a family of concepts that describe two types of situations: dialectical situations and non-dialectical situations. [Freeman 1991][33] defines a dialectical situation as:

'one that involves some opposition among participants to a discourse over some claim, that it involves interactive questioning for critically testing this claim and this process proceeds in a regimented, rule governed manner'.

A dialectical situation involves participants engaged in the process of argument and a protocol to regulate the process. In contrast, a focus on the product of an argumentation process is a non-dialectical view. This involves the linguistic reconstruction of what the argumentation process and procedure have generated. It involves laying out the premises, claims and layout of claims.

The Generic Actual Argument Model (GAAM) ([Yearwood and Stranieri 2004] and [Stranieri *et al* 2001]) is expressly non-dialectical in that it does not model the process of argumentation or protocols that regulate it. The model represents a structured summary of arguments made by judges, defendants, plaintiffs and other stakeholders involved in a legal matter. By omitting dialectical operators, the model lays the structure of reasoning bare, so that constituent elements of the reasoning may be identified. The decomposition of reasoning that occurs in this process is useful for restructuring a data set for mining.

Most argumentation schemes advanced blend dialectical and non-dialectical elements. [Toulmin 1958] drew on arguments conducted in many fields in order to illustrate that reasoning in general, can better be described as a kind of jurisprudence

---

[33] at p20

than as a formal logic. He concluded that arguments display an internal structure that consists of six basic elements: claim, data, modality, rebuttal, warrant and backing.

Figure 2 illustrates a Toulmin argument that makes a claim that *the husband should receive 20% of the property value*. Every argument makes an assertion or claim based on some data. Knowing the data and the claim does not necessarily convince an audience that the claim follows from the data. A mechanism is required to act as a justification for the claim. This justification is known as the warrant. The backing supports the warrant and in a legal argument is typically a reference to a statute or a precedent case.

The claim is made on the basis of three data items, that:
a) the wife's needs for resources is much greater than the husband's need for resources ;
b) the marriage has an average level of income and assets;
c) the wife has contributed much more to the marriage than has the husband

The warrant explains why the claim follows from data: *'The retrospective element, needs is counter-balanced against a prospective element. The impact of needs diminishes with increasing wealth'*

The backing provides authority for the warrant.

Figure 2 depicts a second argument in the layout advanced by [Toulmin 1958]. The claim of the left most argument is one of the three data items of the right most argument. The hierarchy of concepts depicted in the tree in Figure 1 captures the hierarchy of claim/data items and but omits, for brevity the warrant, backing, modality and rebuttal components.

In general, argumentation has been used in knowledge engineering in two distinct ways; with a focus on the use of argumentation to structure knowledge (i.e non-dialectical emphasis) or with a focus on the use of argumentation to model discourse (i.e dialectical emphasis). Dialectical approaches typically automate the construction of an argument and counter arguments normally with the use of a non-monotonic logic where operators are defined to implement discursive primitives such as attack, rebut, or accept. [Carbogim *et al* 2000] present a comprehensive survey of defeasible argumentation.

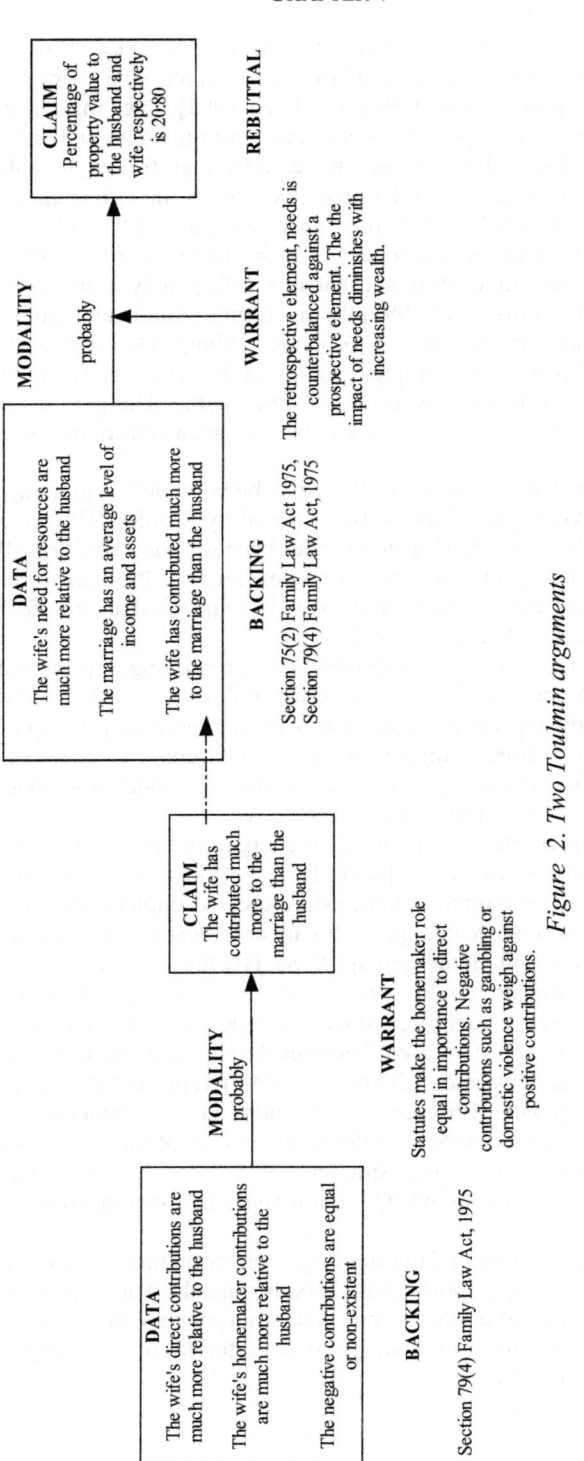

Figure 2. Two Toulmin arguments

Dialectical models have been advanced by [Cohen 1985], [Fox 1986], [Vreeswijk 1993], [Dung 1995], [Prakken 1993], [Prakken and Sartor 1997], [Gordon 1995] and [Fox and Parsons 1998]. [Prakken 1995] notes that, in general these approaches include a concept of conflict between arguments and the notion that some arguments defeat others. Most applications that follow a dialectical approach represent knowledge as first order predicate clauses, though engage a non-monotonic logic to allow contradictory clauses. Mechanisms are typically required to identify implausible arguments and to evaluate the better argument of two or more plausible ones. For example, [Fox and Parsons 1998] analyse and extend the non standard logic LA of [Krause *et al* 1995]. In this formalisation, an argument is a tuple with three components: (Sentence : Grounds : Sign). The sentence is the Toulmin claim, though this may be a simple claim or a rule. The sign is a number or symbol that indicates the confidence warranted in the claim. The grounds are the sentences involved in asserting the claim and can be seen as the reasoning steps used to ultimately reach the conclusion.

The preference for one argument over others has been modelled in a variety of ways. [Prakken 1993] extends the framework proposed by [Poole 1988] in using a concept of specificity. The claim that a penguin flies because it is a bird and all birds fly is less specific that the claim that a penguin does not fly. Preference relations between rules are elicited from experts and explicitly specified in the defeasible reasoning logic described by [Antoniou 1997].

In applications of argumentation to model dialectical reasoning, argumentation is specifically used to model discourse and only indirectly used to structure knowledge. When participants are engaged in a dispute, concepts of conflict and of argument preferences map directly onto a discursive situation. In contrast, many uses of argumentation for knowledge engineering do not model discourse. This corresponds more closely to a non-dialectical perspective.

A non-dialectical representation facilitated the organisation of complex legal knowledge for information retrieval by [Dick 1987]. [Marshall 1989] and [Ball 1994] organised knowledge using the Toulmin structure and implemented hypertext systems to enable a user to readily navigate intricate argument chains. [Clark 1991] represented the opinions of individual geologists as Toulmin structures so that his group decision support system could identify points of disagreement between experts. [Johnson *et al* 1993] identified different types of expertise using this structure, [Bench-Capon *et al* 1991] used Toulmin Argument Structure to explain logic programming conclusions and [Matthijssen 1999] represented user defined tasks with Toulmin Argument Structures. [Branting 1994] expands Toulmin Argument Structure warrants as a model of the legal concept of ratio decidendi. In the Split Up project, [Zeleznikow and Stranieri 1995] used Toulmin Argument Structure to represent family law knowledge in a manner that facilitated rule/neural hybrid development.

Despite the immediate appeal of Toulmin Argument Structures as a convenient frame for structuring knowledge, most researchers that use the Toulmin layout vary the original structure. Each variation can be seen as an attempt to integrate some aspects of dialectical reasoning into a structure that, for knowledge engineering purposes, is largely non-dialectical.

[Freeman 1991] labeled the Toulmin approach as one that provides for a macrostructure of arguments. The key concerns are how statements as a whole enter into arguments and what statements are put forward to support others. In contrast, deductive logic exemplifies a microstructure approach that is concerned with how statements in an argument are built up from constituent parts. For example, in applying modus ponens within a classical syllogism, we must see one premise as an antecedent, another as a conditional and the conclusion is the consequent.

Although, according to [Freeman 1991], a focus on the macrostructure is particularly important for modelling the way in which arguments flow backward and forward between participants in a discourse, the Toulmin layout does not explicitly model discourse. Operators to question, attack or qualify opposition assertions are not explicit. Nor is there the facility to represent an agent's beliefs and how it differs from another agent's beliefs. Not surprisingly, many knowledge engineering applications of the Toulmin framework have not modelled discursive exchanges, but have applied the framework to structure knowledge.

Toulmin proposed his views on argumentation informally and never claimed to have advanced a theory of argumentation. He does not rigorously define key terms such as warrant and backing. He only loosely specifies how arguments relate to other arguments and provides no guidance as to how to evaluate the best argument or identify implausible ones. Nevertheless, the structure was found to be useful as a tool for organising knowledge. For example, [Dick 1991] illustrates how relevant cases for an information retrieval query can be retrieved despite sharing no surface features if the arguments used in case judgements are represented as Toulmin structures. Further, both [Marshall 1989], [Ball 1994] and [Loui 1997] have built hypertext based computer implementations that draw on knowledge organised as Toulmin arguments. Hypertext links connect an argument's assertions with the warrants, backing and data of the same argument and also link the data of one argument with the assertion of other arguments. Complex reasoning can be represented succinctly enabling convenient search and retrieval of relevant information.

[Matthijssen 1999] provides a further example of benefits that arise from the use of the original Toulmin structure. He represented user tasks as Toulmin arguments and associated a list of keywords to the structure. These keywords were used as information retrieval queries into a range of databases. Results indicate considerable advantages in precision and recall of documents as a result of this approach compared with approaches that require the user to invent queries.

Although there are substantial examples of benefits of the use of the argument structure that conform to the original formulation, the majority of applications vary the structure. In the following section four variations are presented. These can be understood as attempts to integrate a dialectical approach into a non-dialectical one.

4.1   Johnson's Toulmin Argument Structure

[Johnson et al 1993] claim that any argument's backing can be classified into one of five distinct types of backing which they label Type 1 to Type 5. Each type of backing corresponds to a distinct type of expertise and also corresponds to a particular philosophical paradigm of reasoning:

a) Type 1 arguments reflect axiomatic reasoning. Data and claim for these arguments are analytic truths. The supporting evidence derives from a system of axioms such as Peano's axioms of arithmetic. Examples of what Aristotle called demonstrations would be captured as Type 1 arguments by [Johnson *et al* 1993] and not as a different type of proof.

b) Type 2 arguments assert a particular medical diagnosis on the basis of empirical judgements from a number of patients who have presented with similar symptoms in the past.

c) Type 3 arguments are characterised by backings which reflect alternate representations of a problem. A medical diagnosis based on a model of the heart as a pump analyses symptoms to be consistent with that model. An alternate presentation that has the heart as a muscle provides other evidence.

d) Type 4 arguments differ from Type 3 arguments in that the alternate representations are conflicting. In this case the argument involves supporting evidence that is conflicting. An assertion is made by creating a composite representation from conflicting ones.

e) Type 5 backings refer to paradigms that reflect a process of inquiry.

The Type 1 and 2 backings that [Johnson *et al* 1993] identifies are markedly different from Types 3, 4 and 5. In the latter group, a claim is ultimately backed by recourse to conflicting or non-conflicting alternate representations of a problem.

The resolution of conflicting representations is akin to a dialectical process. A common solution is sought from the exchange that is stimulated from conflicting representations. In Type 1 (axiomatic) or Type 2 (empirical) arguments, the backing is made from one perspective. There are no alternate representations and no common solutions. This is akin to a non-dialectical perspective.

The [Johnson *et al* 1993] variation does not introduce or eliminate components of the original structure. However, by discerning non-dialectical backings from dialectical ones, it imposes a typology of backing that can be seen as an attempt to extend the structure toward somewhat of a dialectical application. The approach is limited by the unclear nature of the Toulmin warrant.

Broadly speaking, Toulmin formulates the warrant as an inference procedure. It is a procedure for inferring a claim given data. However, the statement that 'Most Saudi's are Muslim' can also be interpreted as a reason for the relevance of the data item 'Mustafa is a Saudi' in the argument depicted in Figure 6. Alternatively, it could be interpreted as an inference procedure, a rule that enables a claim to be inferred from data. We discuss what [Freeman 1991] calls the problematic notion of warrant, at length below, but now note the Johnson typology applies to backings for warrants that are inference procedures but may not necessarily apply in the same way to warrants that are reasons for relevance.

4.2   The Freeman/Farley variation on Toulmin warrants

[Freeman 1994] and [Farley and Freeman 1995] recognised the need to extend the warrant component in order to develop a model of dialectical reasoning more formal than that proposed by Toulmin. Their main objective was to develop a system that could model the burden of proof concept in legal reasoning. The concept of burden of proof is often used to refer to the onus a participant has to supply evidence. So, as [Prakken 2001] notes in modelling this form of burden of proof using a dialogue game model, a judge directs the pleadings phase of proceedings by requiring one litigant or another to supply evidence to support their claims. However, the form of burden of proof that was the focus of attention for [Farley and Freeman 1995] involves the extent to which evidence is required in order to draw a conclusion. In the law of evidence, the burden of proof is the necessity or duty of affirmatively proving a fact or facts in dispute on an issue raised between the parties in a cause. Except as otherwise provided by the law, the burden of proof requires proof by a preponderance of the evidence. In a criminal case, the government, beyond a reasonable doubt, must prove all the elements of the crime. Except in cases of tax fraud, the burden of proof in a tax case is generally on the taxpayer.

[Freeman 1994] distinguished two types of warrants she called wtype1 and wtype2. The first warrant type classifies the relationship between assertion and data as explanatory or sign. Causal links are examples of explanatory warrants because they explain an assertion given data. Fire causes smoke. The consequent is explained by recourse to a cause/effect link. Other types of explanatory warrants include definitional relationships or property/attribute relationships. A sign relationship represents a correlational link between data and assertion.

The second warrant type, wtype2, represents the strength with which the assertion can be drawn from data. Examples of this type of warrant proposed by Freeman represent the strength with which the consequent can be drawn from the antecedent. Default type warrants represent default relationships such as birds fly. Evidential warrants are less certain. Sufficient warrants are certain and typically stem from definitions.

Freeman explicitly represents reasoning methods in addition to the two types of warrant. The reasoning types reside outside the Toulmin structure but interact with warrants in order to produce credible outcomes. Her model incorporates four reasoning mechanisms, modus ponens[34], modus tolens, abduction [35]and contra positive abduction. Some reasoning mechanisms are stronger than others according to heuristics she devised. Modus ponens and modus tolens are assigned a strong link qualification if used with sufficient warrants, whereas the same reasoning types are assigned a 'credible' qualification if used with evidential warrants.

Reasoning types interact with warrant types to control the generation of arguments according to reasoning heuristics. For example, modus ponens/abduction combinations are not permitted for two explanatory warrants unless both are

---

[34] Modus ponens is a form of inference that says if P —> Q holds and P holds, then Q holds.

[35] Abductive reasoning states that from P -> Q and Q it is possible to infer P. It is an unsound rule of inference, in that it is not necessarily true for every interpretation in which the premises are true.

evidential. [Freeman 1994] demonstrates that her model has a capacity to perform dialectical reasoning. An assertion is initially argued for with the use of heuristics she defined. Then, an alternate argument is compared with the initial argument constructed and support for it is ascertained. The comparisons require the notion of level of proof which include beyond reasonable doubt, scintilla of evidence and preponderance of evidence.

Freeman's model is a sophisticated extension to the Toulmin structures that displays impressive dialectical reasoning results. She advances types of relationships between consequents and antecedents (wtpye1) and assigns the link a strength (wtype2). The discernment of two types of warrant is essential, because her model of burden of proof relies upon it. By specifying reasoning types and heuristics for their interaction with warrants, [Freeman and Farley 1995] can be seen to provide a way to extend the Toulmin structure so that it can be applied to model dialogue. The ambiguity in the original Toulmin warrant is dealt with by reserving one type of warrant for the inference rule and the other to indicate the strength of the rule. This adds a representation of uncertainty to some extent, but as we shall describe below, the strength of the data items and strength of claims is not represented. Furthermore, there is no attempt to incorporate information regarding the broader context of the argument.

In contrast, the issue of context is paramount for [Bench-Capon 1998] who is not intent on modelling the burden of proof in legal reasoning but on implementing a dialogue game that engages players in constructing arguments for and against assertions initially made by one party.

4.3   Bench-Capon's variation

[Bench-Capon 1998] does not distinguish types of backing as [Johnson *et al* 1993] do or types of warrant following [Farley and Freeman, K. 1995], but instead introduces an additional component to the Toulmin Argument Structure. The presupposition component of a Toulmin Argument Structure represents assumptions made that are necessary for the argument but are not the object of dispute so remain outside the core of the argument. In our view a presupposition for Toulmin's Saudi argument described above would indicate that the Saudi Arabia in the context of that argument is the modern state.

Making explicit presuppositions in the argument structure are important for the use [Bench-Capon 1998] makes of Toulmin Argument Structure. A program that plays the part of one or both players in a dialogue game is often exposed to utterances in discourse that represent presuppositions and are not central to the discussion at hand. The presuppositions can become critical if parties to a game do not share them. [Bench-Capon 1998] interprets the warrant as an inference procedure much as Toulmin originally did. The dialogue game does not directly add dialectical operators such as rebut, attack or accept into the structure but these are instead encoded into the control mechanism that represent the rules of the dialogue game. The inherent ambiguity in the Toulmin warrant is not addressed however, the context of the argument is modelled by the addition of a presupposition component.

The three variations to the Toulmin structure presented here can be seen to be attempts at clarifying how the structure can be used within a dialogue.   This objective motivated Johnson to add types of backings.   Each new backing type derives from the use of arguments by a discursive community.   [Farley and Freeman 1995] were more direct and developed specific reasoning heuristics so that an argument and counter-argument are constructed as it would be within a discursive community.   Bench-Capon defined a dialogue game that regulated the dialogue between two players who each encode their utterances as Toulmin components and [Freeman 1991] asserted that, in any event, all non-dialectical assertions can be seen to be a dialectical one where there is only one voice.

In the next section a variation of the Toulmin structure is proposed that specifically aims to model the structure of arguments in a non-dialectical manner. This is done in a manner that is at a sufficiently high level of abstraction so as to represent shared understanding between participants to a discourse that ultimately simplifies the specification of a dialectical model.

4.4   The Generic-Actual Argument Model for Restructuring

[Freeman 1991] argues that although Toulmin's contribution was a significant step forward in the recognition that everyday reasoning is not ideally represented with formal logic, the structure he advanced is ambiguous in two main ways. First of all, it is unclear whether the structure represents the product of an argumentative discourse or captures the process of constructing an argument. As a representation of the product of argument, the structure can be seen to be a convenient way to organise the elements of an argument after the fact. This has utility in succinctly summarising a point of view, perhaps for the purpose of easily conveying the argument to others.

The rebuttal element of the Toulmin Structure is explicitly dialectical. The rebuttal is itself a claim of another structure that undoubtedly has its own data, warrant, modality, backing and rebuttal. The way in which an argument's claim is attacked in a dialectical exchange, is explicitly represented by the inclusion of the rebuttal element.

The Toulmin layout without modification is also not suitable for restructuring knowledge, because the nature of the warrant component can be interpreted in different ways. Figure 3 illustrates a sample Toulmin argument. The statement '*Most Saudis are Muslim*' is a warrant that convinces us that the assertion '*Mustafa is a Muslim*' follows from the knowledge that '*X is a Saudi*'. However, this warrant communicates two distinct meanings. On the one hand the warrant indicates a reason for the relevance of the fact *Mustafa is a Saudi*'. On the hand the warrant can be interpreted as a rule which, when applied to the fact that '*Mustafa is a Saudi*' leads us to infer that '*Mustafa is a Muslim*'.

These two apparent meanings are best perceived as different roles the warrant has in the structure of an argument. Drawing the distinction between the two roles a

74

warrant performs in an argument, led to the explicit identification of three features that are left implicit in the Toulmin formulation:
a) an inference procedure, algorithm or method used to infer an assertion from datum;
b) reasons which explain why a data item is relevant for a claim; and
c) reasons that explain why the inference method used is appropriate.

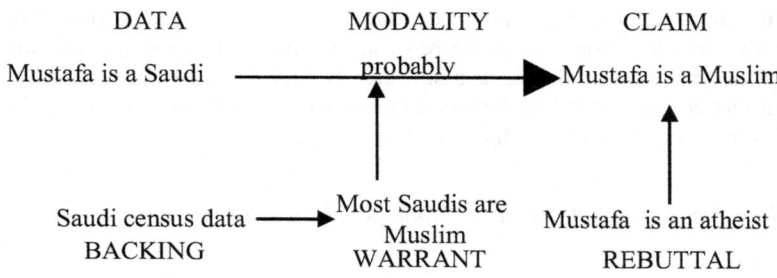

Figure 3. Toulmin layout of arguments

Figure 4 represents a template for a knowledge representation that differs from the Toulmin structure. The template differs from the Toulmin structure in that it includes:
a) a variable-value representation of claim and data items;
b) a certainty variable associated with each variable-value rather than a modality or force associated with the entire argument;
c) reasons for the relevance of the data items in place of the warrant;
d) a list of inference procedures that can be used to infer a claim value from data values in place of the warrant;
e) reasons for the appropriateness of each inference procedure;
f) context variables; and
g) the absence of the rebuttal component present in the original formulation.

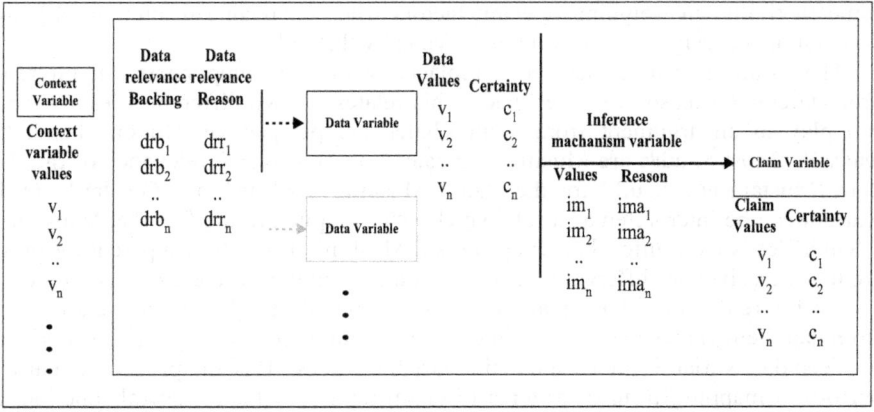

Figure 4. Non-dialectical Argument template

The argument template represents knowledge at a very high level of abstraction. There are two levels of instantiation made in applying the template to model arguments within a domain: the generic level and the actual level. A generic argument is an instantiation of the template where the following components are set:

a) claim, data and context variables are specified but not assigned values;

b) relevance reason values and backing values are specified;

c) inference procedures are listed but a commitment to any one procedure is avoided; and

d) inference procedure reasons are specified for each procedure.

The generic argument is sufficiently general so as to capture the variety of perspectives displayed by members of a discursive community. All participants in a dialogue use the same generic argument so as to facilitate the identification of points of agreement and to constrain a negotiation protocol. This will be discussed further below.

Figure 5 illustrates the Saudi argument as a generic argument. The claim variable has been labelled as 'Muslim' and acceptable values specified. There are three inference procedures known to be appropriate in this example. The first procedure is a rule set that derives from heuristics an expert on Saudi citizenship uses. The second procedure is a neural network trained from past cases, while the third procedure is human inference. This latter inference indicates that a human is empowered with sufficient discretion to infer a claim value from data item values in any way he or she likes.

Discretion is viewed as an instance of open texture. The concept of open texture is significant in the legal domain because new uses for terms, and new situations constantly arise in legal cases. [Prakken 1993] discerns three sources of open texture; reasoning which involves defeasible rules; vague terms; or classification ambiguities. We add judicial discretion as conceptualised by [Christie 1986] and [Bayles 1990], to this list and argue that judicial discretion is a form of open texture distinct from the three above sources. According to this view, decision-makers have some flexibility in weighing relevant factors when exercising discretion, although articulating an assignment of weights is typically difficult.

The Toulmin warrant has been replaced with two components; an inference procedure and a reason for relevance. This relates to two different roles a warrant can play in an argument from a non-dialectical perspective. On one hand, the warrant, 'Most Saudi's are Muslim' indicates a reason for the relevance of the data item 'Mustafa is a Saudi' for the claim 'Mustafa is a Muslim'. On the hand the warrant can be interpreted as a rule which, when applied to the fact that 'Mustafa is a Saudi' leads us to infer that 'Mustafa is a Muslim'. These two apparent meanings are best perceived as different roles the warrant has in the structure of an argument.

An inference procedure is an algorithm or method used to infer a claim value from data item values. Under this interpretation, an inference procedure is a relation between data variable values and claim variable values. It is any procedure that will perform a mapping from data items to claim items. A mathematical function, an algorithm, a rule set, a neural network, or procedures yet to be discovered are examples of inference procedures.

Many inference procedures can be implemented in software. Human agents can sometimes infer claims from data items without the explicit specification of an inference procedure. This occurs frequently in discretionary fields of law where, as [Christie 1986] notes, decision makers weight and combine relevant factors in their own way without articulating precisely how claims were inferred. This situation is accommodated within the Generic Actual Argument framework with the specification of an inference type labelled, simply, human.

The original Toulmin warrant can also be seen to be a reason for relevance or an inference procedure. Past contributions to a marriage are relevant in Australian family law. Past contributions appears as a data item in a generic argument regarding property distribution following divorce, because a statute dictates that contributions are relevant. The level of wealth of an Australian marriage is made relevant by past cases and not by a statute. The hair colour of the wife is considered irrelevant because there is no statutory or precedent basis for its relevance. Further, domain experts can think of no reason that would make this feature relevant.

The concept of relevance is in itself difficult to define. [van Dijk 1989] describes the concept of relevance as it applies to a class of modal logics broadly called 'relevance logics' as the requirement that propositions within the same assertion share a common concept. The consequent in the proposition 'If Harry comes to the party, the grass will be green' shares no obvious concept with the antecedent so is regarded as irrelevant. However, the components of the proposition, 'If it has rained, the grass will be green' seems perfectly acceptable even though no concept is shared between the two propositions.

Given the limitations of a concept sharing definition for relevance, [van Dijk 1989][36] explores an intuitive notion based on referential meaning in that propositions are relevant if they refer to the same thing: 'If Harry comes to the party, he will be pleased'. However even though, referential identity and shared concepts do not explain the relevance of all propositions (e.g. 'if it is spring, the trees will have new

[36] At p29

leaves'), a reason for relevance can be articulated. This view of relevance grounds relevance in the pragmatics of language and is realised in the generic, actual argument model as agreement on what are the valid data items.

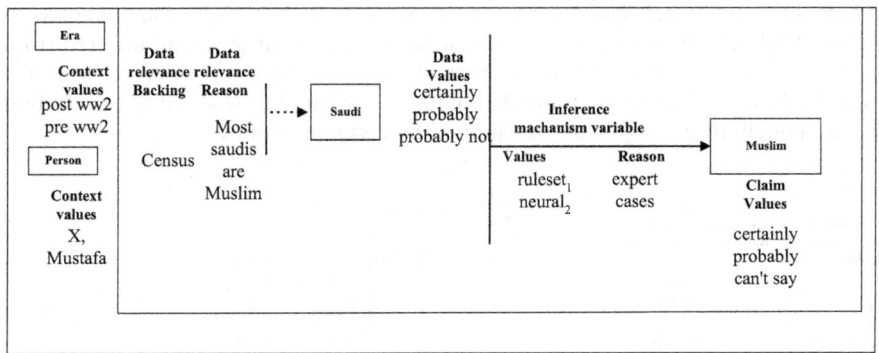

Figure 5. Generic argument for Saudi's

Figure 6 represents an actual argument. This is the second level instantiation of the argument template in Figure 4. An actual argument corresponds to a position held by a participant in a discourse. It is an instantiation of a generic argument. The context variable person in the generic argument is instantiated to 'Mustafa' indicating that the claim only applies to Mustafa and not to others. The data item value in Figure 6 represents the situation that 'Mustafa is probably not a Saudi'. The inference procedure for the actual argument is only that rule that has been selected by the member of the discursive community that constructed the actual argument. As a consequence of applying that rule, the claim value is instantiated to represent that Mustafa may or may not be a Muslim. The claim value reason for this actual argument provides a reason for that value; that many persons outside Saudi Arabia are Muslims therefore no definite conclusion about Mustafa's religion can be drawn.

The claim value reason is not a reason for the inference rule. First, the inference method need not be a rule. If it is a mathematical function or has mechanisms that are not visible, such as a neural network, then the articulation of a reason for the inference method is impossible. Conceptually, it is more accurate to say the claim value reason is a reason for a particular value that has arisen as a result of the application of a an inference method

This framework including the generic/actual distinction, the clear separation of inference procedure from other components and the inclusion of reasons for relevance and context introduces a non-dialectical structure that captures shared understanding within a discursive community, but does not include elements that are clearly needed to model dialectical exchanges. However, the specification of a comprehensive non-dialectical structure constrains the search for an appropriate dialectical representation. In the next section we outline the utility of the non-dialectical variations for knowledge engineering.

4.5   Applications of the generic/actual argument model

Generic and actual argument structures correspond to a non-dialectical perspective. They do not directly model an exchange of views between discursive participants, but rather describe assertions made from premises and the way in which multiple claims are organised. For instance, claim variables are inferred from data item values using an inference procedure. The reasoning occurs within a context and the extent to which the data items correspond to true values, according to the proponent of the argument, is captured by certainty values.

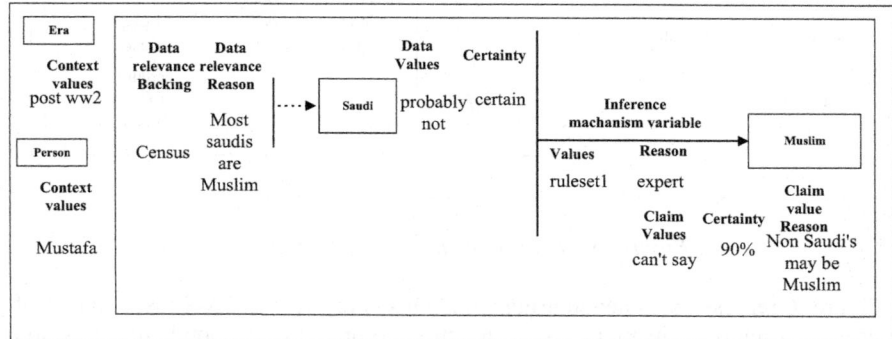

Figure 6. Actual argument

The generic argument provides a level of abstraction that accommodates most points of view within a discursive community and anticipates the creation of actual arguments, by participants, as instantiations of a generic argument. However, it is conceivable that, given the open textured nature of reasoning that a participant will seek to advance an actual argument that is a departure from the generic argument. This can be performed with the introduction of a new variable (data, claim or context) value, with the use of a new inference procedure or, with a new claim value reason.

In the Split Up system, the relevant variables were structured as data and claim items. They system used the generic argument outlined above. The task was decomposed into 35 interlocking arguments, with the claim of one argument being the data item of another argument. Figure 7 illustrates three arguments. Argument A has three features, contributions, needs and wealth. The way in which judges combine these factors to infer a percentage split outcome is discovered as part of a data-mining exercise that is quite separate from that of Argument B and Argument C.

In the Split Up system all claim variable values were inferred from the data item values, using automated inference procedures. In fifteen of the thirty-five arguments, claim values were inferred from data items with an inference procedure that involved the use of small rule-sets that represent expert heuristics. Neural networks, trained on data from past Court cases, were used to infer claim values in the remaining twenty arguments. Split Up performed quite well despite the small number of samples.

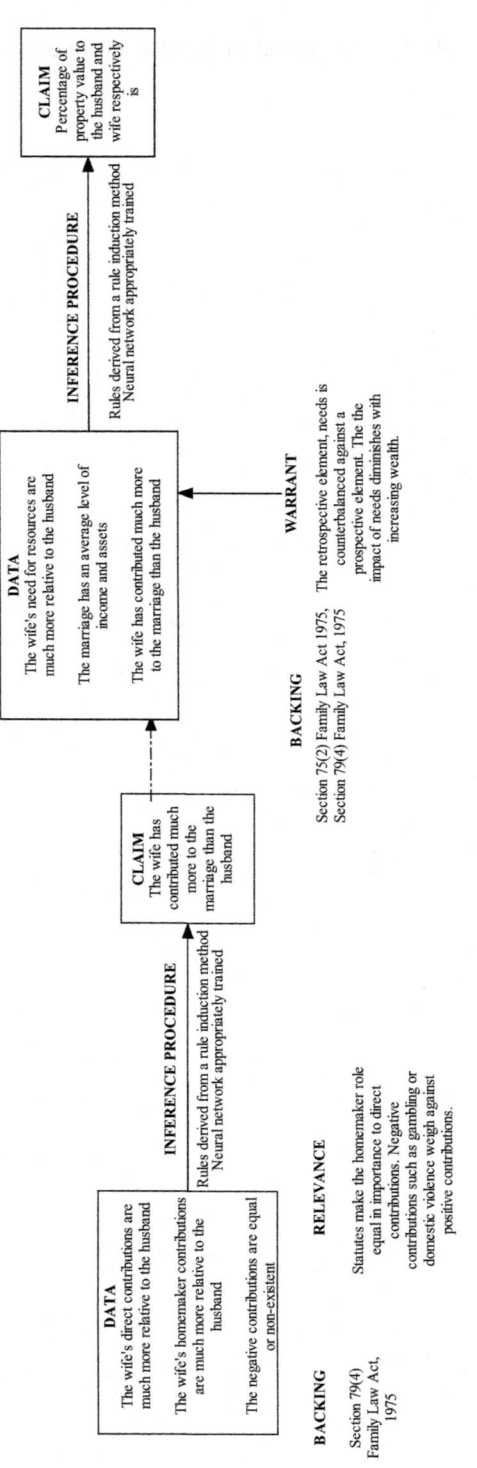

Figure 7. Two GAAM arguments

The use of over ninety features to predict a percentage split outcome without re-structuring the problem was made very difficult because:

a) **Many cases are required**. Even if each feature was present with only two values, perhaps a TRUE and FALSE value then the number of possible different combinations of values representing the number of different cases is astronomical. Even a substantial sample of cases would cover only a small proportion of possible cases. However, by restructuring the problem using an argument tree, each data-mining exercise is performed with only a small number of features. The different number of cases is far small and feasible even with small data-sets.

b) **Legitimate missing values are reduced**. Many marriages in the Split Up do not involve children, yet a number of the 94 features relate to children. Features such as the child's age, residence status and educational level would have missing values for childless marriages. The missing values are legitimate; so replacing the missing value is not appropriate. However, the presence of the missing values is still problematical for many data-mining algorithms. Restructuring the argument tree reduces legitimate missing values. Features that relate to children are represented as a branch of the tree. Data for all data mining along that branch is drawn only from marriages with children so there are no missing values.

c) **Change over time**. The change in law over time is captured within an argument tree by the introduction of a new feature, previously not relevant but now considered relevant, by a statute or precedent cases . According to [Alexander 2000], numerous unsuccessful attempts during the last decade were made to persuade judges to award a more generous property settlement to the victim of domestic violence, despite no statutory or precedent basis existing for such claims. This corresponds to the situation where an argument is advanced that departs from existing generic arguments by the introduction of a new data item. In recent years, a small number of Family Court judges began to accept the domestic violence argument. Many of the early cases were appealed and precedents set by higher Courts so that domestic violence is now undeniably a relevant consideration in property division.

5. CHAPTER SUMMARY

The data transformation phase is the last phase prior to performing data-mining. In this phase, data values are transformed to different values, or the entire KDD exercise is restructured in some way. The transformation of data values is performed so as to improve the meaningfulness of patterns discovered or predictions made in the data-mining phase. The changes involve grouping or aggregating values into categories so that values are not so specific that links with other features are lost in the fine-grained values. For example, date of birth values are transformed into age group values to explore associations of age to other features.

Values may also be transformed by normalisation. This involves transforming values on one scale into values on another scale. Dollar values that range from 0 to many millions may be transformed into values that range from 0 to 1 to bring their influence into a comparable basis with other values also normalised to the same range.

Feature reduction involves removing features that are uninteresting or do not contribute to predictions or classifications in the data-mining phase. Rather than clutter the data-mining exercise with unnecessary features, the features are removed from consideration. Care must be taken in doing so, because although accurate predictions may be made with only a small number of features, explaining the predictions without reference to other features is likely to be unacceptable.

The most important data transformation procedure for KDD in legal databases involves restructuring a problem into many smaller and more feasible KDD exercises. Restructuring enables effective data mining to be performed regardless of the size of the data-set. As legal data-sets are typically small, restructuring becomes very important.

The use of argumentation concepts to generate an argument tree is a convenient mechanism for restructuring. The layout of arguments advanced by [Toulmin 1958] form the basis of the structure of each KDD exercise. The exercises are connected, because items that are claims in one argument are data items in another. Almost all adoptions of the Toulmin layout vary the original formulation. The variations are understandable if a distinction is drawn between dialectical argumentation and non-dialectical argumentation. Non-dialectical argumentation involves concepts that relate to the way in which reasoning is structured. Non-dialectical argumentation provides a convenient mechanism for restructuring a data mining exercise.

In the next chapter, data mining techniques that involve discovering rules from a data set are introduced. The algorithms that discover rules from data perform far better if data is presented that has been appropriately pre-processed and transformed as described in the last two chapters.

CHAPTER 5

DATA MINING WITH RULE INDUCTION

In previous chapters we have investigated how to prepare legal data for the data-mining phase. Tasks prior to data-mining include:
1. **Data selection and pre-processing**– this refers to the pre-processing of data to remove or reduce noise and the treatment of missing values.
2. **Data transformation** – changing the data-set so that the data-mining phase can be more effective.

In this chapter we primarily focus upon one data mining classification and prediction approach, rule induction. In the next chapter, we discuss association rules, fuzzy logic and Bayesian classifiers. Yet another data-mining technique, neural networks is discussed in chapter seven.

Data-mining can be seen as an automated mechanism for learning patterns from a dataset. [Michalski and Larson 1978] identify the following general learning strategies:
a) Direct Implanting of Knowledge,
b) Learning from Instruction,
c) Learning by Deductive Inference,
d) Learning by Analogy,
e) Learning from Examples,
f) Learning by Observation and Discovery.

The learning strategies a-f are presented in order of increasing effort on the part of the learner and decreasing amounts of effort on the part of the teacher. This order also reflects the increasing difficulty of constructing a learning system capable of using the given learning strategy.

The higher the learning strategy, the more inference, and thus the more cost and effort (on behalf of the learner) is involved in deriving the desired knowledge.

Machine knowledge acquisition is easiest if we know how to precisely solve a problem. In this case, to teach the computer by instruction is simpler and better than to engage it in an inductive learning process. There are, however, many application domains where precise algorithms are unknown or difficult to obtain. Law is such a domain.

Inductive learning is a process of acquiring knowledge by drawing inductive inferences from facts provided by a teacher or the environment. This process involves operations of generalising, transforming, correcting and refining knowledge representations in order to accommodate given facts and satisfy various additional criteria. This process has, however one major weakness: except for special cases, the acquired knowledge, cannot in principle, be completely validated[37]. This occurs because inductive inference produces hypotheses with a potentially infinite number of consequences, while only a finite number of confirming tests can be performed.[38]

Thus, to perform inductive inference, we need background knowledge to constrain the possibilities and guide the inference process toward one or a few most plausible hypotheses. This background knowledge must include:

a) The goals of the learning,
b) Criteria for deciding the preference among candidate hypotheses,
c) The methods for interpreting the observations, with corresponding inference rules for manipulating representation.

There are two aspects of inductive inference: the generation of plausible hypotheses and their confirmation. In this chapter, we discuss the first aspect. Plausible hypotheses expressed as rules take the following form:

$$IF <condition(s)> THEN <consequence>^{39}$$

For example, a rule induction algorithm exposed to a data-set of banking records may discover the rule;

$$IF\ credit\text{-}rating = low\ \text{and}\ age > 55\ \ THEN\ credit\_risk = low$$

Rule induction algorithms discover rules that are generalisations from data. The general rule: *if bird then flies* has been induced from a sample of instances of birds and is intended to generalise to all birds.

Rule induction algorithms discover rules that are intended to be applicable as generalizations from sample data. [Zeleznikow and Hunter 1994] note the following benefits of rule induction:

a) Rule induction has the ability to infer new knowledge. A human may be able to list all the factors influencing a decision, but may not understand the impact of these factors;
b) Once rules have been generated they can be reviewed and modified by the domain expert, providing for more useful, comprehensive and accurate rules for the domain.

There are, however, many difficulties in implementing rule induction systems:

---

[37] Validation of knowledge-based systems is an essential task when using knowledge discovery or indeed any statistical techniques to infer knowledge. A discussion of the validation of legal knowledge-based systems can be found in chapter nine. [Hall *et al* 2003] developed the Context Criteria Contingency-guidelines framework for the evaluation of legal knowledge based systems.

[38] The British philosopher David Hume noted this drawback of induction in the eighteenth century.

[39] A rule can be more formally viewed as $p_1\ \&\ p_2\ \&\ \ ...\ \ p_n \rightarrow q$ where $p_1\ \&\ p_2\ \&\ \ ...\ \ p_n$ is the antecedent and q is the consequent

a) Some rule induction programs or training sets may generate rules that are difficult to understand;
b) Rule induction programs do not select the attributes. Hence, if the domain expert chooses inappropriate attributes in the creation of the training set, or there are inconsistent or inadequate examples in the training set, then the rules induced are likely to be of little value;
c) The method is only useful for rule-based, classification type problems;
d) The number of attributes must be fairly small;
e) The training set should not include cases that are exceptions to the underlying law. In law, this requirement may not be feasible;
f) The training set must be sufficiently large to allow the rule induction system to make valid inferences;

Although there are many rule induction algorithms, we now focus upon the ID3 algorithm [Quinlan 1986], which involves the use of information theory and has been extensively applied to many problems. This algorithm, together with an example, is described in the next section.

1. RULE INDUCTION WITH ID3

The ID3 algorithm extracts rules from a dataset by first constructing a decision tree from the dataset and then extracting rules from the tree. A decision tree is an explicit representation of all scenarios that can result from a given decision. The root of the tree represents the initial situation, whilst each path from the root corresponds to one possible scenario. A more formal definition is that a decision tree is a problem representation in which:
a) Each node is connected to a set of possible answers;
b) Each non-leaf node is connected to a test that splits its set of possible answers into subsets corresponding to different test results;
c) Each path carries a particular test result's subset to another node.

Figure 1 illustrates a decision tree that represents sample data in Table 1. This data relates to the property division of six fictitious and overly simple marital splits from [Zeleznikow and Hunter 1994]. The nodes in the decision tree of Figure 1 are variables in the data set. For example, the top most or root node represents the feature *wife_works*. The arcs from each node are possible values of the variable that the node represents. The leaves of the tree represent a distinct category or class of output variable to be classified, in this case *equal_split* and represents whether the split of property between husband and wife is equal. In marriage number 50, the wife works, the marriage is wealthy and there are dependent children. A judge has decided that the property be distributed equally bnetwee the husband and the wife. In a real life example, more than three attributes are relevant and the type of variable is unlikely to be Boolean.

Table 1. Sample data for property split in family law

Case	Asset rich	Children	Wife Working	50/50 split
C50	Yes	Yes	Yes	Yes
C51	No	Yes	No	No
C52	No	Yes	No	No
C53	Yes	No	Yes	Yes
C54	Yes	Yes	No	No
C55	No	No	Yes	Yes
C56	No	Yes	Yes	No

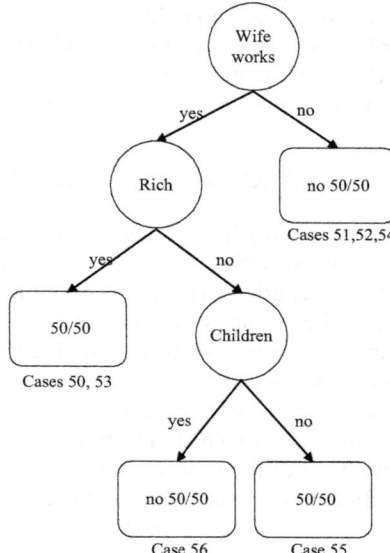

Figure 1. Decision tree with wife works as root

The extraction of rules from a decision tree is trivial once the tree is built as a rule is generated from every path through the tree. For example, the rules that emerge from each path through the decision tree in Figure 1 are:

1. IF wife_works = no THEN 50/50=yes
2. IF wife_works = yes and rich = yes THEN 50/50= yes
3. If wife_works = yes and rich = no and children= no THEN 50/50=yes
4. If wife_works = yes and rich = no and children= yes THEN 50/50=no

A number of different decision trees, and therefore, rules, can be derived from the same data set. Figure 2 illustrates a different decision tree from the same marital data in Table 1. This decision tree has children at the root of the tree.

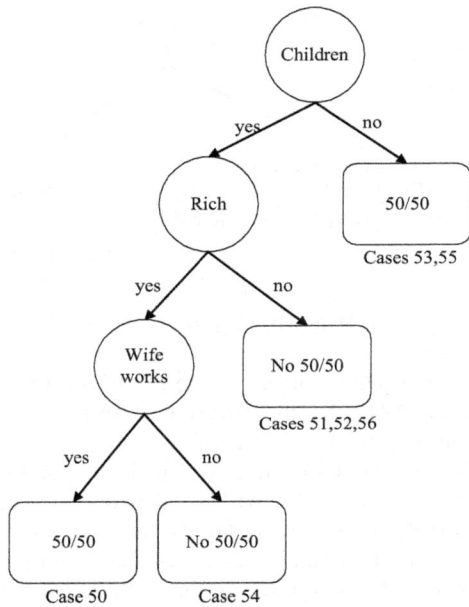

Figure 2. Decision tree from marital data with children as root

Rules derived are quite different from those in the decision tree of Figure 2.
1. IF children = no THEN 50/50=yes
2. IF children = yes and rich = no THEN 50/50=no
3. If children = yes and rich = yes and wife_works = no THEN 50/50=no
4. If children = yes and rich = yes and wife_works = yes THEN 50/50=yes

The ID3 algorithm applies information theory in order to develop a decision tree (from which we can derive rules) that is as simple as possible, so that all examples in the data set are classified by using a small number of short rules. The ID3 algorithm builds a decision tree by following the same three steps:
a) Select an attribute as a node in the tree (often called selecting a feature to split on);
b) Split cases on that attribute's values;
c) Repeat 1 and 2 until the leaves contain the same class.

Figure 3 illustrates the first stage of ID3 if the feature *wife_works* is selected as the root of the tree. The cases on the no arc are all of the same class so the

88

algorithm stops on that branch. The cases on the yes arc contain a mix of values for *equal_split* so the algorithm repeats using only those cases.

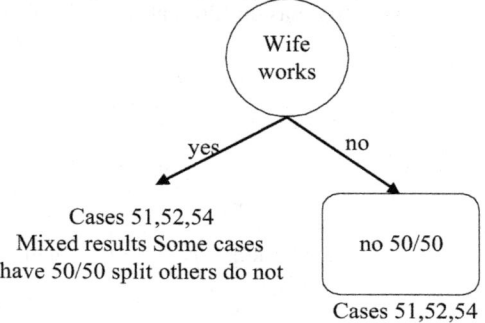

Figure 3. Wife working as root of the tree

The key element of the ID3 algorithm is the use of information theory advanced by [Shannon and Weaver 1949] for the selection of an attribute upon which to split the decision tree. In the next section we provide the intuition underpinning information theory. In his ID3 algorithm [Quinlan 1986] used information gain as a heuristic for selecting the attribute that will best separate the samples into individual classes. Such an information-theoretic approach minimises the expected number of tests needed to classify an object and guarantees that a simple (but not necessarily the simplest) tree is found. This follows the well know principle of Occam's Razor[40]: *prefer the simplest hypothesis that fits the data.*

1.1   Attribute selection using Information Theory

Information theory was developed in order to provide a way to measure information. The theory assumes that information originates at a source and is transmitted, as a message to a receiver. The amount of information in a message is related to how surprised the receiver is to get the message. A motorist would be very surprised to see that the topmost lamp in a traffic light set was blue. A motorist would typically express less surprise on seeing the topmost traffic light was red. The probability of seeing a blue light is in that context is very low.

The information content of a message is inversely related to the probability of receiving the message. The information content in the message 'the top most light is blue' is greater than that of the message 'the top most light is red' because the receiver is more surprised by the occurrence of the blue lamp. Figure 4 illustrates the proposition that the information content of a message is proportional to the probability of receiving the message. Information(M) is inversely proportional to - Probability(M).

---

[40]   Developed by William of Occam circa 1320

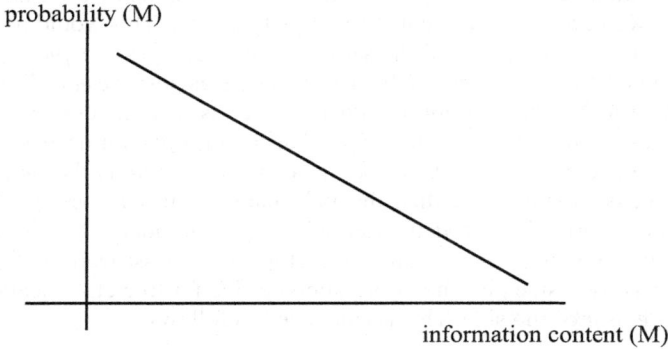

probability (M)

information content (M)

Figure 4. Probability of receiving a message V's. information content

For a number of mathematical reasons, [Shannon and Weaver 1949] believed that the relationship between the information content of a message and the probability of receiving it was not linear, but base 2 logarithmic and that the logarithm of the probability had to be multiplied by the probability itself. The resulting formula is known as the Shannon's entropy formula:

Equation 1

Information (M) = - probability (M) * (log$_2$ probability (M))

In developing the ID3 algorithm, [Quinlan 1986] applied the twin concepts of information needed and information gained to the construction of a decision tree. The true classification for a case is one where the outcome is correctly classified. The information needed for a true classification is taken to be the information content of the message that has the true classification. This can be calculated using Shannon's entropy formula as follows. We see from Table 1 that of the seven divorce cases, three result in a Equal property split and four do not. The probability that a family law case will result in an *equal_split* is 3/7 or 0.429 and the probability of a split other than Equal is 4/7 or 0.571. The information content for a true classification is the information for an *equal_split* outcome plus the information for a non *equal_split* outcome. Feeding these values into the Entropy formula we have:

Information content (i.e
information needed for a true   =   information needed for 50/50=yes
classification   (-0.429 * (log$_2$ 0.429))

                                          +
                                          information needed for 50/50=no
                                          (-0.571* (log$_2$ 0.571))

If the information needed for a true classification is zero, then we would have all the information we need in order to correctly classify a case. This would occur if all the examples in the marital data had the same outcome, say yes to *equal_split*. No information would be needed to correctly classify a case as positive *equal_split*.

The objective in building an optimal decision tree is to first select the optimal attribute to act as the root node of the tree so that the information needed will be a minimum. If, for example, the *wife_works* factor was selected as the first node to split on as depicted in Figure 3, then the information gain can be calculated by determining the information needed after adopting that node. The information needed is calculated as the information needed for a true classification of all cases on the *wife_works* =yes side plus the information needed for true classification of all cases on the *wife_works* =no side. This is calculated as follows:

Cases on the 'yes' arc of *wife_works* are mixed on outcome such that 3/4 (i.e probability 0.75) of the cases display a positive *equal_split* outcome and 1 does not (i.e probability 0.25). Information needed on the 'yes' arc is:

$$= (-0.75 * (\log_2 0.75)) + (- 0.25 * (\log_2 0.25))$$
$$= 0.13$$

The outcomes of the three cases on the 'no' are uniform. So the information needed for a true classification is:

$$= (- 1 * (\log_2 1)$$
$$= 0$$

Combining the information needed at the four 'yes' cases and the three 'no' cases, taking into account the proportion of 'yes' cases and the proportion of 'no'cases results in the following calculation for the information needed if *wife_works* is selected:
$$= (4 * 0.13) + (3 * 0)$$
$$= 0.52.$$

Recall that the information needed before selecting *wife_works* was 0.68 so the information gained by selecting *wife_works* is:

$$= 0.68 - 0.52$$
$$= 0.16.$$

The information gain is calculated for every other available factor and the factor that results in the highest information gain is selected as the root of the tree. Once this is done, the same approach is repeated for the children of the root until the decision tree is constructed.

ID3 also has an inductive bias favouring shorter decision trees

1.2   Decision Tree Pruning

As [Han and Kamber 2001] note, when a decision tree is built, many of the branches will reflect anomalies in the training data due, which are to noise or outliers. Tree pruning methods address this problem of overfitting the data. Overfitting occurs when the data-mining method performs very well with data it has been exposed to but performs poorly with other data. Overfitting is discussed at length in Chapter 9. Such methods typically use statistical measures to remove the least reliable branches, generally resulting in faster classification and an improvement in the ability of the tree to correctly classify independent test data.

There are two common approaches to tree pruning:

a) **Pre-pruning** – in this approach, a tree is pruned by halting its construction early (for example by deciding not to further split or partition the subset of training samples at a given node). Upon halting, the node becomes a leaf. The leaf may hold the most frequent class among the subset samples or the probability distribution of those samples. Measures such as statistical significance, information gain, χ^2 (chi-squared) test, etc. can be used to assess the goodness of a split.

b) **Postpruning** – in this approach, branches are 'removed' from a 'fully grown tree'. A tree node is pruned by removing its branches. The lowest unpruned node becomes a leaf and is labelled by the most frequent class among its former branches. For each non-leaf node in the tree, the algorithm calculates the expected error rate that would occur if the subtree at that node were pruned. Next, the expected error rate occurring if the node were not pruned is calculated using the error rates for each branch, combined by weighting according to the proportion of observations along each branch. If pruning the branch leads to a greater expected error rate, then the subtree is kept. Otherwise, it is pruned. After generating a set of progressively pruned trees, an independent test set is used to estimate the accuracy of each tree. The decision tree that minimises the expected error rate is preferred. Postprunning requires more computation than prepruning, yet generally leads to a more reliable tree.

Rather than pruning trees based on expected error rates, we can prune trees based on the number of bits required to encode them. The 'best pruned tree' is the one that minimises the number of encoding bits.

1.3   C4.5 and C5.0

The ID3 algorithm, [Quinlan 1986], is relatively simple and generates decision trees and rules from datasets in real time, without the use of enormous computing resources. The attribute chosen as the most useful for classifying examples is determined by measuring its information gain. ID3 chooses the first acceptable tree it encounters in its simple-to-complex hill-climbing search through the space of possible trees. The ID3 search strategy:

i) selects in favour of shorter trees over longer ones;

ii) selects trees that place the attributes with highest information gain closest to the root.

ID3's inductive bias is that shorter trees are preferred over longer trees. Trees that place high information gain attributes close to the root are preferred over those that do not.

However ID3 has many limitations including:
a) overfitting the training data – because the training examples are only a sample of all possible instances, it is possible to add branches to the tree that improve performance on the training examples while decreasing performance on other data outside this set;
b) the attributes cannot be continuous;
c) the algorithm is not particularly robust in the presence of noisy or contradictory data;
d) information gain cannot be calculated if values are missing.

C4.5 is an enhancement of ID3 [Quinlan 1993]. C4.5 includes tools:
a) **To deal with missing values on attributes and missing data**. In ID3, two or more identical attribute sets can give different results. C4.5 estimates the most likely value for the missing one by looking at similar records. Methods to deal with missing values as a pre-processing exercise were discussed in Chapter 2.
b) **For pruning decision trees**. C4.5 uses rule post-pruning which involves the following steps:
   – Infer the decision tree from the training set, growing the tree until the training data fits as well as possible and over-fitting is occurring;
   – Convert the learned tree into an equivalent set of rules by creating one rule for each path from the root node to a leaf node;
   – Prune (generalise) each rule by removing any preconditions that result in improving its estimated accuracy;
   – Sort the pruned rules by their estimated accuracy and consider them in this sequence when classifying subsequent instances.
c) **To deal with continuous variables**. Continuous variables have numeric values such as *1.0, 2.1,3.4* as opposed to categorical values such as yes, no or undecided. C4.5 deals with attributes with continuous ranges by examining the values for this attribute in the training set. Say they are, in increasing order, A_1, A_2, .., A_m. Then for each value A_j, j=1,2,... , m, the records are partitioned into those that have C_i values up to and including A_j, and those that have values greater than A_j. For each of these partitions the information gain is computed. and the partition that maximizes the gain is chosen. This is similar to binning, discussed in Chapter 3, although is performed during the data-mining phase.
d) **To deal with rule accuracy**. Perhaps the most common method for estimating rule accuracy is to use a test set that is disjoint from the training set. C4.5 evaluates performance based on the training set itself, using a pessimistic estimate to make up for the fact that the training data gives an estimate biased in

favour of the rules. It determines its pessimistic estimate by calculating the rule accuracy over the training examples to which it applies, then calculating the standard deviation in this estimated accuracy assuming a binomial distribution.

For a given confidence level, the lower-bound estimate is then taken as the measure of rule performance[41] The net effect is that for large data sets, the pessimistic set is very close to the observed accuracy.

C5.0 is a further enhancement of C4.5. The main extensions include the incorporation of boosting techniques, the introduction of more sophisticated ways to measure errors and methods to facilitate the scaling up the algorithm to perform on datasets with millions of records. Boosting, developed by [Freund and Schapire 1997], is a technique for generating and combining multiple classifiers to improve predictive accuracy. Boosting is discussed in Chapter 9. In ID3 and C4.5, an error is defined as a misclassification. However, given that some misclassifications are less desirable than others, C5.0 introduces a variable misclassification cost metric.

The ability for a data-mining algorithm to scale up to very large datasets is not a significant issue in legal databases because most data-sets are not large. However, typically, the performance of decision tree algorithms in databases with millions of records is restricted, because the entire data set needs to be accessed by the algorithm and thus must be kept in memory or swapped in and out of memory. The technique called winnowing, built into the C5.0 algorithm enables attributes that do not contribute substantially to the classification to be ignored.

1.4   CART

Among the earliest work on decision tree learning was Hunt's Concept Learning System (CLS) [Hunt *et al* 1966]. CLS created decision tables rather than decision trees.

Like ID3, CART (Classification and Regression Trees) constructs a classification or decision tree by repeatedly splitting the training set into subsets. CART is described in [Friedman 1977] and [Breiman *et al* 1984]. Its aim is to find a systematic way of predicting to which class a particular object belongs. A distinctive characteristic of the CART system is its pruning algorithm. The construction of the tree depends on:

   a) the selection of splits;
   b) the decision to continue splitting a node or not; and
   c) the assignment of a class to a non-split node (i.e. a non expanded node).

A split in CART partitions the data set into two subsets, similar to the tests ID3 uses for branching. However, CART only has binary splits. When selecting a split, the CART algorithm optimises the class of the resulting subsets. Thus, CART attempts to select a split so that the resulting subsets have examples of only one class.

---

[41] [Mitchell 1997] at page 71, notes that for a 95% confidence interval, rule accuracy is pessimistically estimated by the observed accuracy over the training set minus 1.96 x the estimated standard deviation.

The size of the final tree is a result of a relatively complicated pruning process. Too large a tree may result in over-fitting, whilst too small a tree may have insufficient predictive power for accurate classification.

1.5 AQ11 and the AQ family of algorithms

[Michalski and Larson 1978] developed an algorithm known as AQ11. A description of this algorithm is of historical interest because it is a rule induction algorithm that does not generate a decision tree. There are many situations when one starts with certain initial hypotheses about given data and then, in the process of experimenting with these hypotheses, has to modify them in order to maintain consistency with newly acquired facts. Such situations arise, when in the course of a system's performance, some rules are discovered to be incorrect or incomplete and have to be modified. A process of generating hypotheses or descriptions, in steps, where each step starts with certain working hypotheses, and a set of new data, and ends with appropriately modified hypotheses is called *an incremental generation of hypotheses*.

[Michalski and Larson 1978] used AQ11 on a soybean study to diagnose 15 soybean diseases. The events input to the program were derived from questionnaires completed by experts on plant pathology. One questionnaire was used for each of the fifteen diseases. A set of 630 events was partitioned into a training set and a testing set. The training set was used as data that was input into the AQ11 algorithm, whilst the testing set was used to evaluate the rules derived by AQ11 from the training set. AQ11 was also supplied with some general knowledge of the problem. A description of the algorithm can be found in [Jackson 1990][42].

Given the soybean data, AQ11 produced a set of fifteen decision rules. In parallel, a set of decisions was derived by more conventional knowledge elicitation methods from plant pathologists. The two rule sets differed somewhat in syntax, but the main difference between them was that the expert-derived rules contained weight selectors, while the weights of the selectors in the inductively defined rules was essentially 1. Thus, expects were able to indicate, by attaching weights to selectors, the relative importance of the various conditions of a rule.

The performance of these two rule-sets was systematically compared on a set of 340 test cases. The AQ11 rule set outperformed the rule set directly derived from the expert, with 100% correct diagnoses as opposed to 96% correct. The conclusion drawn was that induction techniques offer a viable alternative to other knowledge acquisition methods, if the domain is sufficiently simple and well defined.

Most programs that perform inductive learning from examples create descriptions that contain attributes that are selected from those present in the original examples. Some programs such as AQ11 and ID3 do not create new attributes or concepts whilst learning. In contrast to such selective induction programs, a constructive induction program is able to generate and use new concepts in the hypothesised description.

---

[42] At p444

AQ15 learns rules from examples represented as sequences of attribute value pairs. The teacher presents to the learner a set of examples of every concept or decision class under consideration. The program outputs a set of general decision rules for each class that cover all the examples of the class and none of the other classes. So the program outputs a complete and consistent description. The rules generated optimise a problem dependent criterion of preference.

AQ15 is based on the AQ algorithm, which recessively employs a star generation procedure. A *star* of an example is the set of all-alternative general rules that cover the example, but do not cover any negative examples. After a star is generated, the best rule in it, as defined by the preference criterion, is selected, and all examples covered by the rule are removed from further consideration. A new example, called the seed, is selected from the yet uncovered examples, and the process is repeated. The algorithm stops when all positive examples are covered. If all the examples of a given class can be covered by just one rule then the algorithm terminates after the first step. In AQ17, the algorithm is combined with a process of iteratively generating new attributes and using them in subsequent learning steps.

In AQ17, [Wnek and Michalski 1991] use the HCI (hypothesis driven constructive induction) method. HCI determines new problem-relevant attributes by analysing the currently held inductive hypothesis. Basic steps of the HCI method are:

a) Induce rules from a selected sample of a training set;
b) For each decision class, generate one candidate attribute that corresponds to a subset of the highest quality rules, and identify irrelevant attributes;
c) Modify the set of training examples by adding the values of the newly generated attributes and removing irrelevant ones;
d) Induce rules from the modified selected sample of the training set;
e) Evaluate the predictive performance of the rules on the remaining training examples. If the performance does not exceed a predefined threshold then go to step 1;
f) Induce rules from the complete training set.
   The AQ15 algorithm performs steps 1, 4 and 6.

The HCI method proved to be a very effective way to improve the performance accuracy of learned rules. Using HCI, the number of rules and the complexity of the rules (measured by the number of conditions) decreased. The algorithm detects irrelevant attributes among those used in a primary description of a problem as well as those introduced during attribute's generation process. Old and new attributes are examined according to classification abilities and new hypotheses are built based on the most relevant attributes.

2. USES OF RULE INDUCTION IN LAW

Three applications of rule induction in law are notable. [Wilkins and Pillaipakkamnatt 1997] demonstrate the potential for data rule induction using standard ID3 algorithms to contribute to predictions that can substantially enhance the efficiency of Courts. The embedding of a rule induction algorithm into a case based reasoning system in the IKBALSIII system [Zeleznikow *et al* 1994] is illustrative of an innovative application of rule induction and the use of decision tree induction using the ID3 algorithm by [Rissland and Freidman 1995] for predicting concept drift is innovative in its application and also in methods for comparing decision trees. Each of these are outlined below.

2.1   Predicting time to case disposition

[Wilkins and Pillaipakkamnatt 1997] illustrate that scheduling of participants to a trial including judges, witnesses, plaintiffs, defendants, interpreters and other staff is very difficult because the duration of a case cannot be easily predicted. This results in inefficient practices that are expensive and wasteful of resources. [Wilkins and Pillaipakkamnatt 1997] assembled a data-set that included 32 variables about the offender, the prosecutor, the court and how the case entered the legal system. Over 700,000 felony cases that reached final disposition in 1990 were included in the data-set.

Early investigation of the data-set revealed very large variations in time to disposition across counties and states so the problem was restructured during the transformation phase to effect a separate rule induction mining exercise for each county. Six counties were selected for the study, three from California and three from New York. The training sets and test sets were comprised of an average of 4500 cases.

Decision trees generated from the six data-sets had an average of 2100 nodes and accurately predicted the time to disposition in 53% of cases not in the training set. The authors suspected that a high proportion of missing values may have prevented a higher predictive accuracy. However, given the number of records, the number of features and the quality of the data the results obtained were quite good and provide hint of the potential that rule induction algorithms have in the legal domain.

2.2   IKBALSIII Reasoning with Credit Law

IKBALSIII described in [Vossos *et al* 1993] and [Zeleznikow *et al* 1994] is an integrated rule-based/case-based reasoner that operates in the domain of Victorian (Australia) Credit Law. Whilst the deductive reasoner covers the total domain of Credit law, the analogical component is confined to advising as to whether a transaction is for a valid business purpose.

Rule induction is used in IKBALS III to generate indices into past cases. Thus, the developer can specify a number of cases, including the relevant factors and the outcome, and the induction algorithm will generate the indices automatically. This is an advance over other systems that require the developer to pre-specify the indices manually.

IKBALSIII uses a rule induction algorithm that extends ID3 with a rule pruning algorithm that makes use of a hierarchy of concepts defined by experts. The approach is interesting because the rule induction is used to dynamically generate an index into cases. A user interacts with IKBALSIII by initially responding to a series of prompts that are driven by rules that are derived manually from statutes. Once an open textured predicate for which no statutory definitions existed, such as 'was the loan for a business purpose' was encountered, the rule induction algorithm builds a decision tree from cases relevant to business uses of credit. By so doing, rules that facilitate the interpretation of open textured terms are generated from the latest case base.

Rule induction was cleverly deployed in the IKBALSIII project to enhance the effectiveness of a knowledge-based system to support legal reasoning by facilitating the integration of reasoning inherent in the latest cases into a current case. An entirely different deployment of rule induction can be seen in the work of [Rissland and Friedman 1995].

2.3   *Detecting concept drift using decision tree induction*

Rule induction was used by [Rissland and Friedman 1995] to analyse a domain in order to detect a change in the way a legal concept is used by Courts. Whilst it is accepted that legal concepts change over time, developing computer techniques to detect such change is non-trivial.

Decision Trees that represented US bankruptcy law cases at various time intervals over a ten-year period were induced by [Rissland and Friedman 1995]. They developed a structural instability metric to compare decision trees. This allowed them to measure the change in the concept of 'good faith' in bankruptcy proceedings by plotting the change over time of Rissland and Friedman's structural instability index.

3. CHAPTER SUMMARY

We commenced this chapter by noting that the knowledge acquisition process could be greatly simplified if an expert system can learn decision rules directly from examples of decisions made by human experts, or from its own errors via feedback. Thus, we focused upon inductive learning the process of acquiring knowledge by drawing inductive inferences from teacher- or environment- provided facts.

The data-mining phase of a knowledge discovery from databases process involves finding patterns within a dataset. The form of the patterns varies with each data-mining algorithm. In this chapter we focus on an inductive types of data mining algorithms that discover patterns in the form of rules: namely rule induction. In chapter six we will discuss fuzzy rules and association rules.

Rule induction algorithms discover rules that are intended to be applicable as generalisations from sample data. Many rule induction algorithms use training sets to learn decision trees that are then converted into rules. [Quinlan 1993] used information theory to decide the root node of his decision tree.

Examples of rule induction systems investigated included CART, AQ11, ID3 and C4. [Zeleznikow *et al* 1994] in (IKBALIII) used rule induction to generate indices into cases. Rule induction was used by [Rissland and Friedman 1995] to analyse a domain in order to detect a change in the way a legal concept is used by Courts. Large numbers of cases were examined by [Wilkins and Pillaipakkamnatt 1997], who used the ID3 algorithm in order to estimate the number of days that are likely to elapse between the arrest of an offender and the final disposition of the case.

CHAPTER 6

UNCERTAIN AND STATISTICAL DATA MINING

In the previous chapter we investigated data-mining techniques that induce rules for use in prediction or classification. In this chapter we describe data-mining approaches that specifically model uncertainty. The four approaches we consider are quite different in their assumptions and implementation though they share superficial similarities.

a) **Association rules.** Association rules are not intended to be viewed as generalisations from data, but indicate that an association exists between features of the data.
b) **Fuzzy rules.** Fuzzy rules are based on fuzzy set theory and attempt to capture the degree of uncertainty inherent in a rule.
c) **Bayesian Classification.** Bayesian classification derives from probability theories used in inferential statistics.
d) **Evolutionary Computing.** Evolutionary computing use artificial intelligence search techniques.

1. DATA MINING USING ASSOCIATION RULES

As we have discussed before, law is open-textured and discretionary. It is rare for crisp rules of the form:

if \<condition(s)\> then \<consequent\>

to naturally exist, except possibly in legislation[43]. Thus algorithms that learn rules via rule induction (whether they be CLS, CART, AQ11, ID3 or C4.5) have their practical limitations.

However, law is full of (often unrealised) associations. Association analysis is the discovery of association rules, showing attribute-value conditions that frequently occur together in a given set of data. Association rules are of the form
A_1 & A_2 & .... & A_m $\rightarrow$ P_1 & P_2 & ... P_n

---

[43] The legislation that if you drink and drive you lose your licence can easily be written as rules, namely, drink(x) & drive(x) $\rightarrow$ licence_loss(x), blood_alcohol_level(x)>.05 $\rightarrow$ drink(x). See [Zeleznikow and Hunter 1994] chapter 6 for details.

Where each A_i and each P_k are attribute-value pairs. The association rule is denoted A ➔ P and is interpreted as 'database tuples that satisfy the conditions in A are also likely to satisfy the conditions in P'.

For example consider the association rule

KILLED=husband &
HISTORY_OF_ASSAULTS=husband &
SHOWS_REMORSE=yes   ➔ NOT_GUILTY=yes

This association rule states that if a wife kills her husband who had a history of assaulting her and she shows remorse, then she will probably be found not guilty of murder. Associated with this association rule, is a confidence factor, that indicates how likely is it, that given the killing of the husband by the wife and the husband's history of wife abuse, that the wife will be found not guilty of murdering her husband. Such a defence to the charge of murder has been called the 'battered wife syndrome.

A second issue is that of the support for the rule. In this case it means what percentage of all killings involve the 'battered wife syndrome'? Of course, if there were very few such occurrences, then no such defence to the killing would be available. Let us say the support for this rule is 1%. This means that 1% of killings involve a battered wife syndrome defence.

An association rule identifies a link between two or more attributes. The rule is drawn directly from the data. It is not a generalisation from the data, but identifies an association between attributes.

[Agrawal *et al* 1993] first described an algorithm for discovering association rules from databases. The difficulty in discovering association rules is not conceptual. In the battered wife syndrome example, we simply count the number of cases where the victim was a violent husband and the wife showed remorse and express the result as an association rule with a level of confidence.

The number of possible association rules is enormous, even in a small dataset, so calculating the confidence of each rule in real time becomes difficult. For example, if a database has only three features, *Sex* that takes values M or F, *Age* with values Elderly and Young and *Split,* with values *Even or Uneven* then there are over 30 association rules with a single feature as consequent. A sample is depicted in Table 1. The number of rules increases astronomically as the number of features and values rises.

Determining the confidence of each rule using a brute force approach of examining every possible association rule. is feasible only with small databases. [Agrawal *et al* 1993] developed the Apriori algorithm, for discovering association rules confidence levels. It is far more efficient than merely calculating each rule by counting all the combinations of features. A description of the algorithm is beyond the scope of this work. However an understanding of three concepts, confidence, support for an item-set and support for a rule is important for the appropriate application of association rules in KDD.

The confidence of a rule is calculated using Equation 6.1:

Equation 1: Confidence of an association rule
$$C_{if\ A\ then\ B} = Pr(A \cap B) / Pr(A)$$

The confidence of the rule *if A Then B* is equivalent to the conditional probability of B given A, $Pr(B \mid A)$. This is interpreted as: What is the probability of event B occurring given that event A has already occurred.

The *if* part and the *then* part of an association rule are sets of features and are called *itemsets*. For example, *(Sex=Male* and *Age=Young)* is an itemset that is involved in the *if* part of rule 27 in Table 1. The itemset *(Age=Elderly)* is the itemset in the *then* part. The frequency of an itemset represents the proportion of examples in the dataset that contain the itemset. This is called the *support* for an itemset and is calculated as depicted in Equation 2:

Equation 2: Support for an itemset
$$S_{\{A,B..\}} = \text{number of occurrences } (A,B,..) / n$$
$$= Pr(A \cap B) / n$$
Where:

$S_{\{A,B..\}}$ = the support for the itemset (A,B,..)
n = number of records in the dataset

The support for a rule is the support for the itemset that contains both the *if* part and the *then* part of the rule. So, the support for rule 27 in Table 1, **If** *(Sex=Male* and *Age=Young)* ***then*** *(Split= Uneven)* is:

number of examples *(Sex=Male* and *Age=Young and Split= Uneven)*
number of records in the dataset

The support for an association rule is the fraction of records covered by the set of features in the association rule. Consider a supermarket that sells nappies and beer amongst other items. If there were 1000 records in total and only 10 of them involved both beer and nappies then support for the association rule; *if nappies then beer* is 10/1000 or 1%. The confidence of the rule may be quite high because almost all customers that did buy nappies went on to buy beer though only 1% of customers bought both.

The Apriori algorithm uses two key devices:
- **The algorithm uses User specified thresholds**. Rather than calculating the confidence and support of every association rule, the Apriori algorithm requires that the user determines the minimum confidence and support thresholds.
- **The algorithm only calculates the confidence and support of rules that exceed the user specified threshold.** If the confidence of the rule *if nappies then beer* does not exceed the user specified threshold then the rule *if nappies and vegemite then beer* need not be calculated as it cannot exceed the threshold.

Table 1. Single consequent association rules with three features

#	IF	THEN
1	*Sex=M*	*Age=Elderly*
2	*Sex=M*	*Age=Young*
3	*Sex=F*	*Age=Elderly*
4	*Sex=F*	*Age=Young*
5	*Sex=M*	*Split=Even*
6	*Sex=M*	*Split=Uneven*
7	*Sex=F*	*Split=Even*
8	*Sex=F*	*Split=Uneven*
9	*Age=Elderly*	*Sex=M*
10	*Age=Elderly*	*Sex=F*
11	*Age=Elderly*	*Split=Even*
12	*Age=Elderly*	*Split=Uneven*
13	*Age=Young*	*Split=Even*
14	*Age=Young*	*Split=Uneven*
15	*Age=Young*	*Sex=M*
16	*Age=Young*	*Sex=F*
17	*Split=Even*	*Sex=M*
18	*Split=Even*	*Sex=F*
19	*Split=Even*	*Age=Elderly*
20	*Split=Even*	*Age=Young*
21	*Split=Even*	*Sex=M*
22	*Split=Even*	*Sex=F*
23	*Split=Even*	*Age=Elderly*
24	*Split=Even*	*Age=Young*
25	*Sex=Male* and *Age=Elderly*	*Split=Even*
26	*Sex=Female* and *Age=Elderly*	*Split=Even*
27	*Sex=Male* and *Age=Young*	*Split=Even*
28	*Sex=Female* and *Age=Young*	*Split=Even*
29	*Sex=Male* and *Age=Elderly*	*Split=Uneven*
30	*Sex=Female* and *Age=Elderly*	*Split= Uneven*
31	*Sex=Male* and *Age=Young*	*Split= Uneven*
32	*Sex=Female* and *Age=Young*	*Split= Uneven*
33	*Sex=Male* and *Split=Even*	*Age=Young*
34	*Sex=Female* and *Split=Even*	*Age=Young*
35	*Sex=Male* and *Split=Uneven*	*Age=Young*
36	*Sex=Female* and *Split=Uneven*	*Age=Young*
37	*Sex=Male* and *Split=Even*	*Age=Elderly*
38	*Sex=Female* and *Split=Even*	*Age= Elderly*
39	*Sex=Male* and *Split=Uneven*	*Age= Elderly*
40	*Sex=Female* and *Split=Uneven*	*Age= Elderly*

The support and confidence of a rule are used to measure the extent to which a rule is interesting. Not all rules are interesting. Rules with a confidence level that is very low are sometimes not very interesting because the association between features is low. However, not all association rules with a high confidence are interesting, because they do not occur often; that is their support is low. Other high confidence rules may be uninteresting because they are fully expected. For example, few data-miners would be surprised to see that the confidence of the association rule *if husband then male* is very high.

The Apriori algorithm has introduced a new data mining approach that has been used extensively in a variety of fields. However, even with a careful selection of confidence and support thresholds, the number of association rules generated is large. Many of the rules that meet the thresholds are not interesting. The extent to which a rule is interesting has become known, with some disregard for English grammar, as the rule's *interestingness*.

There are two types of measures of *interestingness*; objective measures and subjective measures. Objective measures are those that are specified in advance of the data-mining and do not directly use knowledge of the dataset. A decision to label as interesting those rules where the confidence is greater than 70% and the support is greater than 40%, uses an objective measure of interestingness. Other objective measures include various formulae for combining support and confidence such as: a rule is interesting if {(confidence + support) / 2} exceeds 45%.

Objective measures of interestingness are limited in that often knowledge about the dataset can inform the determination of interestingness. Subjective knowledge is brought to bear on the rule *if husband then male* to declare it uninteresting despite a very high confidence. [Ivkovic *et al* 2002] illustrate a subjective determination of interestingness by asking domain experts to estimate the degree of association between features, without seeing the rules. This approach is described in the next section in a discussion of the application of association rules to legal databases.

1.1 Association rules in law

Association rules have not often been applied in law. The studies by [Stranieri *et al* 2000] and illustrated the potential with the small, Split Up dataset drawn family law. [Bench-Capon *et al* 2000] explored their use with a hypothetical dataset representing social security cases. [Governatori and Stranieri 2001] explored the use of association rules to discover default rules for defeasible reasoning. [Ivkovic *et al* 2002], [Ivkovic *et al* 2003] and [Ivkovic 2004] explored the application of association rules in law extensively with large datasets. Those studies have advanced new techniques for grouping and visualising rules.

1.1.1 Mining Association Rules in Australian Family Law

[Stranieri *et al* 2000] illustrated the use of association rules in law. Their case study used the Split Up dataset concerning the distribution of marital property by the Family Court of Australia. This dataset only consisted of one hundred and three litigated cases, so is too small for purposes other to demonstrate the approach. Association rules are far more meaningful if generated from large datasets. However, as we shall discuss at some length in chapter nine, the collection of data that reflects the reasoning process used by legal decision makers is far from routine. Consequently, large legal datasets are rare.

Association rules generators are included within many data-mining program suites. One such example is Mine-set from *Silicon Graphics International*. The majority of these suites are very expensive. The association rules generator used for [Stranieri *et al* 2000]'s study, A-Miner, was developed in house.

Taken from [Stranieri *et al* 2000], Figure 1 illustrates the screen that displays all association rules that have a level of support greater than 0.4, and a level of confidence equal to or greater than 0.7. The analyst explores rules generated from various threshold values of confidence and support. In the sample illustrated in Figure 1, we have restricted rules to those that have the variable *needs_husband* as the antecedent. That variable represents the husband's need for resources in the future. In the Split Up dataset, this variable is an ordinal type that takes values very high, high, some, low and very low.

The first row in Figure 1 represents the rule that is read as:

In 60.9% of the cases where the husband's health is a minor temporary problem or is good then the husband's future needs are very few to few.

This rule meets the predetermined level of confidence and support thresholds and is therefore displayed as potentially interesting. This rule probably does not warrant the articulation of a hypothesis to posit an explanation, because it is, at least to the authors, quite plausible that there ought to be a relationship between good health and low future needs. However, in row 6 in Figure 6.1, a rule that reflects an association between the future needs of the wife and the future needs of the husband, is as follows:

In 73.4% of cases where the wife's needs are some to high then the husband's future needs are few to some.

This discovery of this rule prompts an analyst to pose a plausible hypothesis that if proven, would explain the association. For example, it may be the case that the rule reflects the fact that following divorce, far more women than men remain primary care providers for the children. The women that have *some to high* needs may do so because of their future obligations to children. The ex-husbands of these women would, in general, have fewer needs, because they do not have substantial contact with the children. Hypotheses that explore this issue can readily be advanced in a number of ways.

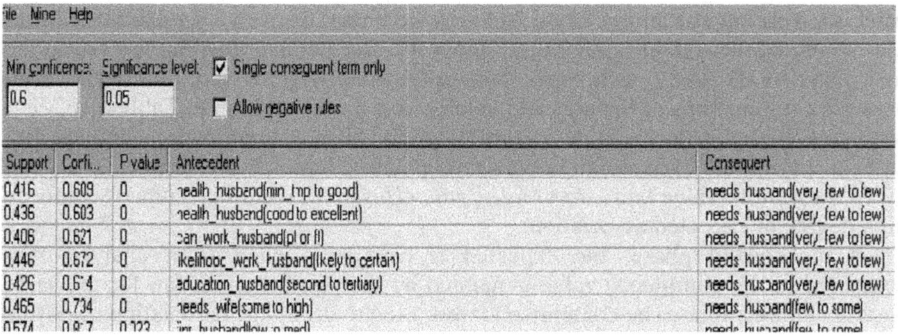

File	Mine	Help

Min confidence:	Significance level:	☑ Single consequent term only
0.6	0.05	☐ Allow negative rules

Support	Confi...	P value	Antecedent	Consequent
0.416	0.609	0	health_husband(min_imp to good)	needs_husband(very_few to few)
0.436	0.603	0	health_husband(good to excellent)	needs_husband(very_few to few)
0.406	0.621	0	can_work_husband(pt or ft)	needs_husband(very_few to few)
0.446	0.672	0	likelihood_work_husband(likely to certain)	needs_husband(very_few to few)
0.426	0.614	0	education_husband(second to tertiary)	needs_husband(very_few to few)
0.465	0.734	0	needs_wife(some to high)	needs_husband(few to some)
0.574	0.9.7	0.323	imp_husband(low to med)	needs_husband(few to some)

Figure 1. A-Miner Association Rule Generator Screen

Association rules do not represent a causal link between the values of variables. Association rules cannot be used in a predictive way to infer an outcome in a particular case. The rules are quite unlike rules discovered by a rule induction algorithm such as C5.0, which are generalisations from the existing data. Association rules generators count the number of records in a dataset that have antecedent X with consequent Y. The utility in generating association rules is not in their predictive power, but because the rules generated are able to draw the attention of a legal analyst to links that may not have been noticed otherwise. The association rules identified from the Split Up data set are of limited applicability, because the dataset is very small. As a consequence, rules discovered are unlikely to motivate the expenditure of resources for rigorous hypothesis testing. Studies described in the next section operate with a much large dataset.

1.1.2   Association rules from a legal aid database

[Ivkovic *et al* 2003] describe the use of association rules from a dataset of over 300,000 records. These records involve applications for government funded legal aid made to Victoria Legal Aid (VLA). In the State of Victoria, Australia, applicants for legal aid must not only pass an income and assets test but must also demonstrate that their case has sufficient merit to justify the expenditure of scant resources[44]. Consequently considerable data is recorded about the applicant and the case.

The objective of the [Ivkovic *et al* 2003] study was to derive a subjective measure of interestingness that overcomes several limitations of objective measures.

---

[44] For example, suppose a wife is found standing over her dead husband, holding a gun that caused the shooting death of the husband. The husband had been asleep when he died. VLA would be unlikely to support the wife to either argue that she did not shoot her husband, or that the killing occurred in self-defence. However, if the wife could convince VLA that the husband had a history of abusing his wife, VLA would support the wife to make an argument that she was not guilty of a charge of murder because she suffered from battered wife syndrome.

Analysts working at Victoria Legal Aid selected a total of twelve significant features used to model the task of modelling whether the case being argued has merit. In the first phase of the study, web pages were automatically generated, that depicted all possible combinations of features and values; in a similar fashion to Table 6.1. VLA analysts were asked to examine a segment of the feature combinations and suggest an expected degree of association between feature values. For example, an analyst given the feature value pair; *sex=Male* ; *role=Husband,* would presumably report a high degree of expected association.

In the second phase, the expected association elicited from analysts was compared to the confidence value generated by the Apriori algorithm for the same feature combination. The comparisons were used to group the association rules into one of three categories thus:

a) Positive level of surprise (PLS). These rules were ones that surprised the analysts because they had expected low associations yet the rules depicted high confidence values;

b) Negative level of surprise (NLS). These rules were ones that surprised the analysts because the expected high level of association was not reflected in a high confidence value;

c) No surprise. These rules had confidence values that were expected.

Figure 6.2 illustrates the depiction of the rules in a grid for all three occurrences: PLS, NLS and no surprise. The threshold boundaries that define the value *no surprise* was arbitrarily set by the analyst. They can be easily readjusted.

This study illustrates that association rules can be useful for analysts if rule confidences are automatically compared with existing knowledge to eliminate those rules that are not interesting from consideration, even if they have high confidence values.

A side effect of the [Ivkovic *et al* 2003] study was the observation that association rules drawn from a real world situation are often difficult to interpret. For example, the following rule is correctly interpreted as: "half of those applicants that are male and apply for criminal matter types are refused aid".

IF   Sex=Male   AND   Matter_type=Criminal   THEN Refused=Yes (50%)

The same association rule can erroneously be interpreted, as "half of those refused are males that apply for criminal matter types". The mis-interpretation arises because the rule is read in the wrong direction. Another type of mis-interpretation arises when more two or more rules are required to be interpreted together. For example, two rules need to be examined together to suggest

More people born in Italy were refused aid than those born in Australia:

if Country_of_birth=Italy THEN Refused=Yes (55%)

if Country_of_birth =Australia THEN Refused=Yes (25%)

The observation that association rules are difficult to interpret motivated the development of the *webAssociate* tool ([Ivkovic 2004] and [Ivkovic *et al* 2003]). This tool groups and presents association rule results in a way that facilitates an informative interpretation.   The objective was to determine whether users of webAssociate could analyse data in order to identify hypotheses that would not otherwise have been considered.   For example, as a result of this study, an association was discovered between the applicant's age and categories of legal aid requested. The association can be summarized as:

89% of applicants between 18 and 21 applied for legal aid for criminal offences, whereas 57% of applicants between 40 and 50 applied for aid for criminal offences.

This result surprised experts in the field who did not expect young applicants to be so highly represented in criminal law matters. This result was advanced to assist in the formulation of hypotheses to explain the associations observed.

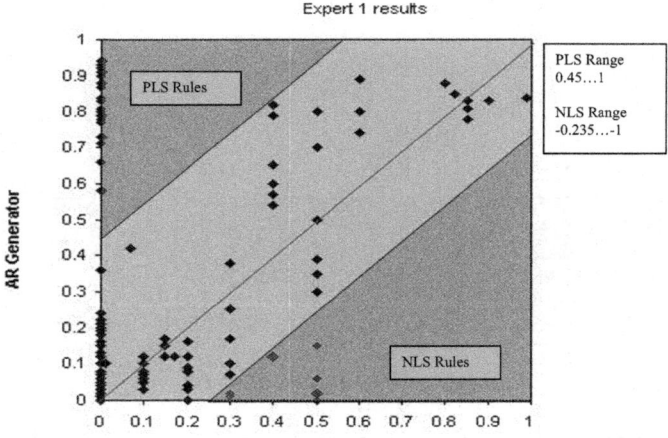

Figure 2. Visual representation of subjective interestingness

WebAssociate enables the expert to focus more directly on the hypothesis under investigation, than concentrating on the rules. The user should be a domain expert, but is not required to have a very extensive data-mining experience. In evaluation studies, domain experts from Victoria Legal Aid found the tool very useful for hypothesis discovery and testing. Figure 3 illustrates a graph from *webAssociate*.

108

The two triangular points at the extreme left of the figure represent the confidence in the two association rules:

if Country_of_birth =Australia THEN age=19-25 (confidence = 26%)
if Country_of_birth =Italy THEN age=19-25 (confidence = 3%)

By presenting the confidence of the two rules together, the user can readily see that a greater proportion of Australian born applicants for Legal Aid were in the 19-25 age group than was the case for those applicants born in Italy. The user may consider this interesting and elect to pursue additional analysis with webAssociate. One of the additional analyses is called *lift*.

Association rules that have an additional element in the IF part are sought that increase or *lift* the confidence of the rule. For example, the following association rule has a higher confidence than the first rule above:

If Country_of_birth =Australia AND matter_type=criminal
THEN age=19-25 (confidence = 33%).

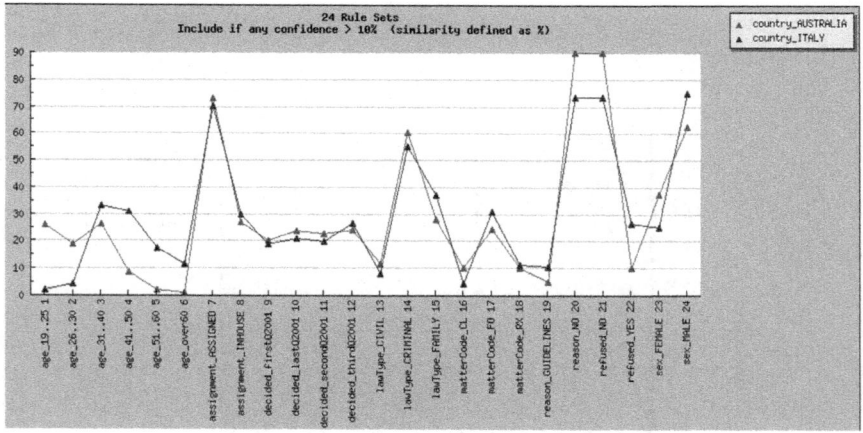

Figure 3. WebAssociate screen

This suggests that matter_type=criminal in some sense, *explains* the association between Australian born applicants and 19-25 year olds. Experienced legal aid analysts had felt that Australian-born applicants tended to be younger and apply for criminal law matters whereas, non Australian born applicants tended to be older and apply for other matters.

The user of association rules by [Ivkovic *et al* 2001], [Ivkovic *et al* 2003] and [Ivkovic 2004] represents a substantial illustration of the potential for association rules to contribute to knowledge discovery in law. [Bench-Capon *et al* 2000] explored the use of association rules in a data-set comprised of hypothetical data and conclude that this relatively new mining technique can make a valuable contribution to data mining in law. In the next section, we describe the use of association rules for the discovery of clauses for the non-monotonic logic default logic.

1.1.3   Using Association Rules for defeasible rule discovery

In the previous section association rules, were used to discover links between features in a data set that were previously unknown. [Governatori and Stranieri 2001] illustrate the use of association rules to discover defeasible rules. Defeasible Logic is a non-monotonic logic advanced by [Nute 1987] and [Nute 1994] which offers natural and intuitive formalisation of reasoning in several fields. The logic consists of *strict* rules that are rules that are always true, and *defeasible* rules that can be defeated by other rules.

In contrast to many other non-monotonic logics, defeasible reasoning is sufficiently simple, elegant and compact to enable real time implementations to be developed. [Maher 2001] has proven that the set of all consequences of a defeasible theory (i.e., a set of facts and a set of rules in Defeasible Logic) can be computed in linear time. [Antoniou *et al* 2000] demonstrated that the logic is flexible enough to deal with several intuitions of non-monotonic reasoning. Further, [Governatori *et al* 2000] illustrate the use of defeasible reasoning within a multi-agent system for automated negotiation. Practical applications of defeasible reasoning have been proposed for executable regulations [Antoniou *et al.* 1999], contracts [Reeves *et al.* 2000], business rules [Grosof *et al.* 1999] and e-commerce [Governatori *et al.* 2000].

Typically, defeasible rules for a real world application are sourced from expert heuristics, regulations, statutes and precedents. Despite the naturalness and intuitiveness of Defeasible logic representations, it is a manually intensive task that involves skilled knowledge engineers and experts. As a consequence, the knowledge acquisition phase is typically extensive and often prohibitively expensive.

The main drawback in the use of defeasible reasoning involves the cost of deriving rules. In most legal modelling, defeasible rules are sourced from regulations, statutes, precedents and expert heuristics. This is a manually intensive task that involves skilled knowledge engineers and domain experts. [Governatori and Stranieri 2001] applied association rules to automatically suggest plausible rules.

Defeasible logic is a sceptical formalism – it does not support contradictory conclusions. Instead, it seeks to resolve differences. In cases where there is support for concluding both p and ~p, the logic does not deduce either of them, hence the term sceptical. If the support for p has priority for support over ~p, then we can conclude p.

A knowledge base in defeasible logic consists of five different types of knowledge:
   a)   Facts,
   b)   Strict rules: of the form p_1 & p_2 ... & p_n $\rightarrow$ q,
   c)   Defeasible rules: are rules that can be defeated by contrary evidence,

d) Defeaters: a special kind of rule used to prevent conclusions rather than to support them,

e) A superiority relation defined over rules: it is used to define priorities among rules, that is, where one rule may override the conclusion of another rule.

An example of a defeasible rule is: *every person has the capacity to perform legal acts to the extent that the law does not provide otherwise.*

This can be written as: person(X) => haslegalcapacity(x)

We know that a person has legal capacity *unless* there is other evidence suggesting the person does not have legal capacity.

An example of a defeater is weakevidence $\rightarrow$ ~guilty. The rule says that if the evidence is weak, then we can prevent the derivation of a guilty verdict. We cannot, however, conclude that the accused is innocent.

Given the following defeasible rules:

α) person(X) => haslegalcapacity(x)

β) minor(X) => ~haslegalcapacity(x)

which contradict one another, no definite conclusion can be made as to whether a minor has legal capacity. If we introduce a superiority relation > with β > α, then we can conclude that a minor does not have legal capacity.

Often, in the knowledge acquisition phase, the emphasis is not on the discovery of rules. The principles are known, but we have to identify the most appropriate rules for the case at hand, especially when the rules are conflicting. In such cases it is important to establish a preference among available rules.

Strict rules can be discovered by a direct application of confidence metric generated by association rule generators. Defeasible rules can similarly be identified. Typically, too many plausible rules emerge. The number of candidate rules can be reduced by applying support, confidence and interest heuristics to the discovery of known types of Defeasible rule groupings.

[Governati and Stranieri 2001] illustrate these findings with a case study relating to the Australian Civil Aviation Regulations 1988 - *when two aircraft are on converging headings at approximately the same height. The aircraft that has the other on its right shall give way, except that (a) power-driven heavier-than-air aircraft shall give way to airships, gliders and balloons.*

As a result of working with sample data, they noted that the application of any KDD technique (including association rules) is limited by the coverage of the dataset. Currently, datasets that represent key attributes of the ratio decidendi do not regularly exist. However, as case management systems become prevalent in courts, it is expected that this situation will change.

[Johnston and Governatori 2003] pursued the automatic derivation of defeasible rules from data sets and reported a heuristic approach that derived rules from a dataset without the use of association rules.

By using a class of rules that is not rigid, the defeasible rules formalism directly represents uncertainty and indeterminacy in law. In the next section, fuzzy rules are described as an approach to capture vague, indeterminate or uncertain concepts. The way that data-mining concepts can be applied to augment fuzzy reasoning is illustrated.

2. FUZZY REASONING

Rule induction methods have been widely applied to analyse and discover general rules from sample data. The most prevalent algorithms utilise information theory to optimise the rules generated. Fuzzy rules are quite distinct from rules generated with rule induction algorithms. Fuzzy rules capture something of the uncertainty inherent in the way in which language is used to construct rules. Although few techniques exist that automatically extract fuzzy rules from data, fuzzy rules have been effectively applied to modelling legal reasoning. We thus introduce the concept of fuzzy rules.

Fuzzy logic and statistical techniques can be used to deal with uncertain reasoning. [Chen 2001] claims that uncertain reasoning focuses on the mechanisms or means used in deriving new knowledge when uncertainty is present, while data-mining emphasises application of results derived from data. Whilst probability theory aims to cope with randomness in reasoning, fuzzy logic deals with vagueness.

Natural language has many terms that are frequently used, but are not precisely defined. For example, the term 'young man' is not precisely defined, yet is useful in many contexts. Fuzzy logic models the way in which imprecise terms in rules can combine with other imprecise terms and imply conclusions which not precise.

To appreciate fuzzy logic and its potential application in law, we must first understand its precursor, fuzzy set theory. [Zadeh 1965] introduced the idea of a fuzzy set as a more general form of classical set theory. In classical set theory, an element either is, or is not, a member of a set. The boundary that demarcates the set from other sets is crisp.

In fuzzy set theory, an element belongs to a set with a degree of probability that ranges from 0, which is equivalent to it not being in the set, to 1, which means the element is in the set. Values between 0 and 1 indicate varying degrees of membership. Table 2 illustrates data that represents the age, in years, of men. Alongside each element is a rating for the degree of membership of each data item, to the set 'young man'.

A male who is 15 years old is clearly a member of the set young man, whereas the 25-year-old male is less clearly a member of the same set. Being 25 years old would be very young for a champion marathon runner, but quite old for a champion swim sprinter.

We are not implying that there is uncertainty regarding the man's age. We may be quite certain the male is 25, yet express the view that the man is not unequivocally young. Interpreting the degree of membership figure as an uncertainty about membership of the set is also misleading. We can be quite certain that that a man aged 25 belongs to the set with a degree that can be quantified as 0.7.

A function that maps the degree of membership for each value of a variable to its degree of membership of a fuzzy set is called a membership function and denoted

112

with the symbol, μ. The membership function for the 'young man' set is illustrated in Figure 4.

Table 2. Degree of membership of 'young man set'

Age in years	Degree of membership in 'young man' set
0	1
5	1
10	1
15	1
20	0.9
25	0.7
30	0.6
35	0.4
40	0.3
45	0.2
50	0
55	0
60	0

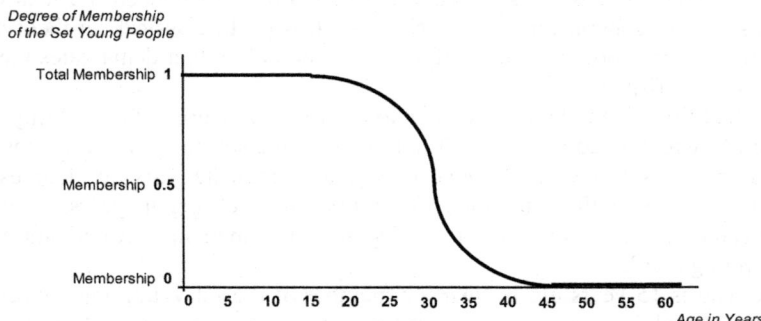

Figure 4. Membership function for the set of young men

A membership function for old and middle-aged men may be superimposed on the same axes as illustrated in Figure 5. We see from Figure 5 that each age has a degree of membership of the young and old sets. So, a person who is 35 years of age has a membership of the 'young' set of 0.2 and of the 'old' set of 0.8.

Fuzzy set theory uses the standard logical operators & (and), v (or), ~ (not). Thus given truth values (or membership values) μ (p) for p and μ (q) for q, we can develop truth values (or membership values) for p & q, p v q and ~p. These values are determined by the following formulas from fuzzy reasoning:

1. $\mu(\sim p) = 1 - \mu(p)$
2. $\mu(p \& q) = \min\{\mu(p), \mu(q)\}$
3. $\mu(p \vee q) = \max\{\mu(p), \mu(q)\}$

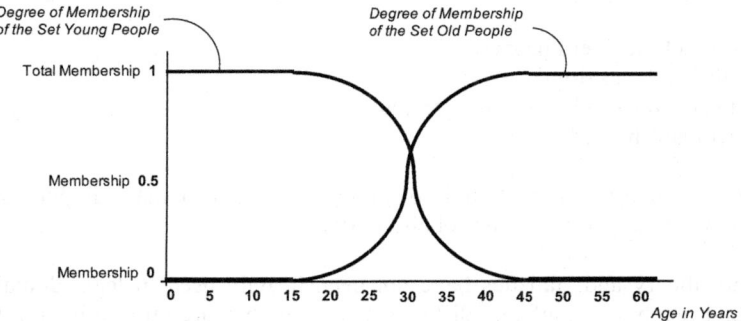

Figure 5. Membership functions for 'young', 'middle aged' and 'old'

[Chen 2001] states that there are at least five important explanations on the role of fuzzy logic in data-mining:

a) **Knowledge Granulation** – Fuzzy sets are conceptual extensions of set theory and are primarily geared towards various aspects of knowledge representation and predetermining most of the activities of data mining, especially knowledge granulation. Fuzzy sets are linguistic information granules capturing concepts with continuous boundaries. They are one of a number of contributing technologies towards data-mining.

b) **Better Tolerance** – Fuzzy sets exploit uncertainty in an attempt to make system complexity manageable. Fuzzy logic can deal with incomplete, noisy and imprecise data and is helpful in developing better uncertain models of the data than is possible with traditional methods. Since fuzzy systems can tolerate uncertainty and utilise language-like vagueness to smooth data, they may offer robust, noise-tolerant models or predictions in situations where precise data is unavailable or too expensive.

c) **Data Classification** – Fuzzy logic works at a high level of abstraction and is thus useful for data-mining systems performing classification [Han and Kamber 2001].

d) **'Indirect' Contribution to Data Mining through its relationship with Artificial Neural Networks** – Fuzzy set theory by itself is neither a machine learning nor a data-mining technique. However, fuzzy set theory does have a close relationship with the weights used in Artificial Neural Networks. As we shall see in chapter seven, Artificial Neural Networks are well known for their learning abilities.

e) **Increased chance of Knowledge Discovery Due to Vagueness** – Fuzzy set theory can be combined with other data-mining and uncertain reasoning approaches. By allowing vagueness, the chance of uncovering hidden knowledge is enhanced.

Fuzzy logic allows for intelligent systems to use probabilities in rules, as developed in the MYCIN system [Shortliffe 1976]. An example of a rule might be:

IF a woman killed her husband
ANDthe husband was drunk
ANDthe husband has a history of wife abuse
ANDthe woman showed remorse

THEN the woman might be found not guilty of murder or manslaughter on a plea of battered wife syndrome with probability 0.8

Probability theory and statistics have not been heavily used in legal domains. Probability and risk have significant differences in how they are utilised in civil law and criminal law. In civil law, the onus of proof is on the balance of probability. In criminal law, the onus of proof is beyond reasonable doubt. To quote [Black 1990], this means that the evidence must clearly, precisely and indubitably convict the accused.

In criminal law, statistics has been used to analyse evidence (see for example [Aitken 1995)] and [Schum 1994]). Areas investigated include DNA testing, fingerprints, footwear and ballistics. [Kadane and Schum 1996] used probability and Wigmore's diagrams of evidence to analyse the trial of the American anarchists Sacco and Vanzetti. [Wigmore 1913] argued that there is a science of reasoning underlying law. Expert evidence with regard to probabilistic reasoning has become common in United Kingdom courts. A British medical expert, Professor Roy Meadows has given evidence that the probability of three infants in one family dying from sudden infant death syndrome (SIDS) is over one in eighty million, and thus in the cases of Trudi Patel and Sally White[45] the infants must have been murdered beyond reasonable doubt. After spending some time in prison, both women were released by the Appeals Court, since it is now believed that there may be genetic reasons why infants die from SIDS. The House of Lords decided that the occurrence of three SIDS deaths in one family is not necessarily a sequence of independent events.

---

[45] Both women had three infants die in their care. Both claimed the cause of the death of all three children was due to illness.

2.1   *Fuzzy Logic in law*

[Philipps and Sartor 1999] argue that fuzzy logic is an ideal tool for modelling indeterminancy. But what is indeterminancy? Indeterminancy is not uncertainty. To quote the Roman maxim – *Mater semper certa est, pater semper incertus* – one can never be certain that a man was the real father of a child, even if he was the mother's husband. But the concept of a father is certainly determinate. [Legrand 1999] has developed guidelines for the use of fuzzy logic to model legal reasoning. [Philipps 1993] has used fuzzy reasoning in modelling traffic accident law. [Borgulya 1999] also uses fuzzy logic methods to model decisions made by judges regarding traffic accidents. He provides information for courts and lawyers about the seriousness of an actual case compared to previously tried cases.

[Xu *et al* 1999] constructed a case-based reasoner to provide advice about contracts under the United Nations Convention on Contracts for the International Sale of Goods (CISG). The cases are represented in the case base with a degree of membership as opposed to traditional case based reasoners where all cases have a degree of membership of 1. In their system, a precedent is described by case rules. The similarity between two cases is assessed by the similarity of judgements on the elements of the case rules. Since there is fuzziness in the judgement of a rule, the judgement can be described as a fuzzy set; then the similarity assessment of cases becomes the similarity assessment of fuzzy sets.

[Shapira 1999] investigates the attitude of Jewish law sources from the second to fifth centuries to the imprecision of measurement. He argues that the Talmudic sources were guided by primitive insights compatible with fuzzy logic presentation of the inevitable uncertainty involved in measurement.

In summary, while fuzzy set theory and fuzzy logic are not data-mining methods in their own right, their use relies on the existence of accurate membership functions. Membership functions can be discovered using data-mining methods if datasets are large enough. Future legal reasoning support systems that encode indeterminate reasoning as fuzzy logic following the examples set by the studies above can conceivably be self adjusting if data mining processes dynamically modify membership functions as cases are decided. In the next section, Bayesian classification is presented as an approach to representing uncertainty in quite a different way from fuzzy reasoning.

3. BAYESIAN CLASSIFICATION

Bayesian methods provide formalism for reasoning about partial beliefs under conditions of uncertainty. In this formalism, propositions are given numerical values, signifying the degree of belief accorded to them. Bayesian classifiers are statistical classifiers that can predict class membership probabilities – such as the probability that a given sample belongs to a particular class. [Han and Kamber 2001] claim that studies comparing classification algorithms have found that the **naïve Bayesian classifier** is comparable in performance with decision tree and neural network classifiers.

Naïve Bayesian classifiers assume the effect of an attribute value on a given class is independent of the other attributes. This assumption is made to simplify computations – hence the use of the word naïve. Bayesian belief networks are graphical models, which unlike naïve Bayesian classifiers allow the representation of dependencies among subsets of attributes. Bayesian belief networks can also be used for classification. They depend upon Bayes' Theorem, which we now discuss.

Suppose we are considering two events A and B. Bayes Theorem states that there is a relationship between the 'after the fact' or posterior probability of A occurring given that B has occurred, denoted as $Pr(A|B)$ and :
a)   the probability that B occurred and,
b)   the probability that A occurred, and
c)   the probability that B occurs given that A occurred:

Eq 1) Bayes thereom

$$Pr(A|B) = Pr(A \& B) / Pr(B)$$
$$= Pr(B|A) * Pr(A) / Pr(B)$$

where

$Pr(A \& B)$ is the probability that A and B occur simultaneously and
$Pr(B)$ is the probability that B occurred

An example outside law is illustrative. Suppose we have a hypothesis that asserts that copper will be discovered at a location:
H_1 We will find copper at location X
E   The rocks at location X are batholithic

The probability of finding copper given that the rocks are batholithic, denoted as $Pr(H_1|E)$ is difficult to estimate directly. However, using Bayes theorem the problem is transformed to one of finding batholithic rocks given there is copper $Pr(E|H_1)$ and the probability of finding batholithic rocks $Pr(E)$ and copper in isolation $P(H_1)$. These probabilities are typically easier to estimate in the real world. We need only to examine past sites where copper was discovered to estimate the probability of finding batholithic rocks given copper $Pr(E|H_1)$. The prevalence of copper and of batholithic rocks overall is also relatively easily estimated. The next example illustrates a Bayesian approach to law.

Let us take for example a hypothesis H, that a man killed his wife and the evidence (each piece of which is independent) consists of the following events:
E_1 – the man will receive $1,000,000 from his wife's insurance policy in the case of her death;
E_2 – the wife was killed by the same make of gun, as one owned by the husband
E_3 – the husband had the wife's blood on his clothes
E_4 – an eyewitness saw the husband leave the marital home, five minutes after he heard a shot fired
The total evidence is $E = E_1 \cup E_2 \cup E_3 \cup E_4$

Pr(H|E) = Pr(H&E) / Pr(E) = Pr(E|H)*Pr(H)/Pr(E)

Again, it is difficult to estimate the probability that the husband killed the wife given the direct evidence. So now, rather than working out the probability of the husband killing the wife given the evidence, we are focusing on the probability that the evidence is true given the husband killed the wife. We can achieve this by noting how many murders of a wife by her husband in the past involved the evidence in the current case.

There are two main problems associated with the use of Bayes theorem in practice:

a)   The probability of each element of evidence and the hypothesis must be known, or accurately estimated in advance. This is often difficult to quantify. For example, how would one estimate the probability that a husband has his wife's blood on his clothes?

b)   Bayes theorem assumes that A is defined to be independent of B if Pr(A&B) = Pr(A) * Pr(B). In this case Pr(A|B) = Pr(A), as would be expected. This is often too strong an assumption to make in practice.

Bayesian Belief Networks developed by [Pearl 1988] are graphs that, by making convenient assumptions about Bayes theorem enable inferences to be drawn in the presence of uncertainty. There are many excellent books on the use of probabilistic reasoning for the construction of intelligent systems. [Schum 1994] is one such text. Figure 6 illustrates a Bayesian Belief network example adapted from [Heckerman 1997] and is related to credit card fraud. The nodes in the network represent relevant factors.

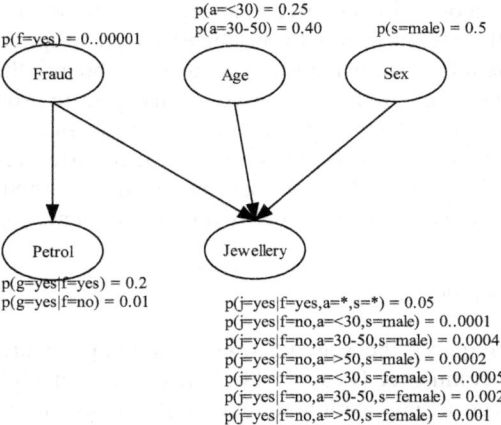

Figure 6. Bayesian belief network example

Building a network involves identifying relevant nodes, assigning a probability to the occurrence of each value on a node and establishing links between nodes that influence each other. The node *Fraud* in Figure 6 has a probability of occurrence of 0.00001 that represents the prevalence of fraud. The probability that jewellery is the object of a fraud is dependent upon the age and sex of the purchaser and the prevalence of fraud. Age and sex are not factors that influence the probability of petrol fraud.

Bayesian belief networks provide a graphical model of causal relationships on which learning can be performed. Bayesian belief networks are also known as belief networks, Bayesian networks and probabilistic networks.

A Bayesian belief network is defined by two components:

a)   A directed acyclic graph where each node represents a random variable and each arc represents a probabilistic dependence. Each variable is conditionally dependent of its non-descendents in the graph, given its parents. The variables may be discrete or continuous.

b)   A conditional probability table (CPT) for each variable, $Pr(X|parents(X))$

The network structure may be given in advance or inferred from the data. The network variables may be observable or hidden in all or some of the training samples. If the network structure is known and the variables are observable, then training the network consists of computing the CPT entries; similar to the case of computing the probabilities involved in naïve Bayesian classification.

When the network structure is given and some of the variables are hidden, then a method of gradient descent can be used to train the Bayesian belief network. The object is to learn the values for the CPT entries. See [Han and Kamber 2001] for details.

Dempster-Shafer theory [Shafer 1976] has been developed to handle partially specified domains. It distinguishes between uncertainty and ignorance by creating belief functions. Belief functions allow the user to bound the assignment of probabilities to certain events, rather than give events specific probabilities. Belief functions satisfy axioms that are weaker than those for probability theory. When the probabilistic values of the beliefs that a certain event occurred are exact, then the belief value is exactly the probability that the event occurred. In this case, Dempster-Shafer theory and probability theory provide the same conclusions.

3.1   Bayesian Approaches in law

Bayesian theory requires the specification of a complete probabilistic model before reasoning can commence [Pearl 1988]. This is not generally possible in the legal domain. However, as applications of Bayesian classification by [Pearl 1988] [Davis and Pei 2003] and [Haliwell *et al* 2003] illustrate, the probabilities required for a Bayesian Belief network can be derived from expert heuristics, physics models or innovative applications of fuzzy sets. As large datasets in law become prevalent, the probabilities required can conceivably be generated directly from real data.

Although the application of Bayesian approaches to modelling reasoning in the legal domain is relatively new, a number of innovative applications illustrate substantial potential. Two approaches will be reviewed here. [Davis and Pei 2003] applied a Bayesian model to reconstruct the most plausible account of a traffic accident and [Haliwell *et al* 2003] applied Bayesian classification in forensics.

3.1.1   Traffic accident reconstruction

The reconstruction of a traffic accident involves the combination of evidence from a number of sources including eye-witnesses, skid marks, speed estimates, and weather conditions. [Davis and Pei 2003] note that counterfactual statements are important for traffic accident reconstruction. These are statements of the form: 'If the vehicle had not been speeding the collision would not have occurred' and are contrasted with statements that assert a fact such as 'the vehicle was speeding'. They identify three steps that are typically deployed in an accident reconstruction a) the vehicle's initial speed is estimated, b) a counter factual value for the vehicle's initial speed is suggested and c) the initial speed estimate and the counterfactual estimate are used to infer the likelihood that the vehicle could have stopped to avoid the collision.

In the [Davis and Pei 2003] study, twin Bayesian Belief networks are built using forensic knowledge and models of mass and movement that derive from physics. The twin networks represent a possible world depicted by a counterfactual statement such as 'If the vehicle had not been speeding the collision would not have occurred'. By comparing the probabilities of key nodes in the belief network with those in the possible world network, an assessment of the plausibility of the alternate world can be made. The study was evaluated using four case studies. The evaluation results were promising.

3.1.2   Bayesian networks for forensic statistics

To attempt to avoid miscarriages of justice forensic statistics has emerged as an increasingly important discipline, by providing techniques, such as the likelihood ratio [Balding and Donelly 1995], to evaluate evidence in term of its relative support of claims made by the prosecution vs. claims made by the defence. [Haliwell *et al* 2003] claim that these methods provide a statistical characterisation of expert testimony. For example, that there is strong support for the defence or prosecution position. Due to the lack of experimental data, inferred probabilities often rely on subjective probabilities provided by experts. Because these are based on informed guesses, it is very difficult to express them accurately with precise numbers. Yet, conventional Bayesian Networks can only employ probabilities expressed as real numbers.

A central component of their work is the use of Bayesian Networks to compute the probability $Pr(E|C)$ of obtaining certain pieces of evidence E given a claim C.

An example of Pr(E|C) is the probability of finding a certain number of glass fragments in the clothes of a person assuming that that person has smashed a window. This is not a trivial task because many factors influence the production of evidence. In this example, the number of glass fragments retrieved in the laboratory from clothes worn by the suspect depends on the way the window was smashed, the movements of the perpetrator after the crime (which may cause some glass fragments to fall from the garment) and the laboratory techniques employed. Bayesian Networks provide an effective way of organising this knowledge. Additionally, they enable the use of efficient algorithms to compute the probability of interest.

A common criticism of the Bayesian approach is that it requires too much information in the form of prior and conditional probability tables, and that this information is often difficult or impossible to obtain. In principle, most values could be obtained through experimentation. Following the scenario above, for example, the probability of glass fragments being transferred to the suspect's garment, might be determined by smashing a representative population of glass panels of the same make as the shop window with a piece of fabric similar to that of the garment in question. But such experiments are obviously difficult to design and conduct correctly and are both time-consuming and expensive. In practice, therefore, it is often necessary to rely on subjective probability estimates provided by experts.

The difficulty of obtaining point estimates of (e.g. prior) probabilities in general has been widely reported. Moreover it has been reported [Zimmer 1986] that verbal expressions of probabilistic uncertainty were more accurate than numerical values in estimating the frequency of multiple attributes through experimental studies. In addition subjective probability assessments are not generally precise and it has been claimed that it is misleading to seek to represent them precisely.

Various studies (e.g. [Budescu and Wallsten 1985]), have concluded that point estimates of probability terms are highly variable between subjects and exhibit great overlap between terms. All this suggests that it would be useful to involve probabilistic terms directly in probabilistic models.

[Haliwell et al 2003] presents a novel approach to the representation of subjective probability assessments known as linguistic probabilities. Fuzzy sets have been widely used to represent the inherent vagueness in linguistic descriptions. Furthermore, a number of psychometric studies have evaluated the claim that fuzzy sets may be used to model qualitative probabilities with generally positive conclusions. So, for example, [Wallsten *et al* 1986] have considered various methodological issues in detail, and established that experimentally obtained fuzzy sets do indeed seem to provide a model for every day probabilistic assessments.

[Haliwell et al 2003]'s approach allows for the expression of subjective probabilities as fuzzy numbers, which more faithfully respect expert opinion. By means of a practical example, they show that the accurate representation of this lack of precision in reasoning with subjective probabilities has important implications for the overall result.

4. CERTAINTY FACTORS

[Shortliffe and Buchanan 1975] developed the use of certainty factors as part of the MYCIN expert system. They argued that a rigorous application of conditional probability and Bayes theorem is unwise. Instead, they used a belief measure that indicates an expert's confidence in her advice. Whilst [Grady and Patil 1987] illustrate an early use of certainty factors in the legal expert system in pension planning, certainty factor approaches to uncertainty are not prevalent. A brief overview of certainty factors is provided because data mining approaches can conceivably be applied to discover certainty factors if data-sets were sufficiently large. They introduced measures of belief, M_B and disbelief M_D for a hypothesis H given evidence E. A new piece of evidence E changes the measures of belief and disbelief thus:

$$M_B\,(H|E) = \begin{cases} 1 & \text{if } Pr(H) = 1 \\ \{\max[Pr(H|E),Pr(H)] - Pr(H)\}/(1\text{-}Pr(H)) & \text{otherwise} \end{cases}$$

$$M_D\,(H|E) = \begin{cases} 1 & \text{if } Pr(H) = 0 \\ \{Pr(H) - \min[Pr(H|E),Pr(H)]\}/(Pr(H)) & \text{otherwise} \end{cases}$$

The certainty factor CF(H|E) is defined by
$$CF(H|E) = M_B\,(H|E) - M_D\,(H|E)$$

The certainty factor varies from -1 to $+1$. A positive certainty factor indicates the new evidence supports the original hypothesis H, a negative certainty factor indicates it opposes the hypothesis.

Suppose we have an example where the original evidence E is that a wife killed her husband with a knife whilst he was asleep. She pleads not guilty by way of battered wife syndrome. New evidence becomes available suggesting that the husband had a history of beating his wife.

Suppose that in general, the wife's probability of being acquitted $Pr(H) = 0.3$. However her probability of being acquitted, given that her husband had a history of wife abuse is $Pr(H|E) = 0.8$.

Then $M_B\,(H|E) = \{\max[Pr(H|E),Pr(H)] - Pr(H)\}/(1\text{-}Pr(H))$
$$= \{\max(0.8,0.3) - 0.3\}/0.7$$
$$= 0.5/0.7$$
$$= 0.71$$
$M_D\,(H|E) = \{Pr(H) - \min[Pr(H|E),Pr(H)]\}/(Pr(H))$
$$= \{0.3 - \min[0.8,0.3]\}/0.3$$
$$= 0$$
Thus $CF(H|E) = 0.71$

Hence the new evidence that the husband had a history of abusing his wife increases our belief that the wife will be acquitted of murder.

There is no theoretical basis underlying certainty factors. Nor do the certainty factors associated with a MYCIN hypothesis correspond to the Bayesian probability model. However, certainty factors have proven to be effective in numerous fields outside law. Below, we discuss evolutionary computing in order to illustrate an innovative use of genetic algorithms in law by [Pannu 1995]. However, before doing this we briefly overview the k-nearest neighbour algorithm that is required for an understanding of the approach [Pannu 1995] uses and more recent data-mining approaches discussed later in this chapter.

5. NEAREST NEIGHBOUR APPROACHES

According to [Ripley 1996], the k-nearest neighbour (k-NN) algorithm is attributed to [Fix and Hodges 1951]. It is a relatively simple algorithm for classifying examples in a sample that uses two basic steps to classify each example:

1. Find the k nearest, most similar examples in the training set to the example to be classified
2. Assign the example the same classification as the majority of k nearest retrieved neighbours.

A trivial example involves classifying whether a young man is likely to be classified with an even split of marital property given the data in Table 3. Say the example to be classified is a young man represented as [1,0,1,0] and that k=3. Assuming each feature is equally important, the three most similar examples are examples 1, 2 and 3. The majority of the k neighbours, (i.e examples 1 and 2) are classified Even so the young man example will also be classified as receiving an even split.

Table 3. Sample data for k^{th} nearest neighbour example

Ex.	Age young	Age elderly	Sex male	Sex female	Split
1	1	0	1	0	Even
2	1	0	1	0	Even
3	0	1	1	0	Uneven
4	0	1	0	1	Uneven

Issues that need to be considered when using the k-NN algorithm include:
- **Choice of Similarity metric.** Typically a Euclidean distance metric is deployed such as $\Sigma(x_e-x_t)^2$ where x_e-x_t is the difference between the example value and the a training set value for each feature. This can be modified by weighting each feature differently $\Sigma w(x_e-x_t)^2$ This metric, which combines the difference between points linearly, is adopted.
- **Optimal choice of k.** The decision about the size of k must be made in advance. A large value of k introduces computational complexity, whereas a small value k is less accurate. Refinements of the algorithms involve dropping examples that are not needed to correctly classify the example.

[Michie *et al* 1994] illustrate that the k-NN compares favourably with respect to error rates in classification tasks against neural networks, Bayesian belief networks and linear or logistic regression. The k-nn approach is embedded in the genetic algorithm of [Pannu 1995] discussed in the next section

6. EVOLUTIONARY COMPUTING AND GENETIC ALGORITHMS

Evolutionary computing refers to the task of a collection of algorithms based on the evolution of a population toward a solution of a certain problem. These algorithms can be used in applications requiring the optimisation of a certain multidimensional function. The population of possible solutions evolves from one generation to the next, ultimately arriving at a satisfactory solution to the problem.

The various algorithms differ in the way in which a new population is generated from the present one, and in how the members are represented within the algorithm. The two most significant evolutionary computing techniques are:

a) Genetic Algorithms – Genetic algorithms are general-purpose search algorithms that use principles derived from genetics to solve problems. A population of evolving knowledge structures that evolve over time – through competition and controlled variation – is maintained. Each structure in the population represents a candidate solution to the concrete problem and has an associated fitness to determine which structures are used to form new ones in the competition. The new structures are created using genetic operators such as crossover and mutation.

b) Genetic algorithms are very useful in search and optimisation problems, because of their ability to exploit the information accumulated about an initially unknown search space in order to bias subsequent searches into useful subspaces, namely their robustness.

c) Evolutionary Algorithms – which can be divided into evolutionary strategies and evolutionary programming. Evolutionary algorithms are computer-based problem solving systems that use computational models of evolutionary processes as key elements in their design and implementation. Examples include evolutionary programming, evolution strategies, classifier systems and genetic programming. Evolutionary algorithms share a common conceptual base of simulating the individual structures via processes of selection, mutation and reproduction.

[Cios *et al* 1998] states that evolutionary computing is useful to data-mining because it can be used to solve optimisation problems. The optimisation processes are based on a population of potential solutions rather than relying on a single search point being moved according to some gradient based or probabilistic search rules.

[Pannu 1995] applied genetic algorithms to discover a prototype, 'perfect' exemplar for cases with a specified outcome. Good exemplars for cases are useful because future cases can be mapped to exemplars with different outcomes to predict likely outcomes and to identify weaknesses in a case. Two elements are required in order to generate a good exemplar; a distance metric to measure the degree of similarity between one case and another, and a search procedure that can explore an very large number of possible exemplars to find the best one.

The approach [Pannu 1995] used integrated k^{th} nearest neighbour distance metric with a genetic algorithm described by [Kelly and Davis 1991]. The distance metric computes a distance between two vectors. The distance algorithm was based on the kth nearest neighbour algorithm.

For [Pannu 1995], the vector elements were a 1 or a 0 and represented whether or not a factor was present in a case. A fitness function that sought to find a exemplar case did so by minimising the distance between itself and all other cases with the same outcome and by maximising the distance between itself and exemplars for cases that had different outcomes.

Evolutionary computing techniques have not been extensively applied in the legal domain though the work by [Pannu 1995] indicates some possibilities. Quite recent data mining techniques broadly categorised as kernel machines are described in the next section, though these algorithms have not yet been applied to law.

7. KERNEL MACHINES

[Muller *et al* 2001] claim that over the past few years, a number of powerful, kernel-based learning machines, such as Support Vector Machines, Kernel Fisher Discrimminant and Kernel Principle Component Analysis have been developed. These approaches have practical relevance not only for classification and regression problems, but also for unsupervised learning. Text categorisation has been a major domain for the successful application of kernel-based algorithms[46].

Whereas histograms are a very simple way for depicting data, they can be misleading because random fluctuations in the values or alternative choices for the ends of intervals, can give rise to very different diagrams. To overcome this problem, [Hand *et al* 2001] suggests the use of kernel estimates, which smooth out the contribution of each observed data point over a local neighbourhood of the point.

[Mitchell 1997] states that nearest neighbour and locally weighted regression are approaches for approximating target functions. Learning involves storing the presented training data and when a new query instance is encountered, a set of similar related instances is retrieved from memory and used to classify the new query instance. The kernel function is the function of distance that is used to determine the weight of each training example. So the kernel function is the function f such that $w_i = f(d(x_i,x_q))$ where d is the standard Euclidean distance function[47]. Kernel functions measure how far apart the estimated value of a data point $x^*(i)$ is from the actual value $x(i)$. The extent of this contribution is dependent upon the shape of the kernel function adopted and the width accorded to it.

---

[46] Other successful application domains include optical pattern and object recognition, time series prediction, gene expression profile analysis and DNA and protein analysis.

[47] Suppose an instance x is described by the feature vector $<a_1(x), a_2(x), \ldots a_n(x)>$ where $a_i(x)$ denotes the value of the ith attribute of instance x. Then the distance between two instances x_i and x_j is defined by $d(x_i,x_j) = sqrt\{ (\Sigma (a_r(x_i) - a_r(x_j))^2\}$ where the sum is from r=1 to r=n.

[Hand *et al* 2001] observes that kernel methods are closely related to nearest neighbour methods. Whereas kernel methods define the degree of smoothing in terms of a kernel function and bandwidth, nearest neighbour methods let the data determine the bandwidth by defining it in terms of the number of nearest neighbours. For example, the simplest nearest neighbour classifier assigns a new object to the same class as its most similar object in the data set, whilst the kth-nearest classifier assigns a new object to the most common class amongst the similar k objects in the data set. More sophisticated nearest neighbour methods weight the contribution according to the distance from the point to be classified, while more sophisticated kernel methods let the bandwidth depend on the data.

Kernel methods are non-parametric because kernel models are largely data-driven with no parameters except for the bandwidth. Data-driven smoothing techniques such as kernel models are useful for data interpretation.

8. SUPPORT VECTOR MACHINES

Support Vector Machines are learning machines that can perform binary classification (pattern recognition) and real valued function approximation (regression estimation) tasks. Support Vector Machines non-linearly map their n-dimensional input space into a high dimensional feature space. In this high dimensional feature space a linear classifier is constructed.

Support Vector Machines are based on the structural risk minimisation principle from computational learning theory [Vapnik 1995]. The idea of structural risk minimisation is to find a hypothesis **h** for which we can guarantee the lowest true error. The true error of **h** is the probability that **h** will make an error on an unseen and randomly selected test example. An upper bound can be used to connect the true error of a hypothesis **h** with the error of **h** on the training set and the complexity of **H**, the hypothesis space containing **h**.

Support Vector Machines are a method for creating functions from a set of labeled training data. The function can be a classification function if the output is binary or the function can be a general regression function.

For classification, Support Vector Machines operate by finding a hypersurface in the space of possible inputs. This hypersurface will attempt to split the positive examples from the negative examples. The split will be chosen to have the largest distance from the hypersurface to the nearest of the positive and negative examples. Intuitively, this makes the classification correct for testing data that is near, but not identical to the training data.

There are various ways to train Support Vector Machines. One particularly simple and fast method is Sequential Minimal Optimisation[48].

[Joachims 1998] states that support vector machines are based on the structural risk minimisation principle from computational learning theory [Vapnik 1995]. The

---

48 Sequential Minimal Optimisation is a fast method to train Support Vector Machines. Training a Support Vector Machine requires the solution of a very large quadratic programming optimisation problem. Sequential Minimal Optimisation breaks this large problem into a series of smallest possible problems. These small problems are solved analytically, which avoids using a time-consuming numerical optimisation

idea of structural risk minimisation is to find a hypothesis **h** for which we can guarantee the lowest true error. The true error of **h** is the probability that **h** will make an error on an unseen and randomly selected test example. An upper bound can be used to connect the true error of a hypothesis **h** with the error of **h** on the training set and the complexity of **H**, the hypothesis space containing **h**. Support Vector Machines find the hypothesis **h** that approximately minimises this bound on the true error. The ability of Support Vector Machines to learn can be independent of the dimensionality of the feature space. Support Vector Machines measure the complexity of hypotheses based on the margin with which they separate the data, not the number of features. Thus generalization can occur, in the presence of many features as long as the data is separable with a wide margin. We do this by using functions from the hypothesis space.

[Joachims 1998] claims Support Vector Machines are excellent for classifying text because of their ability to deal with:

a)   High dimensional input space – when learning text classifiers, we have to deal with a very large number of features. Since Support Vector Machines use overfitting[49], they have the potential to handle these large feature spaces;

b)   Few irrelevant features – one way to avoid high dimensional input spaces is to assume that most features are irrelevant. Feature selection tries to determine these irrelevant features. Text categorization generally involves very few irrelevant features. Through a detailed example, [Joachims 1998] shows that a classifier using only the worst features has a much better than random performance. Since it is unlikely that all the features are completely redundant, he conjectures that a good classifier should combine many features and that aggressive feature selection may result in a loss of information;

c)   Document vectors are sparse – for each document, the corresponding document vector contains only a few non-zero entries. Support Vector Machines are well suited for problems with dense concepts and sparse instances; and

d)   Most text categorisations are linearly separable and thus suitable for the use of Support Vector Machines[50].

[Gonçalves and Quaresma 2003] have developed a methodology for the automatic classification of documents and applied it to a set of documents written in the Portuguese language. Their methodology integrates support vector machines with natural language processing techniques, such as, lemmatization and part-of-speech tagging. They applied their research to a set of Portuguese juridical documents from the Attorney General's Office. This set is composed by 7089 documents and it is being manually classified by juridical experts into a set of concepts from a legal taxonomy.

---

[49] which does not necessarily depend on the number of features.

[50] The concept of linear separability is discussed in chapter seven.

Their current research has only used part-of-speech information to eliminate words from the bag-of-words, but they intend to use syntactical and semantical information and to propose and evaluate specific kernels. They compared their Support Vector Method classification results with other machine learning algorithms, such as C4.5 and Naive Bayes, and also information retrieval measures, namely precision, recall, and f-measure[51]. The obtained results showed to be, at least, equivalent with similar approaches and they proved to be adequate for the Portuguese language and for the legal domain.

9. CHAPTER SUMMARY

In chapter five we investigated data-mining techniques that induce rules for use in prediction or classification. In this chapter we describe data-mining approaches that specifically model uncertainty. The five approaches we considered: a) association rules, b) fuzzy rules, c) bayesian classification d) evolutionary computing and e) kernel methods are quite different in their assumptions and implementation though they share superficial similarities.

Law is open-textured and discretionary. It is rare for crisp rules to exist naturally. Thus algorithms that learn rules via rule induction have their practical limitations. However, law is full of (often unrealised) associations. Techniques for automatically discovering such associations might prove very useful.

An association rule identifies a link between two or more attributes. [Stranieri *et al* 2000] used association rules to discover associations between factors which judges of the Family Court of Australia use to distribute marital property following divorce. [Ivkovic et al 2003] developed WebAssociate to visualise association rules. They discovered useful knowledge about how Victoria Legal aid decides on which cases to fund.

[Governati and Stranieri 2001] showed how association rules can be used to develop defeasible rules. Defeasible logic does not support contradictory conclusions - instead, it seeks to resolve differences. Defeasible logic includes facts, rules, defeasible rules (rules that can be defeated by contrary evidence), defeaters - a special kind of rule used to prevent conclusions rather than to support them, and a superiority relation defined over rules which is used to define priorities among rules, that is, where one rule may override the conclusion of another rule.

In most legal modeling, defeasible rules are sourced from regulations, statutes, precedents and expert heuristics. This is a manually intensive task that involves skilled knowledge engineers and domain experts. [Governati and Stranieri 2001] applied KDD to automatically suggest plausible rules.

Fuzzy logic models the way in which imprecise terms in rules can combine with other imprecise terms and imply conclusions which are also often not precisely defined. [Philipps 1993] used fuzzy reasoning to model traffic accident law. [Borgulya 1999] also uses fuzzy logic methods to model decisions made by judges regarding traffic accidents.

---

[51] See chapter eight for details on information retrieval and text mining.

An overview of Bayes theorem was provided to illustrate another approach to modeling reasoning with uncertainty. Bayesian classifiers are statistical classifiers that can predict class membership probabilities – such as the probability that a given sample belongs to a particular class. Bayesian belief networks are graphical models, which allow the representation of dependencies among subsets of attributes. They can also be used for classification. Dempster-Shafer theory has been developed to handle partially specified domains. It distinguishes between uncertainty and ignorance by creating belief functions. [Davis and Pei 2003] and [Haliwell *et al* 2003] illustrate the potential for legal applications of Bayesian belief networks.

[Xu *et al* 1999] constructed a case-based reasoner to provide advice about contracts under the United Nations Convention on Contracts for the International Sale of Goods (CISG). The cases are represented in the case base as membership of fuzzy sets. Since there is fuzziness in the judgement of a rule, the judgement can be described as a fuzzy set; then the similarity assessment of cases becomes the similarity assessment of fuzzy sets. [Shapira 1999] investigated the attitude of Jewish law sources from the second to fifth centuries to the imprecision of measurement.

We concluded the chapter by considering the k-nearest neighbour algorithm, evolutionary computing and more recent data-mining methods such as kernel methods and support vector machines. Evolutionary algorithms are computer-based problem solving systems that use computational models of evolutionary processes as key elements in their design and implementation. Genetic algorithms are general-purpose search algorithms that use principles derived from genetics to solve problems. A population of evolving knowledge structures that evolve over time – through competition and controlled variation – is maintained. Each structure in the population represents a candidate solution to the concrete problem and has an associated fitness to determine which structures are used to form new ones in the competition. The new structures are created using genetic operators such as crossover and mutation.

In the next chapter, we introduce the data mining technique called neural networks. Like association rules, fuzzy logic and Bayesian classifiers, neural networks are also used to model uncertainty albeit in a quite different way as a result of their origin from machine learning research.

CHAPTER 7

DATA MINING USING NEURAL NETWORKS

The enormous capacity for humans to learn and adapt to new situations led a number of researchers to postulate that a machine, structured in a similar way to the brain, may also learn. [McCulloch and Pitts 1949] explored these ideas by devising a cell that performed the function of a logical AND, and another that performed the function of logical OR. They suggested that higher level reasoning and learning could occur by the combined effect of numerous specialist AND or OR cells.

[Rosenblatt 1958] generalised the McCulloch and Pitts neural network. He developed a neural network called a *perceptron* that could learn a variety of functions including AND and OR. He did so by suggesting dynamic modification of the weights that represent the strength of interconnections amongst neurons.

1. FEED FORWARD NETWORKS

As [Zahedi 1993] notes, neurons are grouped into layers or slabs. An input layer consists of neurons that receive input from the external environment whilst the output layer consists of neurons that communicate the output of the system to the user or the external environment.

Designing the interactions among neurons is equivalent to programming a system to produce an input and produce the desired output. Designing a neural network consists of:

a) Arranging neurons in various layers;
b) Deciding the type of connections among neurons of different layers, as well as among the neurons within a layer;
c) Deciding the way a neuron receives input and produces output;
d) Determining the strength of connections within the network by allowing the network to learn the appropriate values of connection weights by using a training data set.

The neurons of one layer are always connected to the neurons of at least another layer. There are different types of layer-to-layer or inter-layer connections:

i)   **Fully connected** – each neuron on the first layer is connected to every neuron on the second layer;
ii) **Partially connected** – a neuron on the first layer is connected to one or more neurons on the second layer;

129

130

iii)   **Feed forward** – the neurons on the first layer send their output to the neurons of the second layer, but they do not receive any input back from the neurons on the second layer;

iv)   **Bi-directional** – in addition to a set of connections going from neurons of the first layer to those on the second layer, there is another set of connections carrying the outputs of the neurons of the second layer into the neurons of the first layer;

v)   **Hierarchical** – the neurons of the lower layer communicate only with the neurons on the next level;

vi)   **Resonance** – in the resonance type of inter-layer connection, the two layers have bi-directional connection, with the added complexity that they continue sending messages across the connections a number of times until a certain condition is achieved.

Nodes in feed forward networks are organised in layers as depicted in Figure 1

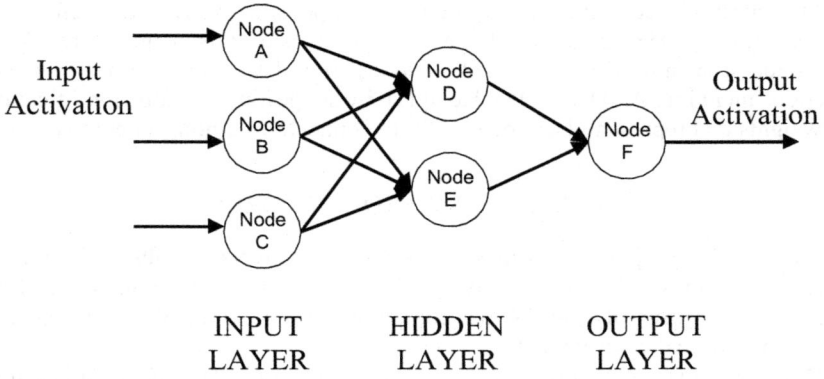

INPUT   HIDDEN   OUTPUT
LAYER   LAYER   LAYER

Figure 1. Feed forward neural network architecture with four layers

The first layer of nodes receives activation input into the network and is called the INPUT LAYER. The input nodes of feed forward networks become activated and forward their activation forwar to nodes in the next layer. Neurons in each layer feed activation forward to subsequent layers. In contrast, recurrent networks, to be discussed in the next section, pass their activation back to input and other nodes to form an internal feedback loop. Of the more than 200 different kinds of neural networks, the feed forward networks are the most commonly used networks. The simplest feed forward network is called the *perceptron*.

Figure 2 illustrates a simple perceptron with three neurons. A perceptron has only two layers, an INPUT and an OUTPUT layer though any number of neurons may be defined in each of those two layers. When the two neurons on the left, A and B are activated, they pass their activation on to neuron C. The link between A and C and B and C is marked with a weight that acts to inhibit (or exalt) the signal. The activation coming into C is calculated by summing the inputs multiplied by the weight. For example, if we set the activation of nodes A and B to 1.0 then the activation reaching C (1 * 0.8) + (1 * 0.8) = 1.6 units, where 0.8 is the weight between A and C and also between B and C. The activation leaving a node is not simply the activation entering the node. Rather, the raw input activation is passed through a function known as the activation function to determine the output. [Rosenblatt 1958], advanced the following activation function:

Equation 7.1
**if input is greater than a threshold then the activation output is 1
else the activation output is 0.**

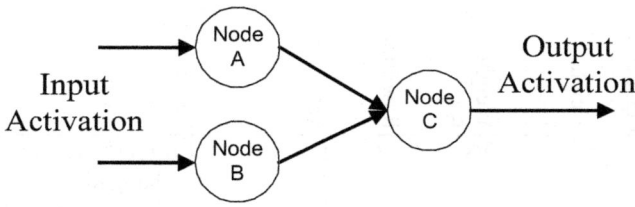

Figure 2. Perceptron

Learning commences in a *perceptron* by setting weights to any random starting point. One by one, examples are presented to the network and a learning rule determines whether the initial weights will produce the output required. If not, the learning rule modifies the weights. Training stops when a set of weights is found that produce the correct output for all inputs.

The *perceptron* learning rule is simple:
a) If the output is correct then do not change any weight
b) If the output is too small then increase the active weight by a constant,
c) If the output is too large then decrease the active weight by a constant,
    [Rosenblatt 1958] demonstrated that starting with any set of initial weights, the *perceptron* learning rule will incrementally modify weights until a set of weights that leads to the desired output is found. The constant, d is called the learning rate and is generally set between 0 and 1. A large learning rate will modify weights each time by a large amount and lead to faster training. However, as we discuss below, this can also lead to sub-optimal training.

Figure 3 illustrates the training of the *perceptron* initialised with weights as depicted in Figure 2. The *perceptron* is required to learn from the data in Table 1.

Table 1. Training data for perceptron example

Example	A	B	C
1	1	1	1
2	1	0	0
3	0	1	0
4	0	0	0

Table 2. Perceptron training

Example	Input at A	Input at B	Weight A/C	Weight B/C	Raw Input at C	Activation at C	Expect Activation	Learning rule outcome
1	1	1	0.8	0.8	1.6	1	1	Correct. Leave weights unchanged
2	1	0	0.8	0.8	0.8	1	0	Output is too large so decrease the active weight
3	0	1	0.5	0.8	0.8	1	0	Output is too large so decrease the active weight
4	0	0	0.5	0.5	0.0	0	0	Correct output so leave weights unchanged
1	1	1	0.5	0.5	1.0	1	1	Correct output so leave weights unchanged
2	1	0	0.5	0.5	0.5	0	0	Correct output so leave weights unchanged
3	0	1	0.5	0.5	0.5	0	0	Correct output so leave weights unchanged
4	0	0	0.5	0.5	0.5	0	0	Correct output so leave weights unchanged

The *perceptron* can be configured with any number of input and output nodes and the learning rule will still find a set of weights, if one exists, that maps the input into the outputs. A great deal of excitement surrounded the introduction of [Rosenblatt 1958]'s *perceptron* as a result of the breadth of applications imaginable. However, the excitement waned when [Minsky and Papert 1969] illustrated how the *perceptron* fails to find a set of weights if the examples are non-linearly separable. This limits the application of *perceptrons* to little more than trivial problems.

Data is linearly separable if a straight line or plane can be drawn to separate examples into different types of outputs. Figure 3 illustrates the plot of points that represent X or Y. The shaded points represent the value 1 on (X OR Y). We see clearly that a straight line can be drawn that separates those X and Y data points that have a value 1 on (X OR Y) from those that have a value 0.

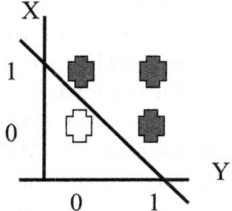

Figure 3. Linear separability of X or Y

In contrast, in Figure 4 we see that a similar straight line cannot be drawn. The exclusive-Or function is said to be non-linearly separable. [Minsky and Papert 1969] demonstrated that the Perceptron cannot learn patterns that are non-linearly separable such as the exclusive-Or function.

[Rumelhart *et al* 1986] and [Werbos 1974] demonstrated that non-linearly separable problems can be learnt by a neural network provided that there were at least three layers of neurons as depicted in Figure 1.

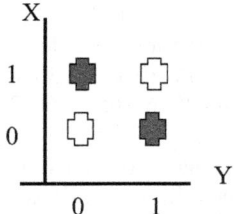

Figure 4. Linear non-separability of X Exclusive-Or Y

A network that has a hidden layer cannot be trained with the *perceptron* learning rule. This is because the error of the nodes in the hidden (middle) layer cannot be known. The error on the output layer is known because the output desired is available in the data set and the network's output is known. However, the desired output on a hidden layer is unknown. Without knowing the error on hidden layers, the weights between input and hidden nodes cannot be adjusted.

[Rumelhart *et al* 1986] developed a new learning rule called the *Generalised Delta Learning Rule* or *Back propagation of errors*. In this learning rule, the error on the hidden nodes, though not known, is estimated from the error at the output layer. The hidden layer error is estimated as the derivative of the output layer error. Using the derivative of the output layer to estimate the hidden layer error turns out to work quite well.

The approach does however assume that the derivative can be calculated on all output values. In order to ensure this, [Rumelhart *et al* 1986] applied an activation function that generated a continuous output. The most commonly used activation function is the sigmoidal or S-curve function.

Since its introduction, the multi-layer feedforward neural network trained with back propagation of errors has been applied in thousands of applications. Many neural network packages are available commercially and others are available as open source programs. The Usenet news group comp.ai.neural-nets maintains a monthly posting of a Frequently Asked Question (FAQ) that lists packages available. Regardless of the package used, the use of a neural network involves two main steps; defining the network and training it with data. These steps are discussed in the next two sections.

1.1   Setting up a neural network

Setting up a neural network involves determining a topology. A network topology is a specification of the number of neurons in the input layer, the output layer and in each of the hidden layers. Decisions regarding the number of nodes in the input and in the output layers depend on the way data is to be encoded for the network.

Data encoding refers to the format of data to be input to the neural network. For example, the percentage split argument in the Split Up exercise encodes:

- A percentage split outcome awarded to the husband, measured with 14 categories; [0-10%, 11-20%, 21-30%, 31-35%, 36-40%, 41-45%, 46-50%, 51-55%, 56-60%, 61-65%, 66-70%, 71-80%, 81-90%, 91-100%] as output.
- An input variable that represents the contributions the husband has made relative to the wife with values on a five point scale: [much more, more, same, less, much less].
- An input variable that represents the level of wealth of the marriage. This is also a five point scale: [very high, high, average, low, very little].
- An input variable that represents the future needs the husband has relative to the wife with values on a five point scale: [much more, more, same, less, much less].

Figure 5 illustrates the topology with fifteen input nodes, five hidden nodes and fourteen output nodes that implements the percentage split network in the Split Up study. Five of the input nodes encode values for the contribution variable. The next five encode the "needs" variable and the remaining five encode the "wealth" variable. A marriage where the judge considers the husband has contributed *much less* than the wife, has future needs *much more* than the wife and is of *average wealth* is encoded as [0,0,0,0,1,1,0,0,0,0,0,0,0,1,0]. This is quite a sparse encoding as the same values could be encoded in a far more compact way. For example, an encoding scheme illustrated in Table 3 could be used to encode the same case using only three input nodes as [-1,1,-0.5].

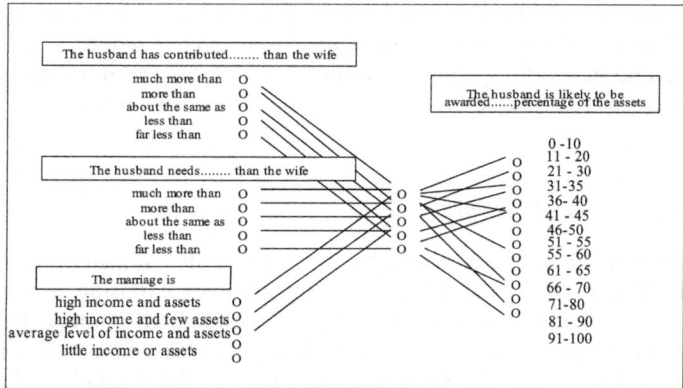

Figure 5. Topology of Percentage Split Network

More compact encoding schemes enable for the development of neural networks with fewer input nodes and connections to be designed. However, the compactness makes training more difficult.

Table 3. Sample encoding

Data value	Encoding
Much less	-1
Less	-0.5
Same	0
More	0.5
Much more	1
Very high income and assets	1
High income and assets	0.5
Average income and assets	0
Low income and assets	-0.5
Little income or assets	-1

Once the input and output encoding is determined, the next decision involves selecting the number of hidden layers and the number of nodes at each layer. [Cybenko 1989] demonstrated that a single hidden layer is sufficient to approximate any (linear or non linear) continuous function. This means that any function between inputs and outputs can be approximated with a neural network that has only one hidden layer. This is not to say that the optimal number of hidden layers is one.

[Haykin 1994] reviews a body of research that has been devoted to the discernment of optimal network architectures. All of the approaches surveyed recognise a relationship between training set size and network size. However, a procedure that can be applied to determine the best topology for any data set has not been found. [Lengers 1995] demonstrates a method based on trying many hundreds of different topologies using artificial intelligence search techniques.

Once a neural network topology is defined, training may commence. In the next section, processes are discussed to ensure training occurs effectively.

1.2   Training a neural network

Multi layer feed forward networks are commonly trained with the back-propagation of errors learning rule. Training involves exposing a network to a training set that is comprised of data examples, with known outputs. The learning rule adjusts the internal weights of a network in a direction that will minimise the errors made by the network on subsequent exposure to the examples. An *epoch* is completed when all training set examples are presented to the network. Typically, a network with many nodes and examples requires many hundreds, thousands or tens of thousands of epochs before the learning rule discovers a set of weights that will minimise the error made on classifying examples.

Training a neural network is as much art as science and requires the adjustment of many parameters during the training. A plot of the errors at each epoch is useful. This is depicted in Figure 6. The error is often measured as the proportion of the training set examples that are incorrectly predicted by the network. For example, an error rate of 0.75 indicates that for 75% of examples in the training set, the output calculated by the neural network did not match the output that was observed in the training set. We see in Figure 6 that the error rate remained quite high for the first 600 or so epochs. By epoch 1000 the rate was quite low. Furthermore, it did not alter terribly much between epoch 1300 and epoch 1700.

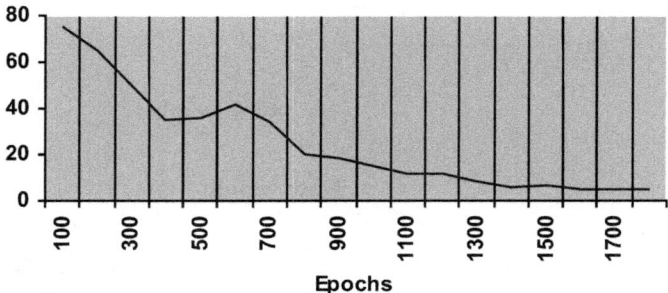

Figure 6. Plot of Error rate vs. epochs

Training a neural network involves making decisions regarding the following parameters:
- Learning rate
- Momentum
- Bias term
- Stopping criteria

1.2.1 Learning rate

The learning rate specifies the speed with which learning occurs. If this is too high, the weight matrix may be caught in a local minima and never find the set of weights that corresponds to an optimal solution. Figure 7 depicts learning as the search for the set of weights that will realise the smallest error. The initial weights, typically selected at random, lead to large errors. As the learning rule adjusts the weights, the error of the network reduces, until no further reduction seems to occur during epoch after epoch. The weights at this point may be the best set that will be discovered; i.e. they represent global minima. However, this cannot be known with certainty because the weights may represent local minima. They do not change from epoch to epoch because any change leads to an error that is worse, so the learning rule re-adjusts the weights back to the local minima.

Many variants introduce additional parameters to tune. Others, such as quickProp [Fahlman 1989] dynamically modify many of the parameters, including the learning rate.

138

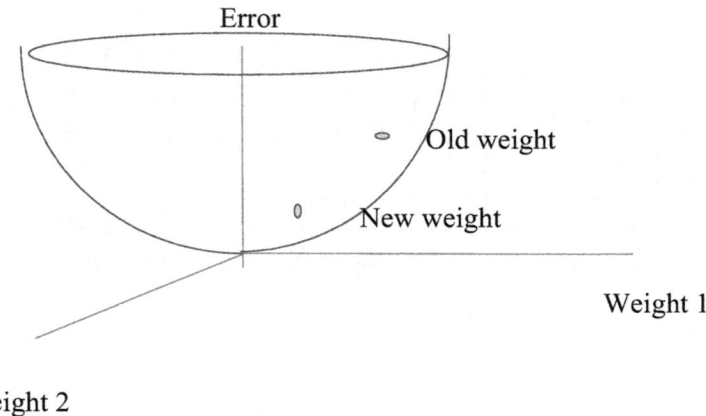

Figure 7. Weight space for error reduction

1.2.2 Momentum and bias.

There is no theoretical way of knowing whether the weights obtained are the best set possible or are an instance of weights stuck in local minima. The generalised delta rule includes a term known as the momentum, to add stability to a network and to guard against being caught in local minima. This term represents the extent to which weight values in previous epochs carry over into subsequent epochs. The user sets the momentum of the learning rule. Momentum values are usually set between 0.3 and 1. A momentum term set too low will result in a network that may not be able to climb out of local minima regardless of the learning rate adjustments. In addition to momentum, terms known as bias represent constants that act as additional inputs to each node. The topology of the network, number of examples and the characteristics of the data all impact on these parameters.

A bias term is included in many implementations of neural networks and can be thought of as a fixed, constant input into each neuron. Bias terms are usually set between -1 and +1. Bias provides additional stability and restricts erratic learning behaviour. Modifying the bias term during training sometimes helps a network seemingly stuck at one error level to begin to make small gains on each epoch.

1.2.3 Stopping criteria

Typically, training ceases when a fixed maximum number of epochs are reached or when the network performance has reached a threshold error level. A stopping criteria based on an error threshold is better than one based on number of epochs, but the error should be measured on examples not seen during training.

The extent to which the trained network will generalise and perform correctly on cases not in the training set depends on the size and coverage of the training set, the architecture of the network and the complexity of the problem. Two extremes are to be avoided if adequate generalisation is to ensue: under-training and over-training.

Under-training of a neural network occurs if the network is not exposed to enough examples. Learning is difficult in this situation simply because the training patterns available are not sufficiently representative of the true population of cases. Another variation of the same extreme occurs if the network is not exposed to the training set for a sufficient number of epochs. The opposite extreme is known as over-generalisation, over-training or over-fitting. If a sufficiently large network has been exposed to an abundance of examples, far too many times, it can learn each input-output pair so well that it, in effect memorises those cases. The network classifies training set cases well but may not perform so well with cases not in the training set. The network is said to be over trained or over-fitted. The concept of over-fitting is discussed at length in Chapter 9.

The objective in training any neural network is to avoid either under-training or over-training. This can be achieved in various ways. In the Split Up project, this goal was achieved by pursuing the cross validation re-sampling method.

However, perhaps the most important consideration in avoiding over-training or under-training involves the discernment of a domain specific appropriate metric for measuring errors. A measure of classifier performance typically used in classifier training in non-legal domains is the number of examples correctly classified. As [Weiss and Kulikowski 1992] point out, this measure of network performance may not be adequate for all domains. They suggest a metric that includes the costs of predicting a positive outcome when the actual outcome was negative (called False positives) and the risks associated with predicting a negative outcome when the actual outcome was positive (called False negatives). For example, a network, trained to discern the presence or absence of a disease will ideally, err far more times on the side of predicting a disease when there is none present than it will err in missing a disease that is actually present. A False positive/False negative analysis of errors is not warranted in family law, because the direction of the error is not as critical as it is in medical diagnostic problems. A network that predicts the husband is to receive 60% of the property errs if the judge in the case actually awarded 55%. However, another network errs in a similar and in a no more or less damaging manner if it predicts the husband is to receive 50% of the assets. Thus, the direction of the error is not critical for our purposes.

The stopping criteria for neural networks that model legal domains are invariably subjective. It is unreasonable to expect perfect performance from neural networks in discretionary domains of law, because networks are trained on data from many judges, and thus cannot always exactly predict the outcome of any one judge on all cases. The measurement of the performance of a neural network, by counting the number of correctly classified examples, leads to a measure of network performance that may be too fine-grained for legal applications and thus increases the risk of over training. Given that a perfect performance is unlikely, other acceptable criteria must be adopted. There seems no theoretical basis to underpin such criteria, so acceptable criteria must be selected heuristically.

A good measure of a neural network's performance in a discretionary legal domain includes an indication of the magnitude of the error. An error of 5% either way when estimating a judge's decision about the percentage of marital assets to be awarded to the wife is, in our view, tolerable. On the other hand, a network which outputs a percentage split which deviates by 20% from that given by a judge, is assumed to have erred. Although the cut off point for declaring that an error has occurred is necessarily subjective it is important that a metric be discerned which can be applied consistently to all neural networks in the Split Up system.

The metric adopted in the Split Up study makes use of the following encoding scheme. Consider a network with five binary outputs. A network output of [1,0,0,0,0] for a particular example indicates that the first bit is set. If the actual output has the fifth bit set [0,0,0,0,1], we consider the network to have made an error of magnitude four. If the actual output sets two bits such as it would in [0,1,1,0,0] we take the average of the positions of the set bits. In this case we say the actual bit set is in position 2.5. If the expected output was [0,0,1,0,0] then the error is of magnitude 0.5 (i.e. 2.5-3). The use of an error heuristic based on the position of the set bit has advantages in that it is simple, easy to calculate and has a direct association with the interpretation placed on the bits. Encoding the five values `much more', `more', `about the same as', `less' and `much less' as bit string could be achieved with as few as three bits. However, a five bit number enables the position of the set bit to correspond directly with one of the values.

The error heuristic we use is central to the training of the neural networks used in the Split Up project. Training is halted in Split Up networks once the proportion of errors of magnitude three or more is observed to be 3% or less. An error of magnitude three represents a significant error for most neural networks. However, the cost of totally eliminating these errors is high, in that the additional training required increases the risk of over-training.

A number of neural networks in legal domains have been trained successfully, although the use of neural networks in law is far from widespread. In the next section we review these attempts in order to argue that many neural networks have not been appropriately trained, and further inappropriate data has been used.

2. NEURAL NETWORKS IN LAW

[Hunter 1994] notes that neural networks are essentially statistical. By this he means that associations between inferred outcomes and facts are represented as statistical associations captured as inter neuron weights. As such, connectionism derives support from the same jurisprudential theories as does any statistical method.

Forty years ago [Kort 1964] and [Nagel 1964] both developed statistical methods for analysing cases. Their goal was to predict decisions. Both authors advanced methods for determining how the courts weighed individual facts to reach a decision. Kort's method was based on the solving of simultaneous equations in order to ascertain the weight of factors, while Nagel used discrimminant analysis. These authors validated their statistical approach by drawing on the jurisprudence of legal realists. As stated in chapter one, we claim that connectionism can be useful for resolving situations that involve open texture, yet their effectiveness depends on the type of open textured situation studied.

The classification of situations characterised as open textured by [Prakken 1993], provides a useful framework for a survey of neural network approaches. We argue that neural networks are best applied to situations that involve the open texture inherent in judicial discretion though some inroads can also be made toward resolving classification difficulties. To recapitulate, [Prakken 1993] identifies situations characterised as open textured as those that involve classification ambiguities, defeasible rules or vague terms. We appended the situation characterised by judicial discretion to that list. We shall survey notable applications of neural networks to each of these open textured situations.

2.1   Neural networks for classification difficulties

[Bench-Capon 1993] applied neural networks to a problem that involved open texture in the manifestation of classification difficulties. He identified six variables as inputs into a neural network that modeled the imaginary domain of social security entitlements in the United Kingdom. The output represented whether or not an applicant was entitled to social security benefits. The open texture in this domain manifested itself as difficulties inherent in classifying whether the applicant was entitled to social security benefits.

Presented with cases that were not used for training, the neural network was able to suggest an outcome that reflected the weightings of input variables in prior cases. However, limitations were apparent in that, in some cases the network was clearly in error. For example for every case in the training set that output a social security benefit, it had, as one of the inputs, the fact that the applicant was over a certain age. This was because the applicant's age was a limiting condition for the granting of a benefit. However, when dealing with some unseen cases, the neural network granted a benefit to some applicants under the limiting age.

A neural network cannot be guaranteed to perform correctly on cases that were not present in the training set. If trained appropriately, then we may estimate the proportion of all possible cases that will be classified correctly. However, we will not know with certainty which class of cases will be incorrectly classified. This is not necessarily a condemnation of neural networks. The limiting condition in the Bench-Capon study is more aptly represented as a rule. Furthermore, the rule seems to be one, which is applied in an all or nothing, way: without any exceptions. In law, very few rules in operate in this way. The Bench-Capon study can thus be seen to apply neural networks to a classification task that is more obviously suited to a series of simple rules.

[Warner 1994] does not explicitly claim that neural networks have the potential to resolve situations in law characterised by classification difficulties. Rather, he maintains that neural networks are appropriate to use in modelling law, because they exhibit the capacity to emulate the parallel reasoning process of a lawyer. He argues that legal problem solving behaviour is often described as a serial process that progresses in a step-by step fashion, from the initial problem description, to the goal of the reasoning. Yet, legal reasoning involves a parallel process of assimilating facts to reach partial solutions and assimilating partial solutions to reach a final solution. Warner's rationale for the use of neural networks in law is open to criticism, in that the distinction between problem solving performed in series and in parallel, is by no means clear. For instance, it is not clear why a parallel process should succeed in law where a serial process will fail. Furthermore, according to [Hunter 1994], there is little support from jurisprudential theorists for the notion that legal reasoning is, in any sense, parallel.

Despite the shortcoming in the rationale that [Warner 1994] uses to justify the use of neural networks, the actual task to which he applies neural network, is one that attempts to deal with classification difficulties in the domain of consideration in contract law. His network attempts to classify a case according to whether the contract involved a consideration. The uses of neural networks for modelling legal reasoning by Bench-Capon and Warner are similar, in that each of these authors applies neural networks to resolve classification difficulties; difficulties that contribute to a perception of law as open textured. The application of neural networks to legal reasoning by [Philipps 1991] and by [Thagard 1989] differ from these approaches, in that their studies can be seen to apply connectionism in an attempt to resolve defeasible rules.

2.2 Neural networks for defeasible rules

[Philipps 1989] demonstrates how neural networks can assist in dealing with defeasible rules by examining a hypothetical example taken from Roman Law. The will of a hypothetical citizen whose wife was pregnant read:

If a son is born to me let him be heir in respect of two thirds of my estate, let my wife be heir in respect of the remaining part; but if a daughter is born to me, let her be heir to the extent of a third; let my wife be heir to the remaining part.

This hypothetical will can be seen to involve two rules, one governing the distribution of the estate in the event of the birth of a daughter and the other governing the distribution of the estate in the event of the birth of a son. Rather than representing these rules as clauses in a logic program or rules in a rule based reasoner, Philipps trained a feed forward neural network with back-propagation of errors to deliver the correct output when exposed to scenarios that involved the birth of a boy and the birth of a girl, but not the birth of both. He then put forward a case that necessarily defeats these rules; one in which twins, a boy and a girl are born. In this case, the network that had not been exposed to this scenario during training, produced an outcome that indicated the mother receives two shares, the son receives three and the daughter receives four.

Philipps argues this outcome is reasonable, in that it represents an equilibrium based on past cases. However, [Hunter 1994] points out that the notion of equilibrium with past cases is jurisprudentially flawed. There is no notion of moral correctness, nor any appeal to reason, that reflect higher principles. We agree with Hunter on this point, because we believe that, in this Roman Law example, reasoning is best modelled as deductions made from known legal rules. However, this is not the case in discretionary domains. Another instance of the application of connectionism for modelling defeasible rules in law can be seen in the work of [Thagard 1989].

He proposed a theory of explanatory coherence that aims to model the way in which competing hypotheses are supported by available evidence. Some nodes in the network he developed represent propositions about each hypothesis. Other nodes represent available evidence. Links exist between evidential nodes and hypothesis nodes. Each has an associated weight that may be excitary or inhibitory. To determine which hypothesis has more support, the network is activated. Nodes feed activation (or inhibition) to other nodes which provide feedback to each other, until an equilibrium is reached. The network is then settled.

Thagard trialed his ECHO program on a murder case in which the competing hypotheses were X was innocent and X was guilty. Propositions associated with these hypothesis included C broke his hand punching X and C broke his hand falling on a rock. Thagard's propositions did not include rules from statutes or from legal principles, but could easily have been extended thus. Propositions that reflected statutes or principles would compete for activation with other propositions and those hypotheses that remained most active after the network settled, would be deemed to have, in Thagard's terms, more explanatory coherence.

In this way, the Thagard approach can be interpreted as one which attempts to resolve those situations in law that are characterised as open textured, because of the presence of defeasible rules. The Thagard approach is certainly intuitively appealing, but requires much further research. Attempts by Thagard and Philipps to use neural networks to model reasoning with defeasible rules can be seen to be overly ambitious if we relate their attempts to the use of Toulmin argument structures. Inputs and outputs of their neural networks correspond to datum and claim of the Toulmin Argument Structure. The force, rebuttal, warrant and backing cannot be represented using conventional connectionist systems. So, in the Roman law example, commentators such as Hunter are unlikely to accept the neural network conclusion, because it cannot supply a warrant or supporting evidence. This does not point to a flaw with the use of connectionism in law, but, in our view only highlights that the procedure used to infer a claim is only one component of the structure used to persuade a reader of the feasibility of the claim.

2.3   Neural networks for vague terms

Law is replete with terms that are vague. A concept such as within reasonable limits, specified in a statute, is labelled a vague term by [Brkic 1985]. The presence of vague terms was enough to entice that author to condemn the use of deduction to model legal reasoning. To our knowledge, connectionism has not been applied to tasks that involve vague terms. Vague terms present difficulties, because there are a number of senses in which a term may be considered vague. A statutory concept such as within reasonable limits, may signify that a decision-maker has recourse to an element of discretion in much the same way that a Family Court judge has some flexibility in distributing marital property. If all relevant principles, rules and factors were made clear to a decision maker who then had to weight the factors in order to determine whether a current case fell within reasonable limits, we would be inclined to regard the resolution of vague terms in much the same way as we see the allocation of discretion.

However, the above paragraph does not describe not all vague concepts appearing in statutes. A vague concept such as within reasonable limits, may be included in a statute, with no supplementary material that would assist a decision maker in defining the term. Legislative drafters often prefer this flexibility, so that Courts will lay down principles to guide future decision makers. A connectionist system can conceivably be developed that has, as inputs, the facts of a case and outputs one of a permitted number of uses of the vague concept. This use of connectionism is not dissimilar to the use of connectionism to resolve classification difficulties.

2.4 Using neural networks to model discretionary legal domains

The application of neural networks to the task of learning the way in which judges weight relevant factors in a discretionary domain does not presume more from neural networks than they can deliver. As we have seen, the use of neural networks to resolve classification ambiguities or to mimic reasoning with defeasible rules makes questionable jurisprudential assumptions. We claim that neural networks can be appropriately applied to learn the way in which judges, have combined factors in past cases. To do this, we adopt a legal realist stance that variations displayed by individual judges on similar cases in a discretionary domain, are not the result of the application of different legal principles. However, a number of obstacles must be overcome if this paradigm is to be usefully applied. [Hunter 1994] and [Aikenhead 1996] identify prominent flaws in the way in which neural networks have been trained for use in past legal applications.

The concerns they raise focus on the explication deficiencies of neural networks, the assembly of appropriate data and methods used for the training of neural networks. We successively survey these concerns in order to describe the steps we have taken to ensure our neural networks are appropriately trained. The lack of explication facility inherent in the connectionist paradigm weighs heavily against their use in law. To overcome this problem we need to return to jurisprudence in order to discover how explanations fit into the scheme of legal reasoning.

The jurisprudence of the legal realism movement is central to the application of the connectionist paradigm, in that this movement advocates a separation of the decision making process from the process of justifying that decision. Thus, reasoning to reach a conclusion and explaining that conclusion can be seen as two distinct processes. Drawing this distinction enables us to design a system that uses neural networks to infer conclusions and another system to explain the conclusions. A decision is made on the basis of facts inputted. We assume that rules and principles are not necessarily factors for arriving at a decision. However, rules, principles and the facts of a case, in addition to the decision itself, are necessary in order for a justification to be advanced.

Discretion, defined as the ability of individual judges to assign different relative weights to relevant factors is accommodated in the first phase, the reaching of a conclusion. The second phase, justification of the decision does not necessarily involve a reproduction of the reasoning steps nor does it necessarily require that all factors that were relevant, even if they are highly weighted, are reported as a justification of the decision.

A barrister who suspects that her client will condemn her performance, will be tempted to offer the client a conservative prediction. Yet, that factor cannot be included in an explanation without defeating the purpose. The justification phase necessarily requires a reference to rules or principles. Decisions explained without reference to established statutes or precedents are totally untenable in liberal democracies. Legal concepts are useful tools for justifying a decision and can be applied by an artificial reasoner to justify or explain any decision. A family law expert displays the same capacity. Given the same set of facts an expert is able to justify a property decision of 70% to the husband and yet, is also able to create a justification for an output of 50% to the husband for the same case.

2.5 Unsupervised Neural networks

The neural networks we have previously discussed are supervised neural networks. This means that during training the network is presented with the example and the output is learnt for that example. For instance, during training of the Split Up percentage split network, input values for contributions, needs and wealth are presented to one network along with a percentage split of assets that the trial judge awarded in that case.

In unsupervised learning the neural network is not presented with inputs and outputs. Rather, the entire data set is presented to the network. The network is required to cluster examples into groups of similar examples. There are many types of unsupervised networks including Self Organizing Maps, Grossberg nets, In-star, out-star, Bi-directional Associational Maps and Hopfield networks[Hecht-Nelson 1990].

Unsupervised neural networks known as Self-organising maps or Kohonen networks have been applied in a text mining KDD by [Merkl and Schweighofer 1997], [Schweighofer and Merkl 1999] and [Merkl et al 1999]. This body of work will be discussed in the next chapter.

3. CHAPTER SUMMARY

This has been our last chapter on the use of data-mining techniques to discover useful patterns of legal knowledge from data sets. Previously, we have considered rule induction, association rules, fuzzy rules and other statistical techniques.

In this chapter, we have investigated alternatives to discovering rules. Instead, we used neural network. A neural network resembles a nervous system in the brain. It consists of many self-adjusting processing elements cooperating in a densely interconnected network. Each processing element generates a single output signal that is transmitted to the other processing elements. The output signal of a processing element depends on the inputs to the processing element: each input is gated by a weighting factor that determines the amount of influence that the input will have on the output. The strength of the weighting factors is adjusted autonomously by the processing element as data is processed. Neural networks are particularly useful in modelling legal domains because they can deal with a) classification difficulties, b) vague terms, c) defeasible rules and d) discretionary domains.

In a feed forward neural network, the neurons on the first layer send their output to the neurons of the second layer, but they do not receive any input back from the neurons on the second layer. We investigated learning patterns in feed forward neural networks.

Our first task in setting up a neural network was to determine a network topology. A neural network topology is a specification of the number of neurons in the input layer, the output layer and in each of the hidden layers.

To train a neural network we need to make decisions regarding the following parameters: a) Learning rate, b) Momentum, c) Bias terms, and d) Stopping criteria.

In supervised learning, the system developer tells the system what the correct is, and the system determines weights in such a way that once given the input it would produce the desired output. The system is repeatedly given facts about various cases, along with expected outputs. The system uses the learning method to adjust the weights in order to produce outputs similar to the expected results. The bulk of our discussion on neural networks for data-mining legal data sets involved a consideration of supervised neural networks.

Most legal data occurs as free text. In the next chapter we shall investigate the use of text mining from legal databases. Issues to be considered will include information extraction, text summarisation, text classification and text categorisation. In unsupervised learning the neural network is not presented with inputs and outputs. Rather, the entire data set is presented to the network. The network is required to cluster examples into groups of similar examples. In the next chapter we will discuss the applications of unsupervised neural networks known as Self-organising maps or Kohonen networks, to law. A case study of the work of Schweighofer and others in the domain of public international law will be presented.

Once we have concluded our investigation of suitable data-mining techniques for discovering legal knowledge, we now need to discuss the final barrier to the use of knowledge discovery from legal databases: *Once we have discovered certain patterns arising from the KDD process, how can we ensure that these patterns are both useful and valid.*

This question is the basis of our final substantive chapter of the book: chapter nine..

CHAPTER 8

INFORMATION RETRIEVAL AND TEXT MINING

Information in the legal domain is often stored as text in relatively unstructured forms. For example, statutes, judgments and commentaries are typically stored as free text documents. Discovering knowledge by the automatic analysis of free text is a field of research that is evolving from information retrieval research and is often called text mining. [Dozier *et al* 2003] states that text mining is a new field and there is still debate about what its definition should be. [Jackson and Moulinier 2002] observe that text mining involves discovering something interesting about the relationship between the text and the world. [Hearst 1999] proposes that text mining involves discovering relationships between the content of multiple texts and linking this information together to create new information. Text mining often includes the following techniques:

a) **Information extraction** is a technique for extracting domain-specific information from texts [Cowie and Wilks 2000]. Text fragments are mapped to field or template lots that have a definite semantic meaning;

b) **Text summarisation** involves identifying, summarising and organising related text so that users can efficiently deal with information in large documents;

c) **Text categorisation** involves organizes documents into a taxonomy, thus allowing for more efficient searches. It involves the assignment of subject descriptors or classification codes or abstract concepts to complete texts;

d) **Text clustering** involves automatically clustering documents into groups where documents within each group share common features.

All text mining approaches utilise information retrieval mechanisms. Indeed, the distinction between information retrieval methods and text mining is blurred. In the next section information retrieval basics are discussed. A number of sophisticated extensions to basic information retrieval advanced in the legal field are described. We then discuss examples of information extraction, text summarisation, text categorisation and text clustering in law.

1.   INFORMATION RETRIEVAL BASICS

The aim of efficient information retrieval should be to retrieve that information, and only that information which is deemed relevant to a given query. [Salton 1989] states that a typical information retrieval system selects documents from a collection in response to a user's query and ranks these documents according to their relevance to the query. This is primarily accomplished by matching a text representation with a representation of the query.

Information retrieval and database systems have some similarities. Whereas database systems have focused on query processing and transactions relating to structured data, information retrieval is concerned with the organisation and information from a large number of text-based documents. The task of querying databases and text retrieval systems is very different. For text retrieval systems, the matching is not deterministic and often incorporates an element of uncertainty. Retrieval models generally rank the retrieved document according to their potential relevancy to the query.

Legal information retrieval considers searching both structured and unstructured content. For structured information, the semantics can be clearly and unambiguously determined and can be described with simple and clear concepts. This information category comprises, for instance, identification data of the texts, data for version management and the function and role of certain components. These data are often added in the form of metadata (i.e., data that describe other data) to the documents.

Unstructured information often occurs in natural language texts, or in other formats such as audio and video and generally has a complex semantics. A detailed analysis of information retrieval in law can be found in [Zeleznikow and Hunter 1994] and [Moens 2001].

[Moens 2001] notes that the majority of existing automatic indexing methods select natural language index terms from document texts. The indexed terms selected concern single words and multi-word phases and are assumed to reflect the content of the text. She claims that a prevalent process of selecting natural language index terms from texts that reflect its content is composed of the following steps:

a) Lexical analysis – the text is parsed and individual words are recognised.

b) The removal of stopwords – a text retrieval system often associates a stop list with a set of documents. A stop list is a set of words that are deemed irrelevant (such as 'a', 'the', 'for') or at least irrelevant for the given query.

c) The optional reduction of the remaining words to their stem form – A group of different words may share the same word stem. The text retrieval system needs to identify groups of words that have a small syntactic variation from each other and only use one word from each group e.g. only use breach instead of breaches, breach, breached. There are different methods of stemming, many of which rely upon linguistic knowledge of the collection's language.

d) The optional formulation of phrases as index terms. Techniques of phrase recognition employ the statistics of co-occurrences of words or rely upon linguistic knowledge of the collection's language.

e) The optional replacement of words, word stems or phrases by their thesaurus class terms – A thesaurus replaces the individual words or phrases of a text by more uniform concepts.

f) The computation of the importance indicator or term weight of each remaining word stem or word, thesaurus class term or phrase term.

The selection of natural language index terms from texts, following the steps above, can be regarded as the pre-processing and transformation phases of text mining. Some pre-processing of text documents may be manual. For example, [Moens 2001] notes that the manual indexing of legal documents is still common, especially when controlled language index terms such as thesaurus class terms and conceptual terms are assigned. Manual indexing also includes the manual assignment of content mark-up, for instance in SGML (Standard Generalised Markup Language) or XML (eXtensible Markup Language).

The effectiveness of full text retrieval is often measured in terms of precision and recall. The precision of a text retrieval query is the percentage of retrieved documents that are relevant to the query (= the number of 'correct' responses) and is defined by:

precision = |Relevant and Retrieved| / |Retrieved|

while the recall of a text retrieval query is the percentage of all relevant documents that are retrieved

recall   = |Relevant and Retrieved| / |Relevant]

where
Relevant is the set of documents relevant to a query,
Retrieved is the set of documents retrieved and
|A| is the number of elements in the set A.

High recall and high precision (ie each as close to 1:1 as possible) are both desirable. There seems to be no optimum relationship between precision and recall. However, it is often observed that there is an inverse relationship between the two, with high recall resulting in low precision, and vice-versa (see [Blair and Maron 1985]).

[Han and Kamber 2001] observe that most information retrieval systems support keyword-based or similarity-based retrieval. In keyword-based information retrieval a document is represented by a string that can be identified by a set of keywords. The user provides a set of keywords such as 'cases dealing with fault in the distribution of property in Australian Family Law'. Whilst keyword-based retrieval is simple to understand and implement it has two major drawbacks.

a)   The synonmy problem : a keyword such as fault may not appear in the case, because the judge used the term 'negative contribution'. Of course fault and negative contribution are closely related.

b)   The polysemy problem: the same keyword such as 'to know' may mean different things in different contexts. One may know a fact or know (be acquainted with) a person.

Similarity-based retrieval finds similar documents based on a set of common keywords. The input into similarity-based retrieval is a document. The output is a set of documents that are most similar to the query document ranked on the degree of relevance, where relevance is measured based on the closeness and the relative frequency of the keywords.

The mechanism for performing the retrieval or matching is drawn from a number of models. In discussing text retrieval for legal practitioners [Turtle 1995] notes that models include:

a) Boolean retrieval;
b) Vector Space retrieval;
c) Probabilistic Retrieval;
d) Rule based Retrieval; and
e) Knowledge based Retrieval.

Each model will be outlined below. [Moens 2001] provides an authoritative review of legal text retrieval.

1.1   The Boolean Retrieval Model

In the Boolean retrieval model [Salton 1989], a query has the form of an expression containing index terms and Boolean operators.   The retrieval model compares the Boolean query statement with the term set used to identify document content. The index terms that satisfy the query are returned as relevant. No ranking of the documents according to relevance is provided. Variants of the model provide ranking based upon partial fulfilment of the query expression.

One of the main criticisms of Boolean information retrieval systems is that they are very strict: they only retrieve documents that meet all the requirements of the search request. A document that contains all the specified search terms except one, or contains all of them but not quite as close together as is specified, will be excluded. A by-product of this fact is that logical connectors provide no method of ranking those documents that satisfy a search request in terms of how likely it is that they will be relevant to the user's request. A document either satisfies the request or it does not. As [Blair and Maron 1985] state, Boolean information retrieval systems retrieve an excess of irrelevant material (low precision).

1.2   The Vector Space Retrieval Model

[Salton 1989]   and [Han and Kamber 2001] describe a vector model for supporting information retrieval.   Commencing with a set of d documents and t terms, each document can be viewed as a vector v in the t dimensional vector space Rt. So $v = (v_1, v_2, \ldots, v_t)$.

v_j measures the association of the jth term with respect to the given document.

v_j is 0   if the document does not contain the term

$\qquad \alpha$ where α is non-zero, otherwise.

There are many ways to define a (the term-weighting). We could define $\alpha = 1$ as long as the jth term appears in the document or allow a to be the term frequency or the relative term frequency .

[Merkl and Schweighofer 1997] deployed a vector space model in their neural network based document clustering system. They generated an index of keywords from a corpora of judgements related to public international law. Each judgement is represented as a vector of numbers where each number represents the frequency that an index word appears in the judgement. Two hypothetical cases are illustrated in Table 1 to reflect this. The term 'international' appears with approximately the same frequency in judgement A and B whereas the term 'environment' appears far more frequently in judgement A. In practice the calculation of frequency can be quite complicated and involves taking into account the length of the document and the frequency of the term in general usage.

Table 1. Sample input vector for Self organising maps

Term	Frequency Judgement A	Frequency Judgement B
International	0.1	0.15
Environment	0.7	0.01
Jurisdiction	0.1	0.33
..		

[Han and Kamber 2001] suggest measuring the similarity among a set of documents or a document and a query based either on similar relative term occurrences in the term frequency matrix (where each row represents a term, each column represents a document vector and each entry registers the number of occurrences of term t_i in the document d_j) or through the use of metrics. One such metric is the cosine metric:

$$\text{sim}(v_1, v_2) = \frac{v_1 . v_2}{|v_1| * |v_2|}$$

where

$v_1 . v_2 = v_{11}v_{21} + v_{12}v_{22} + v_{13}v_{23} + \ldots + v_{1t}v_{2t}$ and

$|v_1| = \text{sqrt}(v_1 . v_1)$

Text-based queries can be represented as vectors which can be used to search for their nearest neighbours in a document collection[52]. However, for any non-trivial document database, the number of terms T and number of documents D is quite large. The high dimensionality of the frequency table, T x D, leads to very sparse vectors and increases the difficulty in detecting and exploiting the relationships among terms (for example synonymy).

Further, the above text-retrieval methods rely on the representation of documents as vectors of term weights. But what happens if users pose queries that involve different concepts for indexing the document? To meet this challenge, the notion of latent semantic indexing [Derweester *et al* 1990] has been introduced. Latent semantic indexing reduces the size of the term frequency matrix by using singular value decomposition (SVD).

---

[52] The nearest neighbour algorithm is discussed in chapter six.

Given a T x D term frequency matrix, the SVD method removes rows and columns to reduce the size of a matrix to a manageable K x K matrix where K is much less than the minimum of T and D. To minimise the amount of information loss, only the least significant parts of the frequency matrix are omitted. Further information can be found in [Hand *et al* 2001].

The vector space model with similarity calculated with a metric such as the cosine metric has been criticised because it does not accurately represent queries and documents [Raghaven and Wong 1986]. The vector space model uses terms as the groundwork of an orthogonal basis of the vector space. It adapts a simplifying assumption that terms are not correlated and term vectors are pairwise orthogonal. Many probabilistic retrieval models discussed in the next section, represent documents as vectors of terms, but include more sophisticated similarity metrics.

1.3 Probabilistic Retrieval Models

The classic probabilistic retrieval model views retrieval as a problem of estimating the probability that a document representation matches or satisfies a query [Baez-Yates and Ribeiro-Neto 1999]. This probability is often computed by learning the weight of the query terms from the documents that are judged relevant for the query and that contain the relevant terms. [Moens 2001] notes that current models use refined statistical techniques such as 2-Poisson distributions and logistic regression to estimate this probability.

Network representations have a long history of use in information retrieval and are well suited for use in legal information retrieval. Such representations have been used to support retrieval functions such as browsing, document clustering and the representation of user knowledge. The inference network model is a probabilistic retrieval model since it uses a probability ranking principle.

In the inference network model [Turtle 1995], document and query content are represented as linked networks that can represent the probabilistic results of different indexing techniques, or represent the probabilistic relation between a term and a concept, or represent the weighted preferences of a user. The networks incorporate knowledge that reflect the properties of the subject domain, possibly using linguistic knowledge and/or knowledge of the supposed retrieval strategies of a user. Inference is based upon the combination of evidence as it is propagated in linked networks. Documents are ranked according to this belief of relevance.

A probabilistic model calculates the probability that a user decides a document is relevant given a particular document and query, Pr(Relevant|{document.query}). The inference network model computes Pr(I|document), which is the probability that a user's information need is satisfied given a particular document. The major difference between the inference network model and other probabilistic models is that the inference network model emphasizes the use of multiple sources to calculate P(I|document).

The most useful techniques for text classification are statistical naïve Bayes methods, nearest neighbour classifiers and Support Vector Machines[53] as well as techniques that learn trees and rules[54]. Hidden Markov Models can perform learning patterns that occur in a sequence.

[Moens 2001] provides a brief description of each of these techniques. We have already considered the naïve Bayes method and learning trees and rules.

a) Nearest Neigbour Classifiers [Masand *et al* 1992] – such classifiers store positive examples of a class. To classify a new object the nearest neighbour classifier compares the feature vector of the new object with the feature vector of each example stored, by using a similarity or distance function. The classifier finds then k closest examples or the examples for which the similarity exceeds a certain threshold.

b) Support Vector Machines [Joachims 1998] – As long as two classes are linearly separable[55], support vector machines determine the hyperplane in the n-dimensional feature space that maximises the margin between the examples of the classes. A new example is classified by computing to which side of the hyperplane the example belongs. The technique can be generalised to examples that are not linearly separable.

c) Hidden Markov Models (HMM) [Manning and Schutze 1999] – HMM are probabilistic finite state automata that model the probabilities of a linear sequence of events. A Markov model is defined by 1) a set of states, 2) a set of transitions, 3) the probabilities of the transitions and 4) a set of output symbols that can be emitted when in a state or transition. For each state or transition, a probability distribution is defined for all symbols that can be emitted.

In a HMM, one only knows a probabilistic function of the state sequence through which the model passes. Given a training corpus in which the information is sequentially structured and which is manually annotated, efficient algorithms learn the probabilities of all transitions and emissions. Typical emissions are the information segments of a text and transitions refer to the sequential structure of the segments. HMM are useful for extracting information that is highly sequentially structured.

As [Greenleaf *et al* 1998] state, the importance of old information to lawyers, both in the form of reported cases and statutes which have not been repealed, is an unusual feature of law in comparison with other professions. Most information used by professions which are based on the natural sciences have little need to retrieve information more than a decade or two old, and in some cases, considerably less. Information has a relatively short 'half-life' in such professions. The 'half life' of legal information is more difficult to determine, even if the idea does have some meaning for legal information. Even statutes that have been repealed must be available so the law in force at the time of a case can be understood. Reported cases that have been accepted as precedents do not lose their authority by virtue of age.

---

[53] See chapter six.

[54] See chapter five.

[55] See chapter six.

In this book we have focused upon how we can use machine learning and knowledge discovery from databases to learn how legal decisions are made. We have hence primarily examined artificial intelligence techniques. The retrieval of relevant cases and statutes is one of the major benefits that information technology can provide for legal professionals. Thus, we need to examine how information retrieval and text mining is used in the legal domain.

2. INFORMATION RETRIEVAL IN LAW

Automated retrieval from large document collections was one of the earliest applications of computer science to law and is a task that over the decades was never absent from the artificial and law community. The early developments originated in government departments, military institutions and university environments where computer technology offered an efficient means to classify large amounts of data.

The first successful demonstration of a legal text retrieval system took place at a conference organised by the American Bar Association in 1960. The system demonstrated was called LITE (Legal Information Through Electronics). There have been very few changes in retrieval software since then. Whilst more efficient file structures have been introduced, the systems are still based on an inverted file and the retrieval is based on Boolean logic.

In the late 1960s, the STATUS project at the UK Atomic Energy Agency developed a system to store all the statutes and regulations. United States legal practitioners created a database that had the capacity to store the whole of the US statute and case law material, LEXIS (now LexisNexis). Westlaw followed in the steps of LEXIS. These commercial systems still exist today as ones of largest providers of legal information offering interactive retrieval through terminals at the customer's office and have gained widespread acceptance by the legal profession. The World Wide Web makes it possible for citizens to access web-based databases of legislation and court decisions [Munro 2002]. The movement to make legislation and court decisions readily accessible via the web is a significant change in the way law is practised and perceived. The movement facilitates such a widespread application of text mining that we digress briefly to illustrate key aspects of this movement.

2.1   AustLII and WorldLII

The World Legal Information Institute (WorldLII) is a free, independent and non-profit collaboration of a number of institutes dedicated to the provision of free access to public legal information throughout the world[56]. Organisations such as

---

[56] The relevant web sites are www.wordlii.org, www.austlii.edu.au, www.bailii.org, www.canlii.org, www.hklii.org, www.paclii.org, www.saflii.org, www.law.cornell.edu and droit.francophonie.org.

Australasian Legal Information Institute (AustLII), British and Irish Legal Information Institute (BAILII), Canadian Legal Information Institute (CanLII), Hong Kong Legal Information Institute (HKLII), Legal Information Institute (Cornell) and Pacific Islands Legal Information Institute (PacLII) receive the text of judgments and statutes on a daily basis from thousands of courts and parliaments world-wide. Within a very short time frame the text is automatically processed and uploaded to the relevant databases making the documents freely available by any internet user. This movement now has a website (in French) relating to law based on the French Civil Code of Law.

The *free law movement* pioneered by AustLII relies heavily on a free-information retrieval engine known as SINO and a hypertext generation facility. This builds components of the early Datalex system described by [Greenleaf *et al* 1996]. The DataLex Workstation Software integrates inferencing (rule-based backward and forward chaining, document generation, and a limited form of case-based inferencing), hypertext and (boolean/proximity) text retrieval into a general-purpose tool for the representation and processing of legal information. The DataLex Workstation Software comprises three distinct engines which share a common interface: a free-text retrieval engine (AIRS), a hypertext engine (HYPE) and an inferencing engine (YSH) which has a quasi-natural language interface that supports document generation using rules. YSH supports backward and forward chaining and procedural inferencing. Applications are written using text editors. The developers have developed a number of Unix-based text processing tools (distinct from the DataLex Workstation Software) to automate the mark-up of legal texts for hypertext and text retrieval by the DataLex software.

[Moens 2000] notes that current commercial retrieval systems either rely on a manual indexing of case texts or upon a full text search. SINO, for example uses a full text search. The disadvantage of the former is the tremendous cost, whilst the latter leads to a lack of reliable retrieval costs.

The precision and recall accuracy results of information retrieval engines have led to major improvement for legal information retrieval. One approach involves using knowledge about the structure of the documents to improve results. Another approach integrates Bayesian reasoning with an information retrieval engine. A third approach integrates neural networks with an information retrieval engine. Examples of each approach are presented in the next section.

2.2   Information retrieval using document structure or domain knowledge

Most judgements are not totally free form text but typically conform to a common structure. [Yearwood 1997] found that determinations from the Refugee Review Tribunal of Australia consist of the same sections: Application, Background, Jurisdiction, Legislative framework and Applicant's case. He explored the extent to which precision and recall improvements could be realised by matching a query with each section of the document separately. This approach realised substantial precision and recall improvements with medical documents, as reported in

[Yearwood and Wilkinson 1997]. Though the improvements were not as dramatic in the case of retrieval of refugee determinations, there was clear evidence that taking the structure of the document into account leads to improved information retrieval results.

In the Olimpo case retrieval system advanced by [Hoeschl *et al* 2001], experts identify terms or phrases within a sample of documents and map them to concepts they regard as important for retrieving cases. In this approach, called structured contextual search, an index is created for each concept. A document is indexed globally and also against each concept index. A similarity metric accommodates the combination of similarities globally with those from each concept. Results in the application domain involving resolutions of the United Nations Security Council were promising. The approach is extended in [Bueno *et al* 2003], with the use of variable weights for each concept. Results on experiments with *súmulas,* three line decision summaries from Brazilian courts demonstrated high recall.

2.3   Information retrieval using a Bayesian network

WIN (Westlaw is Natural) uses a Bayesian network to compute the probabilities that documents in a database are relevant to a query, and returns the relevant documents in order of their significance to the relevant query. Bayesian Networks have been used to analyse criminal evidence (see for example [Aitken 1995] and [Schum 1994]). WIN [Croft and Turtle 1992] has a relatively simple natural language interface that allows users to query the Westlaw database in English sentences. Once the query is specified in English, WIN uses a Bayesian network to compute the probabilities that documents contained in the database are relevant to the query and then returns relevant documents. The higher the probability that the document is relevant to the query, the higher it appears in the order.

In chapter six we discussed Bayesian belief networks. A Bayesian inference network is a directed acyclic graph in which nodes represent prepositional variables or constants and edges represent dependence relations between propositions. If a proposition represented by node p 'causes' or implies the proposition represented by node q, we draw a directed edge from p to q. The node q contains a matrix (a link matrix) that specifies $P(p|q)$ for all possible values of the two variables. When a node has multiple parents, the matrix specifies the dependence of that node on the set of parents and characterizes the dependence relationship between that node and all nodes representing its potential causes. Given a set of prior probabilities for the roots of the directed acyclic dependency graph, these networks can be used to compute the probability or degree of belief associated with all remaining nodes.

2.4   Information retrieval using neural models

[Rose and Belew 1991] argue that any common law legal domain is inherently symbolic. However, they also argue that the legal system can be viewed as connectionist, with legal decisions being unable to be captured by rules. They thus developed a hybrid system SCALIR (Symbolic and Connectionist Approach to Legal Information Retrieval) best described in [Rose 1993]. SCALIR uses the connectionist approach to automate the conceptual structure of a domain.

Three types of nodes are included in a SCALIR network corresponding to terms, cases and statute sections. The nodes are interconnected with two types of links: S-links and C-links. S-links represent symbolic or structural relationships between nodes such as Case A overturned Case B. C-links represent co-occurrence association betweens nodes.

A SCALIR network is constructed by presenting a new case or statute to the network. Terms within the document that do not yet exist in the network are inserted and a weights between other nodes and the new term are calculated using term frequency metrics to form C-links. S-links are inserted manually using world knowledge about the new document.

A user query, generally in the form of a list of terms, 'activates' equivalent terms in the network. These terms spread their activation along C-links and S-links to other nodes that in turn spread activation to other nodes. Once all activation has propagated through the network, nodes that remain most active are those most relevant to the query.

SCALIR represented an innovative architecture for combining machine learning with symbolic reasoning. Although the indexing of a new document required a manual component the approach was clearly scalable to large document repositories.

2.5   Information retrieval using support vector machines

[Al-Kofahi et al 2001] view the task of retrieving similar cases as complex and must be achieved with the integration of more than one method. They used a large dataset of seven million cases and performed similarity matching by invoking a support vector machine trained with over 2000 cases. The support vector machine integrated similarity predictions based on a number of measures. Similarity based on title matching, calculated using optimisation theories from mathematical programming was one measure. Another measure estimated the probability that a example case in a Court A, would have a precedent in another court. The support vector machine was trained using a linear kernel and positive instances were weighted five times more strongly than negative cases. Results demonstrate that recall rates were comparable with those for humans and while precision was not quite at that level, it was sufficiently high to warrant the development.

The distinction between information retrieval and text mining is not definitive. We loosely label information retrieval endeavours that aim to extract, summarise, categorise or cluster text as text mining exercises and describe examples of each category in law in the next section.

3. TEXT MINING IN LAW

Most examples of text mining in law involve information extraction, text categorisation, text clustering or text summarisation. We now discuss each of these four types of text mining and give examples from the legal domain.

3.1 Information extraction

Information extraction involves the automated identification of concepts from text. Two studies are overviewed to illustrate these methods. The first, Smile by [Bruninghaus and Ashley 2001] extracts case factors for case based reasoning. The second, SPIRE locates relevant passages from a judgement.

3.1.1 Smile: Information extraction for case based reasoning

[Bruninghaus and Ashley 2001] present an approach for automatically extracting factors for use in case based reasoning from the text of cases. Indexing of cases to extract factors relevant for case based reasoning is a particularly time consuming manual process. Case based reasoning would, in all likelihood be far more prevalent than it currently is if relevant factors could automatically be extracted from case documents.

In Smile, [Bruninghaus and Ashley 2001] assembled a training set of case summaries from the field of trade secrets law. Sentences in the summaries were marked up as positive instances or negative instances of a factor. A decision tree was then induced using ID3, which could classify whether a sentence was an instance of a factor. This approach, inspired by the method of Support Vector Machines, led to promising if not impressive results. Improvements were advanced based on using natural language parsing to abstract the role performed by key players who were mentioned in the summaries.

3.1.2 SPIRE

The SPIRE system [Daniels and Rissland 1997] was also motivated by the recognition that information extraction methods could lead to a greater use of case based reasoning. SPIRE includes two phases. In the first phase, a case based reasoner is integrated with an information retrieval engine. The case base reasoning system retrieves a very small number of the most on-point cases for the query case. The text of these on-point cases is used as input for the information retrieval. The process of using one method to determine a set of relevant documents that are used as input into another system is known as relevance feedback. The information retrieval engine returns documents that are similar to the fact situation initially entered as the query.

In the second phase, SPIRE gathers excerpts of texts that have been used in past cases to refer to concepts. For example, the phrase 'just over 25 monthly payments' was used in the past cases in relation to a *duration* factor. The location of a passage within a document is performed in a similar way to the location of a document within a collection, by using the text excerpts as query strings.

3.1.3 *Text mining to construct a database of expert witnesses*

[Dozier *et al* 2003] describes how an online directory of expert witnesses was created from jury verdict and settlement documents using text-mining techniques. The authors created an expert witness directory that contains over 100,000 expert profiles, based on approximately 300,000 jury verdict and settlement documents, publicly available professional license information, an expertise taxonomy, and automatic text mining techniques. This directory can be browsed by area of expertise as well as by location and name. In addition, expert profiles were automatically linked to medline articles and jury verdict and settlement documents. The supporting technologies that made this application possible include information extraction from text via regular expression parsing, record linkage through Bayesian based matching, and automatic rule-based classification.

The authors claim that this is the largest expert witness directory of its kind and the first built using automatic text mining techniques. They claim that the application demonstrates how information from disparate sources can be extracted, merged, and organised into a new information resource that is, in some sense, more than the sum of its parts. By collecting and merging expert witness information from a variety of sources, normalising the information, organising and categorising the information, the application has placed expert witnesses within a context that did not previously exist.

3.1.4 *Flexlaw*

Flexlaw [Smith *et al* 1995] used a Vector Space Model for matching. It automatically constructed structured representations from text. Cases and other legal documents are represented by document profiles that preserve the meaning of legal text and contain all the information necessary and sufficient to match documents with a user's query.

In addition to improving legal text indexing and query formulation, the Flexlaw knowledge representation is a documentation tool that automatically generates case headnotes (flexnotes). A flexnote consists of case header information, a classification of the subjects of law being used and a listing of these items. [Gelbart and Smith 1993] contrasted Flexlaw with other information retrieval models: a) the Boolean model; and b) probabilistic models. They performed tests on 1,000 British Columbia (Canada) cases dealing with economic loss. Their conclusions were:

a)   Flexlaw is superior to Boolean search in terms of the knowledge structuring, the user interface, the retrieval effectiveness and the ranking of relevant documents;

b)   Flexlaw, though based on the vector space model, is superior to the SMART implementation of the model in incorporating intelligent structuring of both documents and queries; and

c)   Flexlaw and the inference network model intelligently incorporate structure in the document and query representations offer elegant and easy-to-use interfaces, allow the incorporation of multiple information sources such as thesauri and produce a ranked list of relevant cases.

3.2   Text categorisation

Text categorisation organises documents into a taxonomy, thus allowing for more efficient searches. It involves the assignment of subject descriptors or classification codes to complete texts. Compared to other texts, legal texts are often very complex and text categorisation often involves the assignment of abstract concepts.   The terms of the concepts do not always occur in the texts and might be expressed in a large variety of phrasal expressions. Translating factual descriptions into abstract concepts is very difficult because of the many variant expressions of a concept and their formulations in natural language. Text categorisation has to cope with a large and poorly defined feature set and an often low density of positive training examples [Moens 2001]. .

[Thompson 2001] compared three data mining algorithms in a machine learning exercise to categorise cases use 40 subject descriptors such as bankruptcy, military law, and Tort law:

a)   K[th]-nearest neighbour algorithm[57];

b)   Ripper a rule induction algorithm that avoids decision tree induction [Cohen and Singer 1999]; and

---

[57] Described in chapter six.

c)   C4.5[58].

Results indicated that the Ripper algorithm out-performed k-nn or C.5 on measures of precision and recall.

This study was performed as an example of supervised learning. The training set was classified by exposure to the C4.5 and Ripper rule induction algorithms. In the next section, we survey text clustering approaches, which cluster or group cases in an unsupervised manner.

3.3   Text clustering

As [Moens 2001] notes, a major group of techniques that involves unsupervised learning is the clustering of objects that share common features. Cluster analysis is a multivariate statistical technique that automatically generates groups into data [Kaufmann and Rousseeuw 1990]. Non-hierarchical methods partition a set of objects into clusters of similar objects. Hierarchical methods construct a tree-like hierarchy of objects with the root representing a cluster containing all the objects, the leaves representing the individual objects and the nodes containing the intermediate groupings. The technique of clustering supposes:

- An abstract representation of the object to be clustered, containing the features for the classification;
- A function that computes the relative importance (weight) of the features; and
- A function that computes a numerical similarity between the representations.

Clustering is employed to group terms that regularly co-occur in documents or to group documents if they discuss the same topic terms. A form of neural network, known as self organising maps (SOM), have been successfully applied to text clustering. We discuss SOM in the next section.

3.3.1   Text clustering with self organising maps

[Kohonen 1982] first introduced Self Organizing Maps (SOM) or Kohonen networks. The basic SOM architecture consists of two layers of nodes as illustrated in Figure 1.

---

[58] Described in chapter five

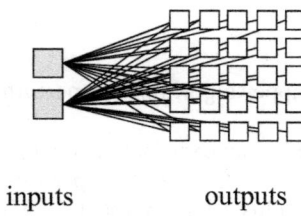

inputs   outputs

Figure 1. Basic Self Organising Map architecture

Each input is connected to every output node. A randomly assigned weight is associated with each connection. The inputs nodes represent feature values that distinguish one example from another.

The data miner sets the size of the SOM output grid. The SOM in Figure 1 contains 25 nodes in a 5 * 5 configuration. There is no systematic way to determining the optimal size of an output grid. Trial runs with grids of varying sizes are generally performed until an appropriate configuration is adopted.

During training, feature vectors are presented to the SOM. Figure 2 illustrates the presentation of a first example that has values [5,5]. Those values represent activation that flows forward along each connection and are attenuated by the weight associated with each connection. The weights are initially set randomly. Each output node receives slightly different activation because the weights are initially different. One of the output nodes received the greatest activation and is called the 'winner'. The weights between the input and the winner are increased so as to ensure the same node is the winner if the same input is presented again. Weights to nodes near the winner are also increased with the use of a *neighbourhood function* illustrated in Figure 3.

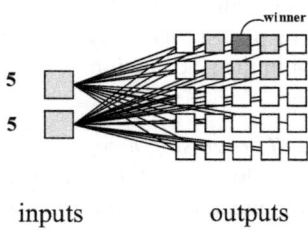

inputs   outputs

Figure 2. Presentation of an example to a SOM

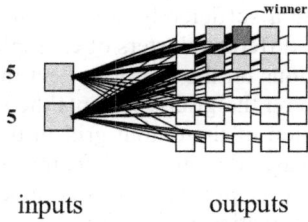

inputs   outputs

Figure 3. Weights strengthened after first example

Figure 4 illustrates the presentation of the second example.

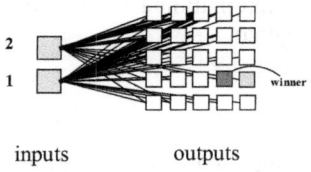

inputs   outputs

Figure 4. Presentation of second example

Figure 4 illustrates that a different node emerges upon presentation of quite different inputs. The weights between that winner and the inputs are strengthened. Figure 5 illustrates the presentation of an input that is more similar to the first instance than the second instance.

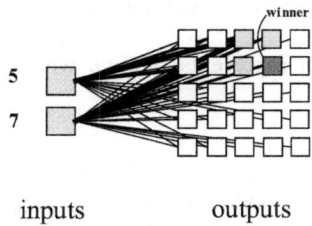

inputs   outputs

Figure 5. Presentation of a third example to SOM

The winning node in Figure 5 is closer to the winning node after presentation of the first example than the second example because the example [5,7] is more similar to [5,5] than it is to [2,1].

After repeated exposure to a sufficiently large number of cases, different areas on the output grid will reflect different clusters of examples. Manual examination is required in order to label regions on the grid to reflect the meaning of each cluster. The distance between regions on the grid represents the similarity between clusters. For example, the top left region of the output grid in the [Merkl and Schwighofer 1997] study corresponded to cases that involved chemical weapons and was labelled 'arms control'. The bottom centre region was labelled 'Human rights' and corresponded to documents on treaties and torture.

[Merkl and Schwighofer 1997] applied a hierarchical variation to the standard SOM. [Miikkulainen 1993] introduced a hierarchical self organising map where the output grid is used as an input grid to another SOM and that output is used as input to yet another SOM. This has benefits in that the higher-level grids represent more abstract clusters. More pragmatically, training time is substantially reduced. For example, the top level grid in the [Merkl and Schwighofer 1997] study discovered four key clusters in public international law: humanitarian law, human rights, environment law and other matters.

3.4   Text Summarisation

Text summarisation involves identifying, summarising and organising related text so that users can efficiently deal with information in large documents. [Sparck Jones 1993] states that text summarisation consists of three steps:

- The text analysis step identifies the essential content of the source text resulting in a source text representation;
- In the transformation step the content of the source text is condensed either by selection or generalisation of what is important in the source. The selected and generalised information is captured in a summary representation; and
- The synthesis step involves drafting and generation of the summary text based upon the summary representation.

The SALOMON project represents seminal work in text summarisation and is discussed next.

3.4.1   The Salomon Project

The SALOMON project [Moens 2000] automatically summarised Belgian criminal cases in order to improve access to the large number of existing and future court decisions. SALOMON extracts relevant text units from the case text to form a case summary. Such a case profile facilitated the rapid determination of the relevance of the case to be employed in text search. Techniques were developed for identifying and extracting relevant information from the cases.

A double methodology was used when developing SALOMON. First, the case category, the case structure and relevant text units were identified based on a knowledge base represented as a text grammar. Consequently, general data and legal foundations concerning the essence of the case were extracted. Secondly, SALOMON extracted informative text units of the alleged offences and of the opinion of the court based on shallow statistical techniques. The application of cluster algorithms based on the selection of representative objects has the potential for automatic theme recognition, text abstracting and text linking, even beyond the legal field.

A major part of the SALOMON research concerns automatic abstracting of text. Document abstracts generated automatically generally belong to two types [Sparck Jones, 1993]. Firstly, the abstract is constructed for easy and fast determination of relevance: it indicates whether the complete text version is of interest (indicative abstract). Secondly, the abstract is a document surrogate expressing the main contents of the document: its components may be used for text search and linking (informative abstract). In this way abstracting is related to indexing. A brief summary may serve as a complex structured index description.

The automatic generation of document abstracts has early been recognised as a potential area for automation [Luhn 1958]. At that time automatic text abstracting and indexing were strongly related. Attempts have been made to extract words, phrases, or sentences that reflect the content of the text. Index terms are weighted depending upon the occurrence in titles and headings [Salton 1989] or upon occurrence frequencies in the text and/or text corpus [Salton and Buckley 1988]. Sentence scores are based on the number of significant and non significant words in it [Luhn 1958], on location heuristics [Baxendale 1958], or on the occurrence of positive or negative indicator phrases [Edmundson 1969], or are computed as the sum of term weights after eliminating stop words [Earl, 1970]. Sentences, the score of which surpasses a certain threshold value, are retained for summary purposes.

[Moens *et al* 1997] note that until recently, automatic abstracting has received little attention, apart from the application of artificial intelligence techniques in restricted text domains. With the current information overload, automation of text summarisation receives renewed interest. An example of the automatic generation of case summaries in the legal field and their use for information retrieval is FLEXICON (Fast Legal Expert Information CONsultant) [Gelbart and Smith, 1993]. FLEXICON extracts relevant text units based on location heuristics, occurrence frequencies of index terms, and the use of indicator phrases.

3.4.2 *Other applications of summarisation in law*

[Grover *et al* 2003] report on the sum project that applies automatic summarisation techniques to the legal domain. In their methodology, sentences from text are classified according to their rhetorical role in order that particular types of sentence can be extracted to form a summary. They describe some experiments with judgements of the House of Lords. They have performed automatic linguistic annotation of a small sample set and then hand-annotated the sentences in the set in order to explore the relationship between linguistic features and argumentative roles.

They use state-of-the-art natural language processing techniques to perform the linguistic annotation using XML-based tools and a combination of rule-based and statistical methods. They focus on the predictive capacity of tense and aspect features for a classifier.

[Farzindar and Lapalme 2004] describe a method for the summarization of legal documents helping a legal expert determine the key ideas of a judgment. Their approach is based on the exploration of the document's architecture and its thematic structures in order to build a table style summary for improving coherency and readability of the text. They present the components of a system, called LetSum, built with this approach, its implementation and some preliminary evaluation results.

They are exploring methods for generating flexible summaries of legal documents, taking as their point of departure the [Teufel and Moens 2002] approach to automatic summarisation. They are working with law reports for three main reasons:

i. The existence of manual summaries means that they have available to them evaluation material for the final summarization system;

ii. The existence of differing target audiences allows them to explore the issue of tailored summaries; and

iii. the texts have much in common with the academic papers that Teufel and Moens worked with, while remaining challengingly different in many respects.

The goals of [Farzindar and Lapalme 2004] are similar to those of the SALOMON project [Moens et al 1997], which also deals with summarisation of legal text. However, their choice of methodology is designed to test the portability of the Teufel and Moens approach to a new domain.

[Farzindar and Lapalme 2004] considered the processing of previous legal decisions and their summaries because a court order generally gives a solution to a legal problem between two or more parties. The decision also contains the reasons that justify the solution and constitute a law jurisprudence precedent from which it is possible to extract legal rules that can be applied to similar cases. To find a solution to a legal problem not directly indicated in the law, lawyers look for precedents of similar cases. For a single query in a database of law reports, one often receives hundreds of documents. Hence, legal professionals require summaries.

In Quebec REJB (R´epertoire ´electronique de jurisprudence du Barreau) and SOQUIJ (Societe quebecoise d'information juridique) are two organizations that provide manual summaries for legal resources, but these services very expensive. For example the price of only one summary with its full text, provided by SOQUIJ is $C7.50. Some legal information systems have been developed by private companies such as QuickLaw in Canada and WESTLAW and LEXIS in the United States, however no existing system completely satisfies the specific requirements of this field.

One reason for the difficulty of this work is the complexity of the domain: specific vocabularies of the legal domain and legal interpretations of expressions produce many ambiguities. For legal judgments, [Farzindar and Lapalme 2004] identify discursive structures for the different parts of the decision and assign some argumentative roles to them. The processing of a legal document requires detailed attention and it is not straight-forward to adapt the techniques developed for other types of document to the legal domain.

Their corpus contains 3500 judgments of the Federal Court of Canada, which are available in HTML at http://www.canlii.org/ca/cas/fct/. They manually analysed fifty judgments in English and fifteen judgments in French as well as their summaries written by professional legal abstractors. The average size of the documents that are input to their system are judgments between 500 and 4000 words long (two to eight pages), which form 80% of all 3500 judgments; 10% of the documents having less than 500 words (about one page) and so they do not require a summary. Only 10% of the decisions have more than 4000 words.

4. WEB MINING

A very significant extension of text mining is web mining, which integrates data mining and text mining within a web site. As [Han and Kamber 2001] state the World Wide Web serves as a huge, distributed global information centre. It contains a rich and dynamic collection of hyperlink information and access and usage information that provides rich sources for data mining. Web mining involves Web link structures to identify authoritative Web pages, the automatic classification of Web documents, building a multilayered web information base and Weblog mining.

[Chen 2003] claims that the term Web mining was coined by [Etzioni 1996] to denote the use of data mining techniques to automatically discover and extract information from Web documents and services. Web mining research can be classified into three categories: Web content mining, Web structure mining, and Web usage mining [Kosala and Blockeel, 2000].

Web content mining refers to the discovery of useful information from Web contents, including text, image, audio and video. Web content mining research includes resource discovery from the Web, document categorisation and clustering and information extraction from Web pages.

Web structure mining studies the model underlying the link structures of the Web. It usually involves the analysis of in-links and out-links information of a Web page, and has been used for search engine result ranking and other Web applications.

Web usage mining focuses on analysing search logs or other activity logs (in a way similar to data mining) to find interesting patterns. One of the main applications of Web usage mining is to learn user profiles. There are a few major differences between Web retrieval and traditional Information Retrieval. First, most Web documents are in HTML (HyperText Markup Language) format. nHTML documents contain many markup tags, mainly used for formatting. Web mining applications must parse the HTML documents to remove these markup tags. But the tags also can provide additional information about the document.

Second, while traditional Information Retrieval systems often contain structured and well-written documents, this is not the case on the Web. Web documents are much more diverse in terms of length, document structure, writing style, and many Web pages contain grammatical and spelling errors. Web pages are also very diverse in terms of languages and domains; one can find almost any language and any topic on the Web. In addition, the Web has many different types of content, including text, images, audios, videos, and executables. There are numerous formats, such as HTML, XML, PDF, MS Word, mp3, wav, ra, rm, avi. Web applications have to deal with these different formats and retrieve the desired information.

Third, while most documents in traditional Information Retrieval systems tend to remain static over time, Web pages are much more dynamic; they can be updated every day, every hour or even every minute. Some Web pages do not even have a static form; they are dynamically generated on request, with content varying according to the user and the time of the request. Such dynamics make it much more difficult for retrieval systems such as search engines to keep an up-to-date search index of the Web.

Another characteristic of the Web, perhaps the most important one, is its hyperlink structure. Web pages are hyperlinked to each other, and it is through hyperlink that a Web page author 'cites' other Web pages. Intuitively, the author of a Web page places a link to another Web page if he or she believes that it contains a relevant topic or is of good quality. Anchor text, the underlined, clickable text of an outgoing link in a Web page, also provides a good description of the target page, because it represents how other people linking to the page actually describe it.

Lastly, the size of the Web is larger, by several orders of magnitude, than traditional Information Retrieval collections. Collecting, indexing, and analysing these documents presents a great challenge. Similarly, the population of Web users is much larger than that of traditional Information Retrieval systems. Collaboration among users can be more feasible because of the availability of a large user base, but it can also be more difficult because users are more diverse.

5. CHAPTER SUMMARY

A theme running through this book is that information in the legal domain is most often stored as text in relatively unstructured forms, as opposed to structured databases. As a consequence information retrieval techniques and text mining has progressed further in the legal domain than other forms of data mining. In this chapter we provided an overview of information retrieval methods and briefly survey some of advances in text mining in law. Text mining includes the topics of information extraction, text summarisation, text categorisation and text clustering. Information extraction involves the automated extraction of concepts from text. Examples include the extraction of expert witnesses from judgements by [Dozier *et al* 2003], and the automated identification of case factors from judgements by [Bruninghaus and Ashley 2001].

Text summarisation involves the automated generation of a summary of a case. A leading example of this approach can be found in the SALOMON project described in [Moens 2000]. [Grover *et al* 2003] use rhetorical patterns to summarise judgements in the House of Lords. [Farzindar and Lapalme 2004] illustrate a summarisation method that is based on the structure of a document and themes contained within it.

Text clustering involves automatically assigning cases to groups where each case within a group shares common elements that distinguish the group from others.

[Merkl and Schwighofer 1997] apply neural networks known as self organising maps for clustering cases in the European Parliament.

Text categorisation involves organizes documents into a taxonomy, thus allowing for more efficient searches.   The Flexlaw system [Smith *et al* 1995] automatically constructs structured representations from text by assigning subject descriptors or classification codes or abstract concepts to complete texts.

All text mining approaches involve information retrieval methods.   Information retrieval engines have proven to be so effective that prospects of uploading all judgement to the internet for global access has become a reality.   The legal movement initiated by the Australasian Legal Information Institute (AustLII) was discussed.   This movement provides free access to significant amounts of legal material.   As this movement gathers momentum and encompasses more and more jurisdictions, the prospect for text mining enormous collections becomes significant.

Innovations in information retrieval methods that do not readily fit into one of the categories of text mining were also discussed. These include approaches by [Yearwood 1997] that take document structure into account, by [Hoeschl *et al* 2001] that take advantage of domain knowledge to improve precision and recall. Extensions using neural networks by [Rose and Belew 1991] and with Bayesian belief networks described at [Westlaw 2004].

We have now concluded our study of when and how to employ knowledge discovery from legal databases. But we have not discussed whethe4r the knowledge discovered is in any way significant or useful. In the next chapter, issues relating the evaluation and deployment of knowledge discovered by data mining is discussed.

CHAPTER 9

EVALUATION, DEPLOYMENT AND RELATED ISSUES

Now that we have completed the task of data-mining, we need to ask ourselves the question '*what do the results of the data-mining task signify?*' If the results are to indicate something more than mere data dredging, then we must provide some justification for our evidence. In this chapter we shall discuss evaluation as a means of justifying the results obtained through statistical endeavours.

Outside the legal domain, the evaluation of models derived with the use of a data-mining technique is often restricted to the measurement of the generalisation performance; the extent to which the model is accurate on examples not in the dataset. Methods for estimating the generalisation performance are illustrated in Section 1. However, the evaluation of a model that derives from legal data-mining is required to be broader than generalisation performance alone. Frameworks for the evaluation of knowledge in law are discussed in Section 2.

1. GENERALISATION

Rules, neural networks or other data-mining techniques learn patterns or weights from a dataset. The extent, to which the discovered knowledge is applicable to data not in the dataset, is unknown. A neural network for example, may accurately predict every case in the dataset; yet fail on every future case. A data-mining method that describes or classifies the dataset very well but does not do so well on cases not in the dataset is said to have over-fit the data. An illustration of over-fitting is provided in Figure 1. Line A and Line B represent two neural networks trained on the dataset represented as black dots. Network B has over-fitted the data. It performs very well with examples from the dataset, but does not do so well with those not in the dataset. In contrast, Network A performs less accurately with the dataset examples, but is more accurate over all cases.

As [Hand *et al* 2001] state: when performing data mining it is necessary to avoid models or patterns which match the database too closely, given that the available data set is merely one set from the sets of data that could have arisen. One does not want to model idiosyncrasies too closely. It is necessary to avoid over-fitting the given data set; instead one wants to find models or patterns that generalise well to potential future data.

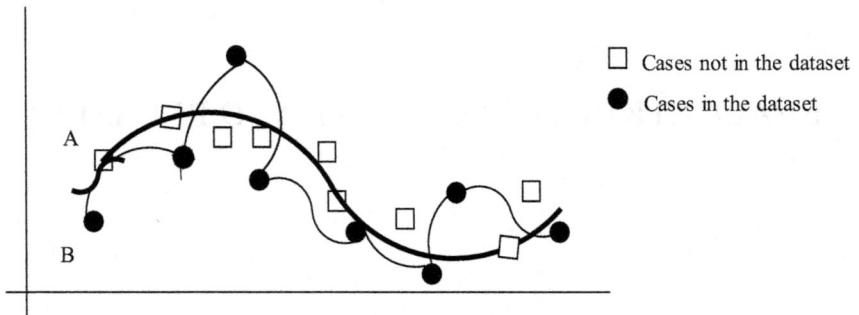

Figure 1. Over-fitting example

Part of the KDD exercise should be to specify the total set of cases to which our developed model should apply. For example, the Split Up data was collected from unreported property cases, decided between 1992 and 1994, in the Melbourne registry of the Family Court of Australia. Neural networks trained with data from these cases are expected to predict other unreported property cases heard in the Melbourne registry during the same years. However, family law specialists were guarded about the extent to which the networks could predict cases heard in the Brisbane registry. In fact, during a demonstration of the Split Up system in Brisbane, remarks were made that the system reasoned like a 'Melbourne' judge.

Requests to use Split Up to predict family law property distribution case outcomes in South African, Canadian and British jurisdictions were met with extreme caution, because the population of cases Split Up was intended to apply never included cases outside the Australian jurisdiction.

Nevertheless, it is interesting to recount one interesting encounter about the 'unwise use' of the Split Up system. On Tuesday July 3 1996, a reporter from the London Daily Telegraph phoned Professor Zeleznikow to enquire about the operation of the Split Up system. A story was to appear in the Information Technology pages of a future edition of the paper. A few hours later the reporter phoned back to say he wanted to run the system on a *prototypical* case: the property split arising from the divorce of Prince Charles and Princess Dianne. Professor Zeleznikow indicated a number of qualms about running Split Up on this case:

1)   The divorce proceedings were not being carried out under Australian family law;
2)   The specific common pool of the couple was unknown; and
3)   The case was not a commonplace case.

Nevertheless, the journalist insisted that he would like to run the system on the case of Charles and Dianne. Split Up classified Princess Dianne as a single mother who had lost her job. As such, she had much greater future needs than Prince Charles, and hence it was suggested that she would receive 70% of the common pool[59]. The next morning, Wednesday July 4 1996, the lead story in the London Daily Telegraph *was Ozzie computer kind to Princess Di.* This was certainly an inappropriate use of Split Up.

The specification of the entire population of cases the Split Up model applies to is:

- *Jurisdiction.* Family Court cases decided in the Melbourne registry. This registry covers cases from Victoria and Tasmania.
- *Type of case.* Commonplace cases that involved disputes solely about property issues. In chapter two we discussed the difference between landmark and commonplace cases and reasons why landmark cases are generally not ideal for KDD exercises.
- *Time window.* Clearly, a model trained with cases over a narrow two-year time period cannot be expected to apply indefinitely into the future. This is particularly the case in discretionary fields of law, because the way in which factors are weighted and combined can be expected to change over time, even in the absence of changes to statutes or precedents. As time goes by, Split Up predictions become less accurate. Currently, the Split-Up tree of arguments is being modified, and new cases included in the training set, in conjunction with domain experts from Victoria Legal Aid, to accommodate recent changes in legislation and practice – in particular:
  - o The recent tendency by Family Court judges to view domestic violence as a negative financial contribution to a marriage;
  - o The re-introduction of spousal maintenance as a benefit to one of the partners. Under the *clean-break* philosophy, judges of the Family Court of Australia were reluctant to award spousal maintenance, since it would mean one partner would continue to be financially dependent on his/her ex-partner. However the increasing number of short, asset-poor, income-rich marriages has led to a re-consideration of the issue of spousal maintenance;
  - o The need to consider superannuation and pensions separately from other marital property.

The degree to which the knowledge discovered generalises from the dataset to the entire specified population can be estimated by re-sampling. There are five main re-sampling methods typically used:

a) Re-substitution,
b) Hold out,
c) Leave one out,
d) Cross validation, and
e) Bootstrapping.

---

[59] The journalist had estimated the value of the common pool.

174

All five re-sampling methods split the dataset into a training set and a test set. Typically, the data-mining is performed with the training set and once completed, is evaluated by measuring the accuracy on the test set. The test set therefore represents the entire population of cases. Each re-sampling method is discussed below. [Weiss and Kulikowski 1992] provides a more detailed discussion.

1.1 Re-substitution

Re-substitution is the simplest re-sampling technique to implement and understand. Re-substitution involves using the entire dataset as the training set and the test set. This is illustrated in Figure 2. Re-substitution is a poor estimate of generalisation performance, because all cases used in the testing have contributed to the data-mining. Generalisation performance depends very heavily on the extent to which the dataset is a representative sample of the entire population. If the data set is quite representative, re-substitution provides good estimates. The method is the simplest re-sampling method to implement and is often used to provide early rough estimates of performance. The hold out technique is more rigorous than re-substitution.

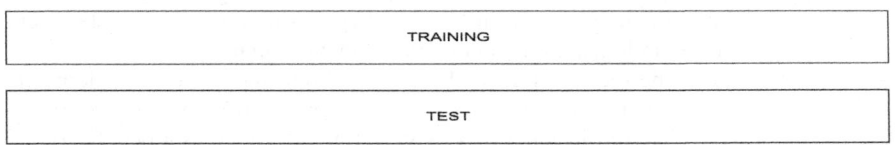

Figure 2. Representation of Re-substitution

1.2 Hold Out

The hold out technique, illustrated in Figure 3, estimates generalisation performance better than re-substitution, because a part of the test set is held out from the training process. Data-mining is performed with the training set and generalisation performance is estimated with the use of the test set. Typically about one-third of the cases, randomly selected from the data-set, are held out for testing.

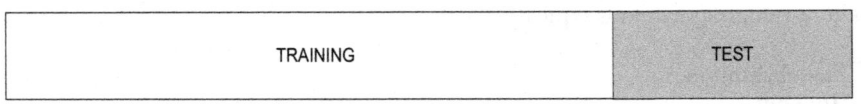

Figure 3. Representation of Hold-out

The hold-out method estimates generalisation better than re-substitution because the test set represents a sample of the population of cases. Table 1 displays results of four hypothetical instances of data mining validated with Hold-Out.

Table 1. Data mining with Hold-out

% of training examples correctly predicted	% of test examples correctly predicted	Analysis of the data mining
95	20	Over-fitting very likely
50	30	Mining ineffective. Poor performance on the test is probably due to under-training or poor data
70	70	Over-fitting unlikely but, depending on the setting, a more accurate predictions is desirable
85	95	Very good result

Estimating validation with the hold-out method is limited, in that the held out set may not be representative of the entire population of cases. Cross-validation, discussed in the next section addresses this limitation.

1.3   Cross-validation

In the cross-validation method, hold-out is repeated a number of times, with a different portion of the data-set held out each time. In four fold cross validation, one quarter of the data-set is randomly selected and held out for the first data-mining exercise. The exercise is repeated with another quarter of the examples that were not included in the previous test set, held out. Four data mining exercises are performed. This process is illustrated in Figure 4. Each example is used in one of the test sets, so there is a greater likelihood that the held-out sets are representative of the entire population. The problem of selecting which model to use for subsequent predictions arises with the repetition of the data-mining phase. Table 2 depicts the hypothetical results from four neural networks trained with each of four cross-validation sets. In the future, one of the four neural networks must be selected to perform predictions.

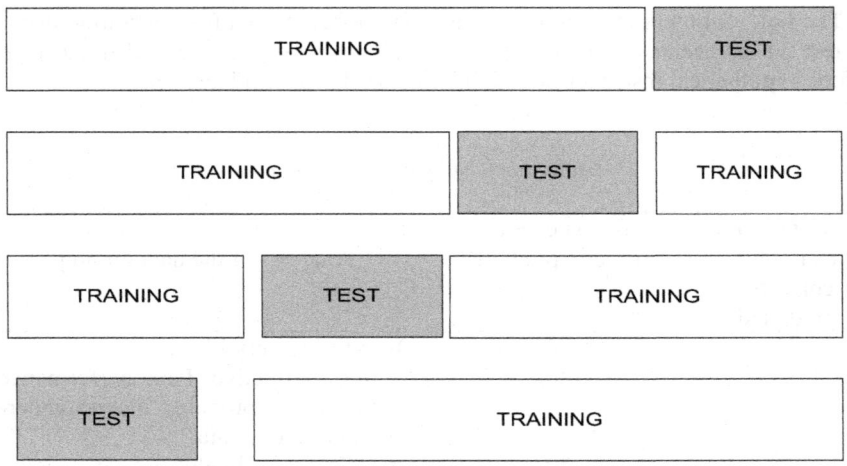

Figure 4. Representation of Cross-validation

In Figure 4, neural network C is the best network for future predictions. With a prediction accuracy of 75% on the test set, network A may not be trained as well as network C. Network B is likely to have over-fitted the data. In contrast, network D's excellent result on the test set is probably due to an aberration inherent in that test set. Overall, network C is the preferred choice for future predictions. Reporting the generalisation performance of network C as the estimate for the entire population may be too optimistic. A better estimate for the performance of network C is calculated as the average of all four cross-validation sets.

Table 2. Cross-validation performance

Neural network	Percentage of training examples correctly predicted	Percentage of test examples correctly predicted	Analysis of the data mining
A	75	70	Over-fitting unlikely but better predictions are possible
B	85	65	Probable over-fitting
C	80	90	Good result
D	70	98	Excellent result on the test set probably indicative of an unrepresentative test set.

Ten fold cross-validation is commonly used. The most effective form of cross –
validation involves holding out only one example as a test set and performing (n-1)
data-mining exercises. This is known as *Leave one out*. Leave one out involves
considerable effort in performing many data-mining exercises. However the
generalisation estimate in Leave one out is very accurate. Only bootstrapping is
more accurate. However bootstrapping requires even more effort and resources.

1.4   Bootstrapping

The bootstrapping re-sampling method was first described by [Efron 1983].
[Efron and Tibshirani 1993] explain the method and the variant most often used in
data mining, the 632 Bootstrap. In the 632 bootstrap illustrated in Figure 5, a data-
mining model is developed with the original dataset and tested by re-substitution.
Let us call the error rate on the test rate.
A training set is then constructed by drawing examples from the dataset, with
replacement until as many examples exist in the training set as there are in the data
set. Drawing with replacement means that some examples will be drawn more than
once, while others will not be drawn at all. Figure 5 illustrates that examples
13,4,8,12 and 2 were not selected at all whereas example 1 was selected three times,
and examples 7, 10 and 3 were selected twice. Those examples that were not
selected form the test set. This process is repeated between 50 and 2000 times, so
that between 50 and 2000 data-mining models can be developed. The error estimate
is calculated using Equation 1:

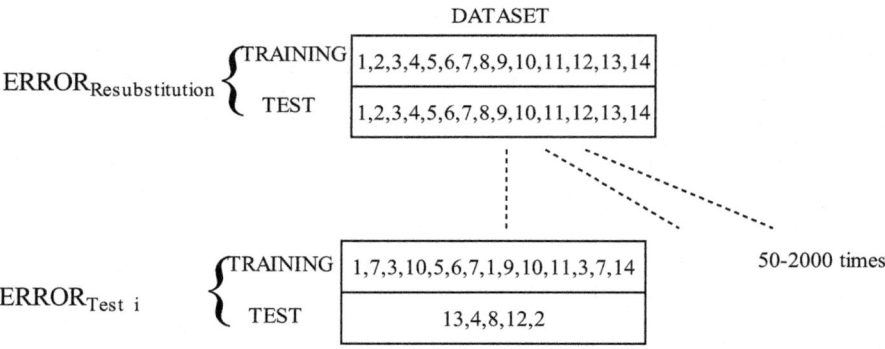

Figure 5. Bootstrapping

[Barai and Reich 1999] generated a data-set as an entire population. They drew
a sample for data-mining in such a way that the true error was known. They then
estimated the generalisation error by using each of the re-sampling methods
discussed above. The horizontal axis in Figure 6 illustrates the true error.
Numerous trials using re-substitution revealed a large range of estimates. Most trials
underestimated the true error. The bootstrap method estimated the true error most

178

accurately, followed by leave one out, five fold cross-validation and hold-out respectively. Using bootstrap or leave-one-out is difficult in practice, because these methods require that the data-mining exercise be repeated hundreds of times. This can be automated to some extent, but still represents a considerable outlay of resources.

Equation 1

$$Error_g = \sum_{i=1}^{n} (Error_i * 0.632 + Error_r * 0.368)/n$$

where :
Error$_g$ is the generalisation performance on the population
Error$_i$ is the error on the test set of the ith model
Error$_r$ is the re-substitution error on the test set trained with original dataset.

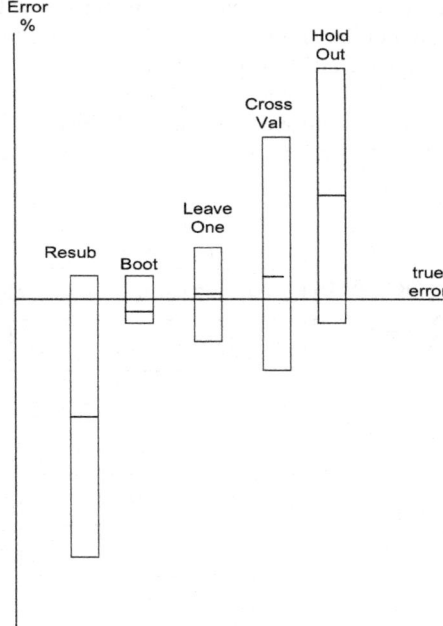

Figure 6. Comparison of re-sampling techniques

[Quinlan 1996] notes that designers of empirical machine learning systems are concerned with such issues as the computational cost of the learning method and the accuracy and intelligibility of the theories that it constructs. Much of the research in learning has tended to focus on improved predictive accuracy, so that the performance of new systems is often reported from this perspective. This emphasis is understandable - accuracy is a primary concern in all applications of learning and is easily measured (as opposed to intelligence, which is more subjective), while the rapid increase in the performance/cost ratio of computers has reduced the emphasis on computational issues.

In chapter five, we noted that pruning could be applied to decision tree induction to help improve the accuracy of the resulting decision trees. Bagging and boosting are recent methods for improving the predictive power of classifier learning systems. Both form a set of classifiers that are combined by voting: bagging by generating replicated bootstrap samples of the data, and boosting by adjusting the weights of training instances. Both bagging and boosting manipulate the training data in order to generate different classifiers. Both approaches are discussed in the next section.

2. BOOSTING AND BAGGING

Boosting had its origins in PAC (Probably Approximately Correct) learning. [Kearns and Valiant 1994] proved that when sufficient data is available, a set of learners, each performing only slightly better than random, can be combined to form an arbitrarily good ensemble hypothesis. [Schapire 1990] provided a polynomial time boosting algorithm. [Freund 1991] improved on this algorithm, while [Freund and Schapire 1995] solved many practical difficulties of earlier approaches with the introduction of the AdaBoost algorithm.

The intuition underpinning boosting can be can be illustrated with the following example. Suppose a novice lawyer, exposed to a sample of cases, learns to predict, somewhat inaccurately, outcomes from a sample of cases. Another lawyer is then asked to perform the prediction on another set of cases, although there may be some cases common to both sets. Two issues must be dealt with in order to improve the lawyers' collective predictive performance; how to select cases for each training session and how to combine the predictions from each lawyer.

The AdaBoost algorithm selects cases for each new training session by including a greater percentage of cases that were misclassified in earlier sessions. This is equivalent to gradually exposing each lawyer to more cases that are difficult to predict. The AdaBoost algorithm deals with the problem of how to combine the predictions from more than one lawyer by assigning each lawyer's opinion a weight proportional to the number of errors made and summing the total weight for each opinion. Boosting occurs if weights can be assigned to each lawyer's opinion. The decision advocated to the client is then a combination of the weighted opinions.

[Meir and Ratsch 2003] state that the underlying idea of boosting is to combine simple rules to form an ensemble such that the performance of the single ensemble member is improved or boosted. [Quinlan 1996] reports results of applying boosting and bagging to a system that learns decision trees and testing the results on a representative collection of datasets. While both approaches substantially improve predictive accuracy, boosting shows the greater benefit. On the other hand, boosting also produces severe degradation on some datasets. A small change to the way that boosting combines the votes of learned classifiers reduces this downside and also leads to slightly better results on most of the datasets considered. Bagging, discussed next is another approach that aims to improve the performance of a classifier.

Bagging [Breiman 1996] produces replicate training sets by sampling with replacement from the training instances. In bagging and in boosting, the multiple classifiers are generated and then combined by voting to form a composite classifier. In bagging, each component classifier has the same vote, while boosting assigns different voting strengths to component classifiers on the basis of their accuracy.

Bagging and boosting improve the predictive accuracy of a classifier without introducing over-fitting appreciably. However, data mining models are typically deployed in a real world context, often embedded in legal knowledge based systems. In a real world legal setting, criteria other than predictive accuracy become important. Frameworks for the evaluation of legal systems, particularly those developed with a data-mining model are discussed in the next section.

3. FRAMEWORKS FOR EVALUATING LEGAL KNOWLEDGE BASED SYSTEMS

As [Hall and Zeleznikow 2002] note, evaluation of human endeavour has a long proud history, from the Stone Age when stone chippers left a track record of gradually improving quality of materials and design through to the last two decades of the 20th century when the Software Engineering community invested considerable effort in the movement towards 'quality' software and established methodologies and standards for software development and evaluation.

[Chelimsky 1997], in the introduction to his book on evaluation for the 21st century, suggests that systems in any discipline should be evaluated for three main reasons: to demonstrate accountability, gain knowledge and enhance development. Evaluation is significant for both legal and computer professionals, both as individuals who build or use legal software applications and as members of the wider legal or system development communities.

Evaluation has much to offer beyond the interests of the individual developer. The Capability Maturity Model (CMM) defines a process maturity framework for software development organisations. It rates organisations where software is developed into five levels of maturity: Initial, Repeatable, Defined, Managed and Optimised. Evaluation of the software product is one work process that distinguishes an organisation operating at a higher level from one at the initial level and the CMM recognizes this as an important step along the way to an effective and scientific solution. There is much can be learned from the evaluations of both successful and less successful systems. Knowledge gained from evaluation can be used to improve the current project and warrant its suitability for use or benefit new projects. Developers should observe and report on what they are doing for the benefit of all who work in the field and any lessons learned should be shared. In the best scenario, past mistakes will be avoided and previous successes repeated [Paulk *et al* 1993].

At the first International Conference on Artificial Intelligence and Law in Boston, in 1987, Professor Richard Susskind suggested that if legal knowledge based systems were to move out of the research laboratory and into the marketplace, their evaluation was essential [Susskind 1987]. However established software evaluation methodologies are not specifically tailored to the legal domain and may be unsuitable for use by those who do not have a sufficient software engineering background. The development and evaluation of legal knowledge based systems is subject to additional challenges beyond those apparent with knowledge-based systems designed to operate in other less open domains. Legal knowledge based system specific issues concerned with knowledge acquisition; different jurisdictions, judicial discretion and the potential for significant social impact are identified below. A more detailed discussion on these issues is available in [Hall and Zeleznikow 2001] and [Hall and Zeleznikow 2002].

As discussed in chapter one and in further detail in [Zeleznikow 2000], *domain knowledge acquisition* issues in law include the possible lack of a strong consensus on the theories of jurisprudence used to develop the model of legal reasoning, the dynamic nature of the knowledge and its open texture requiring interpretation by experts who often have limited availability.

Legal principles vary between *different jurisdictions* with some giving more significance to legislation (rules) and others to precedents (cases). In certain jurisdictions law postulates a fiction of certainty [Koers *et al* 1990]. Here a judge does not have the option to decide that there is insufficient knowledge to reach a decision, or to attach a degree of probability to the correctness of a decision under the law. A decision must be made. *Judicial discretion* can also compound the problem. When there is no concept of 'one correct answer' two assessors given the same details may arrive at a different decision. Software in contrast, will arrive deterministically at a reliable and repeatable outcome given the same inputs. This presents a major difficulty when evaluating the validity of legal knowledge based system.

Finally legal knowledge based systems have a *potential for a significant social impact* both upon individuals and beyond. There is an ethical onus on the knowledge based system designer, developer and evaluator to be accountable and exercise social responsibility.

How should an evaluator of a legal knowledge based systems frame (plan) their evaluation? This is non-trivial. In the Netherlands, the VALENS tool, developed in the POWER-program, has been used to verify legal knowledge [Spreeuwenberg *et al* 2001]. Earlier work on Tessec and ExpertiSZe verified and validated the effects of Dutch Social Security Legislation including technical and environmental aspects [Svensson *et al* 1992]. Other suggestions supporting a broad based evaluation strategy can be found in the International standards or major international projects such as the European SPICE (Software Process Improvement and Capability Determination) and SCOPE (Software Assessment and Certification Program Europe).

International expert system evaluation projects include VALID and VITAL0 in Europe and EVA in the United States. Commercial methodologies, technical books and reports and the academic literature also provide information. Several frameworks have been developed, some applicable to particular domains and others general in design. Many of the newer Knowledge Based System evaluation frameworks and methodologies, extend upon those developed for conventional systems See for example. [Ginsbergand Zmud 1988], [Gregory 1991], [Jung and Min-Suk 1996], [Juristo and Morant 1998] and [Knauf et al 2000].

Many existing evaluation frameworks and methodologies lack specific legal domain content. Typically they are designed for use by evaluators or developers with software engineering expertise and contain terms, references and methods likely to be unfamiliar to the non-computer expert who finds herself charged with evaluating a legal knowledge based system. These existing resources are not all available in one well-publicised, easily accessed location and they may not cover the complete range of activities required. It is difficult for an evaluator to select bits and pieces from different locations, as these materials have partial overlapping content and differing organisation, with no 'common interface'. A common framework to order and organise such knowledge would be of value to evaluators of such systems. This framework should be designed to also assist the framing of specific evaluations. We discuss such frameworks later in this chapter.

The evaluation of all computer software, let alone knowledge discovery from legal databases, is a significant issue. We commence by discussing some early, technical solutions for evaluating legal KDD systems. We then move on to more general techniques for evaluating legal knowledge-based systems.

3.1 The Reich Evaluation Framework

[Stranieri and Zeleznikow 1999] apply an evaluation framework advanced by [Reich 1995] to the legal domain. According to [Reich 1995], the determination of appropriate criteria for a comprehensive evaluation of a knowledge-based system cannot be performed without a conceptualisation of the nature of knowledge. He claims knowledge can be defined in two ways: structurally and functionally. In the structural definition, knowledge is a static entity that includes facts, rules and models that represent real world phenomena. This definition of knowledge enables the direct measurement of knowledge.

In the functional definition, knowledge has a purpose and cannot be measured directly, but only indirectly, by measuring the behaviour of a system that has knowledge. This view of knowledge has been preferred to the structural view by a number of researchers including [Newell 1982]. Defining knowledge as a structural entity alone is quite limiting. [Reich 1995] maintains that only with simple knowledge representation schemes and simple inference mechanisms can a prediction about the expected performance of a system be reasonable. Such a prediction becomes increasingly difficult once the knowledge schema becomes complex.

There are benefits inherent in the structural view of knowledge for the evaluation of intelligent systems despite the limitations raised by [Newell 1982]. An inspection of rules, facts and inferences made is certainly useful in the testing phase of rule based system development. Furthermore, the size of the rule set is often used as an indication of the performance of the system. A knowledge base consisting of 80,000 rules is very large and the system that infers with from such a rule-base is likely to make sophisticated inferences.

In addition to the structural/functional knowledge dichotomy, criteria for the evaluation of knowledge-based systems can be based on quantitative or qualitative metrics. A count of the number of rules in a rule-based expert system is quantitative, while an evaluation of end users' opinion is qualitative. Furthermore, both qualitative and quantitative criteria can be discovered for knowledge that is structural and also for knowledge that is functional. This leads to four categories of evaluation criteria. Examples from these categories are summarised in Table 3.

The extent to which a knowledge base is readable or transparent to engineers is important, because it is difficult to maintain knowledge bases that are overly complex or ill-structured. This is a qualitative measure and assumes the structural view of knowledge. Quantitative measures that assume functional knowledge are more commonly used in evaluating knowledge-based systems. The MYCIN system of [Shortliffe et al 1976] was evaluated by comparing diagnoses, with those of specialists. [Buchanan et al 1995] advocated user acceptance as an appropriate evaluation criteria for their intelligent medical system. User acceptance is a useful criterion because ultimately, the benefits of the system will only be realised to the extent that users actually engage the system.

An extensive empirical study was performed by [Aleven and Ashley 1997] who evaluated their CATO system. They compared learning outcomes from groups of law students who did and did not use CATO. This strategy can be seen as one that assumes the functional view of knowledge using quantitative metrics. Outcomes were thus able to be assessed using statistical tests of significance.

Verification and validation are concepts that are traditionally invoked for the evaluation of any software system including knowledge-based systems [Gonzalez and Dankel 1993]. Verification refers to the process that involves checking for compliance with the system specifications and checking for syntactic and semantic errors in the knowledge base. Specification checking includes measures to ensure that the user interface, explanation facility, real time performance and security provisions reach the requirements specified in the system design. Checking for errors in the knowledge base depends on the knowledge representation. For rule-based systems, this involves checking for redundant, conflicting, unreachable or missing rules. Verification methods assume a structural view of knowledge and use quantitative and qualitative metrics.

The concept of validation refers to the determination of the correctness of the system with respect to user needs and requirements. Validation criteria include comparisons with known results (such as past cases), comparisons against expert performance and comparisons against theoretical possibilities. Validation tests include the Turing Test, user acceptance surveys and the direct comparison on random test cases between inferences performed by experts and inferences performed by the system.

Validation is a broad concept that covers structural and functional views of knowledge and qualitative and quantitative metrics. For example, the comparison of the results of a KDD exercise, against theoretical possibilities, assumes a structural view of knowledge and can be performed with quantitative metrics. The extent to which a user is satisfied by the system assumes the functional view of knowledge and may be measured qualitatively.

The framework suggested by [Reich 1995] avoids the explicit use of the verification and validation concepts, but does not deny that these concepts are useful. Further, the framework, of itself, does not suggest techniques for the evaluation of knowledge-based systems. However, it does provide a useful starting point for the design of an evaluation strategy for a particular knowledge based system. In order to illustrate this we describe evaluation studies conducted on the Split Up system.

Split Up was evaluated in each of the four categories outlined by [Reich 1995]. Each evaluation trial is listed in Table 4 and described in more detail in the following sections.

	Qualitative metric	Quantitative metric
Structural knowledge	1. Readability of knowledge base to knowledge engineers	1. Number of rules 2. Correctness of inferences
Functional knowledge	1. Problem solving behaviour analysed qualitatively	1. Quantitative comparison with experts 2. Quantitative assessment of user acceptance of system

Table 3. Examples of qualitative and quantitative metrics for two types of knowledge

	Qualitative metric	Quantitative metric
Structural knowledge	1. Readability of knowledge base to knowledge engineers	1. Number of rules 2. Correctness of inferences
Functional knowledge	1. Problem solving behaviour analysed qualitatively	1. Quantitative comparison with experts 2. Quantitative assessment of user acceptance of system

Table 4. Split Up evaluation studies categorised according to knowledge type and metric type

	Qualitative	Quantitative
Structural view of knowledge	1. Domain expert assessment of the content and structure of knowledge base. 2. Extent to which the knowledge base is ontologically specified	1. Extent to which a data mining technique has learnt patterns in training data 2. Extent to which a data mining technique generalises well from the training data
Functional view of knowledge	1. Domain expert assessment of the problem solving strategy adopted in Split Up 2. Extent to which the problem solving strategy is based on theoretical perspectives 3. Qualitative feedback from end users in different categories 4. Comparison of predictions made by Split Up with those reported in written judgements of cases	1. Comparison of predictions made by Split Up with those made by eight lawyers on facts from the same three cases

3.1.1   The extent to which the knowledge base is ontologically specified

[Bench-Capon and Visser 1997]   argue that the conceptualisation of legal knowledge stored in a knowledge base ought to be explicitly specified with the use of an accepted ontological framework such as those developed by [van Kralingen 1995], [Visser 1995] and Valente [1995].   The extent to which this has been achieved can be a strategy used to evaluate a knowledge base.   This strategy assumes a structural view of knowledge, even in the case of the ontology proposed by [Valente 1995].   This ontology focuses on the functional aspect of knowledge, because the strategy developed measures something about the knowledge base itself and not its use.   Their metric is qualitative because it is difficult to quantify the extent to which, or the accuracy with which a knowledge base has been specified. The conceptualisation of knowledge used in Split Up, for example, has not, to date, been ontologically specified.   Ontologies in law are important for KDD and are discussed separately below in Section 7.

3.1.2   The measurement of the extent to which a data-mining method has learnt patterns in training data

A measure of classifier performance typically used in classifier training in non-legal domains is the number of examples correctly classified.   As [Weiss and Kulikowski 1992] note, this measure of machine learning model performance may not be adequate for all domains.   They suggested a metric that includes the costs of predicting a positive outcome when the actual outcome was negative (called False positives) and the risks associated with predicting a negative outcome when the actual result was positive (called False negatives). For example, a neural network, trained to discern the presence or absence of a disease, will ideally, err far more times on the side of predicting a disease when there is none present, than it will err in missing a disease that is actually present.

A False positive/False Negative analysis of errors is not warranted in family law, because the direction of the error is rarely as critical as it is in the case of medical diagnostic problems. [Zeleznikow and Stranieri 1997] describe an error metric that is more fine-grained than simply counting the number of examples correctly classified. In this metric, the magnitude of an error was captured, but the direction of the error was not taken into account.

A strategy that measures the extent to which a data-mining method has learnt patterns in training data, can be used to compare dat- mining algorithms. [Michie *et al* 1994] described considerable methodological difficulties inherent in comparisons of data-mining methods.

They reported on an extensive study of a many data-mining algorithms on a range of data sets. Their goal was to attempt to identify what are the significant features of a data set that suggest that on that given data set, one data-mining technique is more appropriate than all other techniques. Results indicate that comparative studies are difficult to formulate and general rules regarding any technique cannot easily be drawn. This experience was confirmed by our attempts to compare linear regression with neural networks on one small data set used by Split Up. The difference between the means of the linear regression and neural network outputs was not significant at the 0.05 level (t = -0.25. tcritical 2 tail = 1.98).

The comparison of linear regression and a neural network is based on the structural view of knowledge. In performing the comparison, [Stranieri and Zeleznikow 1999] were not concerned with the function of the use of the system, but rather examined an aspect of the internal structure of the system's knowledge. The comparison was quantitative; because they exposed the linear regression formula and the neural network to all possible inputs and performed statistical tests of significance and explored descriptive statistics on the outputs.

[Zeleznikow *et al* 1996] compared the use of neural networks, the ID3 algorithm and expert heuristics in examining property distribution following divorce in Australia. The issue examined in detail was a divorcee's ability to find extra employment. ID3 induced thirteen rules. The experts only listed eleven rules. However, when they investigated the output of both the neural networks and ID3 on a test set, they derived a further two rules.

3.1.3 The extent to which the data-mining method generalises well from the training data

Measuring the extent to which a data-mining model trained with sample data can perform on data drawn from the rest of the population, is also a quantitative metric that assumes a structural view of knowledge. Methods for estimating the generalisation performance of a model were discussed in Section 1 above. [Reich and Barai 1999] cite surveys of articles in leading machine learning journals that indicate that less than 75% of articles clearly report the use of any technique that measures generalisation performance, despite the importance of this estimate.

3.1.4   Domain expert assessment of the problem solving strategy adopted

A qualitative analysis that presumes a functional view of knowledge involves the examination of the problem solving behaviour of the system by domain experts. This task was constantly performed with the principal domain expert and occasionally with other domain experts.   All except one domain expert expressed positive comments regarding the problem solving strategy of the Split Up system. Dr Richard Ingleby advocated the implementation of a problem solving strategy that commenced with a 50/50 split of marital assets and inferred appropriate deviations from this starting point. The strategy implemented does not infer deviations from a 50/50 starting point, but rather, infers a percentage split.

3.1.5   The extent to which the problem solving strategy is based on theoretical perspectives

The extent to which the problem solving strategy used by a system is supported by a jurisprudential perspective is a criterion that has fuelled past debates on legal knowledge based systems.   Certainly, a system that makes jurisprudential assumptions based on theory previously expressed, is preferable to one that has no such basis.

Legal realism underpins the data-mining component in Split Up.   Whilst preparing data for use by neural networks, some examples were eliminated from the training and test sets, because they were perceived to represent an inconsistent exercise of judicial discretion. The removal of some cases, legitimately tried, from the sample, seems to infringe the legal concept of stare decisis where any case, whether decided in a higher or equal Court can, conceivably be cited as a precedent. In chapter one, we addressed this concern by drawing the distinction between traditional, local and personal stare decisis.

3.1.6   Qualitative feedback from users in different categories

End users of the Split Up system were Family Court judges, registrars and mediators, lawyers and other parties conversant with Australian family law. Each category of Split Up user has different objectives.   As a consequence, the information need of each user is different.   Registrars of the Family Court are required to attempt to mediate a settlement prior to the dispute being heard by a judge. This process is known as an Order 24 conference. Registrars use the Split Up system in order to convince parties to reach a compromise. They need to inform litigants about the basics of family law and judicial heuristics.

Registrars use explanations for predictions as a convenient way to convince parties that their predictions are accurate. The explanations are often used to educate parties typically unfamiliar with family law, about fundamental principles.

Lawyers are less interested than registrars, in educating their client about family law principles. Instead, they need to validate their own predictions and be reminded of cases and statutes that would strengthen (or weaken) their arguments. These needs derive from a lawyer's primary goal of achieving the best possible result for their client.

Judges are required to arrive at an equitable outcome in the shortest amount of time. They need to ensure adherence to local stare decisis; that their own judgement is consistent with that of other judges of the same Court. Judges are rarely interested in explanations. However they are concerned that their judgements include all relevant matters and only relevant matters[60].

The Split Up system was demonstrated to three judges and five registrars of the Family Court of Australia, along with about fifty other family law specialists. Opinions of the system were largely gathered informally, during open-ended discussions in the course of and after a demonstration. An evaluation feedback form was developed and made available to some users. The evaluation feedback included questions that were loosely adapted from those of a user acceptance survey developed by [Buchanan *et al* 1995].

3.1.7 Comparison of predictions with past judgements in the Family Court

A comparison of predictions made on past judgements, by both the Split Up system and judges, assumes the functional view of knowledge. The metric is typically qualitative rather than quantitative. This is because a written judgement necessarily leaves many points implicit. A judgement that articulates every aspect of every inference would be exceedingly long and unreadable. Yet, leaving many factors implicit may presume too much of the reader. In comparing system predictions with written judgements, interim conclusions leading to the ultimate outcome must typically be read into most judgements. This introduces a degree of subjectivity that necessitates a qualitative assessment.

Split Up predictions were compared with five commonplace cases tried in the Family Court. Results suggest that predictions overall were quite good, though counter intuitive. Some Split Up deviations from conclusions made in judgements can readily be explained by the small sample size (n=102). Other differences revolved around factors such as incest, which is not normally a relevant factor in property proceedings, but may have impacted on a particular judgement.

---

[60] The failure of a Family Court Justice to give adequate reasons for her judgement is sufficient grounds for an appeal against that judgement.

3.1.8   Comparison of predictions made by Split Up with those made by eight
        lawyers on facts from the same three cases.

A comparison of Split Up predictions with those made by a panel of lawyers assumes the functional view of knowledge. This metric was quantitative, as actual predictions were empirically compared and contrasted. Eight family lawyers were asked to confidentially analyse three hypothetical cases and record written predictions and explanations. The cases were hypothetical cases specifically constructed to explore a range of issues, because the same breadth of issues could not be guaranteed with the selection of three random cases. [Lovegrove 1999] found a similar problem in a study of sentencing behaviour of Victorian judges. He invented forty cases for each of eight County Court judges. He justified the use of fictitious cases on the grounds that a full range of issues can be explored if the cases were invented.

Results reported in Table 5 indicate that although predictions amongst lawyers were far from consistent, the predictions made by the Split Up system on all three cases, fell within the range of those made by lawyers.

The generation of an effective explanation for inferences drawn is particularly important for legal knowledge based systems. Issues concerning the evaluation of explication facilities that are finer grained than the Reich framework are described next.

Table 5. Split Up prediction compared with lawyer predictions

	Case A	Case B	Case C
Split Up	50%	40%	55%
Lawyer 1	50%	35%	55-60%
Lawyer 2	50%	35-40%	55%
Lawyer 3	50%	40%	50-55%
Lawyer 4	50%	50%	45%
Lawyer 5	50%	40%	45-50%
Lawyer 6	50%	35%	20-25%
Lawyer 7	50%	35%	45-50%
Lawyer 8	50%	40%	50%

Eight family lawyers gathered at the University of Melbourne Law School to analyse the Split Up system. They were asked to analyse the following three cases:

Marriage A

Couple A has been married 30 years with three independent sons aged 28, 25 and 22. Both ex-partners are 60 years old. Mr. A has worked throughout the marriage being a partner in a pathology practice. He currently earns $250,000 per annum. His wife has not worked during the marriage. Both parties have done little around the house — they have relied on domestic help for maintenance, domestic chores and child-care. They own a house worth $800,000, have $500,000 in shares and the husband is the half owner of a medical practice valued at $1,000,000. They each own cars worth $50,000. Both parties are in good health. Neither party brought any significant finances into the marriage.

Marriage B

Couple B has been married 5 years and have no children. Both ex-partners are 30 years old. The husband earns $30,000 per annum whilst the wife earns $25,000 per annum. They both work as school-teachers. They own a house worth $100,000 and two cars, each worth $15,000. Neither party brought any significant finances into the marriage. The husband has $10,000 in superannuation entitlements whilst the wife has $8,000 in entitlements. The superannuation assets are not realisable for 30 years. Both parties are in good health.

Marriage C

Couple C has been married for fifteen years and have two sons aged thirteen and eleven. Each partner is 45 years old. The husband is the sole partner in a legal company valued at $250,000. They own a house (worth $400,000) and Mrs C's Volvo car (worth $20,000). The legal practice has a Porsche car (worth $100,000) that is driven solely by Mr. C. Mr C. has superannuation entitlements valued at $200,000 and realisable in 20 years time.

Mr C earns $50,000 per annum whilst Mrs C earns $25,000 per annum working as a secretary. Mrs C has performed most of the domestic work and maintenance of the house. She will have custody of both children. Both parties are in good health. Neither party brought any significant finances into the marriage. Mrs C worked full-time for the first 2 years of the marriage and for the past 6 years. She has no superannuation benefits.

All eight lawyers gave the husband in Case B 50% of the Common Pool. This coincided with the determination of the Split Up system. The reasons the lawyers gave for their decisions were also similar to the justifications given by the Split Up system.

In case C, Split Up awarded the husband 40% of the Common Pool. It also suggested that whilst the Family Court could not make any orders with regard to the Porsche owned by the husband's legal practice, it could demand that the value of the Porsche ($100,000) be placed in the pool for later distribution. All eight lawyers suggested the same course of action. With the exception of one lawyer who suggested the husband should receive 50% of the Common Pool, the others suggested Mr. C should receive 35%, 40% or within the range 35-40%. This concurs with Split—Up's reasoning.

The only disagreement within the group and between the group and the Split Up system came in case A. In case A, the Split Up system claimed the husband contributed more financially than the wife, and that they both contributed equally in non-financial terms. It also suggested the wife's resources for the future are much less than the husband. It thus awarded the husband 55% of the large Common Pool. Analysing the lawyers' responses for this case was not easy since they disagreed amongst themselves. One awarded the husband 55-60%, one awarded 55%, one awarded 50-55%, one awarded 45%, two awarded 45-50%, three awarded 40-50% and one awarded 20-25%. Given that we suggest any answer in the range 50-60% is acceptable, then three of the lawyers coincide with our conclusion and another five overlap in an acceptable manner. Two results (45% and 20-25%) are clearly at variance with our system. When we investigated the reasoning of the family lawyers we discovered some interesting factors.

a)   **Choosing the correct data and attributes** — when using neural networks one needs to consult domain experts to choose the correct attributes. In building the Split Up system we then needed to encode free text judicial decisions into our template. But what occurred in Case A was not something that was envisioned when building the system. Examining the lawyers' reasoning in Case A, it appears that many of the lawyers failed to accept the data in the case as valid. They could not believe that in a marriage of thirty years, where the husband was heavily occupied in his medical practice, the wife would not have contributed much more, in non-financial terms, to the family than did the husband. This allowed them to conclude that the husband and wife contributed equally during the marriage.

When we entered into the Split Up system that the wife contributed much more, in non-financial terms, than did the husband, then the system awarded 45% to the husband. This illustrates the dictum that only humans can make decisions with regard to facts and that humans will disregard information they find inconceivable.

b)   **Concept drift** - [Schlimmer 1987] defines concept drift as the change in concepts over time. The commonplace cases used in Split—Up's training set were decided by judges in the period 1992-1994. At that time judges were required to assess the contributions of each partner. Since then, there may have been a considerable change in judges' attitudes to determining past contributions. There have indeed been calls from politicians to amend the Family Law Act to imply a presumption that both parties to a marriage contributed equally. Further a departure from this presumption would occur only in exceptional circumstances.

Currently judges need to make a determination on each partner's contributions. However, the eight lawyers who considered the hypothetical cases believed that except in very asset rich marriages (of which case A was not an example) the presumption of both parties contributing equally should hold. If the legislation were thus amended, the Split Up system would need to include a rule to the effect that contributions are to be considered as equal save for exceptional circumstances.

Both the lawyers and the system agreed that in case A the wife had greater future needs than her husband (due to her limited employment opportunities).

c)   **Political correctness** — lawyers and judges state they believe financial and non-financial contributions should be equally considered when distributing property. But whilst they may utter these politically correct statements our analysis of cases tends to show that in practice judges are more influenced by financial contributions.

As we have noted previously, most of the cases used in the Split Up training set come from the Southern registry of the Family Court of Australia. This is because data from the other registries was unsuitable for inclusion in the system. However this means that the Split Up system models the thinking of judges in Melbourne, rather than the more conservative outlying states. Feedback from users of the system appears to stress this fact. Thus one needs to consider concept drift over both time and location.

The evaluation framework suggested by [Reich 1995] invited a focus on evaluation criteria that were broader than predictive accuracy of classifiers on a data-set. However, the model did not make explicit conceptualisations of quality or social context of the use of data mining models. The Criteria, Context, Contingency model advanced by [Hall and Zeleznikow 2002] discussed next sought to be more comprehensive.

3.2   The Criteria, Context, Contingency Guidelines Framework

[Hall and Zeleznikow 2002] have developed the Criteria, Context, Contingency-guidelines framework (CCCF). CCCF is designed for general use, but it can be specifically tailored to framing (planning) the evaluation of legal knowledge based systems. The CCCF assists an evaluator plan an evaluation in three distinct but interdependent ways. Initially it provides guidance to assess the context of the evaluation i.e. both of the system to be evaluated and of the evaluation itself and to determine the goals of the evaluation. The CCCF also contains a hierarchical four-quadrant model of potential evaluation criteria and offers contingency-guidelines to select appropriate criteria to satisfy the goals of the evaluation and any arising contingency.

The CCCF subsumes and integrates material sourced from the international standards and other frameworks. The CCCF seeks to be wide-ranging in scope and facilitate ordered access for the inexperienced legal evaluator to the multitude of information available. The experienced software engineer should also find it a useful reference to the many general evaluation criteria available, a means of organising their own criteria and a framework upon which to plan, standardise, report and compare their evaluations. It will also facilitate the inclusion of any legal domain specific evaluation requirements.

3.2.1 Contexts

'Context', is concerned with the immediate environment, attendant circumstances, conditions and background of the object under consideration. We consider three relevant areas: the original system requirements, the system operational context and the context of the evaluation itself. The need for these distinctions became apparent during an analysis of software evaluation criteria for inclusion in the criteria model. The operational and evaluation contexts reflect the contingencies of the situation and are major factors impacting upon the choice of evaluation criteria. A sound understanding of these contexts and the system requirements is paramount when establishing the goals of an evaluation and framing it using the CCCF.

a) **System operational context** - The CCCF suggests system properties that should be canvassed to understand the operational context. Application specific factors include the level of management support, application criticality, any consequences of failure, and barriers or encouragement to use the CCCF. Non system-specific factors are either internal or external to the organisation. Internal factors canvas funding and resourcing, constraints, and the work environment. Organisational culture, the managerial and technical climate within which it operates and the ability to tolerate risk is important. Human resource issues include the values, morale and motivation, skills, experience and training of the users. External factors include factors specific to the domain, industry, technology adoption and any involved vendor, national and international affairs and evolving social norms.

In a legal knowledge based system, an understanding of the decision-making environment can be particularly significant; e.g. whether decisions are discretionary or rule-based, whether the jurisdiction conducts litigation in an adversarial or inquisitorial manner and whether the 'fiction of certainty' applies.

b) **Evaluation context** - In addition to taking account of the system requirements and operational context, the CCCF also focuses inward on the properties of the evaluation process itself, including its relationship to the system undergoing evaluation.

The evaluation context considers relevant background issues, intended evaluation outcomes and 'demographic' evaluation factors such as what, why, when, by whom, for whom, etc. Among the more significant background issues are the philosophy of and values inherent in the evaluation process, economic, technical and operational feasibility, any applicable constraints and the political and social environment in which the evaluation takes place.

The *philosophy* of *and values* inherent in the evaluation process should be explicitly considered; as they will have a major impact on the choice of evaluation method e.g. whether the evaluation should be predominantly qualitative or quantitative, subjective or objective and summative or formative. The objective of a formative evaluation is to learn, provide feedback, and to refine and improve the product. A summative evaluation warrants (certifies) that a product has passed some preset barrier, acknowledging it is now fit for use [DeLone and McLean 1992].

The *economic and operational feasibility* of conducting the evaluation is obviously required to be taken into account including appropriate resourcing and any constraints e.g. a requirement to conform to existing corporate evaluation procedures.

The *political and social environments* of the evaluation are also important as organisational culture, power and management style impact not only on the operational context but also on the framing of the evaluation. Evaluation should not only provide an assessment of overall system benefit, but as importantly, should identify who derives that benefit and in what way. For a legal knowledge based system, it is particularly important to identify all relevant stakeholders, both direct and indirect, and to consider not only those for whose use the system has been designed but also those effected by system decisions including clients, sponsors, funding bodies and the wider legal community.

3.2.2 Criteria Model

We use 'criterion' in the philosophical sense of a characteristic attached to something by which it can be judged or measured. Thus evaluation 'criteria' are properties of a software system that can be measured and used in evaluation, similar in concept to the quality characteristics and sub-characteristics (attributes) defined in ISO/IEC 9126. That standard discusses the need for a domain dependent quality model of actual characteristics and the CCCF provides this through a model of evaluation criteria arranged in four quadrants each organized as a tree. The more than one thousand evaluation criteria currently included in the CCCF criteria model have been sourced from international quality software standards, reports in the academic and technical literature, and published restricted frameworks that address subsets of the domain e.g. Delone and McLean's framework [DeLone and McLean 1992]]. Figure 7 below, presents an overview of the CCCF Criteria Model. The four quadrants, containing trees of criteria are delineated by axes representing Technology/People and a Micro/Macro continuum ranging from 'in the small' or focused to 'in the large' or generalised. These axes are included as a conceptual aid to understanding and no implication is intended that they are capable of precise measurement. i.e. the model consists of four hierarchies of groups and sub-groups down to the atomic level (see Figure 8). Atomic level criteria do not require further decomposition and any criterion selected from this level can be measured using an appropriate method, metric and range of acceptability (reference standard). Work is ongoing to combine, order and rearrange these criteria to facilitate access.

3.2.3 User credibility criteria

Figure 8 shows a selection from the criteria tree in the User Credibility quadrant. This quadrant is concerned with the credibility and acceptability of a system to people 'in the small' i.e. at the individual rather than organizational level. The tree has three main branches associated with user satisfaction, utility (usefulness or fitness for purpose) and usability (ease of use). The usability branch is further decomposed into branches associated with operability, understandability, learnability, accessibility, flexibility in use, and other human factors and interface issues. Figure 8 shows the sub-branch concerned with operability criteria partially expanded. The atomic level is concerned with system responsiveness, containing criteria that can be measured using suitable metrics.

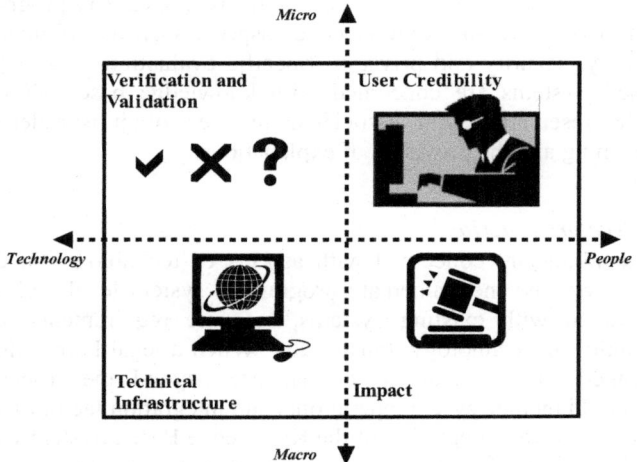

Figure 7. The CCCF criteria model

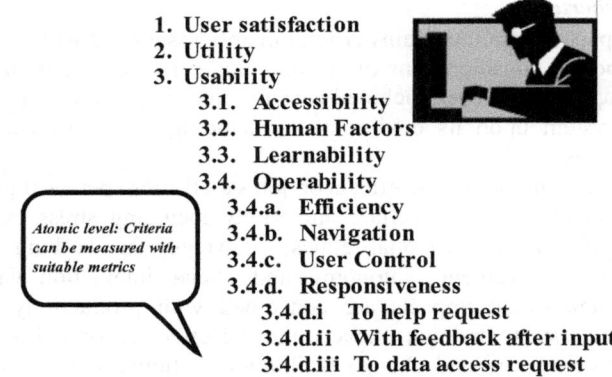

*Figure 8 CCCF Criteria model: User Credibility quadrant. Portion of the
hierarchy of evaluation criteria*

3.2.4   Verification and validation criteria

Criteria in this quadrant are concerned with verification and validation (V and
V). They canvas aspects of technology 'in the small' i.e. at the program rather than
the infrastructure level. Validation is concerned with whether the 'right' product has
been built and verification with whether it has been built 'right' [Boehm 1981].
Validation criteria canvas the match between the system requirements, the provided
functionality and its operational adequacy. Verification criteria consider compliance

and responsibility, and static and dynamic issues. Static issues canvas program quality and software design. Dynamic criteria cover aspects such as efficiency, currency, reliability, safety, security and privacy. Specific evaluation criteria for Legal Knowledge Based Systems are concerned with knowledge base validity, including knowledge representation and associated theories of jurisprudence, inferencing, machine learning and the provision of explanations.

3.2.5 Technical infrastructure criteria

Criteria from this quadrant are concerned with aspects of technology 'in the large' or technical issues beyond the immediate program or system level e.g. the technical fit of the system with existing systems, resource requirements and availability, the opportunity for technology transfer etc. When a legal knowledge-based system is designed for eventual operational use beyond the research laboratory, evaluation should include system operational and integration factors such as provision of adequate hardware, integration of the Knowledge Based System with other user systems, facilitation of effective system maintenance and security.

3.2.6 Impact criteria

The final impact quadrant contains criteria mainly associated with people 'in the large' i.e. beyond the considerations of an individual. However criteria associated with personal impacts have been included here for convenience. Criteria canvas the impact of the system upon its environment, including tasks, people, the parent organisation and beyond.

Personal impact criteria include effects on job satisfaction, personal productivity, motivation and morale, health, welfare and safety including stress exposure and impacts upon privacy and personal ethics. Changes in working conditions, participation and involvement, autonomy and social interaction can also be measured. Organisational impacts are concerned with productivity, quality of service, economic issues, strategic impacts and the effect on organisational goals, organisational restructuring and change facilitation. Impacts in the wider arena beyond the organisation are concerned with industrial relations, effects on other organisations, the formation of new distributed enterprises, globalisation, political, economic and technical issues, intellectual factors and support for certification and professionalism.

Social factors, ethics and integrity, can also be canvassed. These areas can be particularly valuable when evaluating legal knowledge based systems when there is a significant potential for considerable social impact. Therapeutic jurisprudence is the 'study of the role of the law as a therapeutic or anti-therapeutic agent.' It focuses on the law's impact on emotional life and on psychological well being [Wexler and Winik 1996]. Legal knowledge based systems support those who work with the law and the direct and indirect effects of such systems on their clients can be evaluated.

3.2.7   Contingency-guidelines

A 'contingency' is the possibility that something may occur in the future. A 'contingency-guideline' is a suggestion on how to deal with this occurrence. The evaluation contingency-guidelines included in the CCCF are designed to guide evaluators in their choice of appropriate criteria under particular contingencies specified by the goals of the evaluation, properties of the system and most importantly, the evaluation context.

The academic literature includes many reports that consider contingencies (described by their context properties) and offer guidelines for choosing appropriate evaluation criteria.   Typically guidelines are included for evaluations based upon the following evaluation 'demographic' properties:

a) Why – covert and overt evaluation purposes;
b) Where - field or laboratory based;
c) What - product or process, operational system or prototype etc;
d) When - the stage of the product life cycle;
e) How often – frequency i.e. once off or part of a continuous monitoring process;
f) Who by - the capabilities of the evaluation team; and
g) From which viewpoint - the evaluation role

There is general agreement that there is no one 'best' evaluation method or set of evaluation criteria.   [Gregory 1991] suggests a formal contingency framework. The SHOR paradigm and multiview methodology also offer a contingency-based choice of evaluation criteria [Adelman 1989].   Others associate system risk exposure with quality criteria, selected from those suggested by the ISO9126 standard [Rae *et al* 1995].   Currently CCCF contingency-guidelines are presented in word processing documents and models of argumentation. Work is ongoing in this area.

3.2.8   Packaging the CCCF

To use and evaluate the CCCF, it is necessary to make it readily accessible to potential users.   Currently two deployment prototypes are available.   A paper-based version, lists the context properties and set of all evaluation criteria utilizing the 'outline' capability of Microsoft Word.   Contingency-guidelines are also text based. A major challenge is ensuring currency, as neither the contingency-guidelines nor criteria trees are static.   Currently we are in a period of rapid enhancement with criteria being added to or reorganised and contingency guidelines frequently updated. The system is sufficiently large and complex to necessitate its use only by an evaluator who has a sound understanding of the CCCF.   A prototype internet application, designed to meet these challenges, is under development with a few sample criteria currently included.   Evaluation criteria are presented in a decomposable tree structure.   The system also includes a facility to manage and update the trees and prepares questionnaires to canvas system operational and evaluation context properties.

Now that we have provided a detailed investigation of evaluating KDD systems, we turn to the issue of explanation.   Knowledge discovered from legal databases, particularly when embedded in expert system programs, will generate predictions that require an explanation. The quality of the explanation offered is a criterion that is perhaps even more important than the predictive accuracy of our KDD legal systems. However, the nature of an explanation is not straight-forward. Explanations are discussed in the next section.

4. EXPLANATION

The provision of explanations is a central feature of any automated reasoner and especially KDD systems. Because the output of a KDD system is essentially statistical, the only justification for the answer received was that it achieved a certain level of statistical significance. Such an explanation is rarely acceptable to end-users. Thus explanations that are distinct from the inferencing are vital in convincing a user of the value of using a KDD system.

But what constitutes an explanation? [Branting 1991] defines an explanation in legal domains as a collection of reasoning steps that connect the facts of a case to a conclusion. This approach is reasonable; yet, much depends on what is meant by a reasoning step. If, by reasoning step, we mean every part of every inference or calculation that is used to generate an assertion then, our explanation may not always be appropriate. [Wick and Thompson 1992] note that an explanation has a story-like element and typically uses knowledge at a different level of specificity to that used in the line of reasoning. A simple example illustrates that an appropriate explanation may not equate with the line of reasoning used to derive the original answer.

We may engage ourselves with the task of dividing 240 by 16. Using a pen and paper and long division, we reach the conclusion, 15. If asked to explain that result, we are unlikely to reproduce all or even a subset of the algorithm. Instead we perform multiplication in our head and say that the result is 15 because 15 * 16 = 240. In this trivial case, the explanation is provided in a very different and indeed much simpler manner than repeating the reasoning steps used to achieve the result.

[Zeleznikow and Hunter 1994] state that an explanation is an attempt by a computer system to indicate or clarify its actions, reasoning and recommendations. It is a collection of reasoning steps that connects facts to a legal conclusion about those facts.

There are three reasons why explanation is important in legal decision support systems:
a) Users of the system need to satisfy themselves that the program's conclusions are basically correct for their particular use.
b) Knowledge engineers need to satisfy themselves that knowledge is being applied properly.
c) Domain experts need to see a trace of the way in which their knowledge is being applied, in order to judge whether knowledge elicitation is proceeding successfully.

[Moore 1995] provides a thorough review of computer-based systems that generate explanations. She identifies a set of requirements that are intended to act as criteria for the evaluation of explication systems. According to Moore, explanations should have the following qualities:

a) Naturalness. Explanations should appear natural to the user. Explanations that are not structured according to standard patterns of human discourse often make critical elements of an explanation more confusing.

b) Responsiveness. An explanation facility must have the ability to accept feedback from the user and to answer follow-up question(s).

c) Flexibility. An explanation facility must be able to offer an explanation in more than one way in order to accommodate the different knowledge and abilities of the users.

d) Sensitivity. An explication system should take into account the user's goals in the problem solving situation and the previous explanatory dialogue.

e) Fidelity. An explication system must accurately reflect the system's knowledge and reasoning.

f) Sufficiency. An explication system should be able to answer a range of questions users wish to ask and not be limited to those questions predicted by developers.

g) Extensibility. It should be easy to extend the explanation system to accommodate questions not conceived of at design time.

Early explanation systems use pre-written text attached to knowledge chunks or applied simple transformations to produce explanations from program code. This type of explanation is very simple to generate and is natural. However, it is far from responsive, flexible, sensitive or sufficient. Furthermore, this type of explanation may not ensure fidelity in that text associated with a rule set may not necessarily be appropriate for the rule set because of knowledge engineering errors.

The criteria outlined above can only be realised within a dialogue. According to [Moore 1995], the generation of a dialogue requires a natural language generation facility that can generate multi sentential text. This requires knowledge of the domain, knowledge of the rhetorical structure of human discourse and thematic knowledge that governs the shift in focus of attention within an explanatory dialogue.

According to user surveys, the explanation facility in Split Up has been well received. However, it does not engage the user in a dialogue. The facility is intimately linked with the Toulmin Argument Structure and is natural, responsive, and has fidelity to some extent, regardless of whether inferences were performed by neural networks or rule sets. However, the explication facility does not meet any other of the criteria set out by Moore.

Explanation facilities are commonplace in rule based legal decision support systems. Most existing explanation facilities allow the user to ask two types of questions: why and how.

A why question is asked when the user is unsure why the decision support system has asked a particular question.

A how question is asked when the user wants to know the reasoning steps the system has taken to reach the current conclusion.

In most rule based decision support systems, explanations are merely a trace of the rules used to reach the conclusion. Rule-based systems are equivalent to decision trees. Consider the example of a decision tree for determining property distribution in Australian Family Law that was given in chapter five. From it we determined the following rules:

Rule 1. IF NOT wife_working THEN NOT equal_split

Rule 2. IF wife_working AND asset_rich THEN equal_split

Rule 3. IF wife_working AND NOT asset_rich AND children THEN NOT equal_split

Rule 4. IF wife_working AND NOT asset_rich AND NOT children THEN equal_split

This decision tree was in fact learnt using the KDD technique of rule induction. The explanation for reasoning with decision trees (or rules) is indeed to trace through the decision trees (or rules). Such explanations are insufficient when using neural networks.

There has been much research on learning rules from neural networks (see for example [Diederich 1992]). This is however, not a technique [Stranieri et al 1999] wished to use for building connectionist legal decision support systems.

The adoption of a stance that inferencing is a process distinct from the generation of explanation is practically useful in the development of a reasoner for the discretionary domain of family law. It is possible to develop artificial reasoners that operate by invoking neural networks if, another, quite separate process, is invoked to generate an explanation for conclusions reached by neural networks. This notion of how an explanation is generated is in keeping with views on decision-making advocated by proponents of the school of legal realism.

The constitution of an adequate explanation is, in general, a vexed question. The question is particularly important for the development of knowledge-based systems that are required to explain their reasoning. An important assumption [Stranieri et al 1999] make is that the process of explaining reasoning is different from the process of performing the reasoning. The extreme right of Figure 9 illustrates an explanation that is quite separate from the reasoning steps used to solve a problem. Their contention is that many explanations for the type of discretionary reasoning observed in family law are quite separate from the reasoning steps used to infer the conclusion. Take, for example, Hannon J. in *The Marriage of B* ML4336 1995[61] who states:

'Having regard to the relevant contributions of the parties, including substantial financial contribution of the husband from the funds received from the sale of his mother's house, I assess their respective contributions as to 60 per cent to the husband and 40 per cent to the wife'

---

[61] Full name of the parties in this case are confidential. No court reporting service has reported this case. The full text was made available by the Family Court of Australia (Melb). The reference number, ML4336 is the Family Court identification number for this case.

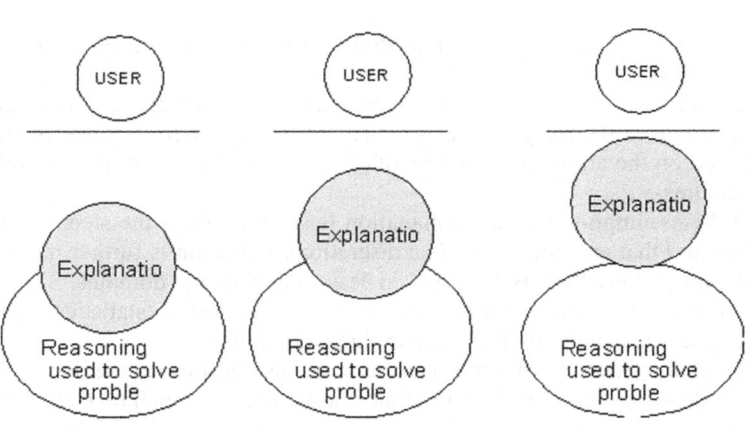

Figure 9. The separation of explanations from reasoning steps

This statement is considered by the Court as an adequate fulfilment of the duty to give reasons. However, the process used by Hannon J. to arrive at a figure that measures the husband's contribution as 60% relative to the wife's 40%, and not 55% for instance, is not articulated. The process is not arbitrary because as stated in Chapter 1, we believe local stare decisis occurs in the Family Court. The judge is not careless in failing to document reasoning steps. Rather, a feature of discretionary domains is that explanations are necessarily further removed from reasoning steps than is the case in domains characterised by traditional stare decisis.

The illustration on the extreme left of Figure 9 depicts explanations that are drawn exclusively from the reasoning steps used to infer a conclusion. Rule trace type explanations first developed for the expert system MYCIN by [Shortliffe *et al* 1976] represents an instance of explanations that closely match the reasoning steps used. As [Johnson *et al* 1987] notes, most human explanations use the same underlying knowledge for explanation and reasoning; but that the knowledge used to construct an explanation is at a different level of specificity. The middle illustration in Figure 9 illustrates this view, but does not separate reasoning from explanations sufficiently to describe explanations, specifically in the task of Property distribution in Australian family law.

Practitioners in family law have considerable difficulty in explaining reasoning. The task of determining whether an asset is included in the common pool of assets is far less discretionary than the task of deciding what percentage of the common pool each partner receives.

The same domain expert, when asked to contribute an explanation for why she expected a particular trial judge to hand down a 45/55% property split would resort to her extensive experience with the Court and report on general legal principles specified in the statute, but not on specific rules, as she did with the common pool task. This suggests that explanations that revolve around predictions about local stare decisis involve statements that refer to the extent of exposure to Court practice:

'I just know that Judge X will hand down a 50:50% judgement because he has tried hundreds of my cases'.

In [Stranieri *et al* 2001], we claim that explanations for discretionary reasoning can be generated if explanatory text is stored within a knowledge representation framework based on the argument structure of [Toulmin 1958] or indeed most other argument structures.

We make the assumption that an explanation is separate from the steps used to infer a solution and that an explanation in a discretionary domain is further removed from the reasoning steps than is the case in less discretionary domains. This is particularly important when using neural networks or other statistical KDD techniques to model reasoning in discretionary legal domains.

In domains characterised with traditional stare decisis, reasons for the decision of a first instance decision often involve principles laid down by appellate Courts. In the absence of traditional stare decisis, explanations cannot be rigidly derived from principles, because appellate Courts have not laid them down in any specific way. Thus, explanations must necessarily be further removed from the sequence of reasoning steps used to infer an outcome.

Once we have considered evaluating legal KDD systems and providing explanation for such systems, we have almost completed our task of investigating Knowledge Discovery from Legal Databases. One question however still remains unanswered: what areas of law are suitable for being modelled using knowledge discovery from databases. In chapter 2, we pointed out that those fields of law that invite judicial discretion are most suited to a KDD exercise. In the next section, we introduce a framework for adding some system to the selection of a suitable field of law.

5. SELECTING SUITABLE FIELDS OF LAW

To use KDD in a legal domain, we have established that the domain must have an abundance of commonplace cases. Whilst this requirement is necessary, is it sufficient? For example, whilst there are plenty of cases involving drink-driving legislation, because the domain has well understood rules[62], it is un-necessary to use KDD to model judicial decision making with respect to drink-driving.

The problem of deciding whether a legal task can be modeled by any existing paradigm (including KDD), and if so, which one, is a problem currently tackled in an ad hoc manner by developers of legal reasoning systems. In an attempt to develop methods for using intelligent systems to model legal decision-making, [Stranieri *et al* 1999] developed a simple classification scheme to classify legal tasks. This methodology was illustrated with examples taken from the domain of property distribution in Australian Family Law.

The classification scheme is based on two dimensions. These are:

a) An estimation of the extent to which a task is open textured; and

---

[62] In Victoria, Australia we have rules: drink(X) & drive(X) $\rightarrow$ licence_loss(X), (blood_alcohol_level(X) > .05%) $\rightarrow$ drink(X)

b) An estimation of the extent to which a task displays a feature that [Stranieri *et al* 1999] call boundedness.

The scheme illustrated in Figure 10 has two dimensions: open texture - well defined and bounded-unbounded.

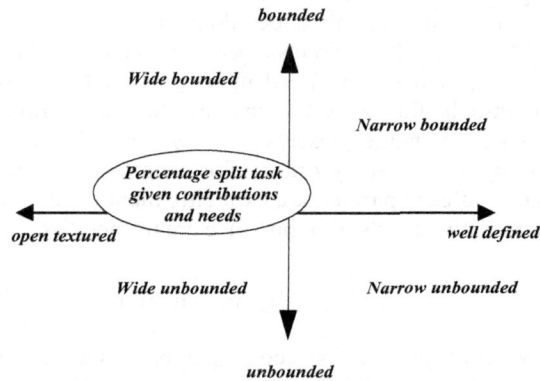

Figure 10. Classification of percentage split task

The open textured - well-defined axis reflects the extent to which experts believed factors known to be relevant in a prediction were open textured. Predicting a percentage split of marital assets was considered open-textured, because of the high degree of discretion given to judges. The bounded dimension refers to an expert's beliefs about the completeness of her knowledge of relevant factors. In Split-Up, ninety-four variables were identified as relevant for predicting a percentage split of assets. Experts were of the view that few factors useful for a prediction were omitted from this list and therefore considered the task to be quite bounded.

Tasks that fall in the narrow bounded quadrant are well suited to implementation with heuristics elicited as rules, because all terms are well defined and all variables relevant for the prediction are known. Discretionary tasks that fall in the wide bounded quadrant (top left in Figure 10) can be modeled using the KDD process.

Unbounded tasks, whether or not they contain open textured terms, cannot be modeled adequately using KDD, since sufficient relevant factors cannot be determined. [Zeleznikow 2000] describes such domains as unfettered discretionary domains. Such domains have no norms and judges are not even told what factors must be taken into account in reaching a decision. We do not believe it is wise to model such domains.

An example of unfettered discretion is the determination of the custody of children in Australian family law. According to the Family Law Act (1975) the only factor to be taken into account is the paramount interests of the child. Following considerable litigation and uncertainty the Australian Federal Parliament made minimal attempts to define what are the paramount interests of a child. They did this by including in the legislation factors such as education, health, and the child's relationship with both parents, and the need to keep siblings together. But there is no clear list of factors. Indeed it is much easier to describe what is not in a child's best interests (for example sexual abuse, violence) than what is in a child's best interests. The granting of refugee status can also be considered to be an example of unfettered discretion and is an unbounded domain.

The *Family Law Act (1975)* directs a decision maker to take into account the past contributions of each party to a failed marriage in addition to their resources for coping with life into the future. Rather than offering one definition for *contributions* and one for *needs*, the statute presents a *'shopping list'* of factors to be taken into account in arriving at a property order. For example, the age, state of health and financial resources of each partner, are explicitly mentioned in the statute as relevant factors, yet their relative levels of importance are unspecified.

6. LEGAL ONTOLOGIES

Whilst the World Wide Web is becoming a major source of information retrieval and a repository of legal knowledge, the uses of web mining to discover legal knowledge has been limited. [Zeleznikow 2002] notes that currently, very few legal decision support systems are available on the World Wide Web. Much current research is focused upon using text mining for Homeland Security and Intelligence and Law Enforcement.

The Australasian Legal Information Institute (AustLII – www.austlii.edu.au) provides free Internet access to Australian legal materials. As discussed in Chapter 8, AustLII's broad public policy agenda is to improve access to justice through better access to information. To that end, AustLII has become one of the largest sources of legal materials on the net, with over 7 gigabytes of raw text materials and over 1.5 million searchable documents.

It does not have any decision support systems on its Internet site. The British and Irish Legal Information Institute (BAILII—www.bailii.org) provides access to the most comprehensive set of British and Irish primary legal materials that are available for free and in one place on the Internet.

In Canada, the Canadian Legal Information Institute project (CANLII) aims at gathering legislative and judicial texts, as well as legal commentaries, from federal, provincial and territorial jurisdictions bin order to make primary sources of Canadian law accessible on the Internet (http://www.canlii.org). The large volume of legal information in electronic form creates a need for the creation and production of powerful computational tools in order to extract relevant information in a condensed form.

The development of Legal Ontologies offers great opportunities for the development of legal decision support that draws on knowledge learnt using KDD on the World Wide Web. An ontology as an explicit conceptualization of a domain is defined in [Gruber 1995]. [Breuker et al 2002] claim that unlike engineering, medicine or psychology, law is not ontologically founded. They claim law is concerned with constraining and controlling social activities using documented norms. They have developed a core upper level ontology LRI-core. This ontology has over 200 concepts and has definitions for most of the anchors that connect the major categories used in law – person, role, action, process, procedure, time, space, document, information, intention, and so on.   The main intended use is supporting knowledge acquisition for legal domains, but a real test of its semantics is whether it enables natural language understanding of common sense descriptions of simple events, as in the description of events in a legal case documentation. This is of the core principle of the Semantic Web initiative of WC3.

The development of legal ontologies has been examined by [Bench-Capon and Visser 1997]. Ontologies have benefits for: a) Knowledge sharing; b) Verification of a knowledge base; c) Knowledge acquisition; and d) Knowledge reuse.

A formal legal ontology was built by [Visser 1995] by developing a formal specification language that is tailored in the appropriate legal domain. He commenced by using Van Kralingen's theory of frame-based conceptual models of statute law [vanKralingen 1995]. Visser uses the terms ontology and specification language interchangeably. He claims an ontology must be:

a) epistemologically adequate;
b) operational;
c) expressive;
d) reusable; and
e) extensible.

Visser chose to model the Dutch Unemployed Benefits Act of 1986. He created a CommonKADS expertise model [Schreiber *et al* 1999]. Specifying domain knowledge is performed by:

a) Determining the universe of discourse by carving up the knowledge into ontological primitives. A domain ontology is created with which the knowledge from the legal domain can be specified.
b) The domain specification is created by specifying a set of domain models using the domain ontology.

A legal ontology based on a functional perspective of the legal system was developed by [Valente 1995]. He considered the legal system as an instrument to change or influence society in specific directions by reacting to social behaviour. The main functions can be decomposed into six primitive functions each of which corresponds to a category of primitive legal knowledge:

a) Normative knowledge – which describes states of affairs that have a normative status (such as forbidden or obligatory);
b) World knowledge – which describes the world that is being regulated, in terms that are used in the normative knowledge, and so can be considered as an interface between common-sense and normative knowledge;
c) Responsibility knowledge – the knowledge which enables responsibility for the violation of norms to be ascribed to particular agents;
d) Reactive knowledge – which describes the sanctions that can be taken against those who are responsible for the violation of norms;

e) Meta-legal knowledge – which describes how to reason with other legal knowledge; and

f) Creative knowledge – which states how items of legal knowledge are created and destroyed.

Valente's ontology, which he described as a Legal Information Server, allows for the storage of legal knowledge as both text and an executable analysis system interconnected through a common expression within the terms of the functional ontology. The key thrust of his conceptualisation is to act as a principle for organizing and relating knowledge, particularly with a view to conceptual retrieval.

Many organizations are now building legal ontologies to provide legal knowledge on the World Wide Web. The Dutch Tax and Customs Administration have developed the POWER (Program for an Ontology-based working environment for rules and regulations) research project [van Engers and Glasee 2001]. POWER develops a method and supporting tools for the whole chain of processes from legislation drafting to executing the law by government employees. The POWER program improves legislation quality by the use of formal methods and verification techniques.

CLIME, e-COURT and FFPOIROT are all legal ontology projects funded by the European Union. Because of the plethora of legal systems, there is a great need to develop legal ontologies that are applicable across the European Union.

In the CLIME project, a large-scale ontology was developed for the purpose of a web-based legal advice system MILE (Maratime Information and Legal Explanation). The system features both extended conceptual retrieval and normative assessment on international rules and regulations regarding ship classification (Bureau Veritas) and maritime pollution (MARPOL). The user can formulate a case using a structured natural language interface. The interface uses only the terms available in the ontology, which ensures that the user formulates a query on a topic known to the system. The ontology also provides a means for adequate knowledge management of the rules and regulations.

The KDE (Knowledge worker Desktop Environment) project reused the CLIME ontology in a knowledge and workflow-management environment. In the KDE system, the CLIME ontology functioned as a domain ontology for the work of those associated with ship classification within the Bureau Veritas organization.

The CLIME knowledge base has two separate components:

a) Domain – A domain ontology of the design, construction, maintenance, repair, operation and construction of ships. The domain ontology incorporates a small abstract top ontology, distinguishing things like artifacts, substances, agents and functions;

b) Norms – A knowledge base of norms: mappings from rules in legal documents to deontic constraints that allow or disallow certain types of cases. These norms are often limited and incomplete interpretations of the norms expressed in the rules. The knowledge acquisition for the CLIME ontology can be split into two phases: (i) the conceptual retrieval phase in which the concepts and their relations are identified, created and defined, and (ii) the phase in which knowledge acquisition for normative assessment takes place.

The e-COURT project [Breuker *et al* 2002] is a European project that aims at developing an integrated system for the acquisition of audio/video depositions within courtrooms, the archiving of legal documents, information retrieval and synchronized audio/video/text consultation. The focus of the project is to process, archive and retrieve legal documents of criminal courtroom sessions. In principle, these documents should be accessible via the World Wide Web. The system has the following major functions:

a) Audio/Video/Text synchronization of data from court trials and hearings;
b) Advanced Information Retrieval – multilingual, tolerant to vagueness. Statistical techniques are combined with ontology based indexing and search;
c) Database management – multimedia documents support retrieval;
d) Workflow management defines and manages rules for sharing relevant information and events among judicial actors; and
e) Security management plays an important role to protect privacy information and to comply with national and international regulations about the interchange of criminal information.

The project is aimed at the semi-automated information management of documents produced during a criminal trial: in particular, the transcription of hearings. The structure of this type of document is determined by the debate/dialogue nature of the hearings, as well as by specific local court procedures. The developers identify and annotate content topics of a document. These annotations can vary from case descriptions in oral testimony to indictments in criminal law. Their first completed task was an ontology for Dutch criminal law, which served as a framework for ontologies on Italian and Polish criminal law.

FF-POIROT is a multi-million euro-dollar venture to develop European standards for the prevention, detection and successful investigation of financial fraud. The goal of the project is to build a detailed ontology of European Law, preventive practices and knowledge of the processes of financial fraud. The FF-POIROT project aims at compiling for several languages (Dutch, Italian, French and English) a computationally tractable and sharable knowledge repository (a formally described combination of concepts and their meaningful relationships) for the financial fraud domain. This knowledge source is being constructed in three ways:

a) Having human experts analyze and model the domain(s), in particular identifying the most abstract notions;
b) Using computers to automatically find relevant notions (the most specific ones) from existing documents and semi-structured corpora including the Internet (text mining);
c) Having humans validate the automatically generated suggestions to combine/merge already existing similar knowledge sources (semi-automatically aligning).

The resulting environment is useful to at least three different and EU-relevant types of user communities:

a) Investigative and monitoring bodies: benefit from the strongly enriched information retrieval made possible by linking e.g. internet or database search facilities to the FF-POIROT ontology in order to detect or investigate instances of attempted or actual financial fraud. Species of fraud (typologies) have been identified so that macro and micro-analysis can be undertaken, the results of which are then used as 'templates of fraud'. These templates can be stored, accessed and used to mine for new instances of fraud, conducted across linguistic and jurisdictional boundaries;
b) Financial professionals: Accountants, auditors, banks, insurance agencies, government departments, regulators and financial experts will benefit from an 'FF-POIROT-style' ontology using it as an authoritative concept base, extensively cross-linked (to other domains, systems and languages) and available for customised applications. Exploitation in this area could be as a high-tech service extending similar services and products (in particular with respect to accounting practices related to European VAT), currently already commercialised by at least two of FF-POIROT's users;
c) Law enforcement: Police and other law enforcement agencies benefit by the availability of relevant parts of the FF-POIROT ontology – for example as an RDF-mapped Semantic Web resource, to support future police-oriented query systems – in a non-technical user-friendly, attractive, and comprehensive manner. Additionally, sharing of information with investigative bodies and understanding of related documents will be substantially enhanced if such communication and documents are hyperlinked to a shared ontology. Optimising the investigation, discovery, prevention and reduction of complex frauds is being made routine and efficient.

The partners in the FF-POIROT projects include universities (in Belgium, Romania and the United Kingdom), software houses (in Belgium and Italy) and two industry partners, CONSOB and VAT Applications who wish to commercialize the consortium's results.

CONSOB is the public authority responsible for regulating the Italian securities market. It is the competent authority for ensuring: transparency and correct behaviour by securities market participants; disclosure of complete and accurate information to the investing public by listed companies; accuracy of the facts represented in the prospectuses related to offerings of transferable securities to the investing public; compliance with regulations by auditors entered in the Special Register. CONSOB conducts investigations with respect to potential infringements of insider dealing and market manipulation law. Within the FF-POIROT project, CONSOB is particularly interested in detecting and prosecuting companies that spread fraudulent information on the internet.

VAT Applications NV is a Belgian software company developing automated software to deal with issues surrounding Value Added Tax at a European level. It has packages for all countries and in eleven languages. The addition of ten new members to the European Union in 2004, has placed a further need for the development software packages to help compliance with VAT requirements across the European Union and the identification, prevention and reduction of fraud across jurisdictions.

The University of Edinburgh's Joseph Bell Centre for Forensic Statistics and Legal Reasoning is performing the following tasks:

a) Prepare for the construction and testing of the financial forensics repository using macro and micro analytical techniques;

b) Gather information on how relevant authorities accumulate and analyse evidence of financial fraud, and analyse the tools auditors and accountants use to maintain up-to-date awareness of financial services regulations; and

c) Collect requirements for the retained data, its validation and the applications needed to optimise the use of the information. User requirements were collected by conducting structured interviews and using consortium expertise to accumulate necessary information for the construction and testing of a financial fraud ontology. Advice was obtained from end-users on how law enforcement agencies and investigative and regulatory bodies accumulate and analyse criminal evidence in domains of financial fraud, and analyse resources by which financial regulatory knowledge is available for auditing and accounting professionals.

7. CHAPTER SUMMARY

In the last substantive chapter of the book, we have investigated what tasks need to be performed once we have mined our legal databases. Our major goal is to answer the question '*what do the results of the data-mining task signify?*

To answer this question, we first conduct an in-depth investigation of the issue of evaluation. Specific evaluation techniques for KDD systems include generalisation, re-substitution, hold out, cross validation and bootstrapping.

We next discussed the work of [Reich 1995] who stated that the determination of appropriate criteria for a comprehensive evaluation of a knowledge-based system cannot be performed without a conceptualisation of the nature of knowledge. He claimed knowledge can be defined in two ways: structurally and functionally. In the structural definition, knowledge is a static entity that includes facts, rules and models that represent real world phenomena. This definition of knowledge enables the direct measurement of knowledge.

Reich's theory was used to analyse the Split Up system in a variety of different ways: a) Domain expert assessment of the problem solving strategy adopted in Split Up; b) Qualitative feedback from users in different categories; c) Comparison of Split Up predictions with past judgements in the Family Court; d) Comparison of predictions made by Split Up with those made by eight lawyers on facts from the same three cases; e) Evaluation of explanations.

[Hall *et al* 2002] developed the Criteria, Context, Contingency-guidelines framework (CCCF). The CCCF assists an evaluator plan an evaluation in three distinct but interdependent ways. Initially it provides guidance to assess the context of the evaluation i.e. both of the system to be evaluated and of the evaluation itself and to determine the goals of the evaluation. The CCCF also contains a hierarchical four-quadrant model of potential evaluation criteria and offers contingency-guidelines to select appropriate criteria to satisfy the goals of the evaluation and any arising contingency.

The CCCF subsumes and integrates material sourced from the international standards and other frameworks. The CCCF seeks to be wide-ranging in scope and facilitate ordered access for the inexperienced legal evaluator to the multitude of information available. The experienced software engineer should also find it a useful reference to the many general evaluation criteria available, a means of organising their own criteria and a framework upon which to plan, standardise, report and compare their evaluations. It will also facilitate the inclusion of any legal domain specific evaluation requirements.

Another significant issue for statistically oriented knowledge based system is that of explanation. We stressed that it is legitimate to separate the explanation of a system's output from the manner in which it arrived at the output.

Our ultimate task was to investigate problem of deciding whether a legal task can be modelled by any existing paradigm (including KDD), and if so, which one. [Stranieri et al 1999] developed a simple classification scheme to classify legal tasks. The classification scheme is based on two dimensions: an estimation of the extent to which a task is open textured, and an estimation of the extent to which a task displays a feature that [Stranieri et al 1999] call boundedness.

Tasks that fall in the narrow bounded quadrant are well suited to implementation with heuristics elicited as rules because all terms are well defined and all variables relevant for the prediction are known. Discretionary tasks that fall in the wide bounded quadrant can be modelled using the KDD process. Unbounded tasks, whether or not they contain open textured terms, cannot be modelled adequately using KDD, since sufficient relevant factors cannot be determined.

CHAPTER 10

CONCLUSION

As we noted in chapter one, over the past decade, there has been a phenomenal advance in the use of knowledge discovery from database techniques. This was quite foreseeable given the volume and size of databases in specific areas. Such examples include astronomy, DNA databases, the human genome project and many databases of commercial transactions.

Not surprisingly, little significant progress has occurred in the area of knowledge discovery from legal databases. This is because of the differences between legal and other data. Legal data is typically unstructured and the amount of such data is small.

This observation gives rise to a number of significant questions, which have hopefully been answered in this book:
a) If legal data is so different, is there any sense in using Knowledge Discovery from Database techniques in legal databases.
b) To perform Knowledge Discovery from Databases requires the domain to have a sufficiency of cases. Reasoning with cases is standard practice in Common Law domains. However this is not the case in civil law domains. Hence is the use of KDD feasible in Civil Law domains?
c) Given that we can use KDD to model legal reasoning, what legal domains are most amenable to the use of KDD?
d) Suppose we have chosen a suitable domain in which to perform KDD from legal databases. How do we massage the knowledge/data so that KDD can be gainfully employed?
e) What data-mining techniques should we use to perform KDD from legal databases?
f) Once we have discovered certain patterns arising from the KDD process, how can we ensure that these patterns are both useful and valid?

We now summarise the material covered in this book by answering these questions.

1. THE VALIDITY OF USING KDD IN LEGAL DOMAINS

[Bench-Capon and Sergot 1988] view the indeterminacy in law as a specific consequence of the prevalence of open textured terms. [Prakken 1993] notes that the following distinct types of situations are difficult to resolve because of the open textured nature of law: a) Classification difficulties; b) defeasible rules, and c) vague terms.

We claim that the existence of judicial discretion contributes to the open textured nature of law. Yet situations that involve discretion cannot be described as instances of a), b), or c) above. We thus argue that the existence of discretion is a distinct form of open texture.

[Hart 1994] assigns judicial discretion a very minor role because rules and principles that derive from statutes or precedent cases can always be seen to underpin any decision that seems, superficially, to involve discretion. Critical legal studies theorists contend that rules and principles are not used to determine an outcome, but are invoked after a conclusion has been reached in order to support and justify an outcome

We claim that there are levels of discretion depending on the domain. There are many domains in which the exercise of discretion cannot be explained by the application of rules and principles. We hold this view because there exist domains such as property division in Australian family law, in which two decision makers may be applying identical rules and principles to facts interpreted in the same way, yet both arrive at different, but legally valid outcomes. Typically, the statute that underlies these domains presents a list of factors to be considered by the decision maker but does not indicate the relative weighting of each factor. [Christie 1986] calls these types of statutes shopping list Acts. Judges, in such domains exercise discretion by assigning a relative importance to each factor.

To develop our argument that KDD can be used in discretionary legal domains, we examined the concept of stare decisis. The principle dictates that the reasoning, loosely, ratio decidendi, used in new cases must follow the reasoning used by decision-makers in courts at the same or higher level in the hierarchy. If legal domains are so discretionary that leading commentators convincingly argue that stare decisis does not apply, then can case outcomes be predicted? If outcomes cannot be accurately predicted, then any attempt at doing so using KDD techniques is futile.

We identified three types of stare decisis:
a) Traditional stare decisis –
b) Personal stare decisis – where judges attempt to be consistent with themselves; and
c) Local stare decisis – where judges tend to be consistent with the decisions of other members of their own region (or registry).

The belief that even in domains where traditional stare decisis does not hold[63], judges at least attempt to abide by personal and local stare decisis, implies that like cases are treated in a like manner, and hence there is some possibility that KDD might be used to discern how judicial decisions are made in discretionary legal domains. We also noted that tasks suited to a KDD exercise are those that involve:

---

[63] Of course, in civil law countries, there is no notion of traditional stare decisis. However, we argue that in such countries judges still attempt to be consistent with themselves and with the decisions of other members of their own region.

a) Many ambiguous or vaguely defined concepts;
b) Many coarse grained rather than fine grained concepts;
c) Tasks underpinned by statutes that embed a *shopping list* of factors;
d) A socio-political environment that encourages ambiguity or discretion;
e) A complete list of relevant concepts for the task.

In general, a KDD analyst adheres to jurisprudential perspectives that are more consistent with the critical legal studies movement or the legal realism movement.

2. KDD AND REASONING WITH CASES

An assessment of the extent to which a KDD is suitable for a task involves identifying the extent to which a task involves open texture. Practitioners seem to estimate the degree to which a field of law is open textured statute in order to offer a prediction. Few practitioners would argue that the concept of a *vehicle* seems less subject to new uses than the concept *a social group* that arises in the determination of refugee status. Similarly, an expert in road laws will suggest that a judge will interpret terms driver, blood alcohol test and legal limit in one and only one way. Drink driving law seems therefore to be more predictable than family law, because it is less open textured than family law.

We noted that a determination of the degree of open texture inherent in a task involves the following considerations:

a)   Ambiguity;
b)   Granularity;
c)   The existence of discretionary statutes;
d)   The jurisprudential perspective presumed;
e)   The social and political context of the reasoning; and
f)   The completeness of the knowledge in the given domain..

Tasks underpinned by discretionary statutes, that adopt ambiguous terms but are essentially complete, are well suited to a KDD exercise. Tasks that are not complete or involve concepts that are not clearly understood are not suited to a KDD exercise, because of the suspicion that relevant variables for the task are not known.

The considerations involved in the selection of records from a domain depend to a large extent on whether the data derives from and represents reasoning processes used by decision makers, or whether the data represents descriptive features of a domain.

The key distinction to be made if data represents the reasoning process used in cases is that between commonplace cases and landmark cases. A landmark case is one that alters our perception about knowledge in the domain. A commonplace case is one that does not provide any lessons by itself, but together with numerous like cases can be used to derive conclusions.

Landmark cases rarely occur in common practice and are reported and discussed widely. These cases set a precedent that alters the way in which subsequent cases are decided   Jurisprudes and developers of legal decision support systems use landmark cases as norms or rules. Commonplace cases can be used to learn how judges exercise discretion. Hence, a training set of commonplace cases is far more suitable for a KDD exercise than the use of landmark cases.

We noted that commonplace cases are suitable for the discovery of knowledge about how judges exercise discretion in family law, whereas landmark cases are not suitable. The distinction between commonplace and landmark cases is not one based on clear definitional categories, since any case that is currently viewed as commonplace could conceivably be used in the future as a landmark case.

Although a case cannot be definitely categorized as either commonplace or landmark, the distinction is a useful one when applying selecting cases for inclusion in a KDD exercise. Most landmark cases are not suitable for the assembly of training sets for data-mining because these cases typically revolve around a definitional issue or they attempt to resolve a classification ambiguity so that a precedent for subsequent cases may be set. Landmark cases heard by appeal courts typically establish a new rule or principle.

Given that to perform KDD from legal databases, we require a sufficiency of commonplace cases and that civil law lawyers do not in general reason with cases, we need to consider whether it is feasible to use KDD in civil law domains. Fortunately, the proliferation of computers and density of legal regulation is leading to a greater use of case reports in civil law domains.

As long as sufficiently many and sufficiently detailed case descriptions exist, we argue that it feasible to use KDD to model the manner in which civil law judges exercise discretion.

3. WHAT LEGAL DOMAINS ARE AMENABLE TO THE USE OF KDD

To use KDD in a legal domain, we have established that the domain must have an abundance of commonplace cases. Whilst this requirement is necessary, is it sufficient? For example, whilst there are plenty of cases involving drink-driving, because the domain has well understood rules[64], it is un-necessary to use KDD to model judicial decision making with respect to drink-driving.

The problem of deciding whether a legal task can be modeled by any existing paradigm (including KDD), and if so, which one, is a problem currently tackled in an ad hoc manner by developers of legal reasoning systems. [Stranieri et al 1999] developed a simple classification scheme to classify legal tasks. The classification scheme is based on two dimensions. These are the estimation of the extent to which a task is open textured, and the estimation of the extent to which a task displays a feature that they call boundedness. The scheme illustrated in Figure 1 has two dimensions: open texture - well defined and bounded-unbounded.

---

[64] In Victoria, Australia we have rules: drink(X) & drive(X) → licence_loss(X), (blood_alcohol_level(X) >.05%) → drink(X)

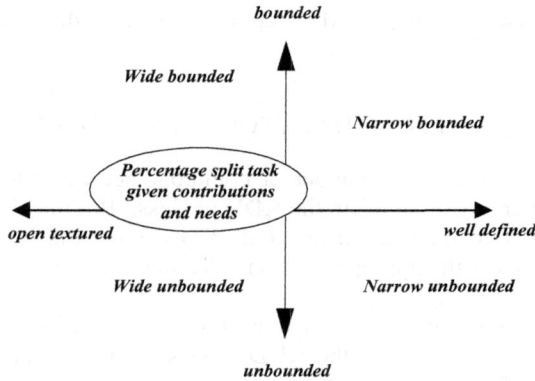

Figure 1 - Classification of percentage split task

In Figure 1, [Stranieri et al 1999] indicated that the task of determining the percentage of the Common Pool that the husband receives is wide bounded (i.e. this task is both open textured and bounded).

The open textured - well-defined axis reflects the extent to which experts believed factors known to be relevant in a prediction of the task of determining the percentage of the Common Pool that the husband received were open textured. For example, predicting a percentage split of marital assets was considered open-textured, because of the high degree of discretion given to Family Law judges. The bounded dimension refers to an expert's beliefs about the completeness of their knowledge of relevant factors.

In the Split-Up project, ninety-four variables were identified as relevant for predicting a percentage split of assets. Experts were of the view that few factors useful for a prediction were omitted from this list and therefore considered the task to be quite bounded.

Tasks that fall in the narrow bounded quadrant are well suited to implementation with heuristics elicited as rules because all terms are well defined and all variables relevant for the prediction are known. Discretionary tasks that fall in the wide bounded quadrant (top left in figure 10.1) can be modeled using the KDD process.

Unbounded tasks, whether or not they contain open textured terms, cannot be modeled adequately using KDD, since sufficient relevant factors cannot be determined. [Zeleznikow 2000] describes such domains as unfettered discretionary domains. Such domains have no norms and judges are not even told what factors must be taken into account in reaching a decision. We do not believe it is wise to model such domains.

Thus, we decided that KDD from legal databases could be most appropriately used in legal domains that are both open-textured and bounded.

The identification of an appropriate field of law and set of cases is a key first step in a KDD exercise. Another early step involves the identification of relevant variables or factors

4. PREPARING LEGAL DATA FOR USE IN THE KDD PROCESS

Once we have a sufficient number of commonplace cases in an open-textured legal domain, we are ready to begin the KDD process. But this does not in any way mean we are ready to mine the data. Indeed, we must first identify background information and select the appropriate data. We may then need to pre-process and transform the data.

Background knowledge is knowledge about the domain to be mined. The knowledge is useful for guiding the KDD process and for evaluating the patterns found. [Han and Kamber 2001] consider concept hierarchies, which are useful in that they allow data to be mined at multiple levels of abstraction. [Yearwood and Stranieri 2004] use a hierarchy of relevant factors derived from the Generic Actual Argument model, which extends the use of Toulmin Arguments described in [Stranieri et al 2001]. This model provides a natural framework for decomposing a task during the data transformation phase. It provides a mechanism for integrating domain knowledge to constrain and enhance the data-mining phase.

[Stranieri et al 1999] developed a sophisticated model about how marital property is distributed in Australia through the use of a Toulmin Argument Structure (see Figure 4 in Chapter 2). In total, the ninety-four variables were dispersed in thirty-five arguments. Twenty of these were classified 'wide bounded' so training sets were assembled for KDD. Heuristics for the remaining fifteen (classified narrow bounded) were sourced from experts for rule sets.

Once a knowledge structure for the relevant legal domain has been developed, we need to identify the relevant variables (on which data will be maintained) and the possible values of these variables. We then need to select a data sample that will enable knowledge about the whole population of interest to be gleaned from the sample.

Given that we have a training set of data, we need to pre-process the data for the data-mining procedure. This step involves dealing with missing values[65], inconsistent data[66] and erroneous data[67]. Data cleaning techniques[68] work to 'clean' the data by filling in missing values, smoothing noisy data, identifying or removing outliers and resolving inconsistencies.

---

[65] Missing values can be treated by: a) ignoring the missing data, b) removing the entire record, c) estimating an appropriate value.

[66] Once detected, inconsistent data may be dealt with in one of three ways: a) All contradictory cases are removed from the dataset, b) No contradictory cases are removed from the dataset, c) Some contradictory cases are removed according to other criteria. [Han and Kamber 2001] state that data smoothing can be performed by: i) binning, ii) clustering, iii) combining computer and human inspection, and iv) regression

[67] Erroneous data may occur because of a) noise, b) judicial error, c) change (in either legislation or landmark cases).

[68] Data cleaning techniques were discussed in chapter three.

Data that has been selected and pre-processed may not necessarily be ready for exposure to a data-mining algorithm. Some transformation of the data may dramatically enhance the benefit of the subsequent data-mining phase. Transformation can take one of three basic forms:

a) The decomposition of the data set into smaller parts where each part will be the subject of an independent data mining exercise;

b) The aggregation of variables and/or values to form a simpler, more general data set; or

c) Changing values of variables in some way.

The decomposition of a data set into smaller parts for independent mining exercises is particularly important for mining from data sets in law. This is due to the lack of availability of large data sets that reflect judicial reasoning. For example, ninety-four variables were identified by specialist family lawyers as relevant for determining property distribution outcomes in Australian family law. To achieve meaningful results, a data-mining exercise with so many variables requires data from many thousands of cases. However the data-mining exercise we conducted was decomposed into thirty-five independent, small and manageable data-mining exercises. Most of these smaller exercises involved less than five variables so that meaningful data-mining was possible with data from around one hundred cases.

Once the data has been pre-processed and adequately transformed, we are now ready to mine the data to find useful patterns. This is the only step of the KDD process that requires the use of computer technology. [Fayyad *et al* 1996] note that the data-mining stage takes less than twenty per cent of the time devoted to a typical KDD project.

5. TECHNIQUES FOR PERFORMING KDD IN LEGAL DATABASES

As outlined in Chapter 1, KDD techniques can be grouped into the following four categories:

a) Classification – where data is grouped into predefined categories.

b) Clustering – where data is analysed in order to group the data into groups of similar data.

c) Series Analysis – where we attempt to discover sequences within the data.

d) Association - where we discover ways in data elements are associated with other data elements.

Neither clustering nor series analysis is regularly used in knowledge discovery from legal databases. The aim of clustering techniques is to group data into clusters of similar items. Research in data clustering comes from biology, machine learning, marketing, spatial databases and statistics. Clustering is an example of unsupervised learning. Unlike classification, clustering and unsupervised learning do not rely on predefined classes and class-labelled training examples.

. The study by [Rissland and Friedman 1995] provides a good indication of the potential utility in using a time series analysis. They collected data from US Bankruptcy cases over a ten-year period and asked whether knowledge discovery techniques could be applied to automatically discover significant shifts in judicial decision-making.

Our first discussion of classification techniques was to consider the automated discovery of rules. Rule induction algorithms discover rules that are generalisations from data[69]. Other examples of automated discovery of rules are fuzzy rules and association rules.

Rule induction has the ability to deduce new knowledge. Once rules have been generated they can be reviewed and modified by the domain expert, providing for more useful, comprehensive and accurate rules for the domain.

A decision tree is an explicit representation of all scenarios that can result from a given decision. The root of the tree represents the initial situation, whilst each path from the root corresponds to one possible scenario. There are many algorithms for learning decision trees from data, and then converting these decision trees into rules. Most use information theory to optimise the rules generated. Algorithms that we considered included CART, the AQ family, ID3, C4.5 and C5.0. We also considered bagging and boosting as methods for improving the predictive power of classifier learning systems. [Zeleznikow *et al* 1994] and [Wilkins and Pillaipakkamnatt 1997] used rule induction to analyse legal concepts.

Fuzzy rules capture something of the uncertainty inherent in the way in which language is used to construct rules. Fuzzy logic and statistical techniques can be used in dealing with uncertain reasoning. [Philipps 1993] and [Borgulya 1999] have used fuzzy reasoning in model traffic accident law. [Xu *et al* 1999] constructed a case-based reasoner/fuzzy logic system to provide advice about contracts under the United Nations Convention on Contracts for the International Sale of Goods. [Haliwell et al 2003] presents a novel approach to the representation of subjective probability assessments known as linguistic probabilities. Fuzzy sets have been widely used to represent the inherent vagueness in linguistic descriptions. They use a combination of fuzzy methods and Bayesian methods to evaluate the usefulness of forensic evidence.

Bayesian methods provide formalism for reasoning about partial beliefs under conditions of uncertainty. In this formalism, propositions are given numerical values, signifying the degree of belief accorded to them. They are very useful for performing classification under uncertainty. [Davis and Pei 2003] used twin Bayesian Belief networks, built using forensic knowledge and models of mass and movement that derive from physics to reconstruct evidence about traffic accidents. WIN (Westlaw is Natural) uses a Bayesian network to compute the probabilities that documents in a database are relevant to a query, and returns the relevant documents in order of their significance to the relevant query.

A neural network receives its name from the fact that it resembles a nervous system in the brain. It consists of many self-adjusting processing elements cooperating in a densely interconnected network. Each processing element generates

---

[69] Inductive reasoning is the process of moving from specific cases to general rules. A rule induction system is given examples of a problem where the outcome is known. When it has been given several examples, the rule induction system can create rules that are true from the example cases. The rules can then be used to assess other cases where the outcome is not known.

a single output signal that is transmitted to the other processing elements. The output signal of a processing element depends on the inputs to the processing element: each input is gated by a weighting factor that determines the amount of influence that the input will have on the output. The strength of the weighting factors is adjusted autonomously by the processing element as data is processed.

Neural networks are particularly useful in dealing with

a)   Classification difficulties;
b)   Vague terms;
c)   Defeasible rules; and
d)   Discretionary domains.

Because neural networks use essentially statistical techniques to learn weights, the issues of explanation and the evaluation of the outcome of neural networks are vital. For example, [Stranieri *et al* 1999] used Toulmin's analysis of argumentation to provide explanations in Split-Up.

[Hobson and Slee 1994] used neural networks to predict the outcome of theft study a cases from the UK theft act and a Brazilian judge (V. Feu Rosa Pedro) has initiated a program for the resolution of traffic accident disputes using neural networks [FeuRosa 2000]. PROLEXS [Walker *et al* 1991] used neural networks in case selection, case abstraction and credit assignment in the domain of Dutch landlord-tenant law. [Stranieri *et al* 1999] used a hybrid rule-based/neural network systems to model how Australian Family Court judges exercise their discretion in distributing marital property. [Borges *et al* 2003] used neural networks to model the legal reasoning of judges about employment contract cases at the Court of Appeal, Versailles, France.

An association rule identifies a link between two or more attributes. Association rules are not intended to be viewed as generalisations from data, but indicate that an association between the condition(s) and the consequent exists. An association rule is of the form A_1 & A_2 & .... & A_m → P. The association rule is interpreted as *database tuples that satisfy the conditions in the A_i are also likely to satisfy the conditions in P*. Associated with each rule, is a confidence factor, which states the likelihood of the rule being true and the support of the rule that states how many of the items in the data set are effected by this rule.

[Stranieri *et al* 2000] used association rules to study the distribution of marital property by the Family Court of Australia. [Ivkovic *et al* 2003] used over 300,000 records drawn from a database of applicants for government-funded legal aid in Australia, to detect trends in the distribution of legal aid grants.

Other statistical techniques that have been used in KDD include evolutionary computing and support vector machines. Evolutionary algorithms are computer-based problem solving systems that use computational models of evolutionary processes as key elements in their design and implementation. Genetic algorithms are an example of evolutionary computing. Genetic algorithms are general-purpose search algorithms that use principles derived from genetics to solve problems. A population of evolving knowledge structures that evolve over time – through competition and controlled variation – is maintained. Each structure in the population represents a candidate solution to the concrete problem and has an associated fitness to determine which structures are used to form new ones in the competition.   The new structures are created using genetic operators such as crossover and mutation.   [Pannu 1995] applied genetic algorithms to discover a prototype, 'perfect' exemplar for cases with a specified outcome.

As long as two classes are linearly separable, support vector machines determine the hyperplane in the n-dimensional feature space that maximises the margin between the examples of the classes. A new example is classified by computing to which side of the hyperplane the example belongs.   The technique can be generalised to examples that are not linearly separable

Once we have discovered the results of our knowledge discovery exercise, we need to make some sense of the result, through providing an explanation, evaluating the results to show they are significant and possibly visualising the results.

6. UNDERSTANDING AND JUSTIFYING THE RESULTS OF THE KDD PROCESS

Because KDD is basically a statistical endeavour, it is essential that KDD systems provide significant explanations. Explanations are particularly important in legal decision support systems because:

a)   Users of the system need to satisfy themselves that the program's conclusions are basically correct for their particular use;

b)   Knowledge engineers need to satisfy themselves that knowledge is being applied properly;

c)   Domain experts need to see a trace of the way in which their knowledge is being applied, in order to judge whether knowledge elicitation is proceeding successfully.

Explanation and Argumentation have become a major research topic in the development of legal decision support systems. [Stranieri *et al* 2001] claim that explanations for discretionary reasoning can be generated if explanatory text is stored within an knowledge representation framework based on the argument structure of [Toulmin 1958], or indeed most other argument structures.   They assume that an explanation is separate from the steps used to infer a solution; and that explanations for discretionary reasoning is further removed from the reasoning steps than is the case in less discretionary domains. This is particularly important when using neural networks or other statistical KDD techniques to model reasoning in discretionary legal domains.

Rules, neural networks or other data-mining phase techniques learn patterns, or weights from the dataset.   The extent to which the discovered knowledge is applicable to data not in the dataset is unknown. A neural network for example, may accurately predict every case in the dataset yet fail on every future case.

The degree to which the knowledge discovered generalises from the dataset to the entire population can be estimated by re-sampling.   There are five main re-sampling methods typically used:

a)   Re-substitution;

b)   Hold out;

c)   Leave one out;

d) Cross validation; and

e) Bootstrapping.

The evaluation of any legal system is fraught with theoretical and pragmatic obstacles. Assumptions regarding the nature of knowledge impact on how knowledge discovered using the process are evaluated. A data-mining system has the potential to generate thousands of patterns or rules. Not all of the patterns are useful or interesting. Hence we need to define what is an interesting pattern and how can we generate all the interesting patterns and only the interesting patterns.

A pattern is also interesting if it validates a hypothesis that the user sought to confirm. An interesting pattern represents knowledge. Several objective measures of pattern interestingness exist, based on the structure of discovered patterns and of the statistics underlying them.   The concepts of support and confidence are examples of objective measures of pattern interestingness.   In general, each interestingness measure is associated with a threshold, which may be controlled by the user.

A major consideration for both the legal decision support system developer and evaluator is the significant social impact that systems can exercise both upon individuals and on the general system environment. Some systems need to be evaluated in a wider forum than that provided by the users, sponsors and their parent organizations [Hall et al 2002].

For an evaluator to understand a system, its benefits, and its constraints, it is necessary to be fully aware of the context in which the system operates. The Context, Criteria, Contingency evaluation framework of [Hall et al 2002] assists an evaluator with this task, suggesting areas that could be fruitful in gaining such an understanding: the parent organization, the application domain, management support, funding, system resourcing and constraints, risk exposure and the work environment.

7. HOW KNOWLEDGE DISCOVERY IN LAW CAN ENHANCE ACCESS TO JUSTICE

It may seem a strange question to pose at the end of a book on knowledge discovery in legal databases, but nevertheless, we need to consider that even if it is technically possible to perform knowledge discovery from legal databases, is there any benefit to the legal community in performing such discovery? Alternatively, is knowledge discovery from legal databases an academic exercise, or are there real benefits for legal professionals?

We believe that knowledge discovery in legal databases can greatly improve access to justice. [Branting 2001] notes that increasing numbers of litigants represent themselves in court. This swelling tide of *pro se*[70] litigants constitutes a growing burden not only to the judiciary but the entire legal process. Typically, unrepresented litigants:

---

[70] A pro se litigant is one who does not retain a lawyer and appears for himself in court.

a) Extend the time taken for litigation – due to their lack of understanding of the process.
b) Place themselves at a disadvantage compared to their opponent(s).
c) Place the judicial decision-maker in the difficult position of deciding how much support and forbearance the decision-maker should offer to the *pro se* litigant.

A recent study conducted for the American Bar Association in the Supreme Court of Maricopa County, Arizona, USA, indicated that at least one of the parties were self-represented in over 88% of domestic relations cases and both parties were self-represented in 52% of the cases. [Meachem 1999] reports that in 1999, 24,416 of the 54,693 cases opened in the US Court of Appeals were filed by *pro se* appellants. This figure, whilst on first glance may not appear alarming, needs to be considered in light of the fact that many pro se appellants have neither the financial resources nor legal skills to conduct their own appeals.

[Quatrevaux 1996] notes that there is a shortfall in legal systems for poor persons in the United States. [Branting 2001] claims that domestic abuse victims are particularly likely to have few resources and little opportunity to obtain the services of a lawyer. He states that the growth of the consumer movement has increased the trend for pro se litigation. The growing availability of books, document kits and computerised forms, together with the increasing availability of legal materials on the World Wide Web, has increased the opportunities for pro se litigants to organise their own litigation.

[Zeleznikow 2002] claims that the development of legal decision support systems has led to:
a) **Consistency** – by replicating the manner in which decisions are made, decision support systems are encouraging the spreading of consistency in legal decision-making.
b) **Transparency** – by demonstrating how legal decisions are made, legal decision support systems are leading to a better community understanding of legal domains. This has the desired benefit of decreasing the level of public criticism of judicial decision-making[71].
c) **Efficiency** - One of the major benefits of decision support systems is to make firms more efficient.
d) **Enhanced support for dispute resolution** - Users of legal decision support systems are aware of the likely outcome of litigation and thus are encouraged to avoid the costs and emotional stress of legal proceedings.

Whilst [Zeleznikow 2002] does not claim that the construction of legal decision support systems will have a drastic effect on improving access to justice, he makes the argument that the construction of such systems for community legal centres will improve their efficiency and increase the volume of advice they can offer. Until

---

[71] Judges of the Family Court of Australia are worried about criticism of the court, which has led to the death of judges, and physical attacks on courtrooms. They believe enhanced community understanding of the decision making process in Australian Family Law will lead to reduced conflict.

recently, most legal decision supports systems were rule-based and developed to run on personal computers. Whereas personal computer based tools are fine for lawyers, they may not be easily accessible to pro-se litigants. Reasons for this difficulty include their lack of an awareness of such systems, and the high cost of purchasing relevant software. Currently, very few legal decision support systems are available on the World Wide Web.

[Zeleznikow 2002] discusses how the provision of web-based systems can enhance access to justice. He shows how two systems built in his laboratory, Split-Up and GetAid improve access to justice. The construction of these systems has led to the development of a start up company JUSTSYS (www.justsys.com.au) which constructs tools for building legal decision support systems on the World Wide Web. Given JUSTSYS' tools, legal knowledge managers can use KDD to build legal decision support systems on the World Wide Web. Such systems can enhance the general public's legal knowledge and hence improve access to justice.

8. CURRENT AND FUTURE RESEARCH IN KNOWLEDGE DISCOVERY IN LAW

Most legal cases are not stored in legal databases. They are generally recorded in free text. Whilst the issue of information retrieval and text mining is not a topic in Artificial Intelligence, the retrieval of relevant cases and statutes is one of the major benefits that information technology can provide for legal professionals. Thus, we need to examine how information retrieval and text mining is used in the legal domain.

Text mining is the discovery of knowledge by the automatic analysis of free text. It includes information extraction, text summarisation, text categorisation and text clustering.

Information extraction is a technique for extracting domain-specific information from texts. Text fragments are mapped to field or template lots that have a definite semantic meaning. [Bruninghaus and Ashley 2001] present an approach for automatically extracting factors for use in case based reasoning from the text of cases. In Smile, [Bruninghaus and Ashley 2001] assembled a training set of case summaries from the field of trade secrets law. Sentences in the summaries were marked up as positive instances or negative instances of a factor. A decision tree was then induced using ID3 that could classify whether a sentence was an instance of a factor. This approach, inspired by Support Vector Machines led to useful improvements, based on using natural language parsing to abstract the role key players mentioned in the summaries derived from text. The SPIRE system [Daniels and Rissland 1997] located passages likely to contain information about legally relevant features of cases found in full-text court opinions.

Text categorisation organises documents into a taxonomy, thus allowing for more efficient searches. It involves the assignment of subject descriptors or classification codes to complete texts. The technique of text clustering supposes: i) an abstract representation of the object to be clustered, containing the features for the classification, ii) a function that computes the relative importance (weight) of the features, iii) a function that computes a numerical similarity between the representations. A case study of legal document classification was performed by [Bench-Capon 1997]. A non-standard neural network model performs the core task of classification with a layered architecture consisting of mutually independent unsupervised neural networks. The resulting system has a remarkably fast training time and explicit cluster representation.

Clustering is employed to group terms if the regularly co-occur in documents or to group documents if they discuss the same topic terms. In unsupervised learning a neural network is not presented with inputs and outputs. Rather, the entire data set is presented to the network. The network is required to cluster examples into groups of similar examples. Unsupervised neural networks known as Self-organising maps or Kohonen networks have been applied in a text mining KDD by [Merkl and Schweighofer 1997]. [Merkl and Schweighofer 1997] discovered four key clusters in public international law; humanitarian law, human rights, environment law and other matters.

Text summarisation involves identifying summarising and organising related text so that users can efficiently deal with information in large documents. In the SALOMAN project, ([Moens *et al* 1997] and [Moens 2000]) aimed to generate a summary of a judgment. This is done by combining text matching using information retrieval algorithms with expert knowledge about the structure of judgments.

[Grover *et al* 2003] report on the sum project that applies automatic summarization techniques to the legal domain. In their methodology sentences from text are classified according to their rhetorical role in order that particular types of sentence can be extracted to form a summary. They describe some experiments with judgements of the House of Lords. They have performed automatic linguistic annotation of a small sample set and then hand-annotated the sentences in the set in order to explore the relationship between linguistic features and argumentative roles. [Farzindar and Lapalme 2004] describe a method for the summarization of legal documents helping a legal expert determine the key ideas of a judgment. Their approach is based on the exploration of the document's architecture and its thematic structures in order to build a table style summary for improving coherency and readability of the text. They present the components of a system, called LetSum, built with this approach, its implementation and some preliminary evaluation results.

[Dozier *et al* 2003] describe how an online directory of expert witnesses was created from jury verdict and settlement documents using text-mining techniques. They created an expert witness directory that contains over 100,000 expert profiles, based on approximately 300,000 jury verdict and settlement documents, publicly available professional license information, an expertise taxonomy, and automatic text mining techniques. This directory can be browsed by area of expertise as well as by location and name. In addition, expert profiles are automatically linked to medline articles and jury verdict and settlement documents. The supporting technologies that made this application possible include information extraction from text via regular expression parsing, record linkage through Bayesian based matching, and automatic rule-based classification.

[Oatley *et al* 2004a] note that computer science technology that can support police activities is wide ranging, from the well known geographical information systems display ('pins inmaps'), clustering and link analysis algorithms, to the more complex use of data mining technology for profiling single and series of crimes or offenders,and matching and predicting crimes. They present a discussion of data mining and decision support technologies for police, considering the range of computer science technologies that are available to assist police activities. The discussion is very practical, with examples taken from the authors' own work with three United Kingdom police forces.

[Oatley *et al* 2004b] discuss data mining and text mining in the domain of the high volume crime of Burglary from Dwelling Houses (BDH) with the collaboration of the West Midlands Police. In [Oatley and Ewart 2003], software was developed to interrogate the database of recorded crimes in order to explore the temporal and spatial characteristics of BDH across the entire operational command unit. The objectives were to allow police to test their beliefs about BDH trends and patterns against the empirical realities, thereby providing a more substantive empirical foundation for the development and implementation of preventative and detection strategies.

[Ashley 2003] argues that judges in civil law jurisdictions do reason with legal cases, but in a very different way from their common law counterparts. Whilst case-based reasoning is particularly suited for modelling reasoning in common law, Knowledge Discovery from Databases is equally suited for use in Civil Law domains. The reason for our claim is that KDD is primarily used to understand how judges exercise discretion. Even in civil law countries, with their emphasis on codifying the law, there exist discretionary acts. The use of KDD in civil law countries can help support transparency and consistency in such countries.

Mixed jurisdictions and mixed legal systems, their characteristics and definition, have become a subject of very considerable interest and debate in Europe, no doubt because of the European Union, which has brought together many legal systems under a single legislature, which in turn has adopted laws and directives taking precedence over national laws. In effect, the European Union is becoming a mixed jurisdiction.

[Ashley 2003] also believes that the proliferation of computers and density of legal regulation will lead to a greater use of case reports in civil law domains. Thus with the development of a European Legal System, and UN conventions and courts there is a need for a uniform application of the same law. As long as sufficiently many and sufficiently detailed case descriptions exist, we argue that it feasible to use KDD to model the manner in which civil law judges exercise discretion.

In summary, we claim that KDD techniques are particularly adept at discovering patterns of judicial reasoning in discretionary fields of law, provided the data that reflects the reasoning processes is collected. Although there is a risk that misleading conclusions can be drawn as a result of a KDD exercise, those risks are offset against potential gains. KDD can promise to make law more accessible, affordable, predictable and transparent.

11

BIBLIOGRAPHY

Adelman, L. 1989. Integrating evaluation methods into the DSS development process. *Information & Decision Technologies* 15(4): 227-41

Agrawal, R., Imielinski, T and Swami, A. 1993. Mining Association Rules between sets of items in Large Databases in Peter Buneman, Sushil Jajodia (Eds.): *Proceedings of the 1993 ACM SIGMOD International Conference on Management of Data*, Washington, D.C., May 26-28, 1993. ACM Press 1993, SIGMOD Record 22(2): 207-216

Aikenhead, M. 1996. The Uses and Abuses of Neural Networks in Law. Santa Clara Computer and High Technology Law Journal. February 1996, 12(1): 31-70.

Aitken, C. 1995. Statistics and the Evaluation of Evidence for Forensic Scientists. John Wiley and Sons, Chichester, UK

Aleven V and Ashley K 1997. Evaluating a Learning Environment for Case-Based Argumentation Skills, *Proc 6th Intl Conf Artificial Intelligence & Law,* Melbourne, Australia, June 30 – July 4, ACM Press, New York: 170 –179.

Aleven, V. and Ashley, K.D. 1995. Doing things with factors. *Proceedings of Fifth International Conference on Artificial Intelligence and Law*, ACM Press: 31-41

Alexander, R. 1992. Mediation, violence and the family. *Alternative Law Journal* 17(6): 276-99

Alexander, R. 2000. *Reflections on gender in family law decision making in Australia* Ph.D Thesis. Monash University. Australia

Alexander, R. 2002. *Domestic violence in Australia : the legal response* 3rd ed. Publisher: Annandale, N.S.W. Federation Press.

Al-Kofahi, K., Tyrrell, A., Vachher, A. and Jackson, P., 2001. A Machine Learning Approach to Prior Case Retrieval. *Proceedings of the 8th international conference on Artificial intelligence and law*. ICAIL'01 St. Louis, Missouri, ACM Press: 89 – 93.

Antoniou, G. 1997. *Nonmonotonic Reasoning with Incomplete and Changing Information.* MIT Press

228

Antoniou, G, Billington, D., Governatori, G, Maher, M, J. and Rock, A., 2000. A flexible framework for Defeasible Logics. *Proceedings of the Seventeenth National Conference on Artificial Intelligence and Twelth Conference on Innovative Applications of Artificial Intelligence.* AAAI Press/ MIT Press. Austin Texas: 405-411

Antoniou, G, Billington, D., and Maher, M, J., 1999. The Analysis of regulations using defeasible rules. *Proceedings of the 32nd Hawaii Internatinal Conference on Systems Science.* Maui, Hawaii: 225

Antoniou, G. and Williams, M. A. 1995. Reasoning with Incomplete and Changing Information: The CIN Project. *Proceedings 2nd Joint Conference on Information Sciences.* Duke University. *Information Sciences* Volume 99 (1-2): 83-99

Ashley, K. D. 1991. *Modelling legal argument: Reasoning with cases and hypotheticals.* Cambridge: MIT Press.

Ashley, K. D. 2003 Case-Based Models of Legal Reasoning in a Civil Law Context. In *International Congress of Comparative Cultures and Legal Systems* at the Instituto de Investigaciones Jurídicas, Universidad Nacional Autonoma de México. Mexico City, Mexico Invited paper. February 2004. Can be accessed at www.juridicas.unam.mx/inst/ evacad/eventos/2004/0902/mesa9/239s.pdf

Baez-Yates, R. and Ribeiro-Neto, B. 1999. *Modern Information Retrieval,* Addison Wesley, Harlow, UK.

Balding, D.J. and Donnelly, P. 1995. Inference in forensic identification. *Journal of the Royal Statistical Society Series A,* 158:21-53

Ball, W. J. 1994. Using Virgil to analyse public policy arguments: a system based on Toulmin's informal logic. *Social Science Computer Review:* 12(1): 26-37.

Barai, S. V. and Reich, Y. 1999 Ensemble modelling or selecting the best model: Many can be better than one. Artificial Intelligence for Engineering Design, Analysis (AI EDAM), and Manufacturing, 13(5): 377-386.

Baxendale, P. B. 1958. Machine-made Index for Technical Literature - an Experiment. *IBM Journal of Research and Development,* 2 (4): 354-361.

Bayles, M. D. 1990. *Procedural Justice. Allocating to Individuals.* Kluwer. Dordrecht.

Bench-Capon T. J. M. 1993a. In Defence of Rule Based Representations for Legal Knowledge Based Systems. *Proceedings of the 4th National Conference on Law, Computers and Artificial Intelligence.* Exeter. UK. 21/22 April.

Bench-Capon, T. J. M. 1993b. Neural networks and open texture. In the Proceedings of the *Fourth International Conference on Artificial Intelligence and Law: an International Journal ,* ACM Press. Amsterdam: 292-297

Bench-Capon, T. J. M., 1997. Argument in artificial intelligence and law. *Artificial Intelligence and Law* 5(4): 249-261

Bench-Capon, T. J. M., 1998. Specification and Implementation of Toulmin Dialogue Game. in Hage, J., C., Bench-Capon, T., J., M., Koers, A., de Vey Mestdagh, C.N.J and Grutters, C., (Eds). *Legal Knowledge Based Systems. Jurix: The Eleventh Conference*. Gerard Noodt Institut (GNI). The Netherlands.

Bench_Capon, T, J, M. 1999. Some observations on modelling case based reasoning with formal argument models. Proceedings of the Seventh International Conference on Artificial Intelligence and Law, ICAIL '99, Oslo, Norway. ACM: 36-42

Bench-Capon, T.J.M., Coenen, F., and Leng, P., 2000. An Experiment in Discovering Association Rules in the Legal Domain. *Proceedings of the 11th International Workshop on Database and Expert System applications (DEXA'2000)*. IEEE Press.

Bench-Capon T. J. M, Lowes, D. and McEnery, A. M. 1991. Argument-based explanation of logic programs. Knowledge Based Systems, 4(3): 177-183

Bench-Capon, T. J. M. and Staniford, G. 1995. PLAID - Proactive Legal Assistance. Proceedings of *Fifth International Conference on Artificial Intelligence and Law: an International Journal* . May 21-24. Boston. ACM Press, USA: 81-87

Bench-Capon, T. J. M., and Sergot, M. J., 1988. Towards a rule-based representation of open texture in law. In Walter, C. (Ed), *Computer Power and Legal Language:* 39-61, New York: Quorum Books

Bench-Capon T.J.M. and Visser P.R.S. 1997 Ontologies in Legal Information Systems: the Need for Explicit Specifications of Domain Conceptualizations, *Proc 6th Intl Conf Artificial Intelligence and Law*, ACM Press, New York: 132-141.

Berman, D. H. 1991. Developer's choice in the legal domain: Thje Sisyphean journey with case—based reasoning or down hill with rules. *Proceedings of the Third International Conference on Artificial Intelligence and Law*, ACM: 307—309.

Berman, D. H. and Hafner, C. D. 1988. Obstacles to the development of logic-based models of legal reasoning. In Walter, C. (Ed) *Computer Power and Legal Reasoning:* 183-214, New York: Quorum Books.

Bing, J. and Harvold, T. 1977. *Legal Decisions and Information Systems*. Tano, Norway.

Black, H. C. 1990. *BLACK'S LAW DICTIONARY*, West Publishing Company, St. Paul, Minnesota.

Blair, D. C. and Maron, M. E. 1985. An evaluation of retrieval effectiveness for a full-text document-retrieval system. *Communications of the Association for Computing Machinery*, 28:289-299.

Boehm, B. W. 1981. *Software Engineering Economics*. Englewood Cliffs, NJ, Prentice Hall

Borges, F., Borges, R. and Bourcier, D. 2003. Artificial Neural Networks and Legal Categorization. *Proceedings of Sixteenth International Conference on Legal Knowledge Based System.* IOS Publications, Amsterdam, Netherlands: 11-20.

Borgulya, I. 1999. Two Examples of Decision Support in the Law. *Artificial Intelligence and Law* 7.(2-3): 303-321.

Branting, L. K. 1991. Building explanations from rules and structured cases. *International Journal of Man Machine Studies* 34(6): 797-838.

Branting, L. K. 1994. A Computational Model of Ratio Decidendi *Artificial Intelligence and Law: an International Journal* 2: 1-31

Breiman, L. 1996. Bagging Predictors. *Machine Learning,* 24(2): 123-140.

Breiman, L., Friedman, J. H., Ohlsen, R. A. and Stone, P. J. 1984. *Classification and regression trees.* Wadsworth International Group: Belmont, Ca

Breuker, J., Elhag, A., Petkov, E. and Winkels, R. 2002. Ontologies for Legal Information Serving and Knowledge Management, *Proc Jurix 2002: 15th Annual Conf Legal Knowledge and Information Systems,* IOS Press, Amsterdam: 73-82.

Brkic, J. 1985. *Legal Reasoning: Semantic and Logical Analysis.* Peter Lang. New York.

Brüninghaus, S. and Ashley, K., 2001 . Improving the representation of legal case texts with information extraction methods. Proceedings of the 8th international conference on Artificial intelligence and law. ICAIL'01 St. Louis, Missouri, ACM Press: 42 - 51

Bruninghaus, S. and Ashley, K. 2003 Predicting Outcomes of Case-based Legal Arguments. Proceedings of the *Ninth International Conference on Artificial Intelligence and Law,* Edinburgh, Scotland: ACM Press: 233-242.

Buchanan, B., Moore, J., Forsythe, D., Carenini, G., Ohlsson, S. and Banks, G., 1995. An Intelligent interactive system for delivering individualised information to patients. *Artificial Intelligence in Medicine.* 7(2); 117-154

Budescu, D. V. and Wallsten, T. S. 1985. Consistency in interpretation of probabilistic phrases. *Organizational Behaviour and Human Decision Processes,* 36:391-405.

Bueno, T. C. Bortolon, A. Hoeschl, H. C. Mattos, E. S. and Ribeiro, M. S. 2003. Analyzing the Use of Dynamic Weights in Legal Case Based System Proceedings of the *Ninth International Conference on Artificial Intelligence and Law,* Edinburgh, Scotland: ACM Press: 136-141.

Callan, J. P., Croft, W. B. and Harding, S. M. 1992. The INQUERY retrieval system. *Proceedings of DEXA92,* Springer-Verlag, New York.

Carbogim, D., Robertson, D., and Lee, J., 2000. Argument-based applications to knowledge engineering. *The Knowledge Engineering Review.* 15(2): 119-149.

Chelimsky, E. 1997. The coming transformations in evaluation. In *Evaluation for the 21st Century: A handbook*. E. Chelimsky and W. R. Shadish (eds.). Thousand Oaks, CAL, SAGE: 1-26

.Chen, P., 2000. An Automatic System for Collecting Crime on the Internet, *The Journal of Information, Law and Technology (JILT)*. 3 http://elj.warwick.ac.uk/jilt/00-3/chen.html

Chen, Z. 2001. *Data Mining and Uncertain Reasoning: An Integrated Approach*. John Wiley and Sons, New York, NY.

Chen, H. 2003. Introduction to the JASIST Special Topic Session on Web Retrieval and Mining: A Machine Learning Perspective, *Journal of the American Society for Information Science and Technology (JASIST)*, 54(7): 621-624.

Christie, G. C., 1986. An Essay on Discretion *Duke Law Journal*. pp747-78.

Cios, K. J., Pedrycz, W. and Swiniarski, R. 1998. *Data Mining Methods for Knowledge Discovery*. Kluwer: Boston, Ma.

Clark, P . 1991. *A Model of Argumentation and Its Application in a Cooperative Expert System*. PhD thesis. Turing Institute. Department of Computer Science. University of Strathclyde. Glasgow.

Cohen, P. 1985. *Heuristic Reasoning about Uncertainty: An Artificial Intelligence Approach*. London, Pitman.

Cohen, W. and Singer, Y. 1999. Context sensitive learning methods for text classification. ACM Transactions on Information Systems, 17(2): 141-173.

Cowie, J and Wilks, Y. 2000. Information Extraction. In Dale, R., Moisl, H. and Somers, H. (eds.), *Handbook of Natural Language Processing*, Marcel Dekker, New York: 240-260.

Croft, W. B. and Turtle, H. R. 1992. Text retrieval and inference. In Jacobs, P. (ed.) *Text-Based Intelligent Systems*, Lawrence Erlbaum, Hillsdale New Jersey: 127-155.

Cybenko, G., 1989. Approximation by superpositions of a sigmoidal function. *Mathematics of Control, Signals and Systems*. 2: 303-314 .

Daniels J. J. and Rissland E. L., 1997. Finding Legally Relevant Passages in Case Opinions. In *Proceedings of the Sixth International Conference on Artificial Intelligence and Law*. Melbourne. ACM Press. New York: 39-46.

David, R. and Brierley, J. E. C. 1985. *Major Legal Systems in the World Today*, (Eds)., Stevens & Sons, London.

Davis, G and Pei, J. 2003 Bayesian Networks and Traffic Accident Reconstruction, Proceedings of the *Ninth International Conference on Artificial Intelligence and Law*, Edinburgh, Scotland: ACM Press, 171-176.

DeLone, W. H. and McLean, E.R. 1992. Information Success: The quest for the dependent variable. *Informations Systems Research* 3(1): 60-95.

Dempster, A. P. 1968. A generalization of Bayesian inference. *Journal of the Royal Statistical Society* ser. B30, 205-247.

Derweester, S., Dumais, S. T., Furnas, G. W., Landauer, T. K. And Harshman, R. 1990. Indexing by Latent Semantic Analysis. *Journal of the American Society for Information Science*, 41(6): 391-407.

Dick, J. P. 1991. *A conceptual, case-relation representation of text for intelligent retrieval*. Ph.D Thesis. University of Toronto. Canada.

Dick, J. P. 1987. Conceptual retrieval and case law. *Proceedings of the First International Conference on Artificial Intelligence and Law*. Boston. ACM Press: 106-115.

Dickey, A., *Family Law*. 1990. 2nd Ed. The Law Book Company Ltd. Sydney.

Diederich, J., 1992. Explanation and artificial neural networks. *International Journal of Man Machine Studies*. 37(3): 335-355

Dozier C, Jackson, P, Guo, X, Chaudhary, M and Arumainayagam, Y 2003 Creation of an Expert Witness Database through Text Mining, *Proc 9th Intl Conf Artificial Intelligence and Law*, Edinburgh, Scotland, ACM Press, New York: 177-184.

Dung, P M. 1995. On the acceptability of arguments and its fundamental role in non-monotonic reasoning, logic programming and n-person games *Artificial Intelligence*. 77 (2): 321-57.

Dworkin, R. 1977. *Taking rights seriously*. Harvard University Press. Cambridge.

Dworkin, R. 1986. *Law's Empire*. Duckworth. London.

Earl, L. L. 1970. Experiments in Automatic Extracting and Indexing. *Information Storage and Retrieval*, 6: 313-334.

Edmundson, H. P. 1969. New Methods in Automatic Extracting. *Journal of the Association for Computing Machinery*, 16 (2): 264-285.

Efron, B. 1983, Estimating the error rate of a prediction rule: Improvement on cross-validation, *J. of the American Statistical Association*, 78, 316-331.

Efron, B. and. Tibshirani, R. J. 1993. *An Introduction to the Bootstrap*, Chapman and Hall, New York..

Eliot, L, B. 1993. Prefilter your neurons. *AI Expert* 8(7): 9

Etzioni, O. 1996. The World Wide Web: quagmire or gold mine. *Communications of the Association for Computing Machinery*, 39(11): 65–68.

Fahlman, S.E. 1989, Faster-Learning Variations on Back-Propagation: An Empirical Study, in Touretzky, D., Hinton, G, and Sejnowski, T., eds., *Proceedings of the 1988 Connectionist Models Summer School*, Morgan Kaufmann Publishers, Inc., 38-51.

Farley, A. M, and Freeman, K., 1995. Burden of Proof in Legal Argumentation. Proceedings of *Fifth International Conference on Artificial Intelligence and Law.* Washington. ACM Press, USA: 156-164.

Farzindar, A. and Lapalme, G. 2004. Legal texts summarization by exploration of the thematic structures and argumentative roles. *Text Summarization Branches Out Conference held in conjunction with The Association for Computational Linguistics 2004*, Barcelona, Spain, July 2004.

Fayyad, U. M. and Irani, K. B. 1993. Multi-interval discretization of continuous-valued attributes for classification learning. *Proceedings of the 13th International Joint Conference on Artificial Intelligence*, Morgan Kaufmann Publishers, Inc., 1022-1027.

Fayyad U, Piatetsky-Shapiro G and Smyth, P., and Uthurusamy, R., (Eds) 1996. *Advances in Knowledge Discovery and Data Mining* AAAI Press/MIT Press. Menlo Park .

Fayyad, U., Piatetsky-Shapiro, G. and Smyth, P. 1996a. From data mining to knowledge discovery: An overview. In *Advances in Knowledge Discovery and Data Mining* AAAI/MIT Press: Cambridge, Massachusetts: 1-36

Fayyad, U., Piatetsky-Shapiro, G. and Smyth, P. 1996b. The KDD Process for Extracting Useful Knowledge from Volumes of Data. *Communications of the ACM*, 39(11): 27-34.

Fayyad, U., Piatetsky-Shapiro, G. and Smyth, P. 1996c. From Data Mining to Knowledge Discovery in Databases. *AI Magazine*, 17(3): 37-54.

FeuRosa P. V. 2000. The Electronic Judge, *Proc AISB'00 – Symp Artificial Intelligence & Legal Reasoning*, Birmingham, UK, April: 33-36.

Fix, E. and Hodges, J. L. 1951. *Discriminatory analysis, nonparametric discrimination consistency properties.* Technical Report 4, Randolph Filed, TX: US Air Force.

Flick, G. A., 1979. *Natural Justice. Principles and Practical Application.* Butterworths. Sydney.

Fox, J. 1986. Knowledge, Decision Making and Uncertainty. In (Ed Gale, W. A.) *Artificial Intelligence and Statistics.* Reading, Massachusetts; Addison-Wesley.

Fox, J., and Parsons, S., 1998. Arguing about Beliefs and Actions. In Hunter, A., and Parsons, S., (Eds). *Applications of Uncertainty Formalisms.* Springer. Berlin: 266-302.

Frawley, W. J., Piatetsky-Shapiro, G. and Matheus, C. J. 1991. Knowledge discovery in databases: an overview. *Knowledge discovery in databases.* AAAI/MIT Press: 1-27

Freeman, J. B. 1991. *Dialectics and the Macrostructure of Arguments* Floris Publications. Berlin.

Freeman, K. 1994. *Toward formalizing Dialectical Argumentation.* PhD thesis. Department of Computer Science and Information Science. University of Oregon.

Friedman, J. H. 1977. A recursive partitioning decision rule for non-parametric classification. *IEEE Transactions on Computers:* 404-408.

Gelbart, D. and Smith, J. C. 1993. FLEXICON: An evaluation of a statistical model adapted to intelligent text management. In the *Proceedings of the Fourth International Conference on Artificial Intelligence and Law*, 142-151, Amsterdam: ACM Press.

Ginsberg, M. J. and. Zmud, R. W. 1988. Evolving criteria for Information Systems assessment. Information Systems Assessment: Issues and Challenges: proceedings of the *IFIP WG 8.2 Working Conference on Information Systems Assessment*, Noordwijkerhout, The Netherlands, Oxford, North Holland.

Gonçalves, T and Quaresma, P. 2003. A preliminary approach to the multilabel classification problem of Portuguese juridical documents. *Proceedings of EPIA'03, the eleventh Portugese Conference on Artificial Intelligence,* Beja, Portugal, December 4-7, Lecture Notes in Computer Science, Springer

Gonzalez, A. and Dankel, D. D. 1993, *The Engineering of Knowledge-Based Systems- Theory and Practice*, Prentice-Hall, Inc.

Gordon, T., F., 1995. The Pleadings Game: An exercise in computational dialectics. *Artificial Intelligence and Law*, 2(4): 239-92

Governatori, G, and Stranieri,A. 2001. Towards the application of association rules for defeasible rule discovery *Fourteenth Annual International Conference on Legal Knowledge and Information Systems Jurix'01. IOS Press. Amsterdam. The Netherlands:* 63-75

Governatori, G., ter Hofstede, H. M., and Oaks, P. 2000. *Defeasible Logic for Automated Negotiation.* Proceedings of CollECTer. Deakin University. Geelong, Victoria

Grady, G. and Patil, R, S. 1987. An Expert System for Screening Employee Pension Plans for the Internal Revenue Service. *Proceedings of the First International Conference on Artificial Intelligence and Law.* ACM Press: 137-143

Greenleaf, G., Mowbray, A. and Lewis, D. 1998. *Australasian Computerised Legal Information Handbook.* Butterworths (Australia)

Greenleaf, G., Mowbray, A. and Van Dijk, P. 1996. Representing and Using Legal Knowledge in Integrated Decision Support Systems: Datalex Workstations, *Artificial Intelligence and Law*, 4: 97-142

Gregory, A. 1991 Which evaluation methodology when? A contingency approach to evaluation., in *Systems Thinking in Europe*, M.C. Jackson, et al. (eds.) Plenum, New York. 435-441.

Grosof, B. N., Labrou, Y. and Chan, H. Y. 1999. . A declarative approach to business rules in contracts: courteous logic programs in xml. In *Proceedings of the first ACM Conference on Electronic commerce*, ACM Press: 68-77.

Grover, C., Hachey, B., Hughson, I. and Korycinski, C. 2003. Automatic Summarisation of Legal Documents. Proceedings of the *Ninth International Conference on Artificial Intelligence and Law*, Edinburgh, Scotland: ACM Press: 243-251

Gruber, T. R. 1995. Towards principles for the Design of Ontologies used for Knowledge Sharing, *Intl J Human-Computer Studies*, 43: 907-928.

Haliwell, J., Keppens, J. and Shen, Q. 2003. Linguistic Bayesian Networks for Reasoning with Subjective Probabilities in Forensic Statistics, Proceedings of the *Ninth International Conference on Artificial Intelligence and Law*, Edinburgh, Scotland: ACM Press, 42-50.

Hall, M. J. J., Stranieri, A. and Zeleznikow, J. 2002. A Strategy for Evaluating Web-Based Discretionary Decision Support Systems. *Proceedings of ADBIS2002 - Sixth East-European Conference on Advances in Databases and Information Systems*, 108-120.

Hall, M. J. J. and Zeleznikow, J. 2001 Current inadequacies in the evaluation of legal Knowledge-Based Systems. Strategies towards a broad-based evaluation model. Proceedings of the *Eighth International Conference on Artificial Intelligence and Law*, St. Louis, Missouri: ACM Press: 147-156.

Hall, M. J. J. and Zeleznikow, J. 2002. The Context, Criteria, Contingency Evaluation Framework for Legal Knowledge-Based Systems. Proceedings *of Fifth Business Information Systems Conference*, Poznan, Poland: ACM Press: 219-227.

Han, J. and Kamber, M. 2001. *Data Mining: Concepts and Techniques*. Morgan Kaufmann Publishers, Inc. , San Francisco, Ca.

Hand, D., Mannila, H. and Smyth, P. 2001. *Principles of Data Mining*. MIT Press, Cambridge Ma.

Hart H. L. A., 1958. Positivism and the separation of law and morals. *Harvard Law Review*: 593-629.

Hart, H. L. A., 1961. *The Concept of Law* Clarendon Press. Oxford.

Hart, H. L. A., 1994. *The Concept of Law* . 2nd Ed. Clarendon Press. Oxford.

Hauck, R., Atabakhsh, H., Onguasith, P., Gupta, H. and Chen, H. 2002. Using Coplink to Analyse Criminal-Justice Data *IEEE Computer,* 35: 30-37

Haykin, S., 1994. *Neural networks: a comprehensive foundation*. Macmillan. New York.

Hearst, M. 1999. Untangling text data mining. *Proceedings of 37th Annual Meeting for Computational Linguistics,* ACM Press, New York, NY.pp3-10

Hecht-Nielson, R. 1990. *Neurocomputing* Addison-Wesley. Massachusetts.

Heckerman , D. 1997. Bayesian Networks for Data Mining, *Data Mining and Knowledge Discovery*, 1:79-119.

Hobson, J. B and Slee, D., 1993. Rules, Cases and Networks in a Legal Domain. *Law, Computers & Artificial Intelligence*. 2(2): 119-135.

Hobson, J. B., and Slee, D. 1994. Indexing the Theft Act 1968 for Case Based Reasoning and Artificial Neural Networks. *Proceedings of the Fourth National Conference on Law, Computers and Artificial Intelligence*. Univeristy of Exeter: 96

Hoeschl, H. C., and Bueno, T, C., Mattos, E, Bortolon, A, and Barcia, R, M. 2001. Olimpo: Contextual Structured Search to improve the representation of UN Security Council resolutions with information extraction methods. *Proceedings of the Eighth International Conference on Artificial Intelligence and Law*. ACM Press: 217-218.

Hunt, E. B., Marin, J. and Stone, P. J. 1966. *Experiments in Induction*. New York: Academic Press.

Hunter, D. 1994. Looking for Law in all the Wrong Places: Legal Theory and Legal Neural Networks. (in) Prakken, H., Muntjewerff, A., Soeteman, A. and Winkels, R. (eds.) 1994. *Legal Knowledge Based Systems. Foundations of Legal Knowledge Systems. Jurix'94*. Koninlijke Vermande The Netherlands: 55-64.

Hunter, D, Tyree, A., and Zeleznikow, J. 1993. There is less to this argument than meets the eye. *Journal of Law and Information Science*. 4(1)46-64.

Ingleby, R. 1991. *In the Ball Park: Alternative Dispute Resolution and the Courts*. Carlton. Australian Institute of Judicial Administration Inc.

Ingleby, R., 1993. *Family Law and Society*. Butterworths. Sydney.

Ivkovic, S., 2004 *Visualisation of generated Association Rules*. MSc thesis. University of Ballarat.

Ivkovic, S., Yearwood, J. and Stranieri, A., 2001. Discovering Interesting Association Rules from Legal Databases. *Information and Communication Technology Law* 11(1): 35-47

Ivkovic S, Yearwood J and Stranieri A 2003 Visualising association rules for feedback within the Legal System, *Proc 9th Intl Conf Artificial Intelligence and Law*, Edinburgh, Scotland, ACM Press, New York: 214-223.

Jackson, P. 1990. *Introduction to Expert Systems*. Second Edition. Addison Wesley, Reading, Ma

Jackson, P. and Moulinier, I. 2002. *Natural Language Processing for Online Applications – Text Retrieval, Extraction and Categorization*. John Benjamins Publishing Company.

Joachims, T. 1998. Text Categorization with Support Vector Machines: Learning with Many Relevant Features. *Proceedings of the European Conference on Machine Learning* (ECML), Springer

Johnson, P. E, Zualkernan, I. A., and Garber, S., 1987. Specification of expertise. *International Journal of Man Machine Studies* 26: 161

Johnson, P. E., Zualkernan, I. A. and Tukey, D., 1993. Types of expertise: an invariant of problem solving. *International Journal of Man Machine Studies* 39: 641-665.

Johnston, B., and Governatori, G., 2003. Induction of Defeasible Logic Theories in the Legal Domain. Eighth international Conference on Artificial Intelligence and Law. ACM Press: 204-213

Jones, W. P. and Furnas, G. W. 1987. Pictures of relevance: a geometric analysis of similarity measures. *Journal of the American Society for Information Science*, 38(6): 420-442.

Juristo, N. and Morant, J. L. 1998. Common framework for the evaluation process of KBS and conventional software. *Knowledge Based Systems* 11(2): 145-159.

Kadane, J. B. and Schum, D. A. 1996. *A Probabilistic Analysis of the Sacco and Vanzetti Evidence* John Wiley and Sons

Kaufmann, L and Rousseeuw, P. J. 1990 *Finding Groups in Data: An Introduction to Cluster Analysis*. John Wiley.

Kearns, M. and Valiant, L. 1994. Cryptographic limitations on learning Boolean formulae and finite automata. *Journal of the Association for Computing Machinery*, 41(1): 67-95.

Kelly, J., and Davis, L., 1991. Hybridizing the genetic algorithm and the K-nearest neighbour. *Proceedings of the Fourth International Conference on Genetic algorithms and their applications*. Morgan Kaufman. California.: 377-383

Kennedy, D., 1986. Freedom and Constraint in Adjudication: A Critical Phenomenology. *Journal of Legal Education* 36(4): 518-562.

Knauf, R., Philippow, I., and Gonzalez, A.J. 2000. Towards validation and refinement of rule-based systems. Journal of Experimental & Theoretical Artificial Intelligence, 12(4): 421-31.

Koers, A. W., Kracht, D., Smith, M., Smits, J. M. and Weusten, M. C. M. 1989. *Knowledge Based Systems in Law*. Computer/Law Series. Kluwer. The Netherlands.

Koers, A.W., Kracht, D., Smith, M., Smits, J.M.,and Weusten, M.C.M. 1990 Criteria for the classification of legal knowledge systems advisory systems on legal questions, in Legal knowledge Based Systems, D. Kracht, C.N.J. De Vey Mestdagh, and J.S. Svensson, Editors. Koninlijke Vermande, Lelystad, Netherlands: 23-35

238

Kohonen, T. 1982., Self-organised formation of Topologically Correct Feature Maps. *Biological Cybernetics.* 43: 59-69

Kolodner, J., 1993. *Case based reasoning.* Morgan Kaufman. San Mateo.

Kort, F. 1964. Simultaneous equations and Boolean Algebra. (in) Schubert, G., 1964. (Ed) *Judicial Behaviour: A Reader in Theory and Research.* Rand McNally and Company. Chicago: 477-491.

Kosala, R. and Blockeel, H. 2000. Web mining research: a survey. *ACM SIGKDD Explorations*, 2(1), 1–15.

Kovacs, D., 1992. *Family Property Proceedings in Australia.* Butterworths. Sydney.

Kraus, S., Wilkenfeld, J. and Zlotkin, G. 1995. Multiagent negotiation under time constraints. *Artificial Intelligence* 75(2): 297-345.

Krause, P., Ambler, S., Elvang-Goransson., and Fox, J., 1995. A Logic of Argumentation for Reasoning under Uncertainty. *Computational Intelligence* 11(1): 113-131

Krause, P., and Fox, J., 1995. Is there a role for qualitative risk assessment? *Eleventh Annual Conference on Uncertainty in Artificial Intelligence.* Montreal: 386-393

Krovetz, R. and Croft, W. B. 1992. Lexical ambiguity and information retrieval. *ACM Transactions on Office Information Systems* 10(2): 115-141.

Lawler, R. 1964. Stare decisis and electronic computers. in Schubert, G. 1964. (Ed) *Judicial Behaviour: A Reader in Theory and Research.* Rand McNally & Company. Chicago: 492-505.

LegalXML 2004. http://www.legalxml.org/ Accessed 15 March 2004.

Legrand, J. 1999. Some Guidelines for Fuzzy Sets Application in Legal Reasoning. *Artificial Intelligence and Law* 7(2-3): 235-257.

Leff, L., 2001. Automated reasoning with legal XML documents. *Proceedings of the 8th international conference on Artificial intelligence and law.* ACM Press: 215 - 216

Lengers, R. J. C. 1995. Evolving Artificial Neural Networks. A Design Approach. *Masters Thesis, Tilburg University. The Netherlands.*

Liang, T., and Moskowitz, H. 1992. Integrating Neural Networks and Semi Markov Processes for Automated Knowledge Acquisition: An application to real-time scheduling *Decision Sciences* 23.(6): 1298-1314

Lovegrove, A. 1999. Statistical information systems as a means to consistency and rationality in sentencing. *International Journal of Law and Information Technology.* 7(1): 31-72.

Loui, R., 1997. Progress on Room 5: A Testbed For Public Interactive Semi-Formal Legal Argumentation. *Sixth International conference on Artificial intelligence and law*. ACM Press: 207 – 214

Luhn, H. P. 1958. The Automatic Creation of Literature Abstracts. *IBM Journal of Research and Development*, 2: 159-165.

Lundmark, T. 1998. Book Review, Interpreting Precedents: A Comparative Study. MacCormick, D. N. and Summers, R. S. (ed.) *America Journal of Comparative Law* 46: 211.

Lustic, I. S and Miodownik, D. 2000. Deliberative Democracy and Public Discourse: The agent-based Argument Repertoire Model. *Complexity*. 5(4): 13-30.

MacCormick, D. N. 1978. *Legal Reasoning and Legal Theory*. Oxford: Clarendon Press.

MacCormick, D. N. 1981. *H. L. A Hart*. Stanford University Press.

MacCormick, D. N. and Summers, R. S. (ed.) 1997. *Interpreting Precedents: A Comparative Study*. Dartmouth Publishing: Aldershot, U.K.

McCulloch. W. S. and Pitts, W. 1943. A logical calculus of the ideas imminent in nervous activity. *Bulletin of Mathematical Biophysics*, 5:115-133.

Maher, M., 2001. Propositional Defeasible Logic has Linear Complexity. *Theory and Practice of Logic Programming* 1(6): 691-711.

Mangasarian, O. L. 1968 Multi-surface method of pattern separation. *IEEE Transactions on Information Theory*, 14:801–807.

Mangasarian, O. L. 1994. *Nonlinear Programming*. SIAM, Philadelphia, PA.

Mangasarian, O. L. 1997. Mathematical programming in data mining. *Data Mining and Knowledge Discovery*, 42(1): 183–201.

Manning, C. D. and Schutze, H. 1999. *Foundations of Statistical Natural Language Processing*. MIT Press, Cambridge, Ma

Marakas, G. 2003. *Modern Data Warehousing, Mining and Visualisation: Core Concepts*. Prentice Hall, Upper Saddle River, New Jersey.

Markesinis, B., 1993 (ed.), *The Gradual Convergence: Foreign Ideas, Foreign Influences and English Law on the Eve of the 21st Century*, Clarendon Press, Oxford

Marshall, C. C, 1989. Representing the structure of legal argument. *Proceedings of Second International Conference on Artificial Intelligence and Law*. New York;ACM Press, USA: 121-127.

Masand, B., Linoff, G. and Waltz, D. 1992. Classifying News Stories Using Memory Based Reasoning. *Proceedings of Fifteenth SIGIR Conference*, ACM, New York: 59-65.

Matthijssen, L. J, 1999. *Interfacing between lawyers and computers. An architecture for knowledge based interfaces to legal databases.* The Netherlands; Kluwer Law International.

Meachem , L. 1999. *Judicial Business of the United States Courts.* Technical Report, Administrative Office of the United States Courts.

Meldman, J. A. 1977. A structural model for computer-aided legal analysis. *Rutgers Journal of Computers and Law*, 6: 27-71.

Meir, R. and Ratsch, G. 2003. An Introduction to Boosting and Leveraging. *Advanced Lectures on Machine Learning.* Springer Lecture Notes in Computer Science, 119-184.

Merkl, D. and Schweighofer, D. 1997. The Exploration of Legal Text Corpora with Hierarchical Neural Networks: A Guided Tour in Public International Law. *Proceedings of Sixth International Conference on Artificial Intelligence and Law*, ACM: Melbourne, Australia, 98-105.

Merkl, D., Schweighofer, E. and Winiwarter, W., 1999. Exploratory analysis of concept and document spaces with connectionist networks. *Artificial Intelligence and Law.* 7 (2-3): 185-209.

Michalski, R. G. 1980. Pattern Recognition as rule guided inductive inference. *IEEE Transactions on Pattern Analysis and Machine Intelligence.* 4:349-361.

Michalski, R.S. and Chilausky, R.L., 1980. Knowledge acquisition by encoding expert rules versus computer induction from examples, *Int. J. Man-Machine Studies* 12: 63-87.

Michalski, R. G. and Larson, J. B. 1978. Selection of most Representative Training Examples and Incremental Generation of VL1 Hypotheses: The underlying Methodology and Desription of programs ESEL and AQ11. *Report No. 867, Department of Computer Science, University of Illinois.*

Michie, D., Spiegelhalter, D. J and Taylor, C.C., (Eds) 1994. *Machine Learning, Neural and Statistical Classification.* Ellis Horwood. West Sussex. England.

Miikkulainen, R. 1993. *Subsymbolic natural language processing: An Integrated Model of scripts, lexicon and memory.* Cambridge, MA: MIT Press.

Minsky, M. and Papert, S. 1969. *Perceptrons: An Introduction to Computational Geometry*, MIT Press, Cambridge, Ma.

Mitchell, T.M. 1997. *Machine Learning.* Mc Graw Hill, New York.

Moens, M., 2000. *Automatic Indexing and Abstracting of Document Texts.* Kluwer Academic Publishers, Boston, Ma.

Moens, M. F. 2001. Legal Text Retrieval. *Artificial Intelligence and Law,* 9(1): 29-57.

Moens, M. F. 2002. What Information Retrieval Can Learn from Case-Based Reasoning in T.J.M. Bench-Capon, A. Daskalopulu and R.G.F. Winkels (eds.), *Legal Knowledge and Information Systems. Jurix 2002: The Fifteenth Annual Conference.* Amsterdam: IOS Press: 83-91.

Moens M. F. 2004. Improving Access to Legal Information: How Intelligent Drafting Can Help. In A. Oskamp & A. Lodder (Eds.), *Information Technology for the Legal Professional* . Boston, Kluwer Academic Publishers (forthcoming).

Moens, M., Uyttendaele, C., and Dumortier, J., 1997. Abstracting of Legal Cases: The SALOMON Experience. *Proceedings of the Sixth International Conference on Artificial Intelligence and Law.* Melbourne. ACM Press. New York: 114-122

Moles, R. N. and Dayal, S. 1992. There is more to life than logic. *Journal of Law and Information Science* 3(2):188-218.

Moore, J., 1995. *Participating in explanatory dialogues: interpreting and responding to questions in context.* MIT Press. Cambridge, Mass.

Muller, K. R., Mika, S., Ratsch, G., Tsuda, K. and Scholkopf, B. 2001. An Introduction to Kernel Based Learning Algorithms, *IEEE Transactions on Neural Networks*, 12(2): 181-202.

Munro, N. 2002 . The ever-expanding network of local and federal databases. *Communications of the ACM*, 45 (7), 17-19.

Nagel, S. 1964. Testing Empirical Generalisations. (in) Schubert, G. 1964. (Ed) Judicial Behaviour: *A Reader in Theory and Research.* Rand McNally & Company. Chicago: 518-529.

Newell, A. 1982. The knowledge level. *Artificial Intelligence.* 18(1):87-127.

Nute, D., 1987. Defeasible Reasoning. *Proceedings of the 20th Hawaiin International Conference on System Science.* IEEE Press: 470-477.

Nute, D., 1994. Defeasible Logic in Gabbay, D, M., Hogger, C., J and Robinsn, J., A. 1994. *Handbook of Logic in Artificial Intelligence and Logic Programming.* Clarendon Press. UK: 353-394.

Oatley, G.C., and Ewart, B.W., 2003. Crimes Analysis Software: 'Pins in Maps', Clustering and Bayes Net Prediction. *Expert Systems with Applications* 25 (4): 569-588.

Oatley, G., Ewart, B. and Zeleznikow, J. 2004. Decision Support Systems For Police: Lessons From The Application of Data Mining Techniques To 'Soft' Forensic Evidence. Submitted to *Journal of Artificial Intelligence and Law.*

Oatley, G., Zeleznikow, J. and Ewart, B. 2004. Matching and Predicting Crimes. *Research and Development in Expert Systems XXIV. Proceedings of AI2004 The Twenty-fourth SGES International Conference on Knowledge Based Systems and Applied Artificial Intelligence,* Springer Verlag, London.

O'Rourke, P. 1982. *A comparative study of two inductive learning systems AQ11 and ID3: Using a Chess Endgame Test Problem.* Report No. 82-2, Department of Computer Science, University of Illinois.

Pannu, A. S. 1995. Using Genetic Algorithms to Inductively Reason with Cases in the Legal Domain. *Proceedings of the Fifth International Conference on Artificial Intelligence and Law. ICAIL'95.* ACM Press. New York: 175-184.

Parliament of the Commonwealth of Australia. *The Family Law Act 1975. Aspects of its Operation and Interpretation. A report of the Joint Select Committee on Certain Aspects of the Operation and Interpretation of the Family Law Act.* November 1992. Australian Government publishing Service. Canberra.

Parliament of Victoria Law Reform Committee. 1999. *Technology and Law Report.* Chairman Victor Perton: ISBN 0-7311-5272-7.

Paulk, M.C. Curtis, B., Chrissis, M.B.and Weber, C V 1993. Capability Maturity Model for Software version 1.1. *Software Engineering Institute.*

Pearl, J. 1988. *Probabilistic Reasoning in Intelligent Systems: Networks of Plausible Inference.* Morgan Kafmann, San Francisco Ca.

Philipps, L. 1989. Are legal decisions based on the application of rules or prototype recognition? Legal science on the way to neural networks. In the Pre-Proceedings of the *Third International Conference on Logica, Informatica, Diritto,* 673-680, Florence: IDG.

Philipps, L., 1991. Distribution of damages in car accidents through the use of neural networks. *Cardozo Law Review* 13(2-3): 987-1001.

Philipps, L. 1993. Vague legal concepts and fuzzy logic. An attempt to determine the required period of waiting after traffic accidents. In *Proceedings of the Computer and Vagueness: Fuzzy Logic and Neural Nets.* Informatica e diritto. 2:37-51, Munich.

Philipps, L. 1999. Approximate syllogisms - on the logic of everyday life. *Artificial Intelligence and Law.* 7(2-3): 227-234.

Philipps, L. and Sartor, G. 1999. From Legal Theories to Neural Networks and Fuzzy Reasoning. *Artificial Intelligence and Law.* 7(2-3): 115-128.

Poole, D. L. 1988. A Logical framework for default reasoning *Artificial Intelligence.* 36: 27-47.

Pound, R. 1908. Mechanical Jurisprudence. *Colombia Law Review.* 8:605.

Prakken, H 1993. *Logical Tools for Modelling Legal Argument.* PhD thesis. Vrije University Amsterdam.

Prakken, H. 1995. From Logic to Dialectics in Legal Argument. *Proceedings of Fifth International Conference on Artificial Intelligence and Law,* ACM Press: 165-174.

Prakken, H. 1997. Logical Tools for Modelling Legal Argument. Dordrecht: Kluwer.

Prakken, H, 2001. Modelling Reasoning about Evidence in Legal Procedure. *Proceedings of the Eight International Conference on Artificial Intelligence and Law.* ACM Press: 119-128.

Prakken, H., and Sartor, G., 1996. A dialectical model of assessing conflicting arguments in legal reasoning. *Artificial Intelligence and Law.* 4: 331-368.

Quatrevaux, E. 1996. Increasing Legal Services Delivery Capacity Through Information Technology (Technical Report No. LSC/OIG-95–035) (Legal Services Corporation). (Available online at http://:oig.lsc.gov/tech/techdown.htm)

Quinlan, J. R. 1986. Induction of decision trees. *Machine Learning.* 1(1): 81-106.

Quinlan, J. R 1989. Unknown Attribute Values in Induction. 164-168. *Proceedings of the Sixth International Workshop on Machine Learning* (ML 1989), Cornell University, Ithaca, New York, USA, Morgan Kaufmann.

Quinlan, J. R. 1993. *C4.5: Programs for.Machine Learning* . Los Altos: Morgan Kaufmann Publishers, Inc.

Quinlan, J. R. 1996. Bagging Boosting and C4.5. *Proceedings of the Thirteenth National Conference on Artificial Intelligence* (AAAI-96), American Association for Artificial Intelligence, Portland, Oregon : 725-730.

Quinlan, J. R. 1997 Decision Trees and Instance-Based Classifiers. *The Computer Science and Engineering Handbook*, 521-535.

Rae, A., Robert, P., and Hausen, H.L. 1995 *Software Evaluation for Certification: Principles, Practice and Legal Liability.* McGraw Hill International, Maidenhead, UK.

Raghaven, V. V. and Wong, S. K. M. 1986. A Critical Analysis of a Vector Space Model for Information Retrieval. *Journal of the American Society for Information Science*, 37(5): 279-287.

Reeves, D., Wellman, P., Grosof, B., and Chan, Y., 2000. Automated Negotiation from Declarative Contract Descriptions. *Seventeenth National Conference on Knowledge Based Electronic Markets KBEM.* AAAI Press. Austin, Texas.

Reich, Y. 1994. Layered Models of research methodologies. *Artificial Intelligence for Engineering Design, Analysis and Manufacturing* 8(4): 263-274 .

Reich, Y., 1995. Measuring the value of knowledge. *International Journal of Human-Computer Studies.* 42(1): 3-30.

Reich, Y., and Barai, S.V. 1999. Evaluating Machine Learning Models for Engineering Problems. *Artificial Intelligence and Engineering* 13(3): 257.

Ripley, B. D. 1996. *Pattern Recognition and Nueral Networks.* Cambridge University Press.

244

Rissland, E. L. and Ashley, K. D. 1987. A case-based system for trade secrets law. In the Proceedings of the *First International Conference of Artificial Intelligence and Law*. Boston. ACM Press: 60-66.

Rissland, E. L., and Friedman, M. T. 1995. Detecting change in legal Concepts. *Proceedings of the Fifth International Conference on Artificial Intelligence and Law. ICAIL'95.* ACM Press. New York: 127-136.

Rose, D. E, 1993. *A Symbolic and Connectionist Approach to Legal Information Retrieval.* Lawrence Erlbaum, Hillsdale, New Jersey.

Rose, D., E, and Belew, R., 1989. Legal information retrieval a hybrid approach *Proceedings of the second international conference on Artificial intelligence and law* ACM Press: 138 – 146.

Rose, D. E. and Belew, R. K. 1991. A connectionist and symbolic hybrid for improving legal research, *Intl J Man-Machine Studies*, 35(1): 1-33.

Rosenberg, F. 1971. Judicial Discretion of the Trial Court. *Syracuse Law Review*, 22:635- 636.

Rosenblatt, F. 1958. The perceptron: a probabilistic model for information storage and organization in the brain. *Psychological Review*, 65: 386-408.

Ross, T. J. 1995. *Fuzzy logic with Engineering Applications.* McGraw-Hill. New York.

Rumelhart, D., Hinton, G., and Williams, R., 1986. Learning Internal Representations by Error Propagation. (in) *Parallel Distributed Processing: Explorations in the Microstructure of Cognition.* (eds) Rumelhart, D., and McClelland, J., Cambridge, MA. MIT Press.

Salton, G. 1968. *Automatic information organization and retrieval.* New York: McGraw-Hill.

Salton, G. 1970. Automatic text analysis. *Science*, 168 (3929) : 335-343.

Salton, G. 1989. *Automatic Text Processing: The Transformation, Analysis, and Retrieval of Information by Computer.* Addison-Wesley Publishing Company, Reading, MA.

Salton, G. and Buckley, C. 1988. Term-weighting Approaches in Automatic Text Retrieval. *Information Processing and Management*, 24 (5): 513-523.

Salton, G., Fox, E. A. and Wu, H. 1983. Extended Boolean information retrieval. *Communications of the Association for Computing Machinery*, 28:1022-1036.

Schapire, R. E. 1990. The strength of weak learnability. *Machine Learning*, 5(2): 197-227.

Schild, U. 1995. Intelligent Computer Systems for Criminal Sentencing. Proceedings of the *Fifth International Conference of Artificial Intelligence and Law*. Washington. ACM Press: 229-239.

Schild, U. 1998. Criminal Sentencing and Intelligent Decision Support. *Artificial Intelligence and Law.* 6(2-4): 151-202

Schlimmer, J. C. 1987. *Concept acquisition through representational adjustment.* Ph.D. diss., University of California, Irvine, California.

Schreiber, J. T., Akkermanis, A. M., Anjewierden, A. A., de Hoog, R., Shadbolt, A., Van de Velde, W. and Wielinga, B. J. 1999. *Knowledge Engineering and Management: The Common Kads Methodology*, MIT Press, Cambridge, MA.

Schum, D. 1993. Argument structuring and evidence evaluation. in Hastie, R (ed) 1993 Inside the Juror Cambridge University Press: 175-191.

Schum, D. 1994. *The Evidential Foundation of Probabilistic Reasoning.* John Wiley and Sons.

Schweighofer, E., and Merkl, D., 1999 A learning technique for legal document analysis. *Proceedings of the Seventh International Conference on Artificial Intelligence and Law*, ICAIL '99, 14-17 June 1999, Oslo, Norway. ACM Press: 156-163.

Shafer, G. 1976. *A mathematical theory of evidence.* Princeton University Press, Princeton N.J.

Shannon, C. E. and Weaver, W. 1949. The mathematical theory of communication. Urbana: University of Illinois Press.

Shapira, R. 1999. Fuzzy Measurements in the Mishnah and Talmud. *Artificial Intelligence and Law* 7(2-3): 273-288.

Shaw, M. L. 1989. Interactive elicitation and exchange of knowledge. *International Journal of Personal Construct Psychology.* 2(2): 215-238.

Shaw, M. L., and Gaines, B. R., 1991. Supporting personal networking through computer networking Human Factors in Computing Systems. Reaching through technology. *CHI'91 Conference Proceedings.* New York USA Addison Wesley.: 437.

Shoham, Y., and McDermott, D., 1988. Problems in formal temporal reasoning. *Artificial Intelligence:* 36(1): 49-90.

Shortliffe, E. H. 1976. *Computer based medical consultations: MYCIN.* New York: Elsevier.

Shortliffe E. H. and Buchanan, B. G. 1975. A method of inexact reasoning, *Mathematical Biosciences* 23: 351-379.

Skabar, A., Stranieri, A. and Zeleznikow, J. 1997. Using argumentation for the decomposition and classification of tasks for hybrid system development. in Kasabov, N., Kozma, R., Ko, K., O'Shea, R., Coghill, G., and Gedeon, T. (eds) *Progress in Connectionist Based Information Systems. Proceedings of the 1997*

246

International Conference on Neural Information Processing and Intelligent Information Systems. Springer-Verlag. Singapore: 814-818.

Smith, J. C., Gelbart, D., MacCrimmon, K., Atherton, B., McClean, J., Shinehoft, M. and Quintana, L. (1995) Artificial Intelligence and Legal Discourse: the Flexlaw Legal Text Management System, *Artificial Intelligence and Law*, 3: 55-95.

Smola, A. J., Bartlett, P. L., Scholkopf, B. and Schuurmans, D. (eds.) 2000. *Advances in Large Margin Classifiers*, MIT Press, Cambridge, Ma.

Sparck Jones, K. 1993. What might be in a summary? *Information Retrieval'93*, Universitatsverlag, Konstanz, Germany: 9-26.

Spreeuwenberg, S., Van Engers, T. and Gerrits, R. 2001. The Role of verification in improving the quality of legal decision-making. Jurix 2001: *the Fourteenth Annual International Conference on Legal Knowledge and Information Systems.* Frontiers in Artificial Intelligence and Applications., Amsterdam, Netherlands, IOS Press.

Stranieri, A. 1999. *Automating legal reasoning in discretionary domains* PHD Thesis, La Trobe University, Melbourne, Australia.

Stranieri, A., Gawler, M., and Zeleznikow, J., 1994. Toulmin Argument Structures as a Higher Level Abstraction for Hybrid reasoning. in Zhang, C., Debenham, J. and Lukose, D. (eds) *Proceedings of the Seventh Australian Joint Conference on Artificial Intelligence. AI'94.* World Scientific. Singapore: 203-210.

Stranieri, A., Massey, P. and Zeleznikow, J., 1994. Inferencing With Legal Knowledge Represented as Diagrams in (eds) Williams A. W. F., *Poster Proceedings of the 7th Australian Joint Conference on Artificial Intelligence:* 25-32. University of New England. Australia.

Stranieri, A., Yearwood, J., and Anjaria, C. 1999. The use of argumentation to assist in the generation of legal documents. *ADCS'99 Fourth Australasian Document Computing Symposium 3rd December 1999* Coffs Harbour, NSW.

Stranieri, A., Yearwood, J., and Pham, B., 1999. Combining knowledge discovery from databases (KDD) and case based reasoning (CBR) to support diagnosis of medical images. *in* Pham, B., Braun, M., Maeder, A., and Eckert, M. (eds) *New Approaches in Medical Image Analysis.* Spie. 3747: 169-177.

Stranieri, A., Yearwood, J., and Zeleznikow, J. 1999. Mapping inference trees to document structure for text generation in refugee determinations. in eds. H.J. van den Herik, M.-F. Moens, J. Bing, B. van Buggenhout, J. Zeleznikow, and C.A.F.M. Grütters. (eds) *Jurix 1999. The Twelfth International Conference on Legal Knowledge Based Systems,*, GNI, Nijmegen, Netherlands: 109-121.

Stranieri, A., and Zeleznikow, J. 1992. Split-Up: Expert System to Determine Spousal *Propertyn: Proceedings of the 5th Australian Joint Conference on Artificial Intelligence.* Hobart. Australia. 1992. World Scientific. Sydney: 51-57.

Stranieri, A., and Zeleznikow, J., 1996. Automating legal reasoning in discretionary domains. (in) Kralingen van, R. W., Herik van den, H. J., Prins, E. J., Sergot, M., and Zeleznikow, J., 1996. *Legal Knowledge Based Systems. Foundations of Legal Knowledge Systems. Jurix'96*. Tilburg University Press. The Netherlands: 101-110.

Stranieri, A. and Zeleznikow, J. 1998. A re-examination of the concepts of open texture and stare decisis for data mining in discretionary domains. *Proceedings of Eleventh International Conference on Legal Knowledge Based Systems,*, Koniklijke Vermand, Gronigen, Netherlands: 101-111.

Stranieri, A., and Zeleznikow, J., 1998. *Split Up: The use of an argument based knowledge representation to meet expectations of different users for discretionary decision making* in Proceedings of Innovative Applications of Artificial Intelligence IAAI'98. American Association of Artificial intelligence: 1146-1152.

Stranieri, A., and Zeleznikow, J. 1999. A survey of argumentation structures for intelligent decision support. in Burstein, R. (Ed) Proceedings of International Society for Decision Support Systems Fifth International Conference ISDSS'99. Monash University, Melbourne.

Stranieri, A., and Zeleznikow, J. 1999. The evaluation of legal knowledge based systems. *Seventh International Conference on Artificial Intelligence and Law. ICAIL'99* ACM Press: 18-24.

Stranieri, A., and Zeleznikow, J. 1999. Knowledge acquisition benefits of a non-conventional rule based reasoning system. *Proceedings of the IASTED International Conference. Law and Technology (LawTech'99)*. ACTA Press. San Francisco: 88-94.

Stranieri, A. and Zeleznikow, J. 2000. Argumentation Structures for Knowledge Management. *Proceedings of the Third International Conference on the Practical Applications of Knowledge Management PAKeM—2000*. The Practical Application Company Ltd, Blackpool, United Kingdom: 51-69.

Stranieri, A. and Zeleznikow, J. 2000. Knowledge discovery for decision support in law. Proceedings of *International Conference on Information Systems (ICIS2000)*, Brisbane, Australia, December 11-13 2000:635-639.

Stranieri, A., Zeleznikow, J., Gawler, M. and Lewis, B. 1999. A Hybrid rule- neural approach for the automation of legal reasoning in the discretionary domain of family law in Australia. *Artificial Intelligence and Law* 7(2-3): 153-183.

Stranieri, A., Zeleznikow, J. and Turner, H. 2000. Data mining in law with Association Rules. Proceedings of IASTED International conference on Law and Technology. IASTED/ACTA Press. California: 129-135

Stranieri, A., Zeleznikow, J. and Yearwood, J. 2001 Argumentation structures that integrate dialectical and monoletical reasoning, *Knowledge Engineering Review* 16(4): 331-348

Susskind, R.E. 1987. *Expert systems in law*. Oxford: Clarendon Press.

Susskind, R. 2000 *Transforming the Law: Essays on Technology, Justice and the Legal Marketplace*, Oxford University Press.

Svensson, J. S.,. Kordelaar, P. J. M., Wassink, J.G.J. and van 't Eind, G.J. 1992. ExpertiSZe, a Tool for Determining the Effects of Social Security Legislation. *JURIX'92: Legal Knowledge Based Systems: Information Technology & Law*, Lelystad Netherlands, Koninklijke Vermande.

Swanson, D. G. 1960. Searching natural language text by computer. *Science*. 132: 1099-1104.

Tata, C. 1997. Conceptions and representations of the sentencing decision process. *Journal of Law and Society*. 24(3): 395,

Tata, C., 1998. The Application of Judicial Intelligence and Rules to Systems Supporting Discretionary Judicial Decision-Making. *Artificial Intelligence and Law* 6(2-4): 203-230

Teufel, S. and Moens, M. 2002. Summarising scientific articles—experiments with relevance and rhetorical status. *Computational Linguistics*, 28(4): 409–445.

Tetley, W. 1999 Mixed jurisdictions : common law vs civil law (codified and uncodified), McGill University, Montreal, Canada as published in thec Official Web Site of the International Institute for the Unification of Private Law. (UNIDROIT), 28 Via Panisperna, 00184 Rome (Italy) http://www.unidroit.org/default.htm Accessed March 23 2004.

Thagard, P. 1989. Explanatory Coherence. *Behavioural and Brain Sciences*. 12(3): 435-502.

Thomasset, C., Blanchard, F., and Paquin, L., 1992. Loge-Expert: Strategies to integrate legal knowledge modelisation, non-expert user interface and textual data base into the development of an expert system in law. *Expert Systems with Applications* 4(4): 379-395

Thompson, P., 2001. Automatic categorization of case law. *Proceedings of the Eigths International Conference on Artificial Intelligence and Law*, ICAIL 2001, May 21-25, 2001, St. Louis, Missouri, USA. ACM Press: 70-77

Toulmin, S. 1958. *The Uses of Argument*. Cambridge University Press. Cambridge

Turtle, H. 1995. Text Retrieval in the Legal World, *Artificial Intelligence and Law*, 3: 5-54.

Valente, A. 1995. *Legal Knowledge Engineering; A modeling approach*. IOS Press. Amsterdam, The Netherlands.

van Dijk, T. A. 1989. Relevance in logic and grammar in Norman, J and Sylvan, R (Eds). *Directions in Relevant Logic*: 25-57.

van Engers, T. M. and Glasee, E. 2001. Facilitating the Legislation Process using a Shared Conceptual Model, *IEEE Intelligent Systems*: 50-57.

van Kralingen, R. W. 1995. *Frame based Conceptual Models of Statute Law*, Kluwer Law International, The Hague, The Netherlands.

Vapnik, V. N. 1995. *The Nature of Statistical Learning Theory*. Springer Verlag, New York.

Visser, P. R. S. 1995. Knowledge Specification for Multiple Legal Tasks: a Case Study of the Interaction Problem in the Legal Domain, Kluwer Computer/Law Series, 17.

Vossos, G. 1995. Incorporating Inductive Case Based Reasoning into an Object Oriented Deductive Legal Knowledge Based System. PhD diss., School of Computer Science and Computer Engineering, La Trobe University.

Vossos, G., Dillon, T., Zeleznikow, J., and Taylor, G. 1990. An object oriented system for legal reasoning—IKBALS. In the Proceedings of the *Tenth International Workshop on Expert Systems and their Applications*, 741-754, Avignon: EC2.

Vossos, G., Dillon, T., Zeleznikow, J. and Taylor, G. 1991. The use of object oriented principles to develop intelligent legal reasoning systems. *Australian Computer Journal* Volume 23(1): 2-10.

Vossos, G. and Zeleznikow, J. 1992. Improving automated litigation support by supplementing rule-based reasoning with case-based reasoning. In the Proceedings of *Third International Conference on Integrating Expert Systems and Databases*, 138-142, Berlin: Springer-Verlag.

Vossos, G., Zeleznikow, J., and Dillon, T. 1990. Combining analogical and deductive reasoning in legal knowledge base systems—IKBALS II. In the Proceedings of the *Third International Conference of the Dutch Foundation of Legal Knowledge Systems (JURIX-90)*, 97-105, Amsterdam: Koninklijke-Vermande.

Vossos, G., Zeleznikow, J., Dillon, T. and Vossos, V. 1991. An example of integrating legal case based reasoning with object oriented rule-based systems—IKBALS II. In the Proceedings of the *Third International Conference on Artificial Intelligence and Law*, 91-101, Oxford: ACM Press.

Vossos, G, Zeleznikow, J. and Hunter, D. 1993. Building intelligent litigation support tools through the integration of rule based and case based reasoning. *Law, Computers and Artificial Intelligence* 2(1):77-93.

Vossos, G., Zeleznikow, J., Moore, A. and Hunter, D. 1993. The Credit Act Advisory System (CAAS): Conversion from an expert system prototype to a C++ commercial system. In the Proceedings of the *Fourth International Conference on Artificial Intelligence and Law*, 180-183, Amsterdam: ACM Press.

Vreeswijk, G., 1993. Defeasible Dialectics: A Controversy-Oriented Approach towards Defeasible Argumentation *The Journal of Logic and Computation*, 3(3): 3-27.

Waismann, F., 1951. Verifiability. (in) Flew, A (Ed). *Logic and Language*. Blackwell.

Walker, R. F. 1991. An expert system architecture for heterogeneous domains: A case study in the legal field. PhD diss., Department of Computer Science, Vrije Universiteit Amsterdam.

Walker, R. F., Oskamp, A., Schrickx, J. A., Opdorp, G. J., and van den Berg, P. H., 1991. PROLEXS: Creating law and order in a heterogeneous domain. *International Journal of Man Machine Studies* Volume 35(1): 35-68.

Wallsten, T. S., Budescu, D. V., Rapoport, A., Zwick, R. and Forsyth, B. 1986 Measuring the vague meanings of probability terms. *Journal of Experimental Psychology: General*, 115(4):348-365.

Wang, P., and Gedeon. T. D., 1995. A new method to detect and remove the outliers in noisy data using neural networks: error sign testing. *Systems Research and Information Science*. 7(1): 55-67.

Warner, D., 1994. A Neural Network-based Law Machine: the problem of legitimacy. *Law, Computers & Artificial Intelligence*. 2(2): 135-147.

Wassestrom, R., 1961. *The judicial decision. Toward a Theory of Legal Justification*. Stanford University Press. Stanford.

Weiss, S and Kulikowski, C. 1992. *Computer Systems That Learn: classification and Prediction Methods from Statistics, Neural Nets, Machine Learning and Expert Systems*. Morgan Kaufman. San Mateo

Werbos, P., 1974. *Beyond Regression: New Tools for Prediction and Analysis in the Behavioural Sciences*. Ph.D. dissertation, Harvard University, Cambridge, MA

Westland, J., C. and Clark, T., 1999. *Global Electronic Commerce*. MIT Press. Cambridge MA.

Westlaw 2004. www.westlaw.com Accessed 15 March, 2004.

Wexler, D.B. and Winick, B. J. 1996. *Law in a Therapeutic Key: Developments in Therapeutic Jurisprudence*, Carolina Academic Press

Wick, M. J., and Thompson, W. B., 1992. Reconstructive expert system explanation. *Artificial Intelligence*. 54(1): 33-70.

Wigmore, J. H. 1913. *The Principles of Judicial Proof*. Little Brown and Company, Boston, Massachussetts

Wigmore, J. H. 1937. *The science of judicial proof as given by logic, psychology and general experience*. Little Brown and Company, Boston, Massachussetts

Wilkins, D. and Pillaipakkamnatt, K. 1997. The Effectiveness of Machine Learning Techniques for Predicting Time to Case Disposition. *Proceedings of Sixth International Conference on Artificial Intelligence and Law*, ACM: Melbourne, Australia, 39-46.

Wnek, J. and Michalski, R. G.. 1991 *Hypothesis Driven Constructive Induction: A Method and Experiments.* Report No. MLI91-4, Machine Learning and Inference Laboratory, George Mason University.

Xu, M. Kaoru, H. and Yoshino, H. 1999. A Fuzzy Theoretical Approach to Case-Based Representation and Inference in CISG. *Artificial Intelligence and Law* 7(2-3):115-128.

Yearwood, J. 1997. Case-based Retrieval of Refugee Review Tribunal Text Cases. Legal Knowledge and Information Systems. JURIX 1997: The Tenth Annual Conference. Amsterdam, Netherlands, IOS Press: 67-83

Yearwood, J., and Stranieri, A., 1999. The integration of retrieval, reasoning and drafting for refugee law: a third generation legal knowledge based system *Seventh International Conference on Artificial Intelligence and Law. ICAIL'99* ACM Press: 117-137.

Yearwood, J., and Stranieri, A., 2000. An argumentation shell for knowledge based systems. Proceedings of IASTED International conference on Law and Technology: 105-111.

Yearwood, J., and Stranieri, A., *2000* Knowledge as Arguments for facilitating E-Commerce Dialogue, *Proceedings of the Sixth CollECTeR Conference on Electronic Commerce, Brisbane, Queensland, Australia.*

Yearwood, J. and Stranieri, A., 2004 The Generic Actual Argument Model of Practical Reasoning. to appear in Decision Support Systems

Yearwood, J., Stranieri, A., and Anjaria, C. 1999. The use of argumentation to assist in the generation of legal documents. *ADCS'99 Fourth Australasian Document Computing Symposium* Southern Cross University Press, NSW, Australia

Yearwood, J and Wilkinson, R., 1997. Retrieving cases for treatment advice in nursing using text representation and structured text retrieval. Artificial Intelligence in Medicine 9(1): 79-99.

Zadeh, L. A. 1965. Fuzzy sets. *Information and Control* 8: 338-353.

Zadeh, L. A. 1983. Commonsense knowledge representation based on fuzzy logic. *IEEE Computer* 16: 61-65.

Zahedi, F. 1993. *Intelligent Systems for Business.* Wadsworth, Belmont, Ca.

Zeleznikow, J. 1991. Building intelligent legal tools—The IKBALS project. *Journal of Law and Information Science* 2(2): 165-184.

Zeleznikow, J. 2000. Building Judicial Decision Support Systems in Discretionary Legal Domains. *International Review of Law, Computers and Technology* 14(3): 341-356.

Zeleznikow, J. 2002. Using Web-based Legal Decision Support Systems to Improve Access to Justice *Information and Communications Technology Law*, 11(1): 15-33.

252

Zeleznikow, J. 2002. Risk, Negotiation and Argumentation – a decision support system based approach. *Law, Probability and Risk*, 1: 37-48.

Zeleznikow, J. 2003. Using Negotiation Support Systems to reduce legal risk. *The Arbitrator and Mediator*, Institute of Arbitrators and Mediators, Australia, 22(1):23-34.

Zeleznikow, J. 2003. An Australian Perspective on Research and Development required for the construction of applied Legal Decision Support Systems, *Artificial Intelligence and Law*, 10: 237-260.

Zeleznikow, J. 2004. The Split-Up project: Induction, context and knowledge discovery in law. *Law, Probability and Risk*, 3: 147-168.

Zeleznikow, J. and Bellucci, E. 2003. Family_Winner: integrating game theory and heuristics to provide negotiation support. in D. Bourcier, (ed.) *Legal Knowledge and Information Systems. JURIX 2003: The Sixteenth Annual Conference.* Amsterdam, Netherlands, IOS Press: 21-30.

Zeleznikow, J., Bellucci, E. And Hodgkin, J. 2002 Building Decision Support Systems to Support Legal Negotiation. Proceedings of the International Conference on Law and Technology (LAWTECH2002), International Society of Law and Technology, ACTA Press. Cambridge, MA: 112-117.

Zeleznikow, J. and Hunter, D. 1992. Rationales for the continued development of legal expert systems. *Journal of Law and Information Science* 3: 94-110.

Zeleznikow, J. and Hunter, D. 1994. *Building Intelligent Legal Information Systems: Knowledge Representation and Reasoning in Law*, Kluwer Computer/Law Series. Deventer-Boston

Zeleznikow, J. and Hunter, D. 1995. Reasoning paradigms in legal decision support systems. *Artificial Intelligence Review* 9(6): 361-385.

Zeleznikow, J. and Hunter, D. 1995. Deductive, Inductive and Analogical Reasoning in Legal Decision Support Systems. *Law, Computers and Artificial Intelligence* 4(2): 141-160.

Zeleznikow, J. Hunter, D. and Stranieri, A. 1994. Reasoning in open textured domains: Benefits of integrating multiple reasoning strategies. in Bramer, M, A,. and Macintosh, A, L,. (eds) *Research and Development in Expert Systems XI. Proceedings of Expert Systems 94,* Cambridge, SGES Publications: 187-198.

Zeleznikow, J. Hunter, D. and Stranieri, A. 1997. Using cases to build intelligent decision support systems. Database Applications Semantics —Proceedings of the IFIP Working Group 2.6 Conference. Stone Mountain, Georgia, USA. May 30 - June 2. 1995. Edited by Meersman, R. and Mark, L. Chapman—Hall: 443-460.

Zeleznikow, J., Meersman, R., Hunter, D. and van Helvoort, E. 1995. Computer tools for aiding legal negotiation. *ACIS95 — Sixth Australian Conference on*

Information Systems, Curtin University of Technology, Perth, Western Australia: 231-251.

Zeleznikow, J. and Nolan, J. 1999. Evaluation of Soft Computing Based Intelligent Decision Support Systems for Building Real World Applications. To appear in *ISDSS'99 — Fifth International Conference of the International Society for Decision Support Systems*.

Zeleznikow, J. and Stranieri, A. 1995. The Split-Up system: Integrating neural networks and rule based reasoning in the legal domain. *Proceedings of Fifth International Conference on Artificial Intelligence and Law*,Washington ACM Press: 185-194.

Zeleznikow, J. and Stranieri, A. 1997a. Modelling discretion in the Split—Up system. *PACIS97 The Pacific Asia Conference on Information Systems*, Information Systems Research Management, Queensland University of Technology: 307-320.

Zeleznikow, J. and Stranieri, A. 1997b. Knowledge Discovery in the Split-Up Project. *Proceedings of Sixth International Conference on Artificial Intelligence and Law*,Melbourne, Australia, ACM: 89-97.

Zeleznikow, J. and Stranieri, A. 1997c. Split—Up: An intelligent decision support system which provides advice upon property division following divorce. *Proceedings of 30th Australian Legal Convention*, Melbourne, September 18-21, Anstat Legal Publishers.

Zeleznikow, J. and Stranieri, A. 1997d. Knowledge Discovery in the Legal Domain. *Proceedings of Ninth IEEE International Conference on Tools for* system which provides advice upon property division following divorce. *Journal of Law and Information Technology*: 6(2): 190-213. Oxford University Press.

Zeleznikow, J. and Stranieri, A. 1998. Split Up: The use of an argument based knowledge representation to meet expectations of different users for discretionary decision making. Proceedings of IAAI'98 — *Tenth Annual Conference on Innovative Applications of Artificial Intelligence*, AAAI/MIT Press: 1146-1151

Zeleznikow, J. and Stranieri, A. 1998. Split—Up: An intelligent decision support system which provides advice upon property division following divorce. *Journal of Law and Information Technology*: 6(2): 190-213. Oxford University Press.

Zeleznikow, J., Stranieri, A. and Gawler, M. 1996. Split-Up: A legal expert system which determines property division upon divorce. *Artificial Intelligence and Law* 3: 267-275.

Zeleznikow, J., Stranieri, A. and Hunter, D. 1995. Beyond Rule Based Reasoning - the Meaning and Use of Cases. In the *Proceedings of the 11th Conference on Artificial Intelligence Applications*, IEEE — Los Angeles: 292-298.

Zeleznikow, J., Stranieri, A. and Lewis, B. 1995. Using induction in legal expert systems. in Bramer, M, A,. Nealon, J. L. and and Milne, R. (eds) *Research and*

Development in Expert Systems XI.Proceedings of Expert Systems 95, Cambridge, SGES Publications: 101-114.

Zeleznikow, J., Vossos, G. and Hunter, D. 1994. The IKBALS project: Multimodal reasoning in legal knowledge based systems *Artificial Intelligence and Law* 2(3):169-203.

Zetie, C. 1995. *Practical User Interface design.* McGraw-Hill. UK. (Pcopy 20 pages)

Zuvela, Peter. 1997. *Family Law Flowcharts.* LBC Information Services. North Ryde. NSW*Artificial Intelligence* (*TAI-97*), Los Alamitos, California, IEEE Computer Society Press: 574-577.

12

GLOSSARY

TERM	DESCRIPTION
abductive reasoning	Abductive reasoning states that from $P \rightarrow Q$ and Q it is possible to infer P. It is an unsound rule of inference, in that it is not necessarily true for every interpretation in which the premises are true.
adversarial case based reasoning	Adversarial case based reasoning involves justifying a conclusion about a problem by drawing an analogy to a similar past case and arguing that the problem should be decided in the same way. This kind of reasoning comprises a variety of tasks, including drawing factual analogies to past cases, distinguishing past cases, citing past cases as counter examples, and evaluating the strength of case-citing arguments.
AIR	Adaptive Information Retrieval is a retrieval system which uses a connectionist network in an adaptive conceptual information retrieval system for bibliographic data.
analogical reasoning	Analogical reasoning is the process of determining the outcome of a current problem (the case at bar) by comparing it to similar past experiences (precedents).
analogy	Drawing an analogy is taking an existing case and seeking to match it with the current case so that one can conclude the outcomes should be identical.
and/or graphs	And/or graphs (or actually trees) are useful for representing the ways in which goals can be expanded into subgoals. The root node represents the main goal, whilst the leaf nodes represent atomic facts. The intermediate nodes represent subgoals. The nodes at any level are all 'ands' or all 'ors' and may alternate from level to level.

TERM	DESCRIPTION
argumentation	Argumentation involves a family of concepts that can be broadly grouped into three categories: a) concepts related to the process of engaging in an argument, b) procedures or rules adopted to regulate the argument process, and c) argument as a product or artefact of an argument process.
association KDD techniques	The objective of association techniques is to discover ways in data elements are associated with other data elements.
association rule	An association rule is of the form A_1 & A_2 & .... & A_m → P . The association rule is interpreted as 'database tuples that satisfy the conditions in the A_i are also likely to satisfy the conditions in P'. Associated with each rule, is a confidence factor, that is how likely is the rule to be true and the support of the rule which states how many of the items in the data set are effected by this rule.
AUSTLII	The Australasian Legal Information Institute (AustLII— www.austlii.edu.au) provides free Internet access to Australian legal materials. AustLII's broad public policy agenda is to improve access to justice through better access to information. To that end, AustLII has become one of the largest sources of legal materials on the net, with over 7 gigabytes of raw text materials and over 1.5million searchable documents.
axioms	In the proof of a theorem, the axioms are those sentences that may be assumed rather than proved.

B

backpropagation of errors	In the Generalised Delta Learning Rule or Back propagation of errors learning rule, the error on the hidden nodes, though not known, is estimated from the error at the output layer. The hidden layer error is estimated as the derivative of the output layer error. Using the derivative of the output layer to estimate the hidden layer error turns out to work quite well.
backward chaining	Backward chaining in a search tree focuses on the goal: given a goal it uses the rules that could possibly lead to that goal and then chains backward through successive rules and subgoals to the given facts.
bagging	Bagging is a method for improving the predictive power of classifier learning systems. It forms a set of classifiers that are combined by voting, by generating replicated bootstrap samples of the data. Bagging produces replicate training sets by sampling with replacement from the training instances. The multiple classifiers are then combined by voting to form a composite classifier. In bagging, each component classifier has the same vote

TERM	DESCRIPTION
base predicate	A base predicate is a predicate that cannot be derived by any other rules, that is they can appear only in the body of the rules. Thus instances of the base predicate appear as facts in the system's rule base. In a legal situation, base predicates can always be resolved as being true or false in a given fact situation.
BATNA — know your best alternative to a negotiated agreement	The reason you negotiate with someone is to produce better results than would otherwise occur. If you are unaware of what results you could obtain if the negotiations are unsuccessful, you run the risk of entering into an agreement that you would be better off rejecting; OR Rejecting an agreement you would be better off entering into.
Bayesian belief networks	Bayesian belief networks are graphical models, which allow the representation of dependencies among subsets of attributes. They can also be used for classification. They are defined by two components: a) a directed acyclic graph where each node represents a random variable and each arc represents a probabilistic dependence. Each variable is conditionally dependent of its nondescendents in the graph, given its parents. The variables may be discrete or continuous; b) A conditional probability table for each variable, $P(X|parents(X))$.
Bayesian classifiers	Bayesian classifiers are statistical classifiers that can predict class membership probabilities – such as the probability that a given sample belongs to a particular class.
Bayesian inference	Bayesian methods provide a formalism for reasoning about partial beliefs under conditions of uncertainty. In this formalism, propositions are given numerical values, signifying the degree of belief accorded to them. Bayes' theorem is an important result in probability theory, which deals with conditional probability. It is useful in dealing with uncertainty, as well as the use of Bayesian inference networks for information retrieval. An application of Bayesian inference networks is the recent WIN (Westlaw Is Natural) legal database.
Bayes theorem	Bayes theorem states that $Pr(A_i|J) = Pr(J|A_i) * Pr(A_i) / [\sum_{k=1}^{k=n} Pr\{(J|A_k) * Pr(A_k)\}]$ and thus allows one to evaluate certain conditional probabilities given other conditional probabilities.
belief functions	Belief functions are an alternative to probability theory, for representing uncertainty in expert systems. Belief functions allow the user to bound the assignment of probabilities to certain events, rather than give events specific probabilities.

TERM	DESCRIPTION
binning or aggregating of data values	Data that has been selected and pre-processed may not necessarily be ready for exposure to a data-mining algorithm. Some transformation of the data may dramatically enhance the benefit of the subsequent data-mining phase. Bining or aggregating of data values involves transforming values into categories or groups. For example, values on an age variable captured in years and months, may be transformed into five pre-defined age groups.
blackboard systems	A blackboard system is a group of knowledge modules collaborating with each other by way of a shared database (blackboard), in order to reach a solution to a problem. Its basic components are: the blackboard, knowledge sources (independent modules that collectively contain the knowledge required to solve the problem) and a control mechanism (or scheduler) which directs the problem-solving process by deciding which knowledge source is most appropriately used at each step in the solution process. The knowledge sources have a condition part and an action part. The condition component specifies the situations under which a particular knowledge source could contribute to an activity. The scheduler controls the progress toward a solution in blackboard systems, by determining which knowledge sources to schedule next, or which problem sub domain to focus on.
Boolean connectives	The basic Boolean connectives are & (and), $\vee$ (or), $\neg$ (not), —> (implies) and <—> (if and only if).
Boolean queries	Boolean queries are queries which are formed using Boolean variables.
Boolean retrieval model	In the Boolean retrieval model, a query has the form of an expression containing index terms and Boolean operators. The retrieval model compares the Boolean query statement with the term set used to identify document content. The index terms that satisfy the query are returned as relevant.
Boolean variables	Boolean variables are variables that take the values T (true) or F (false).
boosting	Boosting improves the predictive power of classifier learning systems by adjusting the weights of training instances. It manipulates the training data in order to generate different classifiers. Boosting uses all instances at each repetition, but maintains a weight for each instance in the training set that reflects its importance; adjusting the weights causes the learner to focus on different instances and so leads to different classifiers. The multiple classifiers are then combined by voting to form a composite classifier. Boosting assigns different voting strengths to component classifiers on the basis of their accuracy.

TERM	DESCRIPTION
bounded domain	A domain may be said to be bounded if the problem space can be specified in advance, regardless of the final definitional interpretation of the terms in the problem space.
breadth-first search	Breadth-first search explores a search space on a level-by-level basis (that is, it examines siblings before children). Only when there are no more states to be explored at a given level does the breadth-first search algorithm move on to the next level.
British Nationality Act	The British Nationality Act as a logic program is a logic programming system built by Sergot and others at Imperial College, London to check if an individual is eligible for British Citizenship under the legislation of the British Nationality Act 1981. It is the major application of logic programming as a tool for constructing legal expert systems.
burden of proof	In the law of evidence, the burden of proof is the necessity or duty of affirmatively proving a fact or facts in dispute on an issue raised between the parties in a cause.
	Except as otherwise provided by the law, the burden of proof requires proof by a preponderance of the evidence. In a criminal case, the government, beyond a reasonable doubt, must prove all the elements of the crime. Except in cases of tax fraud, the burden of proof in a tax case is generally on the taxpayer.
C	
C4.5 algorithm	C4.5 is an enhancement of ID3 that includes tools to a) To deal with missing values on attributes and missing data, b) for pruning decision trees, c) dealing with continuous variables, d) deal with rule accuracy, e) providing alternative measures for selecting attributes.
C5.0 algorithm	C5.0is an enhancement of C4.5 that includes a) Boosting techniques, b) sophisticated ways to measure errors, c) methods to facilitate scaling uyp an algorithm to perform on large datasets.
CABARET	CABARET is a hybrid system built by Rissland and Skalak at University of Massachusetts at Amherst to perform legal interpretation by integrating case based and rule based reasoning. CABARET's application domain is that of income tax law concerning the deduction for expenses relating to an office maintained in one's home. It deals with the circumstances under which a taxpayer may legitimately deduct, on a United States income tax return, expenses relating to an office maintained at the taxpayer's expense. CABARET is an agenda based architecture for integrating case based reasoning and rule based reasoning.

TERM	DESCRIPTION
CART	CART (Classification and Regression Trees) constructs a classification or decision tree by repeatedly splitting the training set into subsets. Its aim is to find a systematic way of predicting to which class a particular object belongs. A distinctive characteristic of the CART system is its pruning algorithm. The construction of the tree depends on: a) the selection of splits; b) the decision to continue splitting a node or not; and c) the assignment of a class to a non-split node (i.e. a non expanded node).
case adaptation	Case adaptation takes a retrieved case that meets most of the needs of the current case and turns it into one that meets all of the case's needs.
case based reasoning	Case based reasoning is the process of using previous experience to analyse or solve a new problem, explain why previous experiences are or are not similar to the present problem and adapting past solutions to meet the requirements of the present problem.
case knowledge base	In a case based reasoner, the case knowledge base is that part of the system that stores the cases.
certainty factor	A certainty factor in an expert system is a probability that the conclusion reached by the system is correct.
civil law	Civil law may be defined as that legal tradition which has its origin in Roman law, as codified in the Corpus Juris Civilis of Justinian and as subsequently developed in Continental Europe and around the world. Civil law eventually divided into two streams: the codified Roman and uncodified Roman law. Civil law is highly systematised and structured and relies on declarations of broad, general principles, often ignoring the details. Civil law systems are closed, in the sense that every possible situation is governed by a limited number of general principles.
class	In the object oriented paradigm a class of objects is a group of objects all with the same characteristics.
Classification KDD techniques	The aim of classification techniques is to group data into predefined categories

TERM	DESCRIPTION
CLIME	In the CLIME project, a large-scale ontology was developed for the purpose of a web-based legal advice system MILE. The system features both extended conceptual retrieval and normative assessment on international rules and regulations regarding ship classification and maritime pollution. The user can formulate a case using a structured natural language interface. The interface uses only the terms available in the ontology, which ensures that the user formulates a query on a topic the system knows about. The ontology also provides a means for adequate knowledge management of the rules and regulations
Clustering KDD techniques	The aim of clustering techniques is to group data into clusters of similar items.
commonplace case	A commonplace case is one that does not provide any lessons by itself, but together with numerous like cases can be used to derive conclusions. Commonplace cases are to be found in the training sets of neural networks and rule induction systems.
common law	Common law is the legal tradition that evolved in England from the 11th century onwards. Its principles appear for the most part in reported judgments, usually of the higher courts, in relation to specific fact situations arising in disputes that courts have adjudicated. common law systems are open, in the sense that new rules may be created or imported for new facts.
concept drift	Concept drift is the change in the view of a concept over time — such as how judges distribute marital property in different registries and at different times.
conceptual retrieval systems	Conceptual retrieval systems are systems that index and retrieve information using conceptual rather than text structures. To allow for conceptual retrieval, the computer must have a knowledge of legal concepts and issues, and their relationship to the structure of case law collections.
cooperation	Cooperation is the process in which a set of information systems utilise intelligence to exchange beliefs, reason about each other and about one another's conceptions, and in general, discuss how they can coordinate their activities to contribute to an information intensive problem.
cooperative problem solving	Cooperative problem solving considers how a particular problem can be subdivided into a number of processing elements that cooperate and interact in terms of partitioning and sharing expertise to develop a solution.

TERM	**DESCRIPTION**
Credit Act Advisory System	The Credit Act Advisory System is a strictly rule based system which represents the statutory provisions of the Victorian Credit Act, 1984. It has was developed by Vossos and others at La Trobe University for Allan Moore & Co, solicitors, and was commercially marketed.
critical legal studies	Critical legal studies theorists contend that rules and principles are not used to determine an outcome but are invoked after a conclusion has been reached in order to support and justify an outcome.
cross validation	*k-fold cross validation* involves partitioning the sample into k training/test set pairs of approximately equal size. k classifiers are trained and the estimate of the true error is obtained by taking the average of apparent error rate on the k test sets.

D

DataLex project	The DataLex project is concerned with building legal expert systems that simulate the advice that a lawyer might give concerning a client's legal rights or which simulate the type of argument which a lawyer might to put to a court. The DataLex Workstation software combines expert systems, hypertext and free text retrieval. It has been developed for use in commercial applications and to teach legal applications.
data cleaning	Data cleaning is the preprocessing of data to remove or reduce noise and the treatment of missing values.
data mining	Data mining is a problem-solving methodology that finds a logical or mathematical description, eventually of a complex nature, of patterns and regularities in a set of data.
data mining pattern	A data mining pattern is interesting if: a) the pattern is easily understood by humans; b) the pattern is valid (with some degree of certainty) on new or test data; c) the pattern is potentially useful;the pattern is novel.
data oriented learning	Data oriented learning programs are systems that aim to develop programs that can search databases for underlying rules.
data pre-processing	Data pre-processing involves preparing the sample data for further phases of the KDD process. This requires attention to two main factors; missing values and erroneous data.

TERM	DESCRIPTION
data selection	The first phase of any KDD process involves the selection of a sample of data from a database of records. Decisions must first be made regarding the nature of the problem of interest in order to assess its suitability for the KDD process. This phase is equivalent to sampling in statistical circles and involves selecting which records to include and which to omit. There are two distinct considerations; how to select records and how to select variables.
data transformation	Data may need to be transformed in order to discover useful knowledge. Transformation can involve changing the categories of values a variable may have. It can take one of three basic forms: a) the decomposition of the data set into smaller parts where each part will be the subject of an independent data mining exercise, b) the aggregation of variables and/or values to form a simpler, more general data set, c) changing values of variables in some way.
decision tree	A decision tree is an explicit representation of all scenarios that can result from a given decision. The root of the tree represents the initial situation, whilst each path from the root corresponds to one possible scenario.
decision tree pruning	When a decision tree is built, many of the branches will reflect anomalies in the training data due to noise or outliers. Tree pruning methods address this problem of overfitting the data. Such methods typically use statistical measures to remove the least reliable branches, generally resulting in faster classification and an improvement in the ability of the tree to correctly classify independent test data.
deduction	Deduction is that inference process that states that if certain premises are true then certain conclusions must follow.
deductive database	A deductive database consists of a set of facts and rules written in first order predicate calculus.
deductive reasoning	Deductive reasoning is the process that commences with a set of pre-determined premises that cannot be derived from the system (axioms) and then uses deduction techniques to derive new conclusions.
deep model	A domain has a deep model if it has a clear underlying model of the mechanisms involved in decision making.

TERM	DESCRIPTION
defeasible logic	Defeasible logic consists of *strict* rules that are rules that are always true, and *defeasible* rules that can be defeated by other rules. A knowledge base in defeasible logic consists of five different types of knowledge: a) Facts, b) Strict rules: of the form p_1 & p_2 ... & p_n → q, c) Defeasible rules: rules that can be defeated by contrary evidence, d) Defeaters: a special kind of rule used to prevent conclusions rather than to support them, e) A superiority relation defined over rules: it is used to define priorities among rules, that is, where one rule may override the conclusion of another rule
Dempster-Shafer Theory	Dempster-Shafer theory has been developed to handle partially specified domains. It distinguishes between uncertainty and ignorance by creating belief functions.
deontic logic	Deontic logic is a form of logic which deals with permissions and obligations. It has two operators in addition to those in first order predicate calculus, O (obligation) and P (permission). It is closely related to the legal reasoning methodology proposed by Hohfeld.
dependency graph	A dependency graph is a means of visualising how knowledge is represented in a logic based (or even rule based) system. In a knowledge base D consisting of facts and rules the dependency graph G_D is the graph whose nodes are predicates in D and there is an arc from q to q in G_D if there is a rule in D with head q for which p is in the body.
depth-first search	In depth-first search, when a state is examined all of its children and their descendants are examined before any of its siblings. Only when no further descendants can be found are its siblings considered.
design oriented case based reasoning paradigm	See planning oriented case based reasoning paradigm.
dialectical argument	A dialectical situation involves participants engaged in the process of argument and a protocol to regulate the process.
dimensions	In a case based reasoner the dimensions are the indices into the case knowledge base. In Hypo, a dimension is a general framework for recording information about a factor for the program to manipulate. Hypo has a library of dimensions for the claim of trade secrets misappropriation, each associated with a factor that identifies a common strength or weakness in a trade secrets claim. Each dimension has a set of prerequisites used to test if the factor applies to a case and a range of values over which the magnitude of the factor in a particular case may vary.

TERM	DESCRIPTION
discretion	Discretion is a power or right conferred upon decision-makers to act according to the dictates of their own judgement and conscience, uncontrolled by the judgement or conscience of others
distributed artificial intelligence	Distributed artificial intelligence deals with the problem of providing coordinated and integrated support to many problem solvers working on multiple simultaneous problems. It also includes attempts to have these processes operating on separate processors.
domain expert	A domain expert is a person involved in the construction of an expert system, who has specific expertise in that domain and who advises the knowledge engineer of the knowledge which is to be placed in the expert system.
domain knowledge	In building an expert system, the domain knowledge is that knowledge specific to the domain being modelled, as distinct from the knowledge necessary to build the inference engine.

E

easy cases	Easy cases are those cases which can be disposed of on the basis of well-established law and where the facts are sufficiently indisputable that no real issue arises.
E-COURT	The e-COURT project is a European project that aims at developing an integrated system for the acquisition of audio/video depositions within courtrooms, the archiving of legal documents, information retrieval and synchronized audio/video/text consultation. The focus of the project is to process, archive and retrieve legal documents of criminal courtroom sessions via the World Wide Web.
encapsulation	In object oriented programming encapsulation is the technical name for information hiding. That is, only the methods of an object have access to its data structure, and a method can only be invoked by sending the object a message. No part of the system can see 'inside' the object, since it does not need to. If an object wants another object to perform some function then it must send a message to the object. It is an important feature of object oriented systems.
evaluation	The final phase of the KDD process involves the evaluation and interpretation of knowledge discovered as a result of the data mining phase.
evolutionary algorithms	Evolutionary algorithms are computer-based problem solving systems that use computational models of evolutionary processes as key elements in their design and implementation.
exemplar based explanation	An inference step that connects the facts of a case to the truth value of an open textured predicate is termed an exemplar based explanation.

TERM	DESCRIPTION
expert system	Expert systems are computer programs capable of providing advice and functioning at the standard of (and sometimes even at a higher standard than) human experts in given fields.
expert system shell	An expert system shell is a tool for developing expert systems that consists of an expert system building language integrated into an extensive support environment.
explanation	Explanation is a collection of reasoning steps that connects facts to a logical conclusion about those facts.
explanation based learning	Explanation based learning addresses the problem of learning generalisations from a single training instance. It uses existing knowledge to form an explanation of why a new instance belongs to the target concept, and saves as a learned concept the generalisation of this explanation.

F

feature reduction	Feature reduction involves the removal of features that are not relevant or make no sizeable contribution to the data mining exercise.
feature selection	Feature selection or relevance analysis attempts to identify features that do not contribute to the data-mining task.
feed forward neural network	In a feed forward neural network, the neurons on the first layer send their output to the neurons of the second layer, but they do not receive any input back from the neurons on the second layer.
FFPOIROT	FF-POIROT is a venture to develop European standards for the prevention, detection and successful investigation of financial fraud. The goal of the project is to build a detailed ontology of European Law, preventive practices and knowledge of the processes of financial fraud. The FF-POIROT project aims at compiling for several languages (Dutch, Italian, French and English) a computationally tractable and sharable knowledge repository (a formally described combination of concepts and their meaningful relationships) for the financial fraud domain.
First Class	First Class is an inductive software tool based on the ID3 algorithm.

TERM	DESCRIPTION
first order predicate calculus	First order predicate calculus is a formal logic language that includes the operators of propositional calculus, functions, predicates, variables, constants and the universal ($\forall$) and existential quantifiers ($\exists$). First order predicate calculus is semi-decidable; that is, if a formula is valid we can prove it is valid, but we cannot necessarily prove a formula to be satisfiable. Its major artificial intelligence use is in the area of representing knowledge and automated theorem proving. Resolution is the theorem proving technique used in first order predicate calculus.
FLEXLAW	Flexlaw used a Vector Space Model for matching. It automatically constructs structured representations from text. Cases and other legal documents are represented by document profiles that preserve the meaning of legal text and contain all the information necessary and sufficient to match documents with a user's query.
forward chaining	Forward chaining in a search tree is the process of moving from IF patterns to THEN patterns, using the IF patterns to identify appropriate situations for the deduction of a new assertion or the performance of an action.
frames	Frames are a knowledge representation method that associates features with nodes representing concepts. The features are described in terms of attributes and their values. They add to the modelling capabilities of semantic networks by allowing complex objects to be represented by single frames, as well as catering for classes, inheritance and default values.
full text retrieval	In full text retrieval, the full text of all of the documents is stored on the computer, so that every character in every document is stored. When the user issues a query to the system, the computer searches for the documents containing the specified word combinations.
fuzzy logic	Fuzzy logic is a many valued propositional logic where each proposition P rather than taking the value T or F has a probability attached (thus between 0 and 1) of being true. It would take the value 0 if it were false and 1 if it were true. Logical operators and probability theory are then combined to model reasoning with uncertainty. Fuzzy rules capture something of the uncertainty inherent in the way in which language is used to construct rules. Fuzzy logic and statistical techniques can be used in dealing with uncertain reasoning.

TERM	DESCRIPTION
fuzzy set theory	Fuzzy set theory uses the standard logical operators & (and), v (or), ~ (not). Thus given truth values (or membership values) μ (p) for p and μ (q) for q, we can develop truth values (or membership values) for p & q, p v q and ~p. These values are determined by (a) μ (~p) = 1 − μ (p), b) μ (p & q) = min{ μ (p), μ (q)}, c) μ (p v q) = max{ μ (p), μ (q)}
G	
GBB	GBB is an expert system shell based on the blackboard paradigm. It provides the blackboard database infrastructure, knowledge source languages and control components needed by a blackboard application. It is used in the construction of the CABARET legal knowledge based system.
genetic algorithms	Genetic algorithms are general-purpose search algorithms that use principles derived from genetics to solve problems. A population of evolving knowledge structures that evolve over time – through competition and controlled variation – is maintained. Each structure in the population represents a candidate solution to the concrete problem and has an associated fitness to determine which structures are used to form new ones in the competition. The new structures are created using genetic operators such as crossover and mutation.
GETAID	GetAid is a web-based decision support system for determining eligibility for legal aid. After passing a financial test, applicants for legal aid must pass a merit test. This assessment involves the integration of procedural knowledge found in regulatory guidelines with expert lawyer knowledge that involves a considerable degree of discretion. KDD was used to model the discretionary task.
goal condition	A goal condition is the solution to a problem instance, particularly in a state space representation.
GoldWorks	GoldWorks is a sophisticated artificial intelligence hybrid shell. GoldWorks is an object oriented knowledge engineering environment based on frames.
GREBE	GREBE is a system for legal analysis that uses legal and common sense rules together with precedent cases to construct explanations of conclusions about cases. It can use either case based reasoning or rule based reasoning. Its current knowledge base is in the domain of Texas worker's compensation law.
H	

TERM	DESCRIPTION
Hidden Markov Models	Hidden Markov Models (HMM) are probabilistic finite state automata that model the probabilities of a linear sequence of events. In a HMM, one only knows a probabilistic function of the state sequence through which the model passes. Given a training corpus in which the information is sequentially structured and which is manually annotated, efficient algorithms learn the probabilities of all transitions and emissions.
hold out estimation of error rates	Hold out estimation of error rates involve partitioning the sample data into a training set and a test set. The classifier is trained with the training set while the test set is held out. Once trained, the classifier is trialed on the test set. The error rate on the test set provides a better estimate of the true error rate than the apparent error figure.
hybrid reasoning	A hybrid reasoning system combines facets of one or more of the following representation schemes into a single integrated programming environment: logical, procedural, network and structured. It usually includes object orientation, rules for representing heuristic knowledge and support for a variety of search strategies.
hypertext	Hypertext is an approach to information management in which data is stored in a network of nodes connected by links. The data can consist of graphics, video, audio or large amounts of textual material.
Hypo	Hypo is a case based reasoner developed by Ashley and Rissland at University of Massachusetts at Amherst. It analyses problem situations dealing with trade secrets disputes, retrieves relevant legal cases from its database, and fashions them into reasonable legal arguments. It has turned out to be the benchmark on which other legal case based reasoners have been constructed.
I	
ID3 algorithm	The ID3 algorithm was developed by Quinlan and is a machine learning algorithm which induces a decision tree for classification problems. The tree is derived from examples in a training set. The ID3 algorithm uses an entropy-based measure known as *information gain*, as a heuristic for selecting the attribute that will best separate the samples into individual classes. The attribute becomes the 'test' or 'decision' attribute at the node.

TERM	DESCRIPTION
IKBALS	The IKBALS Project (Intelligent Legal Knowledge BAsed Systems) at La Trobe University, Victoria, Australia, has as its aim the development of intelligent legal support tools. The original prototype IKBALS I was a hybrid/object oriented rule based system. Its descendants IKBALS II and IKBALS III, provide for integrated rule based reasoning, case based reasoning, and information retrieval by using intelligent cooperating information systems. Machine learning is used to improve case indexing.
indices	In a text retrieval system, indices provide for fast access to data items holding the particular value(s) for which the user is searching.
inductive learning	Inductive learning is a heuristic search through a space of symbolic descriptions, generated by the application of various inference rules to the initial observational statements.
inductive reasoning	Inductive reasoning is the process of moving from specific cases to general rules. A rule induction system is given examples of a problem where the outcome is known. When it has been given several examples, the rule induction system can create rules that are true from the example cases. The rules can then be used to assess other cases where the outcome is not known.
inference	Inference is the process of deriving conclusions from premises.
inference engine	An inference engine is that part of an expert or knowledge based system that contains the general (as opposed to specific) problem solving knowledge. The inference engine contains an interpreter that decides how to apply the rules to infer new knowledge and a scheduler that decides the order in which the rules should be applied.
inference networks	The inference net model is a probabilistic retrieval model; since it uses a probability ranking principle. It computes $Pr(I|document)$, which is the probability that a user's information need is satisfied given a particular document.
information extraction	Information extraction is a technique for extracting domain-specific information from texts. Text fragments are mapped to field or template lots that have a definite semantic meaning.
information system	An information system is a computer system whose basic purpose is to represent/store or manipulate data, information or knowledge.

TERM	DESCRIPTION
information theory	Information theory assumes that information originates at a source and is transmitted, as a message to a receiver. The amount of information in a message is related to how surprised the receiver is to get the message. The information content of a message is inversely related to the probability of receiving the message.
inheritance	In systems adopting the object oriented paradigm, inheritance is the process by which one object takes on or is assigned the characteristics of another object higher up in a hierarchy. It is a mandatory feature of object oriented systems.
integrated expert database systems	In an integrated expert database system the database and artificial intelligence functionalities are totally integrated. This involves rebuilding the entire database management system from source and adding a deductive component.
intelligent and cooperating information system	Cooperative information systems typically involve integrating heterogeneous information sources which span both the database and knowledge based systems domain and which employ heterogeneous data/knowledge representations. The community of information agents that jointly execute a common task is called an intelligent and cooperative information system
intelligent information system	An intelligent information system is an information system which combines knowledge based and database primitives and concepts to support applications that require knowledge directed processing of shared information.
interesting case	For a first instance decision to be interesting it must: 1) be appealed, or 2) includes a new principle, rule or factor in its ratio decidendi, or 3) exhibits an outcome vastly at odds with other similar cases.
interesting KDD pattern	A pattern is interesting if it is a) easily understood by humans, b) valid (with some degree of certainty) on new or test data, c) potentially useful and d) novel. A pattern is also interesting if it validates a hypothesis that the user sought to confirm.
interoperability	Interoperability involves the ability of two or more systems to work together to execute well defined and delimited tasks collectively.
isomorphism	Isomorphism is the principle that any computer comprehensible format must be congruent with the rules being modelled: that is the computer representation must have the same structure as the rules placed in a rule base.
issue	An issue is a legal factor that was known to be relevant to the outcome of a case

TERM	DESCRIPTION
inverted file	An inverted file is a file where the roles of records and attributes are reversed. Instead of listing the attributes of a given record, we list the records having a given attribute. This is useful in database searching.

J

| JUSTSYS | JUSTSYS (www.justsys.com.au) is an Australian start up company which develops legal knowledge based systems for the World Wide Web. Its rationale for developing such tools came from the extended use of Toulmin Argument Structures for representing legal knowledge. JUSTSYS is focusing upon: (i) Tools for the rapid development of decision support; (ii) On line dispute resolution tools and (iii) Data Mining. |

K

Kernel methods	Kernel estimates smooth out the contribution of each observed data point over a local neighbourhood of the point. Nearest neighbour and locally weighted regression are approaches for approximating target functions. Learning involves storing the presented training data and when a new query instance is encountered, a set of similar related instances is retrieved from memory and used to classify the new query instance. The kernel function is the function of distance that is used to determine the weight of each training example. Whereas kernel methods define the degree of smoothing in terms of a kernel function and bandwidth, nearest neighbour methods let the data determine the bandwidth by defining it in terms of the number of nearest neighbours.
knowledge acquisition	Knowledge acquisition is the transfer and transformation of potential problem-solving expertise from some knowledge source to a program.
knowledge based system	A knowledge based system is a computer program in which domain knowledge is explicit and contained separately from the system's other knowledge.
knowledge discovery	Knowledge discovery is the non trivial extraction of implicit, previously unknown and potentially useful information from data
knowledge engineering	Knowledge engineering involves the cooperation of domain experts who work with the knowledge engineer to codify and make explicit the rules or other reasoning processes that a human expert uses to solve real world problems.
knowledge engineering paradox	The knowledge engineering paradox is that the more competent domain experts become, the less able they are to describe the knowledge they use to solve problems.

TERM	DESCRIPTION
knowledge engineering process	The knowledge engineering process is the process of transferring knowledge from the domain experts to the computer system. It includes the following phases: knowledge representation, knowledge acquisition, inference, explanation and justification.
knowledge representation	Knowledge representation involves structuring and encoding the knowledge in the knowledge base, so that inferences can be made by the system from the stored knowledge.

L

landmark case	A landmark case is one which alters our perception about knowledge in the domain — landmark cases are comparable to rules. Landmark cases are the basis of analogical reasoning.
latent semantic indexing	Latent semantic indexing reduces the size of the term frequency matrix by using singular value decomposition (SVD). Given a T x D term frequency matrix, the SVD method removes rows and columns to reduce the size of a matrix to a manageable K x K matrix where K is much less than the minimum of K and D. To minimise the amount of information loss, only the least significant parts of the frequency matrix are omitted.
learning	Learning is any change in a system that allows it to perform better the second time on repetition of the same task drawn from the same population.
legal positivism	Legal positivists believe that a legal system is a *closed logical system* in which correct decisions may be deduced from predetermined rules by logical means alone.
legal realism	Legal realists are jurisprudes for whom the reliance on rules is an anathema. They argue that judges make decisions for a range of reasons which cannot be articulated or at least are not apparent on the face of the judgement given.
lex posterior	Lex posterior is the legal principle that states the later rule has precedence over the earlier rule.
lex specialis	Lex specialis is the legal principle that states the priority is given to the argument that uses the most specific information.
lex superior	Lex superior is the legal principle that states that a ruling of a higher court takes precedence over one made by a lower court.
linear regression	In linear regression, data is modelled using a straight line of the form $y = \alpha x + \beta$. α and β are determined using the method of least squares. Polynomial regression models can be transformed to a linear regression model.
local stare decisis	Local stare decisis is the tendency of judges to be consistent with the decisions of other members of their own region (or registry).

TERM	DESCRIPTION
linearly separable	Data is linearly separable if a straight line or plane can be drawn to separate examples into two different types of outputs.
logic programming	The use of predicate calculus as a programming language is known as logic programming. The best known logic programming language is PROLOG.
logic representation schemes	A logic representation scheme is a knowledge representation scheme in which formal logic is used to represent the knowledge base; rules and proof procedures apply this knowledge to problem instances.

M

machine learning	Machine learning is that subsection of learning in which the artificial intelligence system attempts to learn automatically.
meta-knowledge	Meta-knowledge is knowledge about knowledge.
meta-rule	A meta-rule is a rule that describes how other rules should be used or modified.
method	In an object oriented system a method is a body of code to implement each message. A method returns a value as a response to the message. Each object has a set of messages to which the object responds.
mixed legal system	A mixed legal system has principles derived in part from the civil law tradition and in part from the common law tradition. Scotland is an example of a mixed legal system.
modus ponens	Modus ponens is a form of inference that says if P —> Q holds and P holds, then Q holds.
model based case based reasoning paradigm	The model based approach assumes that there is a strong causal model of the domain task. It generally involves selecting among partially matched cases, in which symbolic reasoning is used to determine the difference between the given problem and the retrieved cases.
multi-agent system	Multi-agent systems coordinate intelligent behaviour amongst a collection of intelligent agents.
multimedia (or hypermedia) system	A multimedia system is an information system that can combine various types of media: such as text, graphics, video or audio

N

naïve Bayesian classifiers	Naïve Bayesian classifiers assume the effect of an attribute value on a given class is independent of the other attributes. Studies comparing classification algorithms have found that the naïve Bayesian classifier to be comparable in performance with decision tree and neural network classifiers.

TERM	DESCRIPTION
nearest neighbour algorithm	The nearest neighbour algorithm is used in information retrieval where data that is closest to the search is retrieved. To perform this search, we need a 'metric' (distance function) between the occurrence of each piece of data. The kth nearest neighbour algorithm classifies examples in a sample by using two basic steps to classify each example: a) Find the k nearest, most similar examples in the training set to the example to be classified; b) Assign the example the same classification as the majority of k nearest retrieved neighbours.
negotiation	Negotiation is the process by which two or more parties conduct communications or conferences with the view to resolving differences between two parties. This process might be formal or mandated as in legal and industrial disputes, semi-formal, as in international disputes or totally informal as in the case of two prospective partners negotiating as to how they will conduct their married life.
network representation schemes	A network representation scheme is a knowledge representation scheme using graphs, in which nodes represent objects or concepts in the problem domain and the arcs represent relations or associations between them. Semantic networks are an example of a network representation scheme.
neural networks	A neural network receives its name from the fact that it resembles a nervous system in the brain. It consists of many self-adjusting processing elements cooperating in a densely interconnected network. Each processing element generates a single output signal which is transmitted to the other processing elements. The output signal of a processing element depends on the inputs to the processing element: each input is gated by a weighting factor that determines the amount of influence that the input will have on the output. The strength of the weighting factors is adjusted autonomously by the processing element as data is processed.
neural networks in law	Neural networks are particularly useful in law because they can deal with a) classification difficulties, b) vague terms, c) defeasible rules and d) discretionary domains.
network topology	A neural network topology is a specification of the number of neurons in the input layer, the output layer and in each of the hidden layers.
normalising data values	A variable with large values measured, for instance in the thousands could dominate a variable with very small values measured in the thousandths in the data-mining phase. Normalising involves transforming both sets of values so that they fall within the same range.

O

TERM	DESCRIPTION
object	An object consists of an encapsulated representation (data structure) and a set of methods (operations or procedures) that can be applied to the object in order to activate it to do something.
object oriented paradigm	The object oriented paradigm is based on encapsulating code and data into a single unit an object. The interface between an object and the system is defined by a set of messages.
Occam's Razor	Occam's Razor, developed by William of Occam circa 1320 states *prefer the simplest hypothesis that fits the data*
ontology	An ontology as an explicit conceptualisation of a domain
onus of proof	In any given scenario the onus of proof indicates the degree of certainty for a given outcome to occur. In a criminal case in Common Law countries such proof must be beyond reasonable doubt, whereas in most civil cases in such countries, the proof required is by a fair preponderance of the evidence (i.e. more than 50% likely to occur).
open textured legal predicate	Open textured legal predicates contain questions that cannot be structured in the form of production rules or logical propositions and which require some legal knowledge on the part of the user in order to answer
outliers	Data objects that are grossly different from or inconsistent with the remaining set of data are called outliers.
overfitting	Overfitting occurs when the data mining method performs very well with data it has been exposed to but performs poorly with other data.
over-training of neural networks	A neural network over-trains if it has been exposed to an abundance of examples, far too many times. In this case it can learn each input-output pair so well that it, in effect memorises those cases. The network classifies training set cases well, but may not perform so well with cases not in the training set.
P	
paradigm	In computer science terms, a paradigm is a model of a theory used to implement a system. Examples include the object oriented paradigm and the paradigm of modularising programs.
perceptron	A perceptron is a generalization of the McCulloch and Pitts neural network which can learn a variety of functions including AND and OR. This occurs by a dynamic modification of the weights that represent the strength of interconnections amongst neurons.
personal stare decisis	Personal stare decisis is the tendency of judges to be consistent with themselves.

TERM	DESCRIPTION
planning oriented case based reasoning paradigm	In the planning (or design) oriented case based reasoning paradigm, cases are instantiated. They record a past problem's solution and are used as templates to map the solution on to a new problem. The focus is on indexing cases according to the planning goals satisfied in the case or the conflicts among planning goals that the case resolves or avoids.
plausible inference	Polya developed a formal characterisation of qualitative human reasoning as an alternative to probabilistic methods for performing commonsense reasoning. He identified four patterns of plausible inference: inductive patterns, successive verification of several consequences, verification of improbable consequences and inference from analogy.
polymorphism	In the object oriented paradigm, polymorphism is the ability of different objects to respond differently to the same message.
precedent based case based reasoning	Precedent based (or interpretive) case based reasoning is where the system establishes whether the current case should be treated like a case in the database. The system gives reasons (both for and against) why the current case should be treated analogously to the retrieved case.
principal component analysis	Principal components analysis (PCA) is the technique most often used to identify features that do not contribute to the prediction from a data-set. PCA involves the analysis of variance between features and the class variable in a prediction exercise. PCA requires specialist statistical software, since the calculations are cumbersome. PCA is applicable only to features that are numeric.
principled negotiation	Principled negotiation promotes deciding issues on their merits rather than through a haggling process focussed on what each side says it will and will not do.
probabilistic information retrieval models	Probabilistic information retrieval models are based on the probability ranking principle which ranks legal documents according to their probability of relevance to the query given every available source of information. The model estimates the probability of relevance of a text to the query, on the basis of the statistical distribution of terms in relevant and irrelevant text, given an uncertainty associated with the representation of both the source text and the information need, as well as the relevance relationship between them.
procedural representation scheme	A procedural representation scheme is a knowledge representation scheme in which knowledge is represented as a set of instructions for solving a problem. Examples of procedural representation schemes include production rules.

TERM	DESCRIPTION
production rule system	Production rule systems are expert systems which consist of a set of production rules, working memory and the recognise-act cycle (also known as the rule interpreter).
PROLEXS	The PROLEXS project at the Computer/Law Institute, Vrije Universiteit, Amsterdam, Netherlands is concerned with the construction of legal expert shells to deal with vague concepts. Its current domain is Dutch landlord-tenant law. It uses several knowledge sources and the inference engines of the independent knowledge groups interact using a blackboard architecture.
Proof beyond reasonable doubt	Proof beyond a reasonable doubt is such proof as precludes every reasonable hypothesis except that which it tends to support and which is wholly consistent with the defendant's guilt and inconsistent with any other rational conclusion.
Proof by a fair preponderance of the evidence	Proof by a fair preponderance of the evidence is the standard of proof required in civil cases; a decision is made according to that evidence which as a whole is more credible and convincing to the mind and which best accords with reason and probability.
Pro se litigant	A pro se litigant is one who represents her/himself.
R	.
ratio decidendi	*Ratio decidendi* is Latin for the 'reasons for decision', that is the legal reasons why the judge came to the conclusion that he or she did. It is the fundamental basis for the rule of law in common law systems. Stare decisis says that the ratio decidendi will apply to subsequent cases decided by courts lower in the hierarchy.
regression	In linear regression, data is modelled using a straight line of the form $y = \alpha x + \beta$. α and β are determined using the method of least squares. Polynomial regression models can be transformed to a linear regression model.
resolution	Resolution is a semi-decidable proof technique for first order predicate calculus, which given an unsatisfiable well formed formula, proves it to be unsatisfiable. If the well formed formula is not unsatisfiable, there is a possibility that the algorithm may not terminate.
rule base	The rule base of a legal (or indeed any) rule based expert system is that part of the system in which the rules are stored. It is kept separate from the other part of the expert system, the inference engine.
rule based expert systems	A rule based expert system is a collection of rules of the form : IF <condition(s)> THEN <action>. Rule based systems include production rule systems, and some would argue, logic based systems as well.
S	

TERM	DESCRIPTION
SALOMON	The SALOMON project automatically summarised Belgian criminal cases in order to improve access to the large number of existing and future court decisions. SALOMON extracts relevant text units from the case text to form a case summary. Such a case profile facilitated the rapid determination of the relevance of the case to be employed in text search.
SCALIR	SCALIR (Symbolic and Connectionist Approach to Legal Information Retrieval) developed by Rose and Belew at University of California at San Diego, uses a hybrid of both symbolic and connectionist links in building an interactive learning system for aiding legal research on copyright law.
Series Analysis KDD techniques	The aim of series analysis is to discover sequences within the data. Sequences typically sought are time series.
Shannon's entropy formula	Shannon's entropy formula: Information (M) = - probability (M) * ($\log_2$ probability (M)) provides a relationship between information of a message and the probability of receiving it. It is the basis of Quinlan's techniques for learning decision trees.
similarity-based retrieval	Similarity-based retrieval finds similar documents based on a set of common keywords. The output of such retrieval is based on the degree of relevance, where relevance is measured based on the closeness and the relative frequency of the keywords.
SPIRE	SPIRE integrates a case based reasoner with information retrieval techniques to locate the passage within a document where a query concept is likely to be found. It uses the INQUERY text retrieval engine
SPLIT-UP	SPLIT-UP is a hybrid rule based/ neural network system developed at La Trobe University that uses textbooks, heuristics, expert advice and cases to model that part of the Family Law Act 1975 (Australia) which deals with property division. Explanation is provided through the use of Toulmin argument structures.
stare decisis	Stare decisis says that the ratio decidendi will apply to subsequent cases decided by courts lower in the hierarchy
statistically oriented case based reasoning paradigms	In statistically oriented case based reasoning paradigms, cases are used as data points for statistical generalisation. The case based reasoner computes conditional probabilities that a problem should be treated similarly to previously given cases.
statutory law	Statutory law is that body of law created by acts of the legislature — in contrast to constitutional law and law generated by decisions of courts and administrative bodies

TERM	DESCRIPTION
statistical reasoning	In contrast to symbolic reasoning, statistical reasoning derives its results by checking whether or not there is a statistical correlation between two events. Examples of statistical reasoning include neural networks and rule induction systems. Whilst rule based systems are considered to be examples of symbolic reasoning; the rules are often derived using statistical tests.
strong discretion	According to Dworkin, strong discretion characterises those decisions where the decision-maker is not bound by any standards and is required to create his or her own standards.
supervised learning	In supervised learning, the system developer tells the system what the correct is, and the system determines weights in such a way that once given the input it would produce the desired output. The system is repeatedly given facts about various cases, along with expected outputs. The system uses the learning method to adjust the weights in order to produce outputs similar to the expected results.
Support Vector Machines	As long as two classes are linearly separable, support vector machines determine the hyperplane in the n-dimensional feature space that maximises the margin between the examples of the classes. A new example is classified by computing to which side of the hyperplane the example belongs. The technique can be generalised to examples that are not linearly separable
symbolic reasoning	Symbolic reasoning is based on the idea that the core of intelligence lies in the explicit, generally sequential manipulation of symbols. Symbolic reasoning systems include rule based systems, logic based systems, frames and semantic networks.
T	
text mining	Text mining is the discovery of knowledge by the automatic analysis of free text. It includes information extraction, text summarisation, text categorisation and text clustering
text categorisation	Text categorisation organises documents into a taxonomy, thus allowing for more efficient searches. It involves the assignment of subject descriptors or classification codes to complete texts.

TERM	**DESCRIPTION**
text clustering	The technique of clustering supposes: i) an abstract representation of the object to be clustered, containing the features for the classification, ii) a function that computes the relative importance (weight) of the features, iii) a function that computes a numerical similarity between the representations. Clustering is employed to group terms if the regularly co-occur in documents or to group documents if they discuss the same topic terms.
text summarisation	Text summarisation involves identifying summarising and organising related text so that users can efficiently deal with information in large documents.
training neural networks	To train a neural network we need to make decisions regarding the following parameters: a) Learning rate, b) Momentum, c) Bias terms, and d) Stopping criteria.
training set	A training set is the collection of example data/cases which is used to train a neural net or induce rules in an induction system.
Toulmin argument structure	Toulmin stated that all arguments, regardless of the domain, have a structure that consists of four basic invariants: claim, data, warrant and backing. Every argument makes an assertion. The assertion of an argument stands as the claim of the argument. A mechanism is required to act as a justification for the claim, given the data. This justification is known as the warrant. The backing supports the warrant and in a legal argument is typically a reference to a statute or precedent case.
U	
undertaining of neural network	Under-training of a neural network occurs if the network is not exposed to enough examples. Learning is difficult in this situation simply because the training patterns available are not sufficiently representative of the true population of cases.
Unsupervised learning	In unsupervised learning, the system receives only the input, and no information on the expected output. The system learns to produce the pattern to which it has been exposed.
V	
valid formula	In logic, a valid formula is a well formed formula that always takes the value $\top$ (true).
vector space retrieval model	The vector space model uses terms as the groundwork of an orthogonal basis of the vector space. Text-based queries can be represented as vectors which can be used to search for their nearest neighbours in a document collection.
W	
weak discretion	According to Dworkin, weak discretion describes situations where a decision-maker must interpret standards in her own way.

TERM	DESCRIPTION
Web mining	Web mining is the use of data mining techniques to automatically discover and extract information from Web documents and services. Web mining research can be classified into three categories: Web content mining, Web structure mining, and Web usage mining
WIN	WIN (Westlaw is Natural) uses a Bayesian network to compute the probabilities that documents in a database are relevant to a query, and returns the relevant documents in order of their significance to the relevant query.

INDEX

Law and Philosophy Library

1. E. Bulygin, J.-L. Gardies and I. Niiniluoto (eds.): *Man, Law and Modern Forms of Life.* With an Introduction by M.D. Bayles. 1985   ISBN 90-277-1869-5

2. W. Sadurski: *Giving Desert Its Due.* Social Justice and Legal Theory. 1985
    ISBN 90-277-1941-1

3. N. MacCormick and O. Weinberger: *An Institutional Theory of Law.* New Approaches to Legal Positivism. 1986   ISBN 90-277-2079-7

4. A. Aarnio: *The Rational as Reasonable.* A Treatise on Legal Justification. 1987
    ISBN 90-277-2276-5

5. M.D. Bayles: *Principles of Law.* A Normative Analysis. 1987
    ISBN 90-277-2412-1; Pb: 90-277-2413-X

6. A. Soeteman: *Logic in Law.* Remarks on Logic and Rationality in Normative Reasoning, Especially in Law. 1989   ISBN 0-7923-0042-4

7. C.T. Sistare: *Responsibility and Criminal Liability.* 1989   ISBN 0-7923-0396-2

8. A. Peczenik: *On Law and Reason.* 1989   ISBN 0-7923-0444-6

9. W. Sadurski: *Moral Pluralism and Legal Neutrality.* 1990   ISBN 0-7923-0565-5

10. M.D. Bayles: *Procedural Justice.* Allocating to Individuals. 1990   ISBN 0-7923-0567-1

11. P. Nerhot (ed.): *Law, Interpretation and Reality.* Essays in Epistemology, Hermeneutics and Jurisprudence. 1990   ISBN 0-7923-0593-0

12. A.W. Norrie: *Law, Ideology and Punishment.* Retrieval and Critique of the Liberal Ideal of Criminal Justice. 1991   ISBN 0-7923-1013-6

13. P. Nerhot (ed.): *Legal Knowledge and Analogy.* Fragments of Legal Epistemology, Hermeneutics and Linguistics. 1991   ISBN 0-7923-1065-9

14. O. Weinberger: *Law, Institution and Legal Politics.* Fundamental Problems of Legal Theory and Social Philosophy. 1991   ISBN 0-7923-1143-4

15. J. Wróblewski: *The Judicial Application of Law.* Edited by Z. Bańkowski and N. MacCormick. 1992   ISBN 0-7923-1569-3

16. T. Wilhelmsson: *Critical Studies in Private Law.* A Treatise on Need-Rational Principles in Modern Law. 1992   ISBN 0-7923-1659-2

17. M.D. Bayles: *Hart's Legal Philosophy.* An Examination. 1992   ISBN 0-7923-1981-8

18. D.W.P. Ruiter: *Institutional Legal Facts.* Legal Powers and their Effects. 1993
    ISBN 0-7923-2441-2

19. J. Schonsheck: *On Criminalization.* An Essay in the Philosophy of the Criminal Law. 1994
    ISBN 0-7923-2663-6

20. R.P. Malloy and J. Evensky (eds.): *Adam Smith and the Philosophy of Law and Economics.* 1994   ISBN 0-7923-2796-9

21. Z. Bańkowski, I. White and U. Hahn (eds.): *Informatics and the Foundations of Legal Reasoning.* 1995   ISBN 0-7923-3455-8

22. E. Lagerspetz: *The Opposite Mirrors.* An Essay on the Conventionalist Theory of Institutions. 1995   ISBN 0-7923-3325-X

Law and Philosophy Library

Law and Philosophy Library

Volumes 56–63 were published by Kluwer Law International.

Law and Philosophy Library

69.   A. Stranieri and J. Zeleznikow: *Knowledge Discovery from Legal Databases*. 2004
ISBN 1-4020-3036-3

SPRINGER – DORDRECHT / BOSTON / NEW YORK